F. Scott Fitzgerald
in the Marketplace

F. Scott Fitzgerald
in the Marketplace

The Auction and Dealer Catalogues
1935–2006

Compiled and Edited by **Matthew J. Bruccoli**
with **Judith S. Baughman**

The University of South Carolina Press

© 2009 University of South Carolina

Published by the University of South Carolina Press
Columbia, South Carolina 29208

www.sc.edu/uscpress

Manufactured in the United States of America

18 17 16 15 14 13 12 11 10 09   10 9 8 7 6 5 4 3 2 1

Library of Congress Cataloging-in-Publication Data

Bruccoli, Matthew J. (Matthew Joseph), 1931–2008.
  F. Scott Fitzgerald in the marketplace : the auction and dealer catalogues, 1935–2006 / compiled and edited by Matthew J. Bruccoli, with Judith S. Baughman.
    p. cm.
  Includes index.
  ISBN 978-1-57003-799-3 (alk. paper)
  1. Fitzgerald, F. Scott (Francis Scott), 1896–1940—Bibliography. I. Baughman, Judith. II. Title.
  Z8301.2B715 2009
  [PS3511.I9]
  016.813'52—dc22
                         2008036740

For Scottie, who deplored my extravagance.

And for Arlyn, who blew our eating money on a $10 copy of *Taps at Reveille*—in dj, of course.

In Memory

C. E. Frazer Clark, Jr.
Charles Feinberg
Peter Keisogloff
John S. Van E. Kohn
Hyman W. Kritzer
Charles Mann
Linton Massey
Jack Neiburg
Michael Papantonio
R. L. Samsell
George Terry
B. George Ulizio
Henry Wenning
John Cook Wyllie

Contents

Preface ix
Acknowledgments xi
Introduction xiii
Overview xxi
Plan and Method xxxv

Catalogue Entries
1930s, 1940s, 1950s 3
1960s 10
1970s 26
1980s 60
1990s 91
2000s 131

Appendixes
1 Fitzgerald–Harold Ober Correspondence and Inscribed Fitzgerald Books 211
2 Fitzgerald-Owens Archive 223
3 Copies of *This Side of Paradise* Inscribed at Princeton 251
4 Advance Copies of *Tender Is the Night* 257
5 T. R. Smith 259
6 Horace Wade 261

Index 267
About the Editors 283

Preface

Writers matter more than anyone else because books and literature matter more than anything else. If you can't be a writer, the next best thing is to be a bookman. I am indebted to the bookmen—collectors, dealers, bibliographers, and curators—who gave me their friendship, encouragement, and knowledge for more than fifty years. They are now dead; and they are irreplaceable.

I have not tried to be impersonal in writing about Fitzgerald collecting. This work is tinctured by the excitement, anger, pleasure, and laughter that went with acquiring books and arguing about them. Fraze Clark took much of the laughter with him.

This volume is not a guide to collecting; but it deals with the formation and dispersal of collections. It is informed by the acquisitions policies I have learned—but have not always adhered to. The books that keep me awake are the ones I failed to get. Fraze wrote this in his introduction to *Hawthorne at Auction*: "Two axioms regarding auction decisions have guided my own adventures in the gallery. The first axiom can be summarized as 'things aren't as expensive as they seem,' and the second axiom, having to do with material you really need, is 'buy it now and worry about how to pay for it later'" (ix). These strictures apply as well to out-of-auction purchases.

A bookman should marry someone who says, "You've got to have it." I did.

M.J.B.

While we were working on *F. Scott Fitzgerald in the Marketplace,* Matthew J. Bruccoli and I referred to it—more accurately than we knew—as "our last big book." MJB died on June 4, 2008, not long after the book had gone into production at USC Press. *F. Scott Fitzgerald in the Marketplace* serves as an appropriate monument to MJB as scholar, collector, and teacher. The book documents his enduring passion for Fitzgerald, his vast knowledge of the book trade, and his commitment, always, to "getting it right" and to having fun doing it.

J.S.B.

Acknowledgments

Many people have provided catalogues, information, and aid for the preparation of this volume: Allen and Patricia Ahearn, Dickerson, Maryland; Bart Auerbach, New York City, New York; Jeanne Bennett, Granbury, Texas; Park Bucker, University of South Carolina Sumter; William Cagle, Paris, France; Rebecca Cape, Lilly Library, Indiana University, Bloomington; Carol Cheschi, Bruccoli Clark Layman, Columbia, South Carolina; Jo Cottingham, Thomas Cooper Library, University of South Carolina, Columbia; R. A. Gekoski, London, England; Terry Halliday, New Haven, Connecticut; Glenn Horowitz, New York City; Thomas Keith, New Directions, New York City; Roger Lathbury, George Mason University, Fairfax, Virginia; Daniel J. and Katharine Kyes Leab, *American Book Prices Current*, Washington, Connecticut; Robert Liska, Exeter, New Hampshire; Ken Lopez, Hadley, Massachusetts; Jeffrey Marks, Rochester, New York; Autumn L. Mather, Newberry Library, Chicago, Illinois; Fernando Peña, Grolier Club Library, New York City; Paul Rassam, London; Jimmy Sellers, Bruccoli Clark Layman; Joel Silver, Lilly Library; Ralph Sipper, Santa Barbara, California; Thomas F. Staley, Harry Ransom Humanities Research Center, University of Texas at Austin; Elizabeth Sudduth, Thomas Cooper Library; Robert Wilson, St. Michaels, Maryland; J. Howard Woolmer, Doylestown, Pennsylvania.

These two helpers are special: Jill Jividen Goff, our trusted research assistant at the University of South Carolina Department of English, and Jeffrey Eger, the learned catalogue specialist in Morristown, New Jersey.

Introduction

F. Scott Fitzgerald in the Marketplace[1] provides a selective survey of Fitzgerald books, manuscripts, typescripts, and letters offered for sale in 106 auction-house and 182 bookseller catalogues from the 1930s through 2006. The best catalogue entries that we found—especially those that facsimile inscriptions and letters—are reproduced. Since many of the items described or illustrated in the catalogues are now unlocatable, this volume provides a record of missing evidence for Fitzgerald study.

The catalogue entries reproduced here constitute a documentary account of the rise of Fitzgerald's posthumous reputation based on the activities of collectors, booksellers, and auction houses. Catalogues become collecting guides and price guides: thus the Jonathan Goodwin (1977) and Maurice Neville (2004) sales catalogues are Fitzgerald reference tools, as well as collectible books themselves. Before *F. Scott Fitzgerald: A Descriptive Bibliography* was published in 1972, the catalogues issued by Henry Wenning and J&S Graphics / J. Stephan Lawrence in the Sixties provided data for collectors and researchers. This record is inevitably incomplete because it is limited to the catalogues we know about. Back-number catalogues are hard to find because research libraries discard or ignore them and book dealers rarely catalogue them for sale. Most of the catalogues utilized here are in the Matthew J. and Arlyn Bruccoli Collection of F. Scott Fitzgerald at the Thomas Cooper Library, University of South Carolina.

Dealer and auction catalogues are neglected resources for literary scholarship and especially for bibliographical research. When Fredson Bowers, the greatest of American bibliographers, was editing Henry Fielding, he asked me to identify a copy of *Tom Jones* that had belonged to "some songwriter." It is in the catalogue for the legendary 1929 Jerome Kern sale—which meant nothing to Bowers. This recollection is not meant to convey disrespect for my teacher and collaborator. Even the great Bowers, like most literary scholars, knew little about the antiquarian book trade. He thought that book collectors were "a little crazy."

John Cook Wyllie, curator of rare books at the University of Virginia—the best bookman I ever knew—trained me and shaped my thinking about bookmanship. He was right about everything book related—except prices. Wyllie's sense of prices was determined by his memory of what comparable material had sold for ten or twenty years earlier. I respectfully disagreed with him in the Fifties, but I am now old enough to have undergone the price-shock experience when Fitzgerald items that I bought or didn't buy for $200 now bring $2,000 or even $20,000. When this happens I recall the sound advice that Charles Feinberg gave me: "They cost more today than they did yesterday, but tomorrow they will cost even more." He was not making a case for books as investments: they are not good investments. The Dow-Jones average has outperformed the rare-book market. Feinberg was instructing me how to build a collection over the course of a lifetime.

When wealthy collectors advised me to stick to Fitzgerald because I wouldn't be able to afford important authors on an academic salary, Feinberg told me that he started buying Walt Whitman with the nickels and dimes he earned as a shoe-shine boy: five cents for black shoes and ten cents for brown shoes. His unsurpassed Whitman collection is now in the Library of Congress through Feinberg's generosity and patriotism. John S. Van E. Kohn and Michael Papantonio, the proprietors of Seven Gables Bookshop at 3 West Forty-sixth Street—a cherished address for bookmen—deprecated my concentration on Fitzgerald, but they found books for me in the Fifties and Sixties at prices I could pay. I first came to them when I was a student with ten dollars to spend, and they treated me as a serious collector.

William Cagle, the former director of the Lilly Library at Indiana University, has stated that libraries were the driving force in the modern-firsts market during the Sixties when federal funding was available. Dealer Glenn Horowitz notes that institutions have now replaced the individual collectors of the nineteenth and early twentieth centuries. The flow of books and manuscripts into libraries inflates the prices for the remaining material; rising prices drive valuable material into the marketplace.

It will trouble some readers of this volume that there is so much about prices in a reference work for literary history. Literature runs on money. Grown-ups know that what they spend their money on defines them. The books, manuscripts, and letters a collector buys establish gauges of his personal values. This statement applies to serious bookmen: not to investors or speculators or conspicuous consumers. Bookmen buy books for their research utility, for their spiritual and cultural significance, and because owning books enriches their lives. Scholar-collectors acquire books because they need them and need to own them. They form collections to support their research—usually bibliographical and textual. Their tribe has diminished because apprentice scholars now lack masters to train them.

Book collecting is not restricted to the affluent. Taste, judgment, courage, determination, and knowledge are more important than money for book collecting. There are abundant opportunities for temporarily impecunious collectors to find the inexpensive editions and reprints ignored by the me-too buyers and the dealers who cater to them. Books are where you find them: in flea markets, in junk shops, in barns, in fancy shops, in cellars and attics, in throw-away catalogues, in elaborate catalogues. Book collecting is book discovery.

The collector-dealer relationship can be close and strong; notable collections often represent collaborations between the collector and a particular bookseller. On a good day Seven Gables Bookshop resembled a symposium, with Kohn and Papantonio tutoring their customers. Kohn, the American literature partner, was genuinely pleased—perhaps triumphant—when he found a ten-dollar variant copy that I didn't know about.

Serious collectors have acquisition plans into which each item fits: everything connects. All serious collections are works in progress. A serious book collection provides evidence for bibliographies, new editions, literary history, publishing history, and literary biography. Books beget books.

A rationale for the function of book collecting is incomplete without the sentimental or spiritual factor: the pleasure of owning a copy of a cultural monument or a work of literature that influenced you, as it was first published. Buying a great book is a way of affirming what is meaningful to you. Bookmanship is a way of life: you live to acquire books. They shape your life. Charles Feinberg said it best: "Without books my life would have been a desert."

In the modern literature field most collections are author collections. An author collection should document the history of the writer's career and reputation, as well as the history of individual works. The best author collectors are completists: every printing of every edition in the English language. Such a collection takes up a lot of room and is very hard to dispose of by sale or even gift because of the library-school shibboleth—*duplication.* John Cook Wyllie held that a duplicate copy is not a duplicate copy until established by bibliographical examination. Even then, two copies are better than one. If a comprehensive collection is broken up, a bibliographical-literary crime is committed.

Collectors—often the ones who are rich enough to back their own judgment—are susceptible to fashion: thus the first-book cult. Some first books have biographical significance; some have literary significance; some have sentimental value; some are worthless apart from their firstness or rarity; and some are artificial first publications. High-spot collectors have driven up the price of *This Side of Paradise*—not a major novel, but a key book in Fitzgerald's career. They want Fitzgerald's first book as an investment, and they want it in mint condition. But *Paradise* is not Fitzgerald's first book; it is his fifth book, preceded by

1. *Fie! Fie! Fi-Fi!*—the 1914 printed acting script for cast use, which survives in two institutional copies;
2. *Fie! Fie! Fi-Fi!*—the published songbook (1914);
3. *The Evil Eye*—the published songbook (1915);
4. *Safety First*—the published songbook (1916).

Fitzgerald was credited with the plot and lyrics for *Fie! Fie! Fi-Fi!*—although he probably wrote most of the libretto as well—and all the lyrics for *The Evil Eye* and *Safety First*. These books are scarcer than *This Side of Paradise*; but dealers have trouble selling them at comparatively low prices. *Fie! Fie! Fi-Fi!* has been catalogued at $3,500 maximum; but *Paradise* in a repaired dust jacket brought $20,000 at auction in November 2002.

Most first books are minor works that have no distinction apart from their firstness. Since many of them were published in short runs or privately printed or produced by obscure publishers, first books tend to be scarce; their value usually derives from their scarcity. At current prices Hemingway's *Three Stories & Ten Poems* (maybe 300 copies: up to $75,000)[2] and *in our time* (170 copies: $50,000) are worth it. Steinbeck's *Cup of Gold* is probably not worth $40,000 on literary grounds. If Faulkner's *The Marble Faun* is worth $60,000, *Fie! Fie! Fi-Fi!* ought to be worth that much. Nonetheless, a book is worth whatever somebody is willing to pay for it.

Collector competition for first books and what dealers refer to as "the nifty fifty"[3] deflects the check writers from seeking material that is bibliographically or critically or textually significant. Heavily revised forty-page Fitzgerald typescripts have sold for less than *This Side of Paradise* in jacket now brings. High-spot buyers do not understand the importance of galleys or proof copies (real proofs—not "advance review copies," which are usually wrapper-bound sheets from the first printing). Proofs provide evidence for establishing the text and tracing the revision of the work; proofs revised or corrected by the author or by an editor are bibliographical treasures.

The fifty-seven galleys for *Trimalchio* were auctioned in 1971 for $2,600. Big money then, but absurdly cheap now (see entry 32). These are the only unrevised galleys for the early version of a pretty good novel Fitzgerald reworked into a masterpiece retitled *The Great Gatsby*.[4] The rejected galleys for *Tender Is the Night* were auctioned in 1992 for $6,600 (see entry 98). Still cheap. Scribners presumably intended to discourage Fitzgerald from revising his novel for book publication by sending him book proofs from the magazine serial. It didn't work: he ignored them.

■

Catalogue descriptions may be unreliable. They are not, in most cases, deliberately misleading, although it is understandable that cataloguers attempt to make items attractive to potential buyers. Apart from exaggerated or invented claims about the provenance or rarity of an item, the chief flaw in catalogue descriptions is the incorrect and reckless application of bibliographical terms. Bibliographies don't always get them right, either.

There are five main terms of bibliographical description as defined in Fredson Bowers's *Principles of Bibliographical Description: edition, printing* or *impression, issue,* and *state*.[5] Many cataloguers use these terms more or less interchangeably to indicate firstness or priority and therefore value.

Edition: All the copies of a book printed from a single setting of type—including all reprintings from standing type, from plates, or by photo-offset.

Printing or *impression:* All the copies of a book printed at one time without removing the type or plates from the press. Printings occur only within editions.

Issue: Issues are created by an alteration of the text that affects *the conditions of publication or sale* (usually a title-page change)—in some copies of a particular printing. Issues occur only within printings. For example, the first printing of *The Beautiful and Damned* was published with the Scribners title page or with the Canadian Copp Clark title page, thereby creating two issues. There cannot be a first issue without a second issue.

State: States are created by an alteration of the text in *some copies* of a particular printing (usually by stop-press correction or by cancellation of leaves in finished books). States occur only within printings. For example, flaws were discovered in the text of *Taps at Reveille* after the first printing was bound; two leaves were canceled and replaced with the revised text in some copies—thereby creating two states. There cannot be a first state without a second state.

These terms apply only to the printed sheets. Catalogues customarily claim issues or states on the basis of bindings or even of dust jackets.

Binding variants are binding variants; they have no bearing on the book sheets and therefore do not apply to issue or state. Honest ignorance in the misapplication of bibliographical terms may be accompanied by creative cataloguing. Some egregious instances of wishful descriptions are noted with the catalogue entries reproduced here.

Some cataloguers may not know how to read a bibliography. *Tales of the Jazz Age* has the most frequently miscatalogued Fitzgerald point. There were three undifferentiated Scribners printings in 1922. The first printing has "and" at 232.6, the reading in the review copy and in the Scribners office copy, both in the Bruccoli Collection. The correction from "and" to "an" was probably made in the third printing. The alteration occurs in "Tarquin of Cheapside," a story about Shakespeare: "So you shall, an you give me pen. . . . " Cataloguers who do not know that "an" was Elizabethan English for "if" assume that "an" is an error; but it is the correction. The point is stipulated in *F. Scott Fitzgerald: A Descriptive Bibliography* thus: 232.6 and [an . The right-pointing bracket signifies *changed to*.

A *manuscript* (MS) is handwritten. A *typescript* (TS) is typed; a typescript with manuscript revisions is a *revised typescript* (RTS) Fitzgerald never typed; but his hand-revised secretarial typescripts have great literary value.

Some dealers don't understand the bibliographical or historical significance of their wares. When I bought a copy of the British *Tender Is the Night* with the Boots rental library label by phone from a London bookseller, it arrived with the label neatly removed. I called the dealer and explained that I had ordered the book because the Boots label provided evidence of the novel's readership and circulation in England. He responded that he had never heard such nonsense—not even from an "Ammerrican."

Some authors are more collectible than others because of their writing habits. Fitzgerald generated a rich archive by rewriting and revising. He wrote everything in pencil, and his manuscripts were typed by secretaries, with carbon copies. He then pencil-revised the ribbon copy and one or more carbons. The best of the revised copies was retyped and re-revised at least one more time. Then—at the point where an author is supposed to be finished—Fitzgerald reworked the proofs until Scribners stopped providing them.

Computers and the writers who have embraced them have diminished literary research by suppressing evidence. Computer revisions are lost—unless writers download them for their archives. Fitzgerald could not have worked on the computer screen. Neither could Thomas Wolfe, who also could not type. Writers have no obligation to generate textual evidence for the use of researchers; nonetheless Fitzgerald's working drafts have enriched scholarship and teaching.

Fitzgerald preserved his manuscripts, revised typescripts, and proofs while moving from hotels and apartments to rented houses at a time when nobody else thought his drafts had literary value. He was motivated by their sentimental significance; but he must have expected—or at least hoped—that some time in the future the manuscript and revised galleys for *The Great Gatsby* or the seventeen stages of *Tender Is the Night* would be studied. Most of the material he saved went to Princeton, through the generosity and wisdom of his daughter, Scottie.

Notes

1. When Frazer Clark and I published *Hawthorne at Auction* (by Clark; 1972), *Hemingway at Auction* (by Bruccoli and Clark; 1973), and *Whitman at Auction* (by Francis and Lozynsky; 1977), there was not enough material to justify publishing *Fitzgerald at Auction*. Now there is an abundance of catalogues—especially from booksellers—necessitating the title alteration.

2. Some dealers and collectors are dubious about the validity of the three-hundred-copy limitation on *Three Stories & Ten Poems* because there are too many surviving copies.

3. In modern American literature these include first books or key books for Fitzgerald, Faulkner, Hemingway, Salinger, Hammett, Chandler, Eliot, and Kerouac.

4. John Kohn, who purchased the *Trimalchio* galleys for me at Parke-Bernet, was reluctant to accept what he regarded as my reckless $3,000 bid.

5. These definitions hold for typesetting before computer typesetting entered the publishing business. Texts set from electronic files are bibliographical crapshoots.

Overview

When F. Scott Fitzgerald died on 21 December 1940, he was generally regarded as a failed writer who had squandered his genius in dissipation and had sold out to the *Saturday Evening Post* and Hollywood. The obituaries were condescending or nostalgic. *The Great Gatsby* was not nominated as a candidate for the great American novel—or even as a great American novel. Potential readers would probably have been unable to find a copy of *Gatsby* in bookstores. Fitzgerald did not die out-of-print; there were unsold copies of his books in the warehouse. In the year of his death Scribners sold only seventy-two copies of his books, and his last royalty check was for $13.13.

Other writers—especially his contemporaries—knew how good Fitzgerald's work was. In 1941 the *New Republic* published tributes or reassessments by John Dos Passos, John Peale Bishop, John O'Hara, Glenway Wescott, Malcolm Cowley, and Budd Schulberg. Dos Passos dismissed the obituaries and wrote: "Many people consider *The Great Gatsby* one of the few classic American novels. I do myself."[1]

Princeton University librarian Julian Boyd grudgingly offered to purchase the entire Fitzgerald archive in 1941 for $750; the archive included the manuscripts, revised typescripts, proofs, and correspondence. When David Randall, head of the Scribner Rare Book Department, protested that the figure was low, Boyd responded that the Princeton Library was not "established to support indigent widows of, and I quote, 'second-rate, Midwest hacks' just because they happened to have been lucky enough to have attended Princeton—unfortunately for Princeton."[2] Randall's appraisal of the archive in 1945 was $2,500, and Boyd offered Scottie Fitzgerald that figure in 1950. She gave the Fitzgerald material to Princeton that year.

Randall was regarded as bullish on American literature prices, but he was unable to accept the growth in the literary and monetary value of Fitzgerald's papers. On 7 June 1965 he told me a version of the dealings with Boyd and the Fitzgerald Estate, in which he set his 1945 appraisal at

$5,000. He was incredulous and angry when I remarked that the Fitzgerald archive at Princeton was now worth three million dollars. My 1965 estimate is conservative in 2008.

Fitzgerald's rise from worthlessness to eminence is unequaled in twentieth-century American literature. It required the recognition of the literary value of Fitzgerald's work; but it also was a matter of timing. Readers in the prosperous years following World War II identified with Fitzgerald's Twenties.

The glamour and heartbreak of his life have attracted Fitzgerald groupies—male and female—who don't know much about him or his work: "I've read all of Scott" usually means that they've read *Gatsby*. They can be identified by their penchant for first-naming him. They're the ones who trivialize Fitzgerald and his work by attending parties in what they think are Twenties costumes and by Charlestoning incompetently. They are not book collectors or even book buyers. Hemingway also has inspired wannabes and look-alike contests, but Faulkner has been spared that nonsense.

The first stage of what became the Fitzgerald revival—more of a resurrection than a revival—developed between 1945 and 1950. It accelerated in the Fifties and Sixties and eventually became a boom that thrives in the twenty-first century. American literary revivals have usually resulted from the efforts of academicians: the Melville rediscovery of the Twenties mainly occurred in the English departments at Columbia and Yale. Scholarly work on Fitzgerald was slow to develop, and graduate students were discouraged from risking their careers on him. The first Fitzgerald dissertations were James E. Miller's "A Study in the Fictional Techniques of F. Scott Fitzgerald" (University of Chicago, 1950) and Henry Dan Piper's "F. Scott Fitzgerald and the Origins of the Jazz Age" (Princeton University, 1950).[3]

The Fitzgerald revival-resurrection was supported by civilian readers and driven by reader word-of-mouth, which required that the books be available for reading. The warmly received 1941 Scribners volume with *The Last Tycoon* and *The Great Gatsby* plus stories (reprinted in 1941, 1945, 1947, and 1948) prepared for the reappraisal of Fitzgerald's position in American literature that began in 1945 as a *Gatsby* resuscitation.

An author's reputation may be fostered by a publisher for literary or commercial reasons: thus the commitment of Random House to the pre-Nobel Faulkner during the Thirties and Forties. There was a small reprinting of *Gatsby* (possibly 260 copies) in 1942; but Charles Scribner's Sons did nothing more for Fitzgerald until 1951, when they reprinted *This Side of Paradise* and published Malcolm Cowley's collection of the *Stories* and his edition "With the Author's Final Revisions" of *Tender Is the Night*. The death of Maxwell Perkins in 1947 impeded Scribner activities on behalf of Fitzgerald's works. The key Fitzgerald publications in the Forties were from other publishers:

The Great Gatsby (Armed Services Edition, 1945—154,663 copies)[4]
The Portable F. Scott Fitzgerald (New York: Viking, 1945)[5]
The Great Gatsby (New York: Bantam, 1945)
The Crack-Up (New York: New Directions, 1945)
The Great Gatsby (New York: New Directions, 1946)
The Great Gatsby in *Great American Short Novels* (New York: Dial, 1946)
"The Diamond as Big as the Ritz" and Other Stories (Armed Services
    Edition, 1946—52,119 copies)
This Side of Paradise (New York: Grosset & Dunlap, 1947)
The Great Gatsby (London: Grey Walls, 1948)
This Side of Paradise (London: Grey Walls, 1948)
Tender Is the Night (London: Grey Walls, 1948)
The Last Tycoon (London: Grey Walls, 1949)
The Great Gatsby (New York: Grosset & Dunlap, 1949)

The chief influence exerted by English teachers on literary reputations is through assigning books as required reading. Scribners did not provide a textbook edition of *The Great Gatsby* until the 1957 "Student's Edition," which was replaced by the bonanza Scribner Library edition in 1960. The Scribner imprint now sells 500,000 copies of *Gatsby* annually; most of them are ordered as textbooks. *Tender Is the Night,* Fitzgerald's most ambitious novel, is undertaught. The same half-dozen stories, especially "Babylon Revisited," are selected for textbooks and anthologies.

The Crack-Up has never gone out of print. Edited by Edmund Wilson, it announced the recognition of Fitzgerald as a literary figure. It is difficult to gauge Wilson's influence on Fitzgerald's comeback. They had been friends at Princeton and remained friends during Fitzgerald's life as Wilson became the most eminent American literary-social critic of his time. He edited *The Last Tycoon* without fee and published *The Crack-Up* with New Directions after Maxwell Perkins declined it for Scribners because the confessional essays made him uncomfortable. But Wilson dropped out as the Fitzgerald revival gained momentum. By the Sixties Wilson came to resent Fitzgerald's fame. Wilson to Bruccoli in 1959: "Do you really believe that Scott was a great writer?" Nonetheless, Wilson was there when needed in the Forties.

Interest in Fitzgerald was stimulated by Budd Schulberg's *The Disenchanted* (1950), a novel whose protagonist is loosely but recognizably based on Fitzgerald, and by Arthur Mizener's *The Far Side of Paradise* (1951), the first biography of Fitzgerald. Or perhaps the success of these two books derived from the revival already in progress. *The Disenchanted* was on the *New York Times Book Review* best-seller list for thirty-four weeks from 5 November 1950 to 1 July 1951 and held the number-one fiction position for eight weeks. That it replaced *Across the River and into the Trees* in first place may account in part for Hemingway's response to the Fitzgerald revival. He was infuriated by it. *The Far Side of Paradise* was on the *Times* list for sixteen weeks from 11 February 1951 to 27 May 1951 and was at the number-two nonfiction slot for two weeks.

F. Scott Fitzgerald in the Marketplace traces the Fitzgerald antiquarian market from 1935 through 2006. Collector interest and literary reputation do not have a clear cause-and-effect relationship. They occur at the same time and stimulate each other. Collectors were not responsible for the Fitzgerald revival; they responded to it. Nonetheless the prices reached at auction and asked in catalogues provide a measure of his growing fame.

Prices rise as collectors compete for the same books that are regarded as desirable and valuable on the basis of literary-historical significance. Other factors affect prices; but books are collected for cultural or emotional reasons. The great bookman-salesman A. S. W. Rosenbach decreed in his first catalogue that "it is not rarity alone that places the value upon a book, although the word sounds entrancing to the ear of the bibliophile. It is the intrinsic worth of the volume itself, its place in literature, history or the arts, that sends the prices up."[6]

Today inexpensive books are not worth bookshop shelf room or catalogue space; but in the Fifties it was possible to book hunt with five dollars all day in used-book stores and come back with finds. Now the Internet has reduced the population of used-book shops and largely spoiled the pleasure of discovery. A collector who doesn't see and handle the books won't be able to recognize the variants he didn't know about. All collectors enjoy finding sleepers, but the main purpose of book hunting is not bargain hunting. Every meaningful book is a bargain. Dealer catalogues and the bookstores that produced them have too often become casualties of the online culture. Some culture.

The early stage of Fitzgerald publishing and reprinting activity was not accompanied by dealer attention. There was no auction of major Fitzgerald material in the Forties and Fifties. The first Fitzgerald book listed in *American Book Prices Current* was the *Gatsby* signed by Christopher Morley that went for eight dollars in 1930—as a Morley item. Randall's 1934 catalogue included a *Gatsby*—jacket not noted—for three dollars. His 1936 Scribner Book Store catalogue offered a *Gatsby* in dust jacket inscribed to

Sinclair Lewis at ten dollars. It did not sell, and he tried it again in 1938 at the same price (see entry 2).

The reader-generated Fitzgerald revival was followed by tardy collector interest and slowly rising prices in the antiquarian book market. Apart from literary reputations, book prices are influenced by what may be called collectibility: the rarity factor (limited editions, signed editions, small printings by small presses) and the sense that the author is a good literary bet. Hemingway was collected in the Twenties, commencing with the instant collectors' items published in Paris. Faulkner was collected in the Thirties and Forties by a cult that believed in his genius. Fitzgerald was not a collected author during his lifetime. In the Thirties he often was deprecated for celebrating the frivolity of the Twenties: *The Great Gatsby* was regarded as a sensational story about a bootlegger, and *Tender Is the Night* was faulted for treating affluent Americans in Paris and on the Riviera. Before the Sixties Fitzgerald was not a good career investment for an ambitious critic or an untenured assistant professor; neither was he considered a good bibliophilic investment. Randall remarked in *Dukedom Large Enough* that at the time of Fitzgerald's death he "had even been dropped from the current edition of Merle Johnson's inclusive book collector's vade mecum, *American First Editions*, and it was pretty impossible to get lower than that." If there are degrees of impossibility, a lower level is never to have been included in Johnson. *American First Editions* was published in 1929 and enlarged in 1932, 1936, and 1942. It provided bibliographical points for the authors included and was consulted by collectors, dealers, and librarians. *American First Editions* represented a rough consensus of writers who warranted collecting in the Thirties and early Forties. In addition to the mandatory nineteenth-century New Englanders, Johnson's 1929 edition included James Branch Cabell, Ben Hecht, Joseph Hergesheimer, Sinclair Lewis, and Carl Van Vechten. The 1932 edition introduced Dos Passos, Faulkner, and Hemingway. The 1936 revision added Pearl S. Buck, Edna Ferber, and Thomas Wolfe. The 1942 edition added Walter D. Edmonds, Katherine Anne Porter, Kenneth Roberts, and John Steinbeck. But never Fitzgerald.

The earliest Fitzgerald checklist was "A Note on the Disenchanted, Francis Scott Key Fitzgerald, 1896–1940" in *Antiquarian Bookman* (20 January 1951), credited to collector C. Waller Barrett. It was followed by scholar Henry Dan Piper's thorough checklists for F. Scott and Zelda Fitzgerald in the *Princeton University Library Chronicle* (Summer 1951). By the early Fifties Fitzgerald collecting interest had reached the point where these guides were needed.

■

The Great Gatsby is the star Fitzgerald work in the auction room and in the classroom. It is the prime desideratum for Gatsbyesque buyers, who have paid up to $250,000 for an uninscribed copy in dj. Fitzgerald was in Europe when the novel was published and sent Scribners inscription slips to be pasted in presentation copies. Five of these copies have been identified: for his mother (see entry 18), for Sinclair Lewis (see entry 2), for Robert Kerr (Kerr family), for H. L. Mencken (Enoch Pratt Free Library), and for Van Wyck Brooks (Bruccoli Collection).[7]

Competition for *Tender Is the Night* has been less active, although it is scarcer than *Gatsby*: 7,600 copies of the *Tender* first printing and 20,870 copies of *Gatsby*. No copy of *Tender* was sold at auction until 1951, when it brought $22—presence of jacket not noted. The first copy stipulated as in jacket was auctioned for $18 in 1957. *Tender* broke three figures at auction in 1964, when a jacketed copy reached $130. This was the top price until a $225 copy was offered by a dealer in 1973. Between 1978 and 2003 dealer catalogue prices for *Tender* rose from $400 to $50,000, when Between the Covers Catalogue 98 offered a copy in the "first issue dust wrapper" at $50,000 and a copy of the "Second edition" (meaning the second printing) in the "second dust wrapper" for $7,500. See appendix 4 for the *Tender* advance copies in wrappers.

In 2000 a *Tender* in "worn and chipped first issue dust jacket" inscribed to Harold Ober brought $26,000 at auction and was recatalogued by Peter Stern at $85,000 in 2001. The copy in an undifferentiated jacket, inscribed to Donald Ogden Stewart, set the auction record for *Tender* at $119,500 in 2002 (see entry 128). *Tender* was a slow starter in the marketplace, but it moved up rapidly in the Nineties—probably indicating the rise of its growing literary stature.

Although there is considerable biographical interest in Fitzgerald's Hollywood years, little of the material generated by Fitzgerald's three screenwriting stints (1927, 1931, 1937–1940) in Hollywood has been catalogued for sale—probably because collectors and librarians were disdainful about the literary value of movie-related material. One Fitzgerald screenplay has been found in a catalogue. In 1987 Swann Galleries sold the mimeographed "1st Draft Continuity" of *The Light of Heart* for $850; Glenn Horowitz recatalogued it the next year at $3,500 (see entry 85). In 2002 the Bruccoli Collection acquired through the William Reese firm some two thousand pages of the manuscripts, revised typescripts, memos, and revised mimeo scripts for Fitzgerald's MGM work during 1937–1938. The $475,000 price was reasonable; but the university administration and the dean of libraries opposed the purchase, which was made with the encouragement of Russell Meekins of the University of South Carolina Educational Foundation. The USC Fitzgerald Collection acquired nothing—apart from the curator's personal purchases—at the Fitzgerald auction sales after 2002 because of a lack of library funding.

■

Well into the Forties dust jackets were regarded as having negligible value, and catalogues inconsistently noted their presence. Jackets properly matter to collectors who want a complete copy of the book as it appeared in bookstores on publication day; but there is no certainty that the jacket now on a book was the one that was there when the copy was originally sold. Jackets are routinely swapped to improve a copy. The preservation of jackets is related to the condition cult, but they may provide literary or historical evidence. A copy of *Gatsby* in mint jacket was sold for $250,000 at the spring 2006 Los Angeles Book Fair. It is gratifying that *Gatsby* in a mint jacket is the most expensive novel in twentieth-century American literature; but the value of a jacket should be related to its literary-cultural significance. Information printed on the jacket can document how the book and its author were regarded by the publisher. The blurbs from other writers are a form of literary history.[8]

■

Dust jackets create terminological nightmares, and the stakes can be very high. Variant jackets are catalogued as issues or states, but they are almost always separate printings.

The Beautiful and Damned: The first twenty thousand jackets have the title printed in white. It was changed to black in the subsequent printing.

The Great Gatsby: The price for the *Gatsby* jacket is determined by the bibliographical point creating two states of the first printing. It was initially printed with a lower-case "j" in "jay Gatsby" on the back panel. These misprinted jackets were salvaged by emending the "j" to capital "J." No unemended jacket has been located; but there must be one. *F. Scott Fitzgerald: A Descriptive Bibliography* (revised edition, 1987) repeats the widely circulated misinformation that the "j" was hand corrected in ink. Wrong. The correction was made by running the jackets through the press to overprint the "j" with a boldface "J" in order to obscure the lowercase piece of type.[9]

A freak *Gatsby* jacket was auctioned by Swann on 9 May 2007. The catalogue description includes the fallacious explanation that the "j" correction was made by a rubber stamp:

> # The Great Gatsby
>
> Here is a novel, glamorous, ironical, compassionate—a marvellous fusion into unity of the curious incongruities of the life of the period—which reveals a hero like no other—one who could live at no other time and in no other place. But he will live as a character, we surmise, as long as the memory of any reader lasts.
>
> "There was something gorgeous about him, some heightened sensitivity to the promises of life...It was an extraordinary gift for hope, a romantic readiness such as I have never found in any other person and which it is not likely I shall ever find again."
>
> It is the story of this Jay Gatsby who came so mysteriously to West Egg, of his sumptuous entertainments, and of his love for Daisy Buchanan —a story that ranges from pure lyrical beauty to sheer brutal realism, and is infused with a sense of the strangeness of human circumstance in a heedless universe.
>
> It is a magical, living book, blended of irony, romance, and mysticism.
>
> **CHARLES SCRIBNER'S SONS**

FIRST EDITION, FIRST PRINTING, OF FITZGERALD'S MASTERPIECE. Only a handful of copies in the rare, famous dust jacket designed by Francis Cugat have ever appeared on the market. Like this copy, most jackets are the second state indicated by the lower case "j" in Gatsby's name in line 14 of the rear panel corrected by hand with a rubber stamp capital "J" applied over it. In this copy, the capital J is curiously misstamped next to the lower case j and so close to the preceding word that it appears "thisJjay Gatsby." Worthy of restoration, and a solid copy of a title which, in a fine jacket, commands upwards of $100,000. Bruccoli A11.1.a; Connolly 48.

It sold for $12,000.

The entire *Gatsby* jacket was reprinted with the correct "J." The 20,970 first-printing copies of the book were almost certainly distributed with the first or second printings of the jacket. The third printing of the jacket—probably for the 1925 second printing of the novel (3,000 copies)—replaces the text with review excerpts.

All the Sad Young Men: The lips of the woman on the *All the Sad Young Men* jacket illustration show progressive batter or wear. There were three printings of the book and probably three printings of the jacket. But the lip batter does not differentiate printings of the book or even of the jacket, as some catalogues wishfully claim.

Tender Is the Night: The earliest jacket of *Tender Is the Night* has statements (not excerpts from reviews) by T. S. Eliot, H. L. Mencken, and Paul Rosenfeld on the front flap. The reprinted jacket replaces them with statements by Gilbert Seldes and Marjorie Kinnan Rawlings and with an excerpt from a review by Mary Colum. *Tender* is the only Fitzgerald work published in his lifetime for which there were advance review copies in wrappers (see appendix 4).

Taps at Reveille: There are two dust jacket issues for *Taps at Reveille*—the first issue without price and the second issue with the price rubber-stamped on the front flap. The stamped price has been noted in two sizes—with no discernable priority.

If you don't have the book, any copy—with or without jacket—is a good copy. Jackets and condition should be negligible factors if the book has an authorial inscription—especially one that says something about the book. Fitzgerald tried to write meaningful or humorous inscriptions. Yet there are buyers who decline a copy with a Fitzgerald inscription because it lacks a jacket. The condition of a *Tender Is the Night* copy in which Fitzgerald advises the inscribee how to read the novel doesn't really matter. See entries 65, 121, 135, and 140.

■

The priciest Fitzgerald material sold at auction has been handled by Parke-Bernet, Sotheby Parke Bernet, Sotheby's (New York), and Christie's (New York). Although seventeen Charles Hamilton Auction sales are noted here, this house did not catalogue any major Fitzgerald collections—except for the Horace Wade material (see appendix 6). Swann Galleries was not a major factor in the Fitzgerald market.

During the Sixties and Seventies no dealer really specialized in Fitzgerald, but Henry Wenning, and Lawrence Kunetka handled more of his material than other dealers—through their catalogues or directly to collectors. Wenning issued ten catalogues (plus supplementary lists) in New

Haven, Connecticut, between 1958 and 1966 and another half dozen in partnership with Stonehill between 1968 and 1971. Much of Wenning's Fitzgerald was sold directly to collectors; his favored customers included Jonathan Goodwin (see entry 52). Wenning provided me with the copy of *Gatsby* inscribed to Van Wyck Brooks with Fitzgerald's letter to Brooks about *The Pilgrimage of Henry James*. Wenning is regarded as the key figure in the modern firsts boom because his catalogues impressed collectors and he asked what were regarded as high prices—which now seem cheap. In 1959 Henry sold me my *Gatsby* in dust jacket for thirty dollars—and let me pay in installments.

Wenning's catalogues provide a gauge of the Fitzgerald market during the second phase of the Fitzgerald revival. He was fussy about condition. His first catalogue had *Tender Is the Night* ("A Beautiful copy in an immaculate dust jacket") at $40. Catalogue 5 had the first and second printings of *The Beautiful and Damned* in "somewhat worn dust jackets" at $40 for the pair. The next item paired the first and second printings of *The Great Gatsby* in "worn dust jackets" at $50 for both.

The best group of Fitzgeralds sold by Wenning appeared in his Catalogue 6 [1965]: twenty-one items, of which thirteen came from Alice Richardson, who had worked for Fitzgerald as a typist in 1935 (see entry 21). The Richardson material included three revised typescripts: "Her Last Case" ($600) and two "Count of Darkness" stories—which were sold to Bruccoli before the catalogue was printed. They were all poor Fitzgerald stories, but the revised typescripts show how he tried to improve them. The rest of the Richardson material consisted of letters and wires from Fitzgerald and inscribed copies of *All the Sad Young Men* ($25) and *Tender Is the Night* ($65).

Commencing in the early Seventies (possibly the late Sixties) Chicago dealer Lawrence Kunetka produced catalogues as J&S Graphics and then as J. Stephan Lawrence. Apart from a few inscribed books and an important letter, Kunetka did not list major Fitzgerald; but he catalogued more Fitzgerald material than anyone else—repeating previously listed items. J&S Graphics Catalogue 8 [1971] offered eighty-eight items ("22 first editions, 24 of Fitzgerald's magazine appearances, 10 appearances in anthologies, 7 items of ephemera, and 20 items concerning Fitzgerald") for $2,500. J&S Graphics Catalogue 11 [1971] listed twenty-seven Fitzgerald and four Zelda Fitzgerald items priced individually. The 1973 J&S Graphics Catalogue 16 had fifty-six items ranging from $3.50 to $650 for an inscribed *Taps at Reveille*. The J. Stephan Lawrence Supplement to Catalogue 38 [1979] was restricted to Fitzgerald: 123 primary items plus nine secondary items. These were the top entries:

Fie! Fie! Fi-Fi!	$ 850
Safety First	$1,200
This Side of Paradise (dj, signed)	$1,500
This Side of Paradise (third printing with "The Author's Apology" tipped in)	$ 650
Flappers and Philosophers (inscribed)	$ 650
The Great Gatsby (dj)	$1,000
The Great Gatsby (second printing, dj)	$ 500
Tender Is the Night (dj)	$ 400
Taps at Reveille (first state, dj)	$ 475

J. Stephan Lawrence Catalogue 45 [1979] listed eighteen separate items and a Fitzgerald collection.

> 749. **FITZGERALD, F. Scott** — An important collection of the work of F. Scott Fitzgerald consisting of First Editions, many in dust jackets, Presentation Copies, first appearances, and critical works about the author. Various places, various dates. Together 112 items. The highlights of the collection are a Presentation Copy of his first book, THIS SIDE OF PARADISE, and a 1-page holograph letter, SIGNED, written while Fitzgerald was at work on THE VEGETABLE, criticizing the work of Waldo Frank and praising Gertrude Stein, Presentation Copies of FLAPPERS & PHILOSOPHERS and TAPS AT REVEILLE. All in very good to fine condition, many in dust jackets. A detailed list is available upon request. $12,000.00

Kunetka's catalogues encouraged what can be called populist Fitzgerald collecting. Collectors who were intimidated by the big-time auctions or the pricey dealer catalogues and could not visit the bookshops in New York or California were able to make a start with Kunetka's affordable books. Lawrence Kunetka's catalogues encouraged and educated apprentice collectors.

Marguerite Cohn of New York's House of Books, Ltd., preferred to work with favored customers and did not catalogue her best material. She demanded loyalty from her customers: "What do you mean by buying books from Henry Wenning?" Since her catalogues from the mid-1940s to 1980 were unnumbered and undated, a chronological summary of the House of Books Fitzgerald offerings cannot be constructed. One of her catalogues, probably from the late Forties, had Fitzgerald's corrected galleys for "Sleeping and Waking" at $17.50 (see entry 8).

■

Very little important Zelda Fitzgerald material has come on the market. She was not a saver. Apart from her paintings, the Zelda Fitzgerald market has been restricted to uninscribed copies of *Save Me the Waltz* and a few letters—but no manuscripts. Ten copies of the novel are recorded in *American Book Prices Current* from 1965 to 2004, reaching $4,500 in the Neville sale. *Bookman's Price Index* lists twenty-one copies from 1979 to 2006, peaking at $7,500 in a 2001 Lame Duck / Jaffe catalogue. One inscribed *Save Me the Waltz* was catalogued at $100 in 1966 (see entry 24). There must have been more inscribed copies. Two books inscribed by both Fitzgeralds have been sold: *The Mind and Face of Bolshevism* by René Fülöp-Miller ($7,500; see entry 97) and *Flappers and Philosophers* ($47,000 with buyer's premium; see entry 123). The only lot of Zelda Fitzgerald's letters—sold at Christie's, New York, Sale Number 9548 (14 December 2000)—brought $3,500 for nine letters.

> **68**
> FITZGERALD, Zelda. Nine autograph letters signed (one "Zelda," the rest "Zelda Fitzgerald") to Paul C. McLendon; written from her mother's home in Montgomery, Alabama, 24 May 1946 to 10 March 1947. *Together 39 pages, 4to, mostly in pencil. [With]*: A mimeographed religious statement signed by Zelda Fitzgerald, *1 page, 4to,* dated 24 November 1946; a telegram from her to McLendon; a typed letter signed from the literary agent Harold Ober to her, *1 page, 4to,* 26 June 1946.
>
> "THE WEARY WORLD IS STREAKED WITH AUTUMN RAIN"
>
> An interesting, if not absorbing, series of letters written — at times in a beautifully mad style — toward the end of her life (she died in a fire on 10 March 1948) to a young man who had sent her manuscripts of his writings for criticism. In the correspondence Zelda Fitzgerald critiques McLendon work, talks of and gives advice on creative writing, voices her religious and spiritual beliefs, and gives news of her own life, and of her daughter Scottie, etc. 24 May 1946: "...This is a fine sense of plot: a quality which I envy you as my own stories are so thematically top-heavy — most editors would't buy them. I would rewrite my favorite story twice more if necessary and send it to *Harper's Magazine.* Both Sherwood Anderson and John Dos Passos have a compelling sense of tragedy-haunted, dark-throated lands which will give you inspiration..." [1 July 1946]: "...At first, most writers just keep on pasteing the rejection slips in their memory-books and stamping white horses and go on saving for a rabbit's-foot, a great public yearn for his philosophy and a neighborhood where there are no children. Controversial issues with vagrant animals, the radio-oblivious and infant-prerogative drove my husband [F. Scott Fitzgerald] half-crazy and I suppose you will suffer likewise as dreams and aspirations bring you dyspepsia and insomnia, stoop shoulders and incommensurate vitamin-reflex..." [5 November 1946]: "...You will...find me singularly unconversant with contemporary letters and even less master of the classics than yourself; probably I *do* know a great deal about the technical approach to writing, painting & dancing and have served an arduous novitiate in all..." [18 November 1946]: "The weary world is streaked with autumn rain and the swooning beatitudes are gone...I will surely — even ominously — come to see you after Christmas. That is a splendid time to visit amidst the skeletons of time and weather and one can happily immerse oneself in the [immensity?] of ideas. We'll discuss the way things ought to be with little reference to ought save memories of salvation...I have sent for [a copy of] *Save Me the Waltz* [her novel published in 1932]: it will probably take Scribner's some time to find it..." (9)
>
> **Estimate: $4,000-6,000**

The end of the twentieth century and the early years of the twenty-first century provided a series of auctions featuring Fitzgerald items at mounting prices: Engelhard (see entry 110), Ballantyne (see entry 125), Rechler (see entry 128), Ober (see appendix 1). The seventeen Fitzgerald items from the collection of dealer Maurice Neville totaled $794,400 (including the 20 percent buyer's premium) in two 2004 sales. The average for F. Scott Fitzgerald items in the Neville sales was $46,729 (see entry 135).

■

In the sixty-eight years since his death F. Scott Fitzgerald has become one of the half-dozen most seriously collected American authors. Single copies of his novels now sell for much more than he earned from writing them. The record constitutes a fulfillment of Fitzgerald's self-assessment expressed to his daughter, Scottie, in 1939 at a low point of his reputation: "I am not a great man, but sometimes I think the impersonal and objective quality of my talent and the sacrifices of it, in pieces, to preserve its essential value has some sort of epic grandeur."[10]

Dr. Johnson identified the disappointments and blighted expectations of authorship. The books that outlive their creators to establish cultural landmarks console readers for "the deceitfulness of hope, and the uncertainty of honour," Johnson declared in *Idler* #59. Now that books are threatened with superannuation, the saga of Fitzgerald collecting provides assurance that books will continue to be cherished and that bookmen will endure. After former libraries have become buildings full of electronic toys, there will be book people who protect and preserve books—possibly in caves. Among the rescued volumes will be *The Great Gatsby* and *Tender Is the Night.*

Notes

1. John Dos Passos, "Fitzgerald and the Press," *New Republic,* 17 February 1941, 213.

2. David A. Randall, *Dukedom Large Enough* (New York: Random House, 1969), 253–55. See Bruccoli, "Where They Belong: The Acquisition of the F. Scott Fitzgerald Papers," *Princeton University Library Chronicle,* 50 (Autumn 1988): 30–37.

3. See W. R. Anderson's dissertation, "The Fitzgerald Revival, 1940–1974: A Study in Literary Reputation" (University of South Carolina, 1974).

4. It is impossible to gauge the effect of the Armed Services Editions of *Gatsby* and *"The Diamond as Big as the Ritz" and Other Stories* on Fitzgerald's new readership. More than two-hundred thousand books were distributed to young men and women with time to read.

5. Viking's *Portable F. Scott Fitzgerald* included *The Great Gatsby, Tender Is the Night,* and nine stories. The first printing was twenty thousand copies at two dollars; sixteen thousand additional copies were printed in 1945 and four thousand in 1949. The collecton was also reprinted in 1949 and 1951 as *The Indispensable Fitzgerald.*

6. Edwin Wolf 2nd with John J. Fleming, *Rosenbach: A Biography* (Cleveland: World, 1960), 52.

7. Thirty-nine of the address slips sent by Fitzgerald to Scribners are in the Lilly Library.

8. See George Garrett, "Some Basic Notes on Three Modern Genres: Interview, Blurb, and Obituary," *Dictionary of Literary Biography Yearbook 2002,* ed. Matthew J. Bruccoli and George Garrett (Detroit: Bruccoli Clark Layman / Thomson / Gale, 2003), 142–64.

9. Information provided orally by Scott Kelly, US Lithographic (13 September 2006).

10. F. Scott Fitzgerald to Scottie Fitzgerald, 31 October 1939, in *A Life in Letters,* by F. Scott Fitzgerald, ed. Matthew J. Bruccoli, with the assistance of Judith S. Baughman (New York: Simon & Schuster, 1994), 419.

Plan and Method

Many dealers refuse to date their catalogues; a few dealers do not even number them. There is no sensible explanation for this policy, which obscures the record. Inferred dates are provided in brackets here. Punctuation has been supplied in catalogue titles, and the typography has been regularized.

Facsimiles of Fitzgerald inscriptions or letters are printed once—except in a few cases where the catalogue entry provides additional information.

Dealers and auction houses do not reveal buyers: private collectors are entitled to privacy. It is impossible to trace the present locations of most of the items described here; but a few purchasers are noted. *Bruccoli Collection* locates items in the Matthew J. and Arlyn Bruccoli Collection of F. Scott Fitzgerald, Thomas Cooper Library, University of South Carolina. Material retained by the Bruccolis in their personal collection is so identified.

Auction prices have been noted on the catalogue entries when known. Missing prices were unobtainable.

Many private collectors and institutional buyers utilize the services of a dealer to bid for them—thereby eliminating a competitor and obtaining the services of an experienced bidder—in which case the bidder charges a 10 or 15 percent fee. The auction houses charge a seller's fee of up to 20 percent, negotiable for very expensive material. In 1976 the auction houses implemented a buyer's premium: 20 percent of the hammer price up to $100,000 and 10 percent above $100,000. The auctioneers now charge two commissions on the same item, totaling up to 40 percent. A collector who employs a bidder ends up paying $13,000 for a $10,000 item: $10,000 + $2,000 (buyer's premium) + $1,000 (bidder's fee). The auction prices noted in this volume that are taken from *American Book Prices Current* are the hammer prices—that is, the highest bid without an added-on premium—unless otherwise stipulated. Depending on the auction house, the prices reported by the house may be hammer or premium-added prices. The BP notation here designates a price that includes the buyer's premium.

Sources and Tools

American Book Prices Current. New York: Bancroft-Parkman [etc.], 1930– .
Book Auction Records. London: Henry Stevens, Son & Stiles, 1940– .
Bookman's Price Index. Detroit: Gale Research, 1964– .
Book Prices Current. London: Elliot Stock, 1930– .
Bruccoli, Matthew J. *F. Scott Fitzgerald: A Descriptive Bibliography.* Rev. ed. Pittsburgh: University of Pittsburgh Press, 1987.
———. *Some Sort of Epic Grandeur: The Life of F. Scott Fitzgerald.* 2nd rev. ed. Columbia: University of South Carolina Press, 2002.
Bucker, Park, comp. *The Matthew J. and Arlyn Bruccoli Collection of F. Scott Fitzgerald at the University of South Carolina: An Illustrated Catalogue.* Columbia: University of South Carolina Press, 2004.
Fitzgerald, F. Scott. *Correspondence of F. Scott Fitzgerald.* Edited by Matthew J. Bruccoli and Margaret M. Duggan, with the assistance of Susan Walker. New York: Random House, 1980.
———. *A Life in Letters.* Edited by Matthew J. Bruccoli, with the assistance of Judith S. Baughman. New York: Simon & Schuster, 1995.
Fitzgerald, F. Scott, and Harold Ober. *As Ever, Scott Fitz— : Letters between F. Scott Fitzgerald and His Literary Agent Harold Ober, 1919–1940.* Edited by Matthew J. Bruccoli, with the assistance of Jennifer McCabe Atkinson. Philadelphia: Lippincott, 1972.

Catalogue Entries

1930s
1940s
1950s

1. American Art Association/Anderson Galleries Sale Number 4160 (13–14 March 1935)

The earliest Fitzgerald items located in an auction catalogue. Item 166 was sold again by Parke-Bernet in December 1941: see entry 5, item 183. It was recatalogued by House of Books [1976] at $625.

> 166. FITZGERALD (F. SCOTT). This Side of Paradise. 12mo, original cloth, uncut; 2 margins slightly damaged.
> New York, 1920
> FIRST EDITION. PRESENTATION COPY FROM THE AUTHOR, with autograph inscription on the end-paper: *"For John Myers O'Hara who first introduced me to Sappho in his Translations, with a thousand thanks. 'Much have I travelled in the realms of gold'* . . . *his most cordially F. Scott Fitzgerald, Washington D. C."*
>
> 167. ——— The Beautiful and Damned, N. Y., 1922 ❖ The Chinese Nightingale (Lindsay), N. Y., 1917 ❖ The Passing God (Kemp), N. Y., 1919 ❖ The New Adam (Untermeyer), N. Y., 1920, and others similar. Together 25 vols., 12mo and 8vo, cloth, calf, boards, boards with cloth backs, and wrappers. V.p., v.d.
> NEARLY ALL FIRST OR LIMITED EDITIONS. A MOST INTERESTING COLLECTION OF BOOKS. ELEVEN VOLUMES ARE PRESENTATION OR INSCRIBED COPIES AND SOME CONTAIN LETTERS BY THE AUTHORS IN ADDITION TO THE SIGNATURES. The other fifteen volumes contain letters or manuscripts by the various authors, compilers, and translators.

2. *Scribner Firsts: 1846–1936*. Catalogue 108 [1936]

Fitzgerald sent Scribners inscription slips from France to be pasted in presentation copies of *The Great Gatsby*. This copy did not sell and was listed at the same price in Scribner Catalogue 114 [1938]. It was included in the inventory of the R. L. Samsell library by Heritage Bookshop (6 April 1976): see entry 49, item 36. Scribner Catalogue 108 also listed *The Beautiful and Damned* in dust jacket and *The Vegetable* in dust jacket at $2.50 each.

> [No. 125]
> —— THE GREAT GATSBY. 12mo, First Edition, original green cloth, uncut. New York: Charles
> Scribner's Sons, 1925. $10
> Published April 10, 1925, in an edition of 20,870 copies.
> A fine copy in the original dust wrapper.
> Laid in is an autograph note: "Dear Sinclair Lewis: I've just sent for Arrowsmith. My hope is that The Great Gatsby will be the second best American book of the spring. F. Scott Fitzgerald."

Fitzgerald/Hemingway Annual 1971

3. "*Autographed by the Author.*" Goodspeed's Catalogue 303 [1938]

Both items were offered again in the December 1941 H. Bertram Smith Sale at Parke-Bernet: see entry 5, items 184 and 185.

> 61 FITZGERALD, F. Scott. The Beautiful and Damned. 12mo, cloth. New York, 1922. $3.50
> First edition. "For Charles T. from F. Scott Fitzgerald. This lowsy, uneven, rambling, stumbling, tumbling, rattling, groaning, coughing novel—from the author, who once considered it the best book ever written. 'Ellerslie' Edgemoor, Delaware. April 18, 1927."
>
> 62 FITZGERALD, F. Scott. The Great Gatsby. 12mo, cloth. New York, 1925. $4.50
> First edition. "For Charles T. Scott. Gatsby was never quite real to me. His original served for a good enough exterior until about the middle of the book he grew thin and I began to fill him with my own emotional life. So he's synthetic—and that's one of the flaws in this book. F. Scott Fitzgerald, Ellerslie, Edgemoor, Delaware, 1927."

4. *We Moderns: Gotham Book Mart, 1920–1940* [ca. 1941]

This influential catalogue provided headnotes for important authors, but Fitzgerald did not merit such recognition. It listed ten Hemingway items—including *Three Stories & Ten Poems* and *in our time* at $100 each.

> 381. FITZGERALD (F. SCOTT): The Great Gatsby—8vo, cloth. N.Y., 1925. $2.00
> 382. ———. Tender Is the Night—8vo, cloth. N. Y., 1934. ($2.50) $1.00

5. *First Editions of American and English Authors Mainly in Superb Condition: The Distinguished Collection of H. Bertram Smith, New York.* Parke-Bernet, New York, Sale Number 325 (10–11 December 1941)

> 183. FITZGERALD, F. SCOTT. This Side of Paradise. 12mo, original cloth, uncut. In a cloth folder. New York, 1920
> FIRST EDITION. PRESENTATION COPY FROM THE AUTHOR, inscribed on the front end-leaf: "*For John Myers O'Hara who first introduced me to Sapho in his Translations, with a thousand thanks 'Much have I travelled in the realms of gold . . .' F. Scott Fitzgerald . . .*"
>
> 184. FITZGERALD, F. SCOTT. The Beautiful and Damned. 12mo, original cloth, uncut. In a cloth folder. New York, 1922
> FIRST EDITION. PRESENTATION COPY FROM THE AUTHOR to Charles T. Scott, with a 6-line autograph inscription regarding the book on the front end-leaf, signed, and dated: "*April 18th 1927.*"
>
> 185. FITZGERALD, F. SCOTT. The Great Gatsby. 12mo, original cloth, uncut. In a cloth folder. New York, 1925
> FIRST EDITION. PRESENTATION COPY FROM THE AUTHOR to Charles T. Scott, with a 7-line autograph inscription by the author regarding the book on the front end-leaf, signed, and dated "1927."

6. *First Editions, 1643–1943, Including 53 First Books of American and British Authors.* Charles S. Boesen Catalogue 9 [1943]

> 100. FITZGERALD, F. SCOTT. **Tales of the Jazz Age.** 12mo, cloth. New York, 1922. $40.00
> FIRST EDITION. On the first flyleaf, in ink, in the autograph of the author, is the following inscription: For Mamma
> from
> Her Angel Child
> Scott
> This book is dedicated "Quite inappropriately To My Mother" so this copy of the book is, of course, the "Dedication Copy." A fine copy.

7. Literary Manuscripts and Autograph Letters of Eminent Authors. Scribner Book Store (1946)

The first Fitzgerald revised typescript located in a catalogue: $2.10 per page for "Crazy Sunday." Faulkner's revised typescripts in this catalogue were comparably priced.

> 62. FAULKNER, WILLIAM.
>
> Typescript of *Hair*. 21 pages, 4to. Apparently typed by the author, and with some autograph corrections and changes in his hand; there are also a number of editorial emendations. $45
>
> One of the first of Faulkner's short stories to be published, this originally appeared in *The American Mercury*, May, 1931, and was subsequently collected in *These Thirteen*. Faulkner has named *Hair* as being one of the three stories he likes best in that collection, and it properly belongs with *Sanctuary* as part of the chronicle of the town of Jefferson. One of the central characters in it, Maxey, the barber, reappears in *Light in August*.
>
> 63. ——— Typescript of *Centaur in Brass*. 24 pages, 4to. Apparently typed by the author and with a few autograph changes in his hand.
> $27.50
>
> This story appeared in *The American Mercury*, February, 1932. It is part of the "Snopes Saga" but was not used in that section of it which was published as *The Hamlet*.
>
> Faulkner autograph or typescript material is exceedingly scarce; none connected with any of his published books appears to have been offered for sale in the past.
>
> 64. FITZGERALD, F. SCOTT.
>
> Original typescript of *Crazy Sunday*. 26 pages, 4to, corrected throughout by the author. $55
>
> First published in *The American Mercury*, October, 1932, and reprinted as one of the five short stories to be included in *The Last Tycoon* (1941). Edmund Wilson considers this one of Fitzgerald's finest achievements.

8. House of Books Catalogue [ca. 1946]
Presumably the first Fitzgerald galleys offered for sale.

> *First Edition. Mint copy, dust-wrapper.*
>
> 92 FITZGERALD. Original galley proofs of SLEEPING AND WAKING. Chicago, 1934. These are the galley proofs of this article which appeared in *Esquire* magazine, December 1934, with all Fitzgerald's corrections in pencil appearing thereon. In the margin is a letter from the editor of the magazine querying Fitzgerald concerning corrections which were thereupon made. Three galley sheets and the proof of the table of contents of *Esquire* magazine. This article was later published in THE CRACK-UP. $17.50

9. *The Earle J. Bernheimer Collection of First Editions of American Authors Including . . . Robert Frost.* Parke-Bernet, New York, Sale Number 1207 (11 December 1950)

The inscribed copy of *This Side of Paradise* was included in the 6 April 1976 Samsell list: see entry 49, item 4.

> 58. FITZGERALD, F. SCOTT. This Side of Paradise. 12mo, original cloth. In a pig-skin backed case. New York, 1920
>
> FIRST EDITION. THE AUTHOR'S FIRST BOOK. With an 8-line signed autograph inscription by the author on the end-leaf, pertaining to the book. With bookplate of M. O. Green, on which he has written "*F. Scott Fitzgerald crowds to the nice fireplace*".
>
> 59. FITZGERALD, F. SCOTT. The Beautiful and Damned. 12mo, original cloth, uncut; inner hinges cracked; with dust jacket (repaired). In a pig-skin backed case. New York, 1922
>
> FIRST EDITION. Inscribed by the author on the front end-leaf "*The phrase: 'Beautiful but dumb' was this book's contribution to its time. F. Scott Fitzgerald. It has awful spots but some good ones. I was trying to learn*". With bookplate of E. C. May.

10. Jack Potter Catalogue [1952]

The first catalogued group of Fitzgerald letters. Sam Marx was story editor at MGM; Fitzgerald had worked there in 1931. Item 51 brought $210 in the 1963 Chord sale: see entry 14, item 162. Item 52 was relisted in Charles S. Boesen Catalogue 27 [ca. 1953] for $25.

JACK POTTER, 4506 BROADWAY, CHICAGO 40, ILLINOIS   5

---

50 **FITZGERALD** (F. Scott). Five Typed Letters written to Mr. Samuel Marx, script director of Metro-Goldwyn-Mayer, in the Spring of 1934. All of the letters were written from Baltimore, and two are accompanied by their original envelopes addressed in hand by Fitzgerald. The lot: $110

A most interesting group of letters. The first one is a letter of transmittal, Fitzgerald asking Marx to give something to George Cukor, the motion picture director . . . evidently a proposal or suggestion regarding a film version of *The Great Gatsby*, for the second letter begins: "*The letter to Cukor dealt with the idea of Gable playing "Gatsby."* He continues: "*Tender is the Night*" *is still an unknown quantity*, (it was published the following month). *Would rather like to come out there now that the main chore is finished. It seems to be that or the Saturday Evening Post and I long for variety—but at any price (and I am cherishing none of the illusions of 1931 about money) I wouldn't come out there with any such line-up as I had to face last time. Who is this Joan Crawford? Is she the one who preaches in the Los Angeles temple, or is that Greta McArthur?*"

The third letter reads: "*It's just occurred to me, in regard to a letter I have from Carl Laemmle asking if I had any old silent productions that I thought could be done over into a talkie, that you own the first two stories I ever sold to pictures. They were Saturday Evening Post stories that appeared in 1920 and later in a book called "Flappers and Philosophers." The first one, "Head and Shoulders" you made with Viola Dana and Garret Hughes (it was the start of his short-lived career) under the title of "The Chorus Girls Romance." I believe it was a big hit at the time. The second was called "The Offshore Pirate" and was made with Viola Dana and I have forgotten what man. If you still have the originals in your library it might be worth while to look them up."*

The fourth letter transmits a copy of a treatment of "*Tender Is the Night*", and states that he has "abandoned the idea of coming to the coast even if urged."

The fifth letter is the most interesting of all. Fitzgerald writes: "*Apropos of a proposed treatment of my book (Tender Is the Night) which went to you (by the way Publishers Weekly lists it third best seller this week) you will remember that I collaborated on that first treatment with a kid named Charles Warren who has shown a remarkable talent for the theatre in writing, composing and directing two shows which have packed them in and had repeat weeks here in Baltimore and in Princeton. My intention, if Tender Is the Night was sold immediately, was to back him in going out there and seeing if he could help round it into shape. So far the offers have been unsatisfactory considering the work put on it—nevertheless Warren has planned to brave Hollywood even without the permit to enter which a definite connection would be to him. He will be without acquaintance there save for such letters as I can give him. I would be much in your debt if you will see him, give him what advice you can about finding an opening. His talents are amazingly varied—he writes, composes, draws and has this aforesaid general gift for the theatre—and I have a feeling that he should fit in there somewhere within a short time and should go close to the top, in fact I haven't believed in anybody so strongly since Ernest Hemingway. Incidentally, he is not a highbrow, his instincts are toward practical showmanship which is why I engaged him, as a sort of complement to me. Perhaps you could arrange to let him look around the lot for a few hours, lend him a few sample treatments that he could take back to his hotel and study and also some story that he could work on without salary . . . Ever your friend, Scott Fitzgerald.*"

51 —— The Vegetable. 12mo, green cloth, New York, 1923. $35
FIRST EDITION. Presentation copy, inscribed by the author: "*For Edna Hooper from F. Scott Fitzgerald—On the eve of the first performance of this great moral document. Atlantic City, Nov. 20th, 1923.*"
Following its unsuccessful premiere in Atlantic City ("It was a colossal frost," wrote Fitzgerald) *The Vegetable* was withdrawn. It is its author's only play. The spine lettering is very dull, else a very fine copy.

52 —— This Side of Paradise. 12mo, blue cloth, New York, N.d. $35
A reprint, with the following fine inscription by the author: "*For Sam Marx, who has just arranged my future for me—very different from the future of Amory Blaine. From his friend, F. Scott Fitzgerald, Hollywood 1931.*" Amory Blaine is, of course, the hero of this book. Spine is sun-faded, else a mint copy.

11. *Rare Books, First Editions.* **Charles S. Boesen Catalogue 24
[ca. 1952]**

Bruccoli acquired the inscribed *Beautiful and Damned* in 1969 from John F. Fleming for $485—but without the ALS.

> 139. FITZGERALD, F. SCOTT. The Beautiful and the Damned.
> 12mo, original green cloth. New York, 1922. $75.00
> FIRST EDITION, First Issue. On the first flyleaf, in ink, in the autograph of the author, is the following inscription: "To a bookseller/ Who declares himself to be ⅜ tight and promises the other ⅝ before night and says he wouldn't try to be too damn clever if he was me—after compromising with you on this description, A. L. Sugarman, I officially declare myself to be— F. Scott Fitzgerald/ and swear from this day forward to take all books to be autographed into the next room." Laid in is an autograph letter, signed, to the same man reading: "Your letter makes me feel guilty—as if I had enviegled you into my book under false pretenses. The title is bad but I regret you only reached p. 71, for on p. 72 . . . however . . . / I am struggling over some Bodenheim verse as you suggest. I think I have a great future at it./ Faithfully/ F. Scott Fitzgerald."
> On the bottom of the page are two drawings by Fitzgerald headed "Advertisement ! ! !" The one sketch shows a man with a happy smile on his face. The caption below reads: "The man who read beyond p./ 71 of the B & D." The other sketch is that of a frowning man. Below it Fitzgerald has written: "The man who abandoned the B & D at p. 71." Below the drawings Fitzgerald has written: "The Beautiful & Damned! A tale for red-blooded he-men! Read it here! See it in the movies! Play it on the phonograph! Run it on the sewing machine!" To A. J. Sugarman. esq. Northwest Bk. Co. 625 Boston Block. Minneapolis.' A very fine copy in the dust wrapper.
>
> 140. FITZGERALD, F. SCOTT. The Great Gatsby.
> 12mo, original green cloth. New York, 1925 $15.00
> FIRST EDITION. New in the dust wrapper. The dust wrapper is in the First State, with the capital "J" in Jay Gatsby on the back of the wrapper printed over the small "j." New in the dust wrapper.
>
> 141. FITZGERALD, F. SCOTT. The Great Gatsby.
> 12mo, original green cloth. New York, 1925. $7.50
> FIRST EDITION. A very fine copy in a dust wrapper of the Second State.

1960s

12. Goodspeed's Catalogue 491 [1960]

Fitzgerald inscribed multiple copies of *The Vegetable* to actor Ernest Truex at the Atlantic City tryout of the play. The copy described below is the first located in a catalogue or at auction.

> 138 Fitzgerald, F. Scott. The Vegetable. 12mo, cloth. New York, 1923. $50.00
> First edition. Inscribed by Fitzgerald and signed by Ernest Truex on the disastrous opening night at the Apollo Theatre. Fitzgerald has recorded his enthusiasm for Truex's performance as the star of the play by quoting its last line, "The best postman in the world", followed by his full signature and "Nov 19th, 1923, Atlantic City". Above the author's inscription Truex has signed his own name, evidently with the same pen. The association of the two names, plus the fateful date, makes this a most desirable copy. Very good condition.

This or another copy inscribed to Truex was offered in Black Sun Catalogue 33 [ca. 1975] for $750. This or another copy inscribed to Truex was offered by Allen Ahearn First Editions at the Quill & Brush, Catalogue 36 (August 1979) for $2,500. This or another copy inscribed to Truex was auctioned in Christie's, New York, Sale Number 5059 A (22 May 1981) for $1,800. This or another copy inscribed to Truex was sold in the 13 April 2004 Sotheby's New York auction (the first session of the Neville sale) for $11,000: see entry 135, item 59. Other inscribed copies are in the Bruccoli Collection and at the University of Virginia.

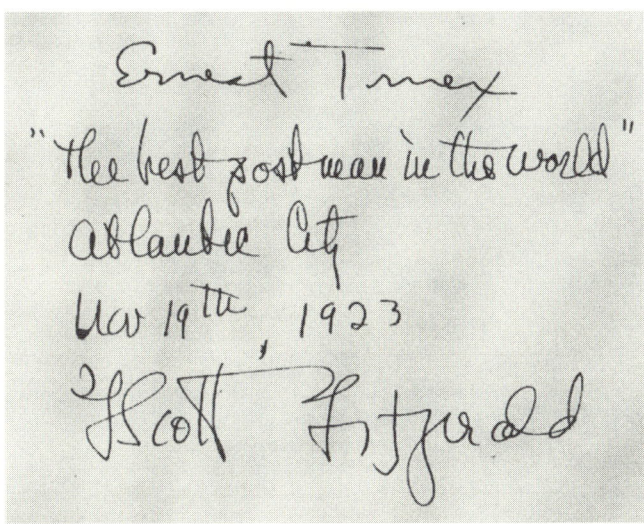

Bruccoli Collection

13. *First Editions, Association Copies, Autograph Letters, and Manuscripts.* House of Books Catalogue [ca. 1961]

> 167 FITZGERALD (F. Scott). THIS SIDE OF PARADISE. New York, 1920. 12mo, cloth. $250.00
> *First Edition. The author's first book. With full-page inscription on front end paper: "This book is a history of mistakes—something never retracted yet, in a way, to be ashamed of, by a conscientious worker ... Scott Fitzgerald." Again signed and with some added words on the former owner's bookplate. Almost new, enclosed in half morocco slip case.*

14. *First Editions & Manuscripts . . . Belonging to J. T. Chord.* Parke-Bernet, New York, Sale Number 2184 (9–10 April 1963)

The Chord sale included the best group of Fitzgerald books to be auctioned to that time, including the first copy of *Fie! Fie! Fi-Fi!* noted in an auction catalogue.

[NUMBER 158]

158. FITZGERALD, F. SCOTT, and others. Fie! Fie! Fi-Fi! A Musical Comedy . . . presented by the Princeton University Triangle Club. 4to, cloth-backed light boards; covers stained, an inked correction on first page of score (see below). [New York] 1914

Piano and vocal score, Plate Mark 17389. Copyright date is given as 1914 on the title-page; copyright is repeated at the foot of the first page of score, and apparently was here dated incorrectly, for there has been an erasure and the two figures of the Roman numeral "IV" have been written in in ink. Fitzgerald plotted the piece and contributed 15 lyrics.

[See illustration]

KINDLY READ CONDITIONS OF SALE IN FOREPART OF CATALOGUE

$50- 159. FITZGERALD, F. SCOTT. This Side of Paradise. 8vo, original cloth. A very good copy, the gold lettering on the spine bright. New York, 1920
FIRST EDITION of the author's first published novel. Laid in at the back (and offset on the endpapers) is a newspaper clipping with a contemporary review of this title by Burton Rascoe.

$55- 160. FITZGERALD. This Side of Paradise. 8vo, original cloth; a clean, sound copy, the gold lettering on the spine a little dull. New York, 1920
Third Impression, with one-leaf printed insert SIGNED BY THE AUTHOR. Copies with this insert were distributed by the publishers at a meeting of the American Booksellers Association; in the text, Fitzgerald admits that much of the material of the novel is autobiographical.

$55- 161. FITZGERALD. The Beautiful and Damned. 8vo, original cloth, in original dust jacket. The book FINE, the jacket slightly soiled. New York, 1922
FIRST EDITION, without later terminal leaf of ads. Mr. and Mrs. Fitzgerald are said to have modelled the couple pictured on the dust jacket, and to have been highly dissatisfied with the resulting drawing.

A PRESENTATION COPY

$240- 162. FITZGERALD. The Vegetable or from President to postman. 12mo, original cloth; the spine lettering dulled, otherwise a clean, crisp copy. In cloth case. New York, 1923
FIRST EDITION, INSCRIBED BY THE AUTHOR, "*For Edna Hoopes from / F Scott Fitzgerald / on the eve of the / first performance of / this great moral / document / Atlantic City / Nov 20th, 1923*". The "great moral document", a satirical extravaganza, was not presented elsewhere.

$160- 163. FITZGERALD. The Great Gatsby. 8vo, original cloth, in dust jacket; the book FINE, with text and covers bright, the jacket with traces of shelf wear. In cloth case. New York, 1925
FIRST EDITION of the author's most widely read novel, rarely found in dust jacket.

$60- 164. FITZGERALD. All the Sad Young Men. 8vo, original cloth, in original dust jacket; a good copy, the minor defects noted below. New York, 1926
FIRST EDITION. The front endpapers have a faint offset and a previous owner's name in ink, and there is a small defect in the bottom margins of the front endpaper and half-title. The jacket has one small repair and is strengthened in two or three places.

$85 165. FITZGERALD. Tender is the Night. 8vo, original cloth, in original dust jacket; a clean copy, firm in covers, with 2 defects noted below.
New York, 1934
FIRST EDITION of the novel with which the author was never fully satisfied and which he attempted to improve by extensive re-writing after publication. The dust jacket is in good condition and the covers and text of the book are bright; however, there is a marginal tear at p. 5, affecting a few letters without actual loss, and the bottom margins of a few leaves at the front are faintly stained.

34

| FIRST SESSION | TUESDAY AFTERNOON, APRIL 9TH |

166. FITZGERALD. Taps at Reveille. 8vo, original cloth, in original pictorial dust jacket. FINE; the jacket with minor traces of shelf wear. *$70-*
New York, 1935
FIRST EDITION, rare complete with the dust jacket.

15. Parke-Bernet, New York, Sale Number 2207 (1 October 1963)

This sale included twelve Fitzgerald books from the collection of newspaper columnist George Matthew Adams.

> INSCRIBED COPY
>
> 95. FITZGERALD, F. SCOTT. This Side of Paradise. 8vo, original cloth. A very good copy. In half leather folding slipcase. (*Adams*)   New York, 1920
> FIRST EDITION. The gilt lettering on the spine a little dull. A delightful inscription on the flyleaf to "*Dear Uncle & Aunt—The Great American Novel at Last. Scott.*"
> 19

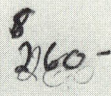

16. Swann Galleries Sale Number 639 (16 January 1964)

W. E. Hill illustrated the dust jackets for *This Side of Paradise, Flappers and Philosophers,* and *The Beautiful and Damned.* Item 160 brought $120.

> WITH A FULL-PAGE INSCRIPTION
>
> 160 FITZGERALD, F. SCOTT. This Side of Paradise. 8vo, cloth, rubbed. FIRST EDITION.   New York, 1920
> WITH A FULL-PAGE INSCRIPTION, written on a sheet of Scribner letterhead and tipped in — "Dear Mr. Hill — If my book was half as good as your cover I'd sell a million copies . . . Very gratefully one of your many admirers. F. Scott Fitzgerald."

17. Paul C. Richards Autographs Catalogue 11 [ca. 1964]

Relisted at the same price in the *Beacon Bulletin*, Catalogue 13, Issue 5 (Paul C. Richards Autographs Catalogue [ca. 1964]) and the *Beacon Bulletin*, Catalogue 14, Issue 6 (Paul C. Richards Autograph Catalogue [ca. 1964]). Offered again in Argosy Books Catalogue 506 [ca. 1973] at $200. Relisted in Glenn Horowitz Catalogue 24 (1991) at $5,500: see entry 94, item 58.

> 118. FITZGERALD, F. SCOTT. *The Vegetable,* New York, 1923. First edition. Inscribed *For Fanny Hurst/from hers admiringly/F. Scott Fitzgerald/May 4th 1923.* Very fine copy with the Hurst bookplate. QUITE SCARCE! $225.00

Richards Autographs Catalogue 11

18. *Baltimore Symphony Auction* (9 October 1964)

This benefit sale was amateurishly catalogued and badly managed. Scottie Fitzgerald donated two books: the copy of *The Great Gatsby* (item 281)—not a manuscript—inscribed "It's a masterpiece, Mother. Write me how you like it." brought $1,000; and *Death in the Afternoon* (item 284) inscribed "To Scott with much affection Ernest" went to the University of Texas Humanities Research Center for $800. The copy of *Taps at Reveille* (item 311) inscribed to Curtis Carroll Davis—"For Carroll Davis from an old editor of The Nassau Litt. to a young Editor of the Yale Litt F. Scott Fitzgerald / Baltimore 13   1936"—was acquired by Scottie for $275 and is now in the Bruccolis' personal collection.

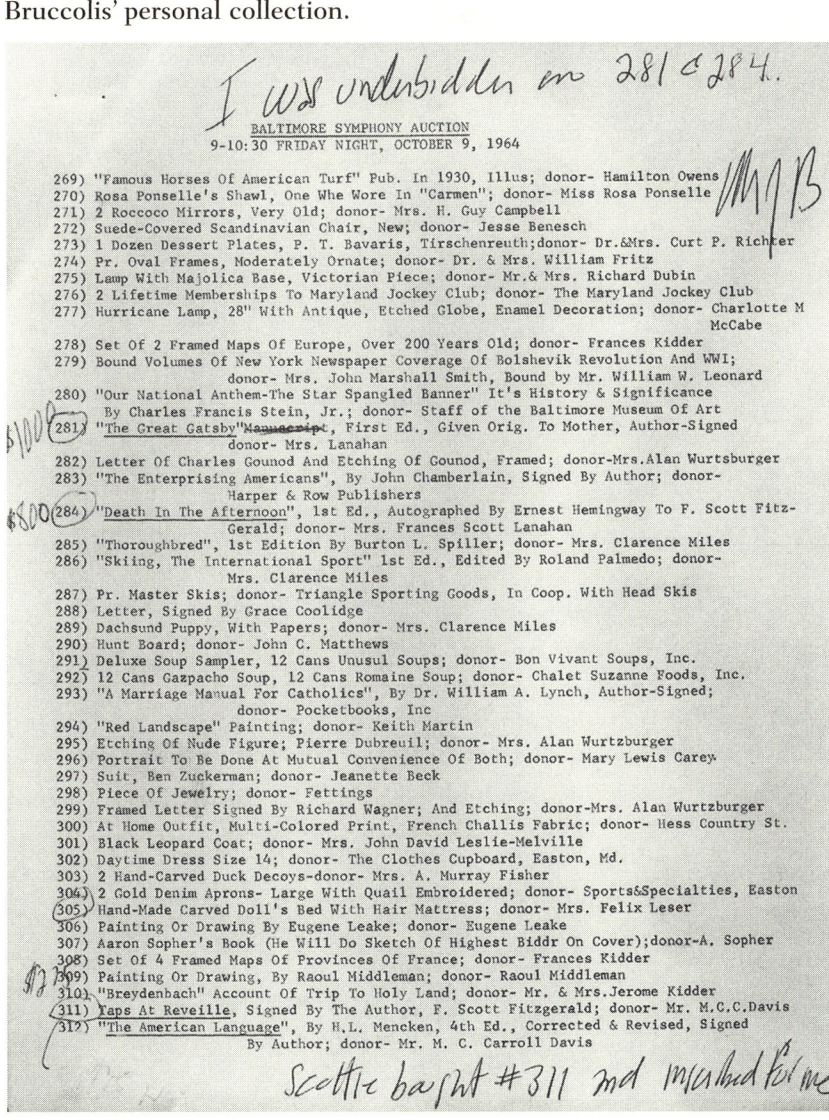

19. Heritage Book Shop (Long Grove, Illinois) Catalogue 3 (Winter 1964–1965)

These two items were later offered by Lew David Feldman as lot 289 in his *Catalogue Sixty Six A* (1966) for $500. Location: Harry Ransom Humanities Research Center, University of Texas, Austin.

> A-19. FITZGERALD, F. Scott. American novelist. Autograph letter signed, one page, Great Neck, L. I., no date. To Mr. Emmerich. Declining a lecture engagement. "Only last week I tried making a speech and almost collapsed from sheer terror. I guess we'd better call off the idea." A magnificent letter on gray laid paper and a beautiful example of Fitzgerald's bold holograph style. $75.00
>
> SIR SHANE LESLIE'S "DISCOVERY" OF SCOTT
> FITZGERALD: A LITERARY LETTER OF IMPORTANCE
>
> A-20. (FITZGERALD, F. Scott.) Leslie, Sir Shane, Irish author, and J. H. Edge. An exchange of correspondence concerning Leslie's discovery of Fitzgerald as a writer. Two items: Autograph letter signed, one page, (London), May 20, 1926, by Shane Leslie, asking to see a "paragraph" about which Edge has inquired so that he can tell "how much truth lies in it." Leslie adds: "I was interested in Scott Fitzgerald and took his first book to Scribner's with striking results. If one has no genius one should discover the genius of others." Autograph letter signed, two pages, from Edge, London, June 2, 1926, sending the clipping referred to and asking Leslie to tell "how you discovered him"; on the back of these two pages, Leslie has written his explanation and signed his initials "S. L." Monsignor Fay, head master of the Newman School, "begged me to look over Fitz's first novel," says Leslie. "I left the manuscript with Scribner.... When the book was a success, Fitz and Zelda crossed the Atlantic to pay me a visit of thanks." (Leslie refers in this letter to the manuscript "The Romantic Egotist," which was the first draft of "This Side of Paradise." See page 82 of Andrew Turnbull's "Scott Fitzgerald," which confirms that Leslie sent the novel in to Scribner's.) Included is the clipping referred to in the letters, in which a columnist had reported that Leslie "was first responsible" for the publication of "This Side of Paradise." With the original envelope addressed to J. H. Edge in Sir Shane's hand. A magnificent documentation of one of the significant literary events of modern times. $350.00

Heritage Book Shop Catalogue 3

20. Charles Hamilton Auction Number 9 (30 September 1965)

Recatalogued at the same price by Hamilton in his Auction Number 16 (13 December 1966).

The novel to which Fitzgerald refers in this ALS is both mistitled and misdated by the cataloguer. Fitzgerald notes the following "errors" or inconsistencies in *The Beautiful and Damned* (1922):

p. 276: "Gloria would be twenty-six in May."
p. 391: "She would be twenty-nine in February."
p. 192: "—she would be twenty-four in August. . . . "

> 55a FITZGERALD, F. SCOTT. American author. A.L.S., ¾ page, 8vo, St. Paul, Minnesota, with addressed, stamped envelope postmarked June 10, 1922. To Zella R. Kimball. _____(100.00)
> Amusing letter on his printed letterhead, "F. Scott Fitzgerald/Hack Writer and Plagiarist/Saint Paul, Minnesota." Apparently commenting on errors in *The Beautiful and the Damned* (1921), Fitzgerald writes: "You mention pages 276 & 391. But—look on page 192 and see the worst! August! God! How come, indeed!"
> Worn at top with several small tears (not affecting text) caused by removal from an album.

Hamilton Auction Number 9

21. *Catalogue Number Six: Modern Authors.* Henry W. Wenning [1965]

The best group of F. Scott Fitzgerald materials catalogued by a dealer. See "Overview" for commentary on Wenning's book-selling activities.

Henry W. Wenning

NOTE

The Fitzgerald material that follows is from the collection of Alice Richardson and for that reason has been separately listed out of the usual order. Miss Richardson (then Alice Richardson Wooten) worked for Fitzgerald as a typist for less than a month in the early winter of 1935. A graduate of the University of Alabama, she had directed publicity for the Maryland Tercentenary in 1934 and hoped to write fiction. The author gave her his revised typescripts of the three short stories listed below to use as a guide in rewriting her own work. When Miss Richardson left Baltimore in 1935, Fitzgerald provided her with letters of introduction to friends in New York, in an effort to assist her in finding a position in publishing or promotional work. A sporadic correspondence was maintained; the last letter that he wrote to her was dated five months before his death. There emerges from these minor events a sizeable portrait of the author as a kind and gracious man.

370. FITZGERALD (F. Scott). THE COUNT OF DARKNESS. A 40pp. triple-spaced typescript, very heavily revised in pencil. This story is Part Two of a four part series that Fitzgerald wrote under the general title THE COUNT OF DARKNESS. It appeared in the June 1935 issue of REDBOOK.   [Sold]

371. ———A KINGDOM IN THE DARK. A 50 pp. triple-spaced typescript, very heavily revised in pencil, as above. Although the text is continuous, the pagination reads 1-8 and then 10-51. Pages 35-51 were originally numbered 10-26. Apparently there are two typescripts conflated here. This story is Part Three of THE COUNT OF DARKNESS and appeared in the August 1935 issue of REDBOOK.   [Sold]

372. ———HER LAST CASE. A 43 pp. (the pagination reads 42) triple-spaced typescript, very heavily revised in pencil. This is accompanied by five additional pages (also typed with autograph corrections) that provide two further conclusions to the story, each of them differing from each other as well as from the main draft described above. The story was published in the SATURDAY EVENING POST for November 3, 1934. $600.00

373. ———Telegram dated Nov. 28, 1934 to Alice Richardson. 80 words beginning *"I got up out of more sickness than you ever saw in this house and you saw plenty to crawl down to the B and O to send this..."* Ending *"with dearest love Scott"*. The *"this"* referred to was a group of letters of recommendation, some of which are listed below.   [Sold]

44

282 York Street, New Haven, Conn.

374. ———One page typed letter, signed December 8, 1934, addressed to Mary Brown requesting a place for Alice Richardson in *"your paternal store"* (Wanamaker's). *"Both Zelda and I are very fond of her and would appreciate anything you could do for her ... starting out on her own in New York."* Signed *"Scott"*. $25.00

375. ———One page typed letter, signed January 20, 1935, addressed to *"Dear Cupie"* (Horace F. Simon). A letter of recommendation on behalf of Alice Richardson. *"I boasted to her of having been a classmate of yours at Princeton."* Two words are inserted in holograph and the signature reads *"Scott Fitzgerald"*. $25.00

376. ———One page typed letter signed, March 2, 1935, addressed to Charles MacArthur (*"Dear Charlie"*) asking for a job as script girl for Alice Richardson. Signed *"Scott Fitz"*. $25.00

376a. ———One page typed letter signed, March 2, 1935, addressed to Max Perkins with similar content and signature. [Sold]

377. ———Two page typed letter signed with a few trivial corrections in ink, to Alice Richardson, dated February 28, 1935. Approximately 370 words— including a short lesson on writing. Apparently Miss Richardson had written a story dealing with the life of a famous writer and forwarded the ms to Fitzgerald for his views. His very gentle critique runs in part:
"It won't do, Alyce. It is in part too personal and in part not personal enough. It is not really English to write such a sentence as 'Her tonsils were in terrible shape,' which gives a rather revolting picture of the lady's throat. I appreciate your sparing me on the alcoholic side, at the same time the picture of a writer living in a dressing gown isn't sufficiently new or startling to give personality interest. Due to the fact that my books no longer have the national circulation they used to have, but sell chiefly in big cities, the interest in such articles would be limited to magazines such as THE NEW YORKER, whose readers would not consider the company of an author very exciting after all. This is sad but true . . . .
In the above text the word *"national"* was inserted before the word *"circulation"* as a correction. Signed *"Scott Fitz"*. $150.00

378. ———Two page typed letter signed, to Alice Richardson, dated May 14, 1935. Approximately 175 words. A gay letter: *"The establishment here is breaking up and I am going south to recuperate. I dont drink anymore (4 mos) and you would like me better. No possible news. Mrs. Owens and I often think of you riding in the park on your roan stallion. I have put a 'tail' on your husband and find he is running around with a lovely high yellow girl named Sally Washington. No other news really. Scottie has leprosy. Mrs. Owens is in prison for assault and battery."* $75.00

Henry W. Wenning

379. ———One page typed letter, single-spaced, to Alice Richardson, July 29. 1940. Approximately 175 words. A poignant letter, written five months before the authors death. He states that he is in Santa Barbara *"working on a story for little Miss Temple. Santa Barbara is supposed to have some escape magic like Palm Springs but no matter how hard you look it's still California."* He reminisces a little about the past including *"Gertrude Stein's passage through Baltimore. It was a solemn winter but there were worse to come and in retrospect those months have an air of early April."* He states that he is sorry not to have seen her and is glad that things turned out as she hoped and intended. The letter concludes *"Your old friend"* and is signed *"Scott"*.

A post script follows: *"Isn't Hollywood a dump—in the human sense of the word. A hideous town, pointed up by the insulting gardens of its rich, full of the human spirit at a new low of debasement."* $150.00

380. ———ALL THE SAD YOUNG MEN. Small 8vo, cloth. New York 1925. First Edition. A bad copy: spine and covers soiled; front hinge repaired and about a half an inch missing from back joint. A presentation copy that Fitzgerald gave to Alice Richardson upon the occasion of her leaving Baltimore. *"God speed thee FSF"*. $25.00

381. ———TENDER IS THE NIGHT. Small 8vo, cloth. New York 1934. Not the first printing. Covers rubbed; otherwise a good sound copy. With a fine presentation inscription: *"For Alyce Wooten/with high regards and many thanks from that old & experienced bully F. Scott Fitzgerald Nov 5th 1934 Baltimore, Md"*. $65.00

22. *Collector*, Volume 79, Numbers 7–10 (1966)

The first catalogued letter from Fitzgerald to Maxwell Perkins with editorial content. But this is not the actual document; it is the facsimile distributed by Charles Scribner's Sons for the 1963 publication of *The Letters of F. Scott Fitzgerald*, edited by Andrew Turnbull. The original letter at the Princeton University Library is in black ink; the facsimile is printed in blue. It has been catalogued several times as the real thing.

> **F. SCOTT FITZGERALD**
> **(1896-1940)**
>
> American novelist. Author of THE GREAT GATSBY, THE BEAUTIFUL AND DAMNED, etc. ALS, 8pp. 16mo, St. Paul, Minn., Sept. 18, 1919. Signed twice, once in full and once with initials. To Maxwell E. Perkins, who had just notified him that his first book, THIS SIDE OF PARADISE, had been accepted for publication. Fitzgerald eagerly desired to have the book appear by Christmas. "... *I have so many things dependent on its success — including of course a girl — not that I expect it to make me a fortune but it will have a psychological effect on me and all my surroundings and besides open up new fields. I'm in that stage where every month counts frantically and seems a cudgel in a fight for happiness against time...*" The book, published the following spring, had a great success, and he and his Zelda were married. He continues: "... *I'm beginning (last month) a very ambitious novel called* THE DEMON LOVER *which will probably take a year. Also I'm writing short stories. I find that what I enjoy writing is always my best... I'm writing a marvellous after-the-war story....*" Fitzgerald's title was rejected by the publisher and THE DEMON LOVER appeared in 1922 as THE BEAUTIFUL AND DAMNED. In a postscript, he inquires: "*Who picks out the cover? I'd like something that could be a set look, cheerful & important like a Shaw Book. I notice Shaw, Galsworthy & Barrie do that. But Wells doesn't — I wonder why...*" As fine a letter of this noted author as one could find, written before his career had yet begun.
> $525.00

23. Charles Hamilton Auction Number 15 (3 November 1966)

This book was subsequently listed by Robert K. Black in the *11th Co-operative Catalogue of Members of the Middle Atlantic Chapter of the Antiquarian Booksellers Association of America* [1967] for $150.

> 311 FITZGERALD, F. SCOTT. American author. *The Beautiful and the Damned*, Charles Scribner's Sons, New York, 1922, bound in gilt-stamped green textured cloth, first edition, inscribed by Fitzgerald on front fly-leaf (not signed). _____ (110.00)
> Excessively rare inscribed copy of one of Fitzgerald's best known works. Although Fitzgerald did not sign the inscription, his bold handwriting fills the entire front fly-leaf, "To Mary Craven, who doesn't think it's fun to be rich — from one who's one idea is GOLD, from a sincere admirer of Mary & Frank Craven (& what's more — an imitator of the latter) Nov 17th 1(9)22." Frank Craven is the American actor and playwright.
> Shaken, with the binding somewhat worn and spotted, but a remarkable inscription revealing a little-known aspect of Fitzgerald's personal philosophy.

$90 — Black [handwritten annotation]

Hamilton Auction Number 15

24. *Catalogue Sixty Six A*. Lew David Feldman (1966)

Rosalind Sayre Smith was Fitzgerald's sister-in-law who came to despise him. He reciprocated.

> PRESENTATION COPY
> 288. FITZGERALD, F. Scott. *The Beautiful and Damned*. 12mo, green cloth, fore edges uncut, green cloth case. New York, 1922. First Edition, Presentation Copy, inscribed by the author on the front free endpaper: "For Rosalind Smith, Wanderer on the face of the earth — from F. Scott Fitzgerald, St. Paul, Minn. This is *not* autobiography." Small tear on spine neatly repaired, 2 small spots on back cover where faded.   250.00

Nell Brooks is unidentified.

> PRESENTATION COPY INTIMATELY INSCRIBED
> 290. FITZGERALD, F. Scott. *Tender is the Night. A Romance.* Decorations by Edward Shenton. 12mo, green cloth (front cover somewhat spotty, back cover slightly wrinkled), fore edges untrimmed, green cloth box. New York, 1934. First Edition, Presentation Copy, signed and inscribed on the front free endpaper and fly-leaf: "For Nell: as we (lie) sit here on the old (bed) swing we often think of you. Miss Garbo realizes that you had no past & feels no real jealousy when I speak of our "platonic" friendship (You remember our encounter in the family wastebasket?) But all is over between us (Nell Mary) Nell, and Greta feels the same way I do—we wish you the best of happiness (and Marlene joins us), even if you weren't (sic) able to make F. Scott Fitzgerald" Also on the title page, after the printed "A Romance," Fitzgerald wrote in ink: "about Nell Brooks" and signed his name again   500.00

Item 540 was later auctioned by Sotheby Parke Bernet (29 March 1977) for $1,800 (see entry 52, item 105) and then by Christie, Manson & Woods (22 May 1981) for $2,400.

> CRISP PRESENTATION COPY OF AUTHOR'S FIRST BOOK
> 540. FITZGERALD, F. Scott. *This Side of Paradise*. 12mo, green cloth. New York, 1920. First Edition of the author's first book, Presentation copy inscribed and signed for Harold Davis, July 2, 1920.   150.00

Item 565 is the only inscribed copy of *Save Me the Waltz* located in a catalogue. The recipients were the Ludlow Fowlers; he was the best man at the Fitzgeralds' wedding and a model for Anson Hunter, protagonist of "The Rich Boy" (1926). Feldman sold this book by phone to Bruccoli, and then resold it to someone else who offered more money for it.

> 565. [FITZGERALD, F. Scott]. FITZGERALD, Zelda. **Save Me the Waltz.** 12mo, green cloth (spine a trifle faded). New York, 1932. First Edition, Presentation copy with a note laid in inscribed to "Elsie and Ludlow" and signed by the author. 100.00

25. Charles Hamilton Auction Number 21 (28 September 1967)

> 276 FITZGERALD, F. SCOTT. Amusing original Autograph Manuscript of eight lines, written in pencil (but signed and dated in ink), July, 1933. On verso of an engraved wedding invitation. _____ (150.00)
> Delightful original verses, with revisions. "Don't expect me/I've gone fancy/I'm all set/With Bryan Dancy./Scotty's Windbag—/Michell's Berries/Back at midnight/Out with fairies." In the left margin appears the signatures, in ink, of Jake Mitchell (with a small drawing) and Bryan, both mentioned in the poem.

The poem was subsequently listed in Robert F. Batchelder Catalogue 48 (1984), where its description is pure invention.

> AMUSING ORIGINAL F. SCOTT FITZGERALD AUTOGRAPH
> POEM SIGNED, PROBABLY MEANT AS A NOTE FOR ZELDA
> 33. FITZGERALD, F. SCOTT. American author. Autograph Manuscript Signed with revisions, 1 page, 8vo, July, 1933, probably a note written while drunk to his wife, Zelda. Fitzgerald pens an amusing eight line verse which reads: "Don't expect me/I've gone fancy/I'm all set/With Bryan Dancy./Scotty's windbag/Michell's Berries/Back at midnight/Out with fairies." The verse is in pencil while Fitzgerald's signature at the conclusion and the date "July, 1933" which he wrote at the top are in ink. The poem is on the back of a wedding invitation of May, 1933. In the left margin appear signatures in ink of Jake Mitchell with a little drawing of what apparently is a fairy, and of Bryan, the two men mentioned in the poem. Fitzgerald had probably left this note for Zelda when he went out to meet Dancy and Mitchell. One of them undoubtedly saw the note and asked Fitzgerald to sign it for him. Fitzgerald obliged, sloppily signing it and dating it, with Dancy and Mitchell signing it as well. This manuscript is illustrated in Charles Hamilton's book "The Signature of America" on page 144, and he has captioned it "F. Scott Fitzgerald. Handwritten verses signed, obviously penned while drunk." At this time Fitzgerald was finishing his last complete novel, Tender is the Night, at the same time trying to cope with Zelda's creeping insanity, which left him in poor condition both physically and emotionally. In addition, Zelda was at this time challenging his masculinity, and if Dancy and Mitchell were not "fairies," i.e. homosexuals, Fitzgerald may have meant the term to look like a sarcastic comment to Zelda.   1500.00
> [SEE ILLUSTRATION ON OPPOSITE PAGE]

[Horseshit]

26. *An Important Gathering of Autographs & Manuscripts American and European.* Parke-Bernet, New York, Sale Number 2763 (13 November 1968)

This inscription with drawing was recatalogued in Heritage Catalogue 114 [ca. 1968] for $550; in Literary Heritage Catalogue 11 (Spring 1969) for $550; and in Literary Heritage Catalogue 14 (May 1970) for $525.

> 67. FITZGERALD, F. SCOTT. Ms. satiric quotation, with signature in text. 1 p, 12 lines, small 8vo; picture postal card pasted to verso. Dated May 31st, 1922. Together with an A.L.s. 1 p., 4to, old folds.
> The quotation reads: "For Harry W. Winslow, A.B., M.D., Ph.D. from The Very Reverend F. Scott Fitzgerald Archbishop of the Church of St. Voltaire Patterson, New Jersey. 'Now is the time for all good men to come to the aid of their party.' Ezeliel III v.2 May 31st, 1922 [comic drawing of bearded old man with spectacles.] A self portrait of Mr. Fitzgerald just after the battle of Gettysburg."
> The A.L.s. reads: "Dear Mr. Winslow: Be glad to autograph your book. I know [John] Farrar slightly. Sincerely F. Scott Fitzgerald 626 Goodrich Avenue. St. Paul, Minn. May 21st 1922."
>   [See illustration]   *$350-*

Parke-Bernet Sale Number 2763

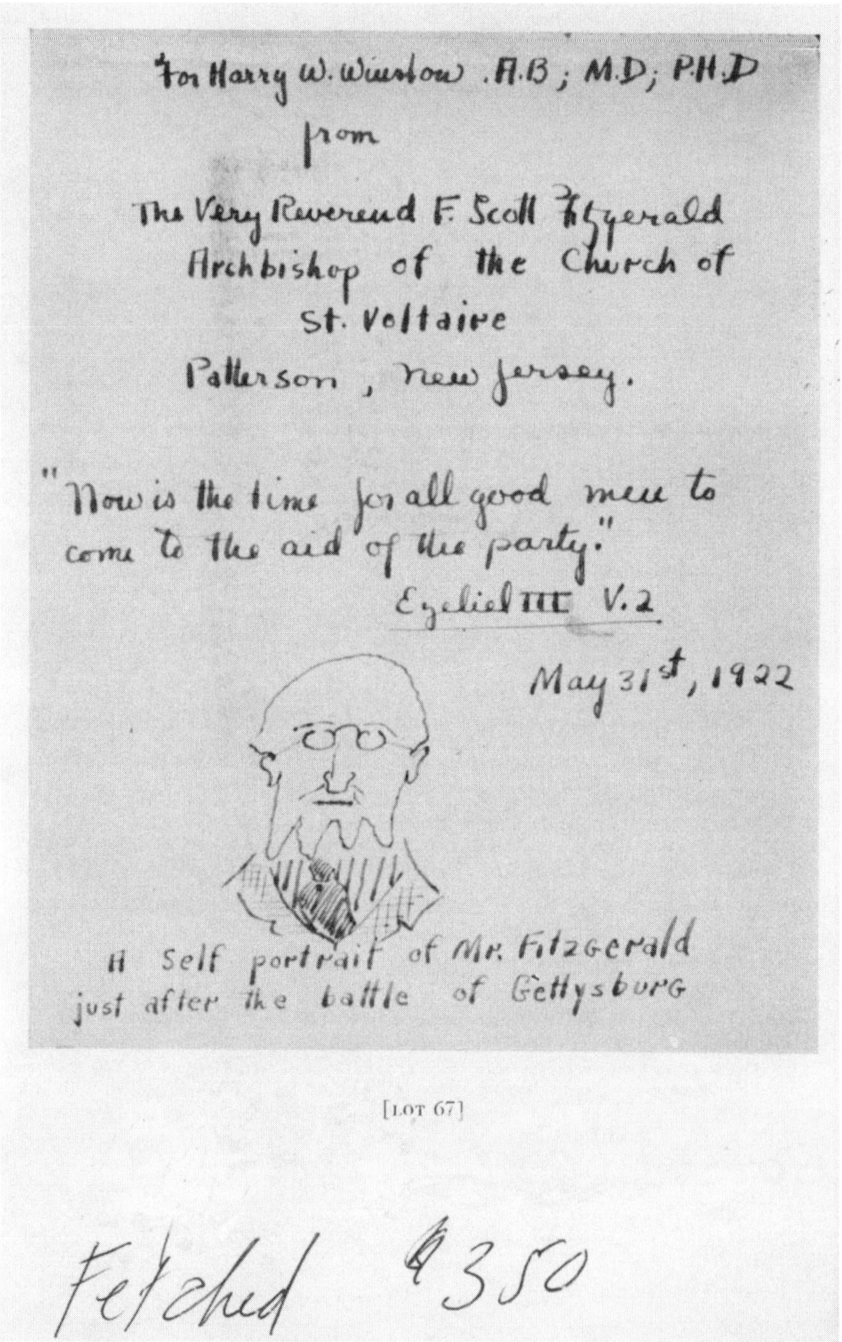

> For Harry W. Winston, A.B; M.D; P.H.D
> from
> The Very Reverend F. Scott Fitzgerald
> Archbishop of the Church of
> St. Voltaire
> Patterson, New Jersey.
>
> "Now is the time for all good men to come to the aid of the party."
>   Ezekiel III V.2
>
>   May 31st, 1922
>
> A Self portrait of Mr. Fitzgerald just after the battle of Gettysburg

[LOT 67]

Fetched $350

27. *Beacon Bulletin,* **Catalogue 23, Issue 14 (Paul C. Richards Autographs [ca. 1969])**

Item 963 was catalogued at $350; it was recatalogued at the same price in Paul C. Richards Autographs Catalogue 46 [ca. 1970] as item 61.

> Of wonders is Silas M. Hanson the champ
> He asked for an aut'graph and sent me a stamp
> But none of his pleadings would go on a shelf
> If he'd added an envelope 'dressed to himself
>
> F Scott Fitzgerald

61. FITZGERALD, F. SCOTT. 1896-1940. American fiction writer. Autograph Manuscript Occasional Verse Signed. 1/2p., 4to. [Paris, June 26, 1925]. With original stamped envelope addressed by Fitzgerald to "Silas M. Hanson / The Autograph King /...Chicago, Ill. / Etats Unis." Very unusual poem written by Fitzgerald at the request of an autograph collector. See illustration above.   350.00

1970s

28. Bennett & Marshall Catalogue 9 [1970]

This copy of *Taps at Reveille* was included in the 6 April 1976 Samsell list: see entry 49, item 78.

> 55. FITZGERALD, F. SCOTT. Taps at Reveille. New York. 1935. SOLD
>
> First Edition. 12mo. Cloth. Lettering on spine faded. Author's presentation on front free end paper: "For Sylvia Lewis/in memory of those/days when she/translated *A Rebours* for me/in my cork-lined/converted Pullman/F. Scott ("Huysmans") Fitzgerald/The Flood — 1938".

29. Black Sun Books Catalogue 10 [ca. 1970]

> "A PIECE OF INSOLENCE"
>
> 110. FITZGERALD (F. Scott). The Beautiful & Damned. N.Y. 1922. 8vo, cloth. First edition, first issue. Some minor foxing, else nearly fine in a fragmentary dw. With Fitzgerald's full page presentation: "For _____/with best wishes/from/F. Scott Fitzgerald/This was a book about/things I knew nothing/about, a drawing upon/experiences that I had/not had. Much more than/my first book this/was a piece of insolence." Tipped in to the front pastedown is a 1 page TLS from Fitzgerald. Probably the finest Fitzgerald presentation to be catalogued in recent years.   1,000.00

30. *An Auction of Literary and Artistic Materials for the Benefit of Antiwar Congressional Candidates* (8 October 1970)

Marya Mannes was the daughter of David Mannes and Clara Damrosch Mannes, musicians and educators. This item was subsequently auctioned in the 13 April 2004 Neville sale for $90,000 BP: see entry 135, item 60.

44. FITZGERALD, F. SCOTT. A fine Autograph Letter Signed, 2½ pages 4to, with envelope, to Marya Mannes, Paris, Oct. 21, 1925. Fitzgerald writes: "Thank you for writing me about *Gatsby*—I especially appreciate your letter because women, and even intelligent women, haven't generally cared much for it. . . . America's greatest promise is that something is going to happen, and after a while you get tired of waiting because nothing happens to American people except that they grow old, and nothing happens to American art because America is the story of the moon that never rose. . . . My new novel is marvellous. I'm in the first chapter. . . . Can you name a single American artist except James & Whistler (who lived in England) who didn't die of drink? . . ."

Donated by Marya Mannes.

31. Charles Hamilton Auction Number 45 (22 October 1970)

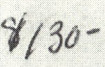

119 FITZGERALD, F. SCOTT. American author. His book, *Tender is the Night*, Charles Scribner's Sons, N.Y., 1934, *first edition*, inscribed by FITZGERALD on front flyleaf: "Tom Rennie from/his friend Scott." Dr. Thomas Rennie, distinguished psychiatrist on the staff of Johns Hopkins Hospital and a director of the Mental Health Foundation, was the psychiatrist for Fitzgerald's wife, Zelda. Binding very slightly worn, else in fine condition and an interesting association piece. _____ (90.00)

32. Parke-Bernet, New York, Sale Number 3209 (18 May 1971)

See the introduction for an account of this sale. Acquired for the Bruccoli Collection.

Galley Proofs of *The Great Gatsby*

22 FITZGERALD, F. SCOTT. Uncorrected galley proofs of *The Great Gatsby* (New York, Scribner, 1925), 57 galleys (complete), in a half morocco slipcase.

The title on each galley is *Trimalchio* (from the noveau-riche party-giver in Petronius' *Satyricon*). On the first galley *Trimalchio* has been crossed out and *The Great Gatsby* has been pencilled in. The galleys differ importantly, and often extensively, from the text of the first edition: two-thirds of the galleys vary *at least* in a sentence or two from the printed text; about one-half show major changes (paragraph deletions or additions, altered dialogue, etc.); and blocks of material in a few galleys have been left out of the book entirely. For example, the crucial party scene in the Plaza Hotel (Chapter VII), as evident from the galleys, was virtually rewritten by Fitzgerald. Another vital difference between the galleys and the book is the transposition of material in various chapters, e.g., information about Gatsby's previous life is presented in Chapter VI of the book, but appears with differences in Chapter VIII in the galleys. EXTREMELY RARE, no more than a few sets of galleys having been printed.

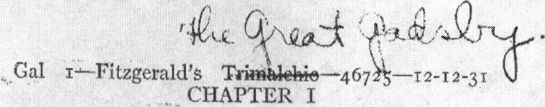

Gal 1—Fitzgerald's Trimalchio—46725—12-12-31

CHAPTER I

In my younger and more vulnerable years my father told me something that I've been turning over in my mind ever since.

"When you feel like criticising any one," he said, "just remember that everybody in this world hasn't had the advantages that you've had."

He didn't say any more, but we've always been unusually communicative in a reserved way, and I understood that he meant a great deal more than that. In consequence, I'm inclined to reserve all judgments, a habit that has opened up many curious natures to me and also made me the victim of not a few veteran bores. The abnormal mind is quick to detect and attach itself to this quality when it appears in a normal person, and so it came about that in college I was unjustly accused of being a politician, because I was privy to the secret griefs of wild, unknown men. Most of the confidences were unsought—frequently I have feigned sleep, preoccupation, or a hostile levity when I realized by some unmistakable sign that an intimate revelation was quivering on the horizon; for the intimate revelations of young men, or at least the terms in which they express them, are usually plagiaristic and marred by obvious suppressions. Reserving judgments is a matter of infinite hope. I am still a little afraid of missing something if I forget that, as my father snobbishly suggested, and I snobbishly repeat, a sense of the fundamental decencies is parcelled out unequally at birth.

Top section of the first galley page

33. *First Editions: Modern American Literature.* Joseph the Provider Catalogue 2 [July 1971]

```
181. FITZGERALD, F. SCOTT. This side of paradise. New York,
Scribner's Sons, 1921. Reprint edition of the author's first
book. This copy bears the following interesting inscription
on the front fly leaf: "For---This immature product of which,
did I not feel an unnatural affection for it, I would be
somewhat ashamed. F. Scott Fitzgerald, April 22nd 1922, St.
Paul, Minn." Bookplate of the recipient on front pastedown.
An almost fine copy with faint traces of shelf wear.      250.00
```

34. Charles Hamilton Auction Number 55 (3 February 1972)

Hamilton catalogued this letter at $60. It was recatalogued by Ira and Larry Goldberg Auctioneers (18 November 2006) as item 158.

F. SCOTT FITZGERALD SOBERS UP AND RETHINKS AN OFFER

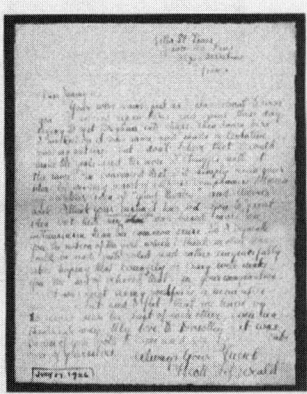

158   Fitzgerald, F. Scott (1896-1940) American writer; the premier novelist of the Jazz Age. Autograph Letter Signed, 1 p., 10¾x8¼", Villa St. Louis, Juan-les-Pins, Alpes Maritime, France, 17 July 1926. Very good; uneven toning and some fading of ink to a few words. Written while *The Great Gatsby* was on the bestseller list, to "Dear Jimmy," probably James Rennie, the actor who played the lead in the Broadway production of *The Great Gatsby*, regarding Fitzgerald's attempts to convert the book *Brigham Young* by M.R. Werner into a play. "...*I sobered up in Paris and spent three days trying to get Brigham into shape. Then down here I worked on it some more and made a tentative working outline. But I don't believe that I could make the grade and the more I struggle with it the more I'm convinced that I'd simply ruin your idea by making a sort of half-ass compromise between my amateur idea of 'good theatre' and Werner's book. I think your instinct has led you to a great idea but that my unsolicited offer was based more on enthusiasm than on common sense. So I bequeath you the notion of the girl which I think in other hands could be made quite solid, and rather ungracefully retire hoping that Connolly or Craig will make you the sort of vehicle of it that's in your imagination....You're a man after my own heart and I feel that we have by no means seen the last of each other, even in a theatrical way. My love to Dorothy - it was so nice of you both to come and see Zelda....*" Zelda was recovering from an appendectomy at this time. According to Fitzgerald biographer, Andrew Turnbull, the author went out on the town every night with James Rennie during the two weeks Zelda was in the hospital.
Estimated Value $2,000-3,000

Fitzgerald's "Craig" is probably George Kelly, author of the popular 1925 play *Craig's Wife*. Ira and Larry Goldberg Auctioneers (18 November 2006)

35. Charles Hamilton Auction Number 60 (3 August 1972)

66-A FITZGERALD, F. SCOTT. American author. L.S., 1-1/3 pages (on two 4to leaves), 1307 Park Ave., Baltimore, Md., April 24, 1935. To Mr. C.A. Wright. "I was on the *Tiger* staff at Princeton for three years and got out many issues...though I was not chairman. It was never as big a thing at Princeton as was the *Record* at Yale...because most of the local wit was concentrated on producing the hullabaloo of the Triangle show, and lately the "Intime" reviews. My time was chiefly notable for the first acknowledgment in print that girls would be girls and the first use in the east of such words as 'necking' and 'petting' exemplified by a series which I started...called *International Petting Cues*..." Fine, bearing two words of holograph corrections. ....(225.00)

36. Charles Hamilton Auction Number 61 (14 September 1972)

160 FITZGERALD, F. SCOTT. American author. Interesting L.S., 1-1/2 pages (on two 4to leaves), Baltimore, Md., Jan. 7, 1934. To Mr. E.S. Oliver. "The first help I ever had in writing in my life was from my father who read an utterly imitative Sherlock Holmes story of mine and pretended to like it. But after that I received the most invaluable aid from...[the] headmaster of the St. Paul Academy...from Courtland Van Winkle in freshman year at Princeton...he gave us the book of *Job* to read and I don't think any of our preceptorial group ever quite recovered from it...Most of the professors seemed to me old and uninspired, or perhaps it was just that I was getting under way in my own field. I think this answers your question. This is also my permission to make full use of it with or without my name..." Trivial paper-clip stain, otherwise fine. ....(200.00)

161 FITZGERALD, F. SCOTT. L.S., 2/3 page, 4to, Baltimore, Md., Feb. 1, 1935. To Mr. E.S. Oliver, "...I don't want to be quoted...anything you may want to use from my letter is to be summarized..." Fine. ....(75.00)

37. Sotheby Parke Bernet, New York, Sale Number 3476 (20 February 1973)

Individual pieces of this lot were subsequently catalogued in Bernard Quaritch Catalogue 931 (1973) and Kenneth W. Rendell Catalogue 102 [ca. January 1975].

The eighteen-line poem beginning "My Very Very Dear Marie" and sent to Marie Hersey, a St. Paul friend of Fitzgerald's, first appeared in the Sotheby Parke Bernet sale and was then included in the 1973 Quaritch Catalogue and the 1975 Rendell Catalogue—see illustrations below. It was subsequently offered in William Young Catalogue 617 [1975]: see entry 43, item 51. Its final catalogue appearance to date was in Sotheby's, New York, Sale Number 5563 (18 June 1987), where it brought $2,200.

Sotheby Parke Bernet Catalogue 3476

Fitzgerald and His 'First Loves'

207 FITZGERALD, F. SCOTT. A very early group (7 items) of unpublished Fitzgerald manuscript material and ephemera (dated ca. Jan. 1915, or earlier) connected with two girl friends of his undergraduate days—Marie Hersey and Ginevra King—and consisting of: (1) Autograph Letter in Verse Signed, 1 p. 8vo, 107 Patton Hall, Princeton University, on stationery with the Princeton seal, Jan. 1915, to Marie Hersey at The Westover School in Middlebury Conn.; with envelope. The letter is in 18 lines of verse: ". . . *The letter that you sent, Marie,/ Was neither swift nor fair./I hoped that you'd repent, Marie,/Before the start of Lent, Marie,/But Lent could not prevent Marie/From being debonnaire/ . . . So write me what you will, Marie,/ Altho' I will it not./ . . . And tho' you treat me ill, Marie,/Believe me I am still, Marie,/Your fond admirer/Scott.*"
(2) Autograph Letter in the form of a collage (with clippings of advertisements—a few risque—pasted in the letter), 8 pp. 8vo; N.d., n.p. [probably Princeton, ca. 1915], to Marie Hersey. In this collage-letter Fitzgerald humorously tells the history and fate of Miss Hersey, Miss King and three other girls who were mutual friends.
(3) Autograph Note, 1 p. 8vo, headed "Sacred to the memory of Xmas 1911 . . . for Marie Hersey."
(4) Autograph Note by Ginevra King to Fitzgerald, 1 p. 18, asking him to phone her in the morning; N.p., n.d. [ca. 1915].
(5) A dance card belonging to Ginevra King on which Fitzgerald has signed his name ("Scot Fitz") for two dances; together with Miss King's and Fitzgerald's calling cards. [St. Paul, Minn., ca. 1915].
Fitzgerald had grown up with Marie "Midge" Hersey in St. Paul and it was with her, in 1911, that he "experienced his first faint sex attraction." She became the model for Imogene Bissel in "The Scandal Detectives," the autobiographical short story about Basil Duke Lee's first crush. In 1936 Fitzgerald was writing to her: ". . . I think of you as about my oldest real friend, certainly my first love."
Fitzgerald met Ginevra King while she was a house guest of Marie Hersey's in St. Paul during Christmas vacation of 1914 and a romance flared up. She became the model for Judy Jones in "Winter Dreams," Isabelle in *This Side of Paradise* and prefigured later versions of the Fitzgerald heroine. See Arthur Mizener's *The Far Side of Paradise, The World of F. Scott Fitzgerald* and Andrew Turnbull's *Scott Fitzgerald*. (1500/2000.)

[See illustration]

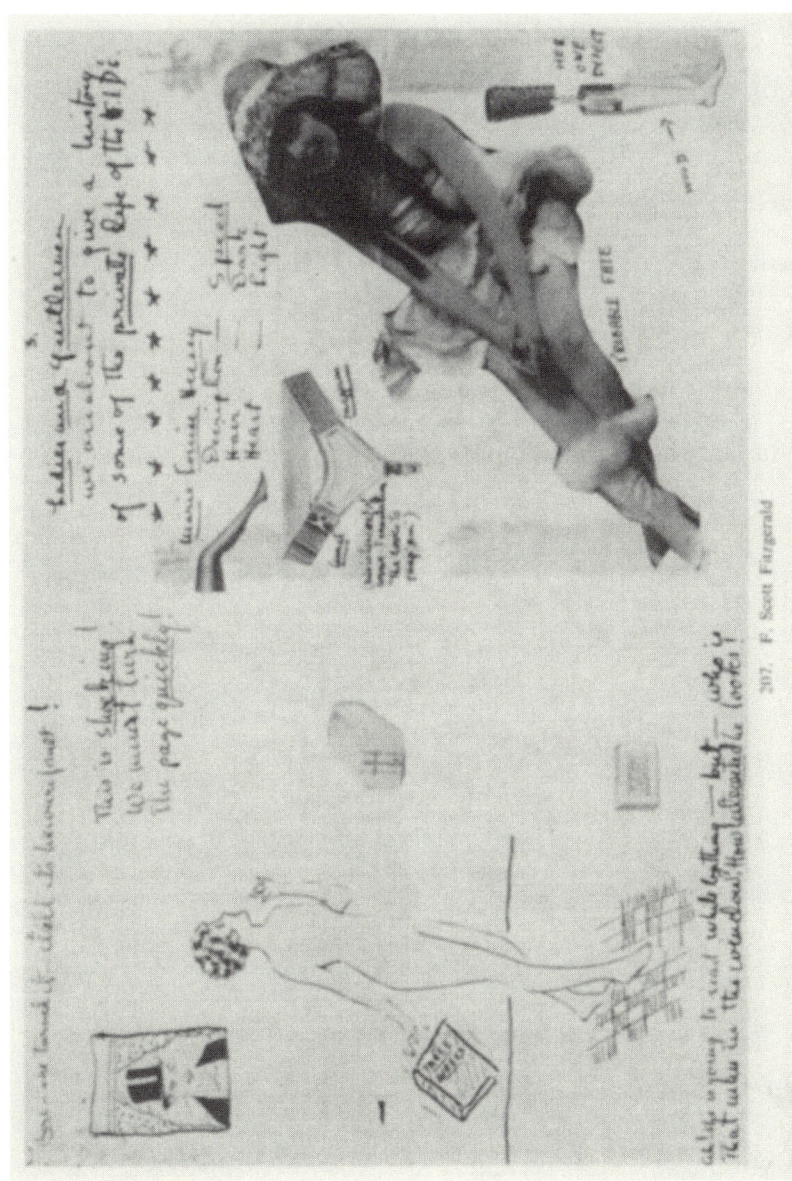

207. F. Scott Fitzgerald

Quaritch Catalogue 931

Scott Fitzgerald and His First Loves

176 **FITZGERALD (F. Scott).** Small card calligraphically signed, to his "first love," Marie Hersey, with representations of *"The mistletoe"* and three amoeboid "tears," surrounding an inscription "Sacred to the memory/ of/Xmas 1911."

3 x 5 inches, *mounting traces*, n.p. [*probably Newman Academy, New Jersey, early* 1912].

£150

Fitzgerald met Marie Hersey in his home town of St. Paul sometime in the spring of 1911, and experienced "his first faint sex attraction" (Fitzgerald, quoted by Turnbull). Later she was to figure as Imogene Bissel in *The Scandal Detectives*, and writing to her in 1936, Fitzgerald declared "I think of you as about my oldest friend, certainly my first love." This Christmas was his first vacation home from boarding school in the East; Turnbull in *The Letters* publishes none to Marie Hersey earlier than 1920, and only one letter at all (a note to his mother from camp) earlier than the present card, written at age fifteen.

177 **FITZGERALD (F. Scott).** Spectacular A.L., constructed as a collage with pictorial advertisements and drawings (some risqué) to Marie Hersey, but with individual pages dedicated to Ginevra King and three other girls, all at the Westover School: each segment tells, with a gifted sophomore's wit, the probable fate of the girls, or predicts their activity at Westover. "Signed" with a drawing of a blackface minstrel, the "Trade Mark" of Fitzgerald, even then a mainstay of the Triangle Dramatic Club at Princeton.

8 pp., 8vo., *some wear, and considerable residue on two pages of mounting tape, rather sticky, through which the text can however be read perfectly*. [*Princeton*], *n.d.* [*but certainly early January* 1915].

£1,000

In addition to the quality of the text and the sentimental appeal of its initial recipient, it is very probably the first letter written (albeit in part) to Ginevra King, who shares with Zelda the responsibility of creating Fitzgerald's "ideal" woman: she is Isabelle in *This Side of Paradise*, Judy Jones in "Winter Dreams," and more than a little of Daisy in *The Great Gatsby* (see Turnbull, p. 150); even in 1937—rather in contrast with what he tells Marie Hersey herself—Fitzgerald refers to Ginevra in a letter to his daughter as "the first girl I ever loved." Their relationship has been carefully charted by Turnbull and by Mizener, who remarks that she "gave substance to an ideal Fitzgerald would cling to for a lifetime; to the end of his days the thought of her could bring tears to his eyes." They met on the last day of Fitzgerald's return to St. Paul over Christmas, 1914-15, where Ginevra, a junior at Westover and roommate of Marie Hersey, was visiting; he "monopolized her" for two hours, as he later recalls. For various peccadilloes Ginevra was expelled from Westover, to which Fitzgerald here certainly alludes, with a clipping of an advertisement for Lassell Seminary for Young Women—"not a *finishing school* but it will be *her* finish!"—and predicting the change of academy will qualify her to become a nurse. One suspects that this quizzical communication, through Marie Hersey and with other messages, must precede the "voluminous correspondence" which Turnbull speaks of, or the "daily . . . incoherent letters" Mizener mentions, *not one of which however appears* in the 1963 *Letters*.

178 [**FITGERALD (F. Scott)**]. A group of memorabilia linking Fitzgerald and Ginevra King, probably assembled by Marie Hersey, comprising (1) calling card of "Miss Ginevra King"; (2) an A.N.s. ("Ginevra") asking the recipient to call her up in the morning ("arrived just a second ago from Virginia Hot Springs . . ."); and (3) a program for a dance, on two small cards, with "Scot Fitz" signed up for two dances (corners worn, tape traces).

4 pp., 12mo., *probably St. Paul*, ?1911 and 1915-6.

£65

It is intriguing to guess whose dance-card this is, but the entries are in different hands. One doubts that Fitzgerald (or his old friend Marie) would mis-spell his own first name. At least one of the other signers, Bob Schmurmeier, was Fitzgerald's close friend in St. Paul during the spring of 1911, when both met Marie Hersey.

Rendell Catalogue 102

AN EXTRAORDINARY AUTOGRAPH MANUSCRIPT

37. FITZGERALD, F. Scott. American writer; author of *The Great Gatsby*. Autograph Manuscript Signed, [his black-faced minstrel trademark], eight full pages, octavo, undated, [early 1915]. Addressed on the first page to Marie Hersey, with individual pages dedicated to Ginevra King and three other girls at the Westover School. Fine condition, except for narrow stains around the border of four pages [the tape which caused the stains, and all residue, has been removed]. The stains do not, in any way, affect the legibility, but do detract slightly from the appearance which is otherwise fine. [See illustrations.] $3000.00

A highly interesting manuscript constructed as a collage with pictorial advertisements interspersed with text and drawings by Fitzgerald. It is headed *Letter for Hersey!* and commences: "My heavens, who'd write to her - must be a mistake. What are the initials - M. L. - well, that's write (a pun). However I would advise Miss Hersey if she wants to keep her peace of mind and moreover her modesty not to look at middle pages of this sheet.... There - she turned it.... This is shocking! We must turn the page quickly...." Fitzgerald has illustrated this page with cut-out pictures of a nude woman, a bathtub, and a man in the background peering through a window which Fitzgerald has drawn around him. He has written: "Ah! She's going to read while bathing - but - who is that man in the window? How *interested* he looks!" Fitzgerald continues with comments about Miss Hersey: a picture of a garterbelt bearing the notation that "This is her coat-of-arms. Translation 'She loves to snap 'em.'," is followed by a page dedicated to her roommate, Marjorie Howey Muir.

The fifth page is dedicated to Ginevra King. "Poor Ginevra! This is some school she's going to next year! It's not a finishing school but it will be her finish! By that time she'll be well-fitted to [printed] Become a Nurse! Poor Ginevra!" In the right portion of this page, Fitzgerald has mounted an advertisement for the Lasell Seminary for Young Women. The remaining pages are dedicated to three other girls at the Westover School and are written in the same manner.

Ginevra King appeared in *This Side of Paradise* as Isabelle and in *Winter Dreams* as Judy Jones, and probably formed part of the character of Daisy in *The Great Gadsby* [see Turnbull, page 150]. Fitzgerald's relationship with Ginevra has been chronicled by Turnbull and Mizener who remarks that she "gave substance to an ideal Fitzgerald would cling to for a lifetime; to the end of his days the thought of her could bring tears to his eyes." Fitzgerald had met her on the last day of his visit to St. Paul for Christmas of 1914 where she was a junior at Westover and a roommate of Marie Hersey, whom he was visiting. As he later recalled, he "monopolized her" for two hours, and in a letter to his daughter in 1937 referred to her as "the first girl I ever loved."

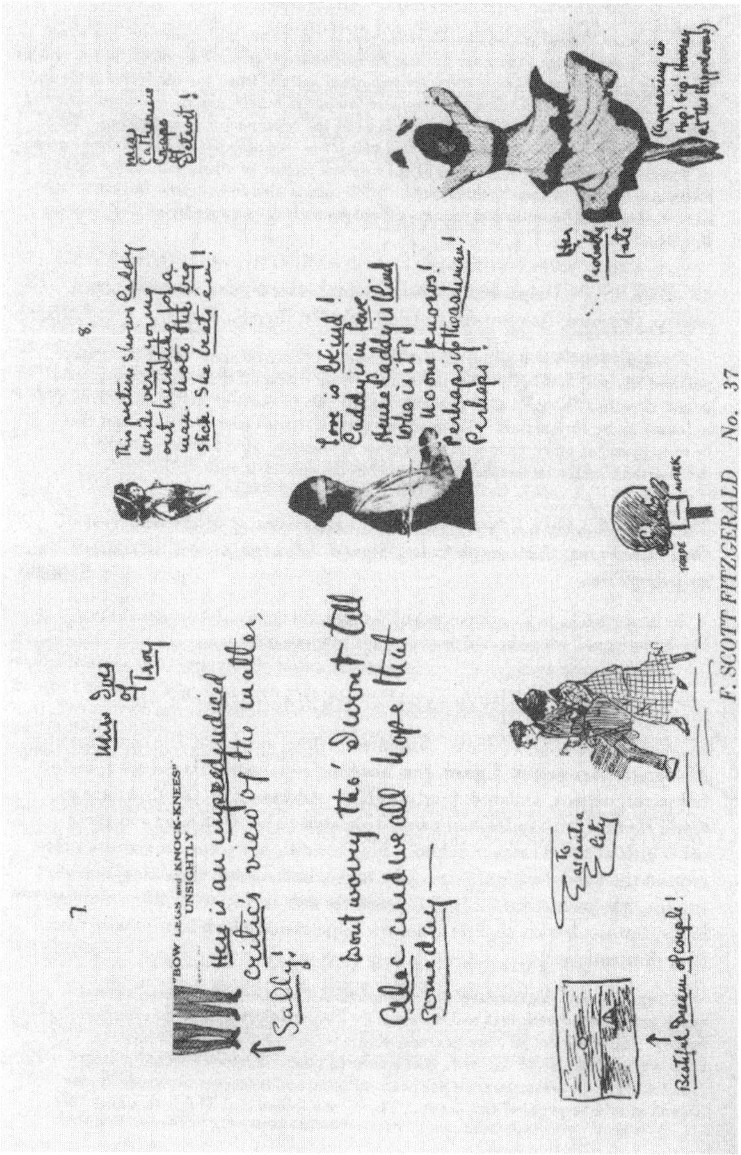

38. *Modern Literature: First Editions & Presentation Copies of American & English Authors.* **Black Sun Books Catalogue 20 [1973]**

The Newman School textbook annotated by Fitzgerald was recatalogued in the 13 April 2004 Neville sale at Sotheby's: see entry 135, item 55.

'WITH APOLOGIES FOR LIVING'

F. SCOTT FITZGERALD AT FIFTEEN

70. FITZGERALD (F. Scott). Fitzgerald's prep school textbook. "The Gateway Series Of English Texts" (Washington's Farewell Address & Websters First Bunker Hill Oration). N.Y. 1911. Sm 8vo, red cloth. Pages torn at edges. Signed by Fitzgerald on the title page: "Francis Scott Fitzgerald/Newman School/Hackensack/New Jersey.". On the first blank page following, Fitzgerald has written a column of 4 numbers (probably his marks). He has also numbered in Roman numerals the chapter headings on pages 21, 22, 23, 24, 25, 26, 33, 34, 35, & 37. He has also sarcastically written above the printed text of Washington's address on pages 22-23, where Washington says: "Not unconscious, in the outset, of the inferiority of my qualifications..." the following comment: "Your most humble & obedient servant/Geo. Washington". Fitzgerald has made a small interpretive note on page 33 and has underlined passages on pages 34, 35, 37, & 43. He has also drawn a picture on page 43 and practised signing his name in a fancy script. In addition to further small doodles and drawings and minor rhyming attempts, he has written a full page autobiographical report on the rear pastedown. The autobiography, prophetic for its contradictions of character and ability, ends: "With apologies/for living/Francis Scott Fitzgerald.". Extremely scarce. There is, we are informed, almost no surviving

holograph material of merit from this period in the author's life. School textbooks, with notes, from Fitzgerald, at age 15, are very rare. This prophetic autobiography is probably the earliest surviving piece of personal importance. $3,500.00

INSCRIBED

71. FITZGERALD. This Side Of Paradise. N.Y. 1920. 8vo, cloth. Slight nick on front flyleaf, else a nearly fine, bright copy. With the author's signed and dated presentation on title page, and APCs laid in. 450.00

Black Sun Books Catalogue 20

39. Maurice F. Neville Rare Books Catalogue 1 [ca. 1974]

358 FITZGERALD, F. SCOTT. Tender is the Night. New York: Charles Scribner's Sons, 1934. $425.00

8vo ,cloth covered boards. *With the author's presentation inscription on front flyleaf*: 'Her fri(e)d Friend is very fond of her, & she will just *half* to except his bad puns, F Scott Fitzgerald, 1934, The Art Museum, Philadelphia, "With Audible Screams" '. Early edition, a good copy.

40. *Americana Mail Auction.* George M. Rinsland Auction 56 (25 May 1974)

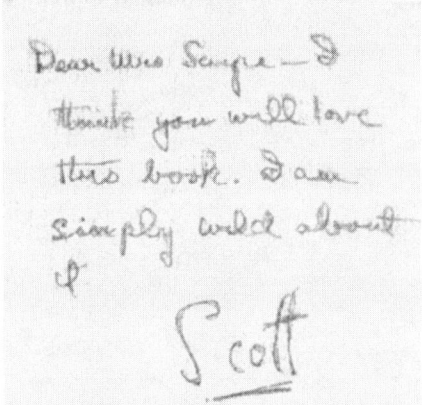

Bruccoli Collection

41. Sotheby Parke Bernet, Los Angeles, Sale Number 127 (23 June 1974)

"Curtis" was probably William Curtis, who had favorably reviewed *The Great Gatsby* for *Town & Country*. The book was offered again in Sotheby Park Bernet, New York, Sale Number 3482 (25 February 1976) and brought $825. It was recatalogued for Christie's, New York, Sale Number 1579 (2 December 2005) where it sold for $10,200 BP.

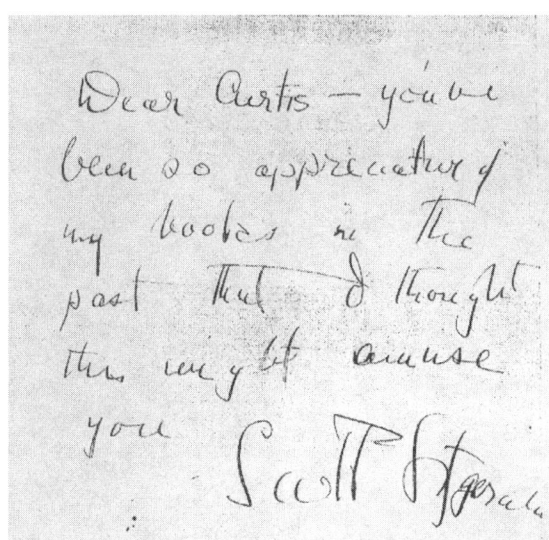

Sotheby Parke Bernet Sale Number 127

42. *The William E. Stockhausen Collection of English & American Literature, Part II.* Sotheby Parke Bernet, New York, Sale Number 3708 (14 December 1974)

> *"I'd rather watch a good shimmee dance than . . . Pavalowa"*
>
> 577 FITZGERALD, F. SCOTT. Autograph letter signed, 1½ pp. 4to. Westport, Conn., 19 June 1920 to David Balch. Mounted on card (blank portion of second page cut away).
>
> David Balch was editor of *Movie Weekly* in the 1920s, and Fitzgerald's letter is apparently in response to an inquiry from Balch for a magazine article. Most of the letter deals with a story called "Head and Shoulders" which Fitzgerald mentions *"will be republished in my collection of short stories 'Flappers and Philosophers' which the Scribners are publishing this fall."* He goes on to mention, in true Flapper and Philosopher fashion, that he would *"rather watch a good shimmee dance than Ruth St. Dennis & Pavalowa combined. I see nothing at all disgusting in it"*. He also tells Balch that his story *" 'The Camel's Back' in the S.E.P. (which you may be buying) was the fastest piece of writing I've ever heard of. It is twelve thousand words long and it was written in fourteen hours straight writing and sent to the S.E.P. in its original form."* The letter closes with Fitzgerald's regret that he has *"no good picture. I expect to have some soon though & will send you one."*

Recatalogued in Kenneth W. Rendell Catalogue 289 [ca. 2001] at $45,000

43. *Modern First Editions: 20'th Anniversary Catalogue.* William Young Catalogue 617 [1975]

The Fitzgerald poems were listed again, one at $2,600 and the other at $4,500, in Young Catalogue 618 [1975].

Item 51 is "My Very Very Dear Marie": see entry 37.

Item 52 is the poem to Carmel Myers and Ralph Blum published in F. Scott Fitzgerald's *Poems, 1911–1940* (Bloomfield Hills, Mich.: Bruccoli Clark, 1981), 145. This item was recatalogued in Sotheby's, New York, Sale Number 5563 (18 June 1987), where it brought $2,500, and subsequently in Profiles in History (Joseph M. Maddalena) Catalogue (1988).

> 51. FITZGERALD, F. SCOTT. Unpublished manuscript poem in holograph. Dating from January, 1915 when he was at Princeton. Written on a sheet of Princeton stationery and giving his room number as '107 Patton Hall'. Signed at the end "Scott". An eighteen line poem to a girl friend of the moment. Very clever word usage. The rhythm is good enough to have made the lyrics for a song. This manuscript, at the beginning of his life, full of spirit and joy de vivre and the next manuscript written in the last years of his life clearly show the shocking contrasts the intervening years brought about. Manuscript enclosed in a slipcase. I don't think we need dwell on the rarity of Fitzgerald manuscript material, especially anything unpublished.
>
> 52. FITZGERALD. Unpublished manuscript poem written in a tragi-comedy style. Signed and dated 1937. Twenty four line poem dwelling on his heavy drinking as the background theme. Presumably written to some friends who kept the free booze flowing. Inasmuch as liquor was the major influence in his life and an important factor in his early demise, this is a most revealing and important manuscript. Entirely in holograph and the only manuscript of this period, unpublished and holographic, that we have ever seen offered for sale.

Young Catalogue 617

Fitzgerald met Carmel Myers in Rome in 1924 when she was acting in the silent *Ben-Hur*. He saw her again when he was working in Hollywood in 1937. Ralph Blum was her husband.

> **51. FITZGERALD, FRANCIS, SCOTT.** 1896-1940. American novelist and short-story writer. Author of The Great Gatsby, his masterpiece, concerning a bootlegger obsessed with making a fortune. Autograph Manuscript Poem Signed, One full page, Quarto, 1937. Titled *"Lines on reading through an autograph album."* Fitzgerald writes:
>
> *Carmel and Ralph——(Four grand guys)—*
> *Paid plenty soup for these sweet lies poured*
> *plenty gin to make this collection*
> *Cut plenty cake to win this "affection"*
> *Lots of these "darlings," lots of these "dears"*
> *Foamed from the tops of costly beers*
> *How many men who shook hands like fishes*
> *Winked when they set down tese lovely wishes?*
> *Minds clearly vacant—thoughts quite alarming*
> *Charming—CHARMING—OH SO CHARMING!*
> *Watch these—see their elbows bend,*
> *Fill 'em up again and they call you friend.*
>
> *There's just one who is writing here*
> *Thanks your a lucky lad and lass*
> *(hey, gal, please fill up that glass)*
> *Pages sad with remembered dead*
> *Who have drunk your wine and broken your bread*
> *Sign right here, boys, please don't shove*
> *"Sweetest people" love-Love-LOVE*
> *But they couldn't very well all be liars*
> *So there must be something about these Myers*
> *Oh! What a jaux pas! Sure am dumb*
> *What was that name now? Bloom or Blum?*
>
> A wonderful poem. Fitzgerald was obviously looking through a friend's autograph album. Inspired by what he saw, he penned these lovely lines. This is a rare opportunity — first to own a full signed page of Fitzgerald's unpublished poetry; secondly, the wonderful autograph collectors association. The condition is fine, with one small paper tear, at the lower left of the page, not affecting any of the writing. SUPERB!! 5,000.00

Profiles in History (Joseph M. Maddalena) Catalogue (1988)

44. Charles Hamilton Auction Number 85 (27 February 1975)

180-A **FITZGERALD, F. SCOTT.** American author. Amusing brief A.L.S., four lines penned on a small sheet (about 3" x 4"), undated. To Miss Lang, declining a request because, "...I have gone to Zion City for the horse races and won't be back until next June." Trimmed, with mounting traces on verso, and a marginal tear in blank portion, otherwise very good. Accompanied by a similar A.L.S. of ZELDA SAYRE FITZGERALD, six lines to Miss Long, date-lined "Sing Sing," explaining, "The warden is very particular about letting forged signatures be sent in the mail from here so I regret that I am unable to oblige you." Trimmed, with mounting traces on verso, otherwise very good. Two pieces.
....(150.00)

$250

45. Doris Harris Catalogue 18 [June 1975]

```
63    FITZGERALD, F. SCOTT (1896-1940).   American author.  Wrote
The Great Gatsby, etc.    Letter Signed, "Scott", 1 page, 4to,
Baltimore, 26 July 1934; Autograph Letter Signed, "Scott Fitz",
1½ pages (2 leaves), 4to, Grove Park Inn, Asheville, [c. July
1935].   Both to Don [Swann].                 The two,   $750.00
     In the Letter Signed, Fitzgerald turns over his
preface to Swann's book, Colonial and Historic Homes of Maryland.
He notes that, after publication, all rights revert to him.  He
allows Swann some leeway on changes but none "...that would
utterly defeat the rhythm and so the purpose of the introduction
...."
     In the Autograph Letter Signed Fitzgerald explains his pref-
erence for Swann's etching of Tudor Hall, giving at the same time
some of his family background.   "...The reason I didn't want the
one of Hampton was because the Pleausance Ridgely from whom I am
descended, antedated the present mansion by a generation & I
thought it would be pretentious of me to hang it for that reason.
But direct ancestors did live in Tudor Hall so you can imagine
the pleasure it gives me...."
     Not published in Andrew Turnbull's Letters of F. Scott
Fitzgerald.
```

The 1934 TLS was recatalogued in Profiles in History Catalogue 39 [2005].

Marylander F. Scott Fitzgerald provides a wonderful Foreword to a famous book about historic Maryland homes

54. FITZGERALD, F. SCOTT. 1896-1940. American novelist and short-story writer. Typed Letter Signed *"Scott"*, One page, Quarto, dated July 26, 1934 from Baltimore, Maryland. Written to Don Swann, author of Colonial & Historic Homes of Maryland (privately published in 1939), regarding the Foreword to the book which Fitzgerald was asked to write. In full:

"*Dear Don:*

This is the best I can do. Only thing I want to ask you is first, that after your book is published all rights to use this in any way, such as in a collection of stray pieces, etc. reverts to me.

Secondly, that you do not make any changes, that is, if you want to change the word "mansion" to the word "manor" that is O.K. with me, but if you want to change 'beautiful mansion' to 'magnificent manor' that would utterly defeat the rhythm and so the purpose of the introduction. It would be exactly as if I took one of your etchings of Holder Hall at Princeton and drew a black oblong around one of the windows to indicate to my mother where I lived.

Ever yours,

Scott"

Colonial & Historic Homes of Maryland was published as a collection of etchings of Maryland homes built between 1642 and 1830 by famed Baltimore etcher Don Swann. Each etching is accompanied by a descriptive monograph written by his son, Don Swann Jr., which records the histories of the houses, legends about their previous owners, and specific architectural features. F. Scott Fitzgerald was asked to write the Foreword, which he submitted to Don Swann, Sr. with the above letter. Each of Fitzgerald's writings – both the Foreword and this accompanying letter – are wonderful snippets of prose by one of America's most treasured and gifted authors. The Foreword as printed in the book – and which presumably was left unaltered by Swann (one should hope) – reads (in full):

"The undersigned can only consider himself a native of the Maryland Free State through ancestry and adoption. But the impression of the frames and the domains, the vistas and the glories of Maryland followed many a young man West after the Civil War and my father was of that number. Much of my early childhood in Minnesota was spent asking him such questions as:

'—and how long did it take Early's column to pass Glenmary that day?' (That was a farm in Montgomery County.)

'—what would have happened if Jeb Stewart's [sic] cavalry had joined Lee instead of raiding all the way to Rockville?'

and:

'—tell me again about how you used to ride through the woods with a spy up behind you on the horse.'

or:

'Why wouldn't they let Francis Scott Key off the British frigate?'

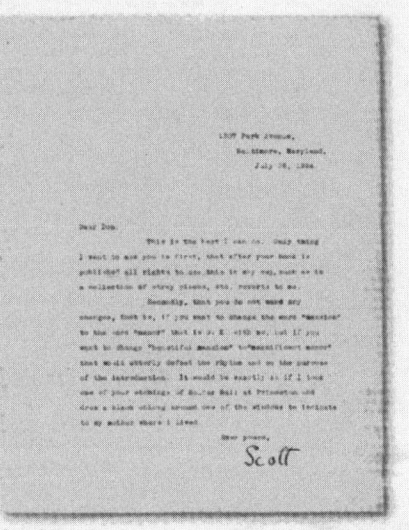

And since so many legends of my family went west with father, memories of names that go back before Braddock's disaster such as Caleb Godwin of Hockley-in-ye-Hole, or Philip Key of Tudor Hall, or Pleasance Ridgeley – so there must be hundreds and hundreds of families in such an old state whose ancestral memories are richer and fuller than mine.

But time obliterates people and memories and only the more fortunate landmarks survive. In the case of this fine book, it is upon the home above all that Don Swann has concentrated his talents and his painstaking research – the four walls (or sixteen, as it may be) of Baronial Maryland, or the artistic result of the toil and sweat that some forever anonymous craftsman put into a balcony or a parquet. And outside this general range, the etcher has also paused here and there to jot down some detail of plainer houses that helps to make this permanent record of the history of the Free State.

His work, naturally, will speak for itself, and, to allow it to do so, I cut short this prelude with the expression of high hopes for this venture by one of the State's adopted sons."

A great letter from F. Scott Fitzgerald – who himself was named after famous Marylander Francis Scott Key – revealing his rich heritage and close ties with his ancestral home. In fine condition. (#24365) $3,950.00

46. Charles Hamilton Auction Number 89 (24 July 1975)

> 130 FITZGERALD, F. SCOTT. American author. A.L.S., 1/2 page 4to, Paris, undated. To Harry Hansen (of the *Chicago Daily News*), with original holograph envelope, stamped and postmarked Paris, June 13, 1925: "Thank you for your kind letter about *Gatsby*. You have always been so nice about my stuff that I'd hoped this would please you too. Thanks for letting me know it did." Attractive and fine, penned on violet paper. Two pieces. ....(170.00)

47. Charles Hamilton Auction Number 91 (2 October 1975)

> 197 FITZGERALD, F. SCOTT. American novelist. Scarce A.L.S., six lines penned on message-portion of a picture postcard (depicting Nice, France), undated. To Miss Virginia Brooks, sending thanks for, "...the kind, encouraging letter. It's nice to hear things like that and I appreciate your writing it..." Slightly creased, with postage stamp removed and mounting traces on picture side, otherwise very good. ....(100.00)

48. House of Books [1976]

This letter was written to Boni & Liveright editor Thomas R. Smith from Paris, probably in May 1925; Fitzgerald declines Smith's invitation to leave Scribners and praises Hemingway and Cummings: see entry 135, item 303.

> 152 FITZGERALD. A.L.S. To Tom (Smith, editor at Liveright). Paris, N.d. (1925). Thanks for kind letter about *Gatsby*, afraid it is not going to sell like the others. His relations with Max Perkins and Scribners have always been so cordial he could not imagine breaking them but if anything happens will surely come to his firm. "But it would be a monopoly in restraint of trade . . . you already have the only other two Americans under thirty who promise a great deal—Hemingway and Cummings. . . ." Will be in Paris the rest of 1925. "As ever your friend Scott Fitz". The letter had been pasted to something, possibly for framing; while the paste marks show there is no damage to the text. About 200 words. $850.00

49. Inventory of the Robert L. Samsell Collection of F. Scott Fitzgerald. Heritage Bookshop (6 April 1976)

Samsell, an attorney, was sightless as the result of his World War II wound; he was a fastidious collector and worked with the help of Jeanne Bennett.

Samsell's was the only comprehensive Fitzgerald collection offered for sale en bloc. Heritage Bookshop, Los Angeles, prepared a list of 469 items of the 602 total items—including 127 of the A entries in *F. Scott Fitzgerald: A Descriptive Bibliography* (1972). This collection was priced en bloc at $25,000—a bargain, even in 1976—but it did not sell and was broken up.

```
4.  THIS SIDE OF PARADISE. New York: Scribners, 1920.
    First edition, first issue. Presentation copy: "This
    book is a/ history of mistakes/ --something never/
    retracted yet, in/ a way, to be ashamed/ of, by a
    conscientious/ worker.
        I am glad you/ like it. A lot went/ into it.
                                    Scott Fitzgerald"
    Bookplate of Margarate Orr Green (picture of books
    either side of fireplace), written on Bookplate:
    "F Scott Fitzgerald/ crowds to the/ nice fire-place."
    Fine, front inside hinge loose, boxed. MJB #___
```

```
23. Another copy. New York: Scribners, 1922. First edition,
    first issue. Presentation copy inscribed two days before
    March 4 publication:
    "For Bernard Vaughn
    Inspired concocter of/ headlines, from his/ collaborater.
    F. Scott Fitzgerald/ St. Paul,/ March 2nd."
    Very fine, boxed. MJB #___
```

```
36. THE GREAT GATSBY. New York: Scribners, 1925. First edition,
    first issue. Presentation copy. Because Fitzgerald was
    abroad at Great Gatsby's publication date, thereby making
    inscribed presentation copies impracticable, Fitzgerald,
    instead, sent Scribners slips of paper with holographic
    sentiments to the named recipients. One of these copies
    sold at auction for $1,000.00 in 1964. "Two important
    F association books were auctioned for the benefit of the
    Baltimore Symphony Orchestra on 9 October. A first print-
    ing GG with a paste-inscription by F to his mother brought
    $1,000: 'It's a masterpiece, Mother. Write me how you like
    it.'" Fitzgerald Newsletter, Washington, D.C.; Microcard
    Editions, 1969, page 164.
        This copy has a glued-in presentation slip to Sinclair
    Lewis: "Dear Sinclair Lewis: I've just sent for/ Arrow-
    smith. My hope is that this the/ Great Gatsby will be the
    second best/ American book of the Spring./ F. Scott
    Fitzgerald."
        Fine in badly chipped dust jacket, boxed. MJB #___
```

```
37. Another copy. New York: Scribners, 1925. First edition,
    second printing. Presentation copy: "F. Scott Fitzgerald/
    for Lajya Ryan/"(band-aided in magazine blurb) "Will you
    try to explain/ this to your husband/ --Baltic Siren--/
    after a glance at/ you & a slap-down/ from your tennis
    muscle/ no wonder the Nazis/ covet your land./ Affly,
    Scott" Very fine in repaired dust jacket, boxed.
    MJB #___
```

```
        57.  Another copy.  New York: Scribners, 1926.  First edition
             first issue.  Presentation copy:
             "For Walter Bruington/ from F. Scott/ Fitzgerald.
             --one sad young/ man to another?/ Hollywood, 1940"
             Fine, gold on spine rubbed.  MJG #____

        78.  Another copy.  New York: Scribners, 1935.  First edition,
             first state, only printing.  Presentation copy: "For Sylvia
             Lewis/ in memory of those/ days when she/ translated A
             Revours for me/ in my cork-lined/ converted pullman/ F
             Scott ("Huysmans") Fitzgerald/ The Flood--1938"  Good.
             MJB #____
```

50. *Collector*, Whole Number 853 (1977)

Published in *The Correspondence of F. Scott Fitzgerald*. Francis Scott Key was Fitzgerald's second cousin, three times removed: see Scottie Fitzgerald Smith, "The Colonial Ancestors of Francis Scott Key Fitzgerald"; reprinted in *Some Sort of Epic Grandeur: The Life of F. Scott Fitzgerald*.

K-746 **FITZGERALD, Francis Scott Key** (1896-1940). American novelist. Author of *The Beautiful and Damned, The Great Gatsby*, and other works. LS, 4to, La Paix, Rodgers' Forge, Towson, Md., July 18, 1933. To a Mrs. H.H. Prouse. A most interesting letter about their common ancestry. *"The Keys settled in Maryland with a tremendous grant about 1698 in St. Marys County. They were rich with no special record of service to the state until after the Revolution. You and I are both descended from Philip Key, who died about 1800, you through his grandson Francis Scott Key, and I through Francis Scott Key's uncle Philip Barton Key...In my branch of the Key family (descendants of Philip Barton Key) there has been no money or achievement of note for four or five generations though some of the descendents have married well....I am told here in Baltimore that two men bearing the Key name, descendents of the aforementioned Philip Key, died poverty stricken in the Confederate Home at the beginning of the century. So I am afraid we must forget past glories, if there were any, and look forward to the future".* Fitzgerald has made three corrections in this tightly written single-spaced letter. A splendid item and scarce. $875.00

51. Bennett & Marshall Catalogue 19 [1977]

Recatalogued in Peter L. Stern Catalogue 28 [early 1997] at $4,000.
   This description is fanciful: Buck was not a model for Gatsby.

> **INSCRIBED**
>
> 63.
>   FITZGERALD, F. SCOTT. **The Vegetable or from President to Postman.** New York: Scribner's, 1923.
>   FIRST EDITION. Inscribed by Fitzgerald to Gene Buck. Spine a little faded, otherwise a fine copy. Gene Buck was a neighbor and friend of Fitzgerald who gave lavish parties. It is often speculated that he was the model for "The Great Gatsby."
>
> $375

Bennett & Marshall Catalogue 19

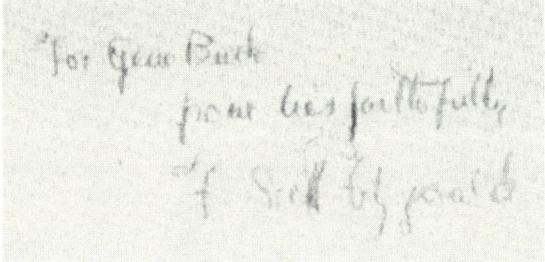

Bruccoli Collection

52. *Important Modern First Editions . . . The Collection of Jonathan Goodwin.* Sotheby Parke Bernet, New York, Sale Number 3966 (29 March 1977)

The Jonathan Goodwin collection was sold in three parts in 1977; the first catalogue included his Fitzgeralds. The strength of this collection was the twentieth-century American writers. Hemingway was represented by fifty-four lots, some of which were batches of letters. The $18,000 price for Pound's *A Lume Spento* was described at the time as the most ever paid at auction for a modern American book.

   The fourteen Fitzgerald lots totaled $17,375—the priciest group of his materials to that time. The top item was the *Gatsby* in dust jacket with a routine inscription to the Newman Smiths, which brought $4,250. The rarest printed Fitzgerald item in this sale was the third known copy of *The True Story of Appomattox,* Fitzgerald's spoof account of Grant's surrender to Lee. The only copy ever catalogued for sale, it brought $1,800 from a dealer who acquired it for stock; it is now in the Carter Burden Collection at the Morgan Library.

   Goodwin, a Connecticut businessman, acquired most of his modern literature from Henry Wenning and the House of Books. He had earlier presented his Clemens collection to the Mark Twain House in Hartford; disgusted by the treatment of his books there, he decided to sell his remaining collections.

■ 102 FITZGERALD, F. SCOTT. Fie! Fie! Fi-Fi! A Musical Comedy in Two Acts...Plot & Lyrics by F. Scott Fitzgerald   New York, &c., [1914] 4to. Original cloth-backed pictorial boards (a little soiled). Cloth case
First edition of the score of Fitzgerald's first show for the Triangle Club at Princeton University. Very scarce

■ 103 FITZGERALD, F. SCOTT. Safety First. A Musical Comedy in Two Acts...Lyrics by F. Scott Fitzgerald   New York, &c., [1916] 4to. Original cloth backed pictorial boards. Cloth case
First edition of the score of Fitzgerald's third Triangle Club musical. A very nice copy of an elusive book

■ 104 [FITZGERALD, F. SCOTT]. A Book of Princeton Verse II. 1919   Princeton, [1919] 8vo. Original cloth, with the dust jacket. Morocco-backed case
First edition. Contains the first book appearance of three Fitzgerald poems. An exceptionally fine copy

■ 105 FITZGERALD, F. SCOTT. This Side of Paradise   New York, 1920 8vo. Original cloth, with the dust jacket (strengthened on verso). Morocco-backed case
First edition of the author's first book. Presentation copy, inscribed "For Harold Davis with Best Wishes from F. Scott Fitzgerald, July 2nd, 1920." A nice copy in the very scarce jacket

Item 105 was first offered in 1966 by Lew David Feldman for $150: see entry 24, item 540. It then appeared in the 22 May 1981 Christie's, New York, Sale 5059 at $2,400.

Item 108 was resold in the 27 October 1995 Engelhard sale for $4,370: see entry 110, item 41.

Number 109 was sold by Christie's, New York (2 December 2005) for $9,000. It was recatalogued by Peter L. Stern (February/March 2006) for $17,500.

Number 110 was resold at the 1995 Engelhard sale for $55,000: see entry 110, item 42.

Number 113 was recatalogued by Maurice A. Neville in 1980 for $4,500.

Number 114 was auctioned by Christie's, New York, on 22 May 1981 for $4,200.

Number 117 was resold in the April 2004 Neville sale for $10,000: see entry 135, item 65.

[103]

■ 106 FITZGERALD, F. SCOTT. Flappers and Philosophers　　　　　　　　　　　New York, 1920
8vo. Original cloth, with the dust jacket (slightly frayed). Morocco-backed case
First edition. A very good copy

$375

■ 108 FITZGERALD, F. SCOTT. Tales of the Jazz Age　　　　　　　　　　　　　New York, 1922
8vo. Original cloth. Cloth case
First edition. Presentation copy, inscribed five days after publication "For Kenneth Brightbill from F. Scott Fitzgerald who purchased this book for presentation to said gent. on this sunny day of September 27th, 1922"

$700

■ 109 FITZGERALD, F. SCOTT. The Vegetable
New York, 1923
8vo. Original cloth, with the dust jacket (chipped). Cloth case
First edition of this play. Presentation copy, inscribed about a week after publication "For Kenneth Brightbill from F. Scott Fitzgerald, May 4th, 1922 [sic]." Very scarce in the dust jacket

$1200

[107]

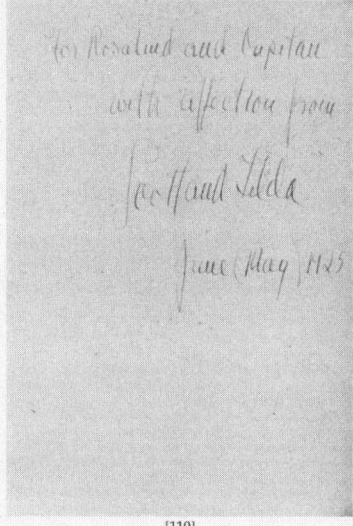

[110]

■ 107 FITZGERALD, F. SCOTT. The Beautiful and Damned　　　　　　　　　　　New York, 1922
8vo. Original cloth, with the dust jacket (the variant printed in white with black outlines). Cloth case
First edition. A fine, fresh copy
[SEE ILLUSTRATION]

$600

■ 110 FITZGERALD, F. SCOTT. The Great Gatsby
New York 1925 $4,250-
8vo. Original cloth, with the dust jacket (frayed). Cloth case.
First edition, first printing of text and jacket. Presentation copy, inscribed to Zelda's sister and her husband Newman Smith: "For Rosalind and Capitan with affection from Scott and Zelda, June (May) 1925"
Connolly, The Modern Movement: One Hundred Key Books, 48

[SEE ILLUSTRATION]

■ 111 FITZGERALD, F. SCOTT. The Great Gatsby
New York, 1925
8vo. Original cloth. Cloth case $1,000-
First edition, first printing. Malcolm Cowley's copy with a note laid in reading: "This is the copy of Gatsby I used in preparing a new text (with FSF's revisions) for Three Novels by F. Scott Fitzgerald (Scribner, about 1951).--Fitzgerald's copy, from which I took the changes is in the Princeton University Library. Malcolm Cowley, July 1964." Cowley has inscribed the book on the flyleaf and has made extensive corrections throughout the text to conform with Fitzgerald's own copy

■ 112 FITZGERALD, F. SCOTT. All the Sad Young Men
New York, 1926 $225-
8vo. Original cloth, with the dust jacket (rubbed). Cloth case
First edition. A very good copy

■ 113 [FITZGERALD, F. SCOTT]. The True Story of Appomattox. Columnist Discovers That It Was Grant Who Surrendered to Lee...
[Baltimore: Privately Printed, 1934]
Broadside, 8½ x 2, simulating a newspaper clipping. Morocco-backed case. First and only edition of this rare spoof that Fitzgerald had "faked up" by the Baltimore Sun. In fine condition $1,800-
Boxed with a Typed Letter Signed ("Scott"), 1 page 4to, Baltimore, December 8, 1934, to "Dearest Ceci" [possibly his cousin, Cecilia Taylor]: "Thought this might amuse you. It is a fake, set up by courtesy for me by some newspaper friends...Don't let it get in the real press!..."

[SEE ILLUSTRATION]

THE TRUE STORY OF APPOMATTOX

Columnist Discovers That It Was Grant Who Surrendered To Lee Instead Of Lee Surrendering To Grant

Circumstances Divulged For The First Time By Captain X

We have learned that when Grant had decided to surrender his milk-fed millions to Lee's starving remnants and the rendezvous was arranged at Appomattox Court House, Lee demanded that Grant put his submission into writing. Unfortunately Grant's pencil broke, and, removing his cigar from his mouth, he turned to General Lee and said with true military courtesy: "General, I have broken my pencil, will you lend me your sword to sharpen it with?" General Lee, always ready and willing to oblige, whipped forth his sword and tendered it to General Grant.

It was unfortunately just at this moment that the flashlight photographers and radio announcers got to work and the picture was erroneously given to the world that General Lee was surrendering his sword to General Grant.

The credulous public immediately accepted this story. The bells that were prepared to ring triumphantly in Loudoun county were stilled while the much inferior Yankee bells in Old North Church in Boston burst forth in a false paean of triumph. To this day the legend persists, but we of the Welbourne Journal are able to present to the world for the first time the real TRUTH about this eighty-year-old slander that Virginia lost its single-handed war against the allied Eskimos north of the Mason and Dixon line.

[113]

[114]

■ 114 FITZGERALD, F. SCOTT. Tender Is the Night
New York, 1934
8vo. Original cloth. Cloth case
First edition. Presentation copy, with a poignant inscription to Malcolm Cowley (then with the New Republic): "Dear Malcolm: Please don't review this–I know how you'd do it. Put a young man on it–oh hell–use your own judgement, as you will anyhow. Ever Yours, Scott." With his private life cracking-up and so much riding on the success of 'Tender Is the Night' to re-establish his popular and critical reputation, Fitzgerald was apprehensive about Cowley's reaction to the novel. Cowley did in fact review the novel in The New Republic (as "good", but not "great"), and there are marginal notes in his hand
Connolly, The Modern Movement: One Hundred Key Books, 79
[SEE ILLUSTRATION] $3,200

■ 115 FITZGERALD, F. SCOTT. Taps at Reveille
New York, 1935
8vo. Original cloth, with the dust jacket. Cloth case
First edition, first state. A particularly fine copy
[SEE ILLUSTRATION] $425

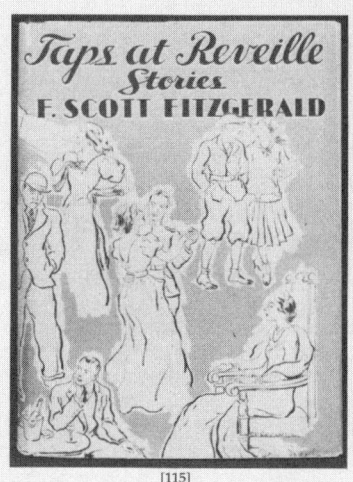

[115]

■ 116 FITZGERALD, ZELDA. Save Me the Waltz
New York, 1932
8vo. Original cloth, with the dust jacket. Cloth case
First edition of Zelda's first and only book. A very good copy
[SEE ILLUSTRATION] $300

■ 117 FITZGERALD, ZELDA. Autograph Letter Signed, 4 pages 4to, in pencil, [Paris, c. July 2, 1926], to Madeleine, wife of the critic Ernest Boyd. Written from a Paris hospital where she had just had her appendix removed, this is a rambling, chatty letter in which Zelda gives news of the Paris and Riviera scenes and tells of Scott's writing

"...I swim all day and enjoy tremendously a vague nostalgia that comes from living in a perfect place and wishing there was somewhere to go...We are coming home in Nov. or Dec.–neither Scott nor I quite know why. Perhaps to stay– Scott's writing an amazingly good novel ['Tender Is the Night'] which goes so slow it ought to be serialized in the Encyclopedia Britannica...give my love to Ernest and Lewey Collins is a bitch and everybody hates the Bromfields and life is, after all, very complicated"

[116]

53. Charles Hamilton Auction Number 104 (7 April 1977)
William C. Lengel was an agent and editor.

138 FITZGERALD, F. SCOTT. American novelist. A.L.S., 1 full page, 4to (penned in blue ink on blue paper), 14 Rue de Tilsett, Paris, undated but docketed in pencil Dec. 3, 1925. To Bill (Lengel), an editor. "...Ober...thinks it would be unwise of me to leave the *Post* at this time just when they have been so liberal in raising my price and in running my stories in first position...I would like to

[handwritten letter with signature F Scott Fitzgerald]

do some stories for Ray Long despite the fact that there I am simply one of many, because in several ways he is more liberal in what he allows than Lorimer is. On the other hand they have always been by far my staunchest friends and I imagine they have conveyed to Ober that they are most anxious to retain my work...I'm awfully sorry that our negotiations should have turned out this way..." Pencil dockets, with one marginal tear and in internal tear (slightly affecting a few words of text), otherwise good. Literary letters of Fitzgerald are uncommon. ....(300.00)

139 FITZGERALD, F. SCOTT. A.L.S., 1 full page, small 8vo (on printed letterhead of Savoy Hotel, London), undated. To (Bill) Lengel, an editor and literary agent. "Sorry I missed you...Have called up twice this morning but no answer so I presume you waited in Paris & will try you at the St. Regis there...Do write me the dope..." Docketed, otherwise a fine attractive example, penned in black ink. ....(180.00)

54. Sotheby Parke Bernet, New York, Sale Number 4057 (6 December 1977)

Item 85 was apparently unsold; it was recatalogued in the Engelhard sale at Christie's (27 October 1995): see entry 110, item 40.

> ■ 85 FITZGERALD, F. SCOTT. The Beautiful and Damned   New York, 1922
> 8vo. Original cloth, with the dust jacket (the variant printed in black). A very good copy
> First edition. Presentation copy, inscribed by the author to the critic Harry Hansen 'Dean of the Middle-West from his friend F. Scott Fitzgerald'

55. Maurice F. Neville Rare Books Catalogue 4 [ca. 1978]

> INSCRIBED *GATSBY*
> 381 FITZGERALD, F. SCOTT. The Great Gatsby. London: Chatto and Windus, [1926]. $1100.00
> FIRST ENGLISH EDITION, REMAINDER BINDING. Signed presentation copy with the humorous inscription, "For Edith M. Brown, in memory of those dear old days at Ward-Belmont where we were schoolmates together, F. Scott Fitzgerald, Paris 1930." Ward-Belmont was a school exclusively for women. Binding rubbed and spine faded. Chipping to top and bottom of spine with some repaired tears. Edith M. Brown was a friend of William Faulkner and had helped to edit *Soldier's Pay*. *Gatsby* is the most elusive of the author's novels to find inscribed.

56. Charles Hamilton Auction Number 111 (23 March 1978)

Brown illustrated the *Beautiful and Damned* serial (*Metropolitan Magazine*, September 1921–March 1922) and Fitzgerald stories in *Metropolitan Magazine* and the *Saturday Evening Post*.

Item 110 provides Fitzgerald's ideas for illustrating "Winter Dreams" (*Metropolitan Magazine*, December 1922). This letter was resold for $4,600 by Christie's in the Engelhard sale (27 October 1995): see entry 110, item 46.

54 F. Scott Fitzgerald in the Marketplace

109 FITZGERALD, F. SCOTT. American novelist. A.L.S., 2/3 page, 4to, Great Neck, L.I., Nov. 15, 1922. To illustrator Arthur W. Brown. "Hovey gave me an advance copy of the magazine — almost his last official act before leaving the *Metropolitan*. The drawings...were excellent — careful, beautifully done and 'appetizing,' like everything you do. If you had heard me beg Hovey in letter after letter to have you do *The Beautiful & Damned* you would know how much I appreciate your work..." Some chipping of blank margins and fold breaks, otherwise good, the handwriting bold and dark. *The Beautiful & Damned*, a major Fitzgerald work, was published in 1922. .... (375.00)

110 FITZGERALD, F. SCOTT. A.L.S., 3 full pages (penned on three 4to sheets), undated. To illustrator Arthur W. Brown, about illustrations for a Fitzgerald story. "...I'm sorry my suggestions are so few & so fragmentary but Mr. Hovey has asked me for them right away & it has been a most peculiar story—not nearly so obvious as it sounds here. I like all your work very much and was tremendously pleased at your illustrations for *The Camel's Back* and for *The Jellybean*..." Fitzgerald outlines the plot of his story at considerable length; in part, "The story concerns a poor boy, his rise and his attempts to win a rich girl. He first sees her when he is a caddy about 14 years old...The sight of her stirs the poor boy to give up his job of caddying—He is too proud to caddy for a little girl as young as that—He rises in the world. At 25 he is a guest at the golf club where he has been a caddy. She comes by in a motor boat & they go surf-board riding under the moon...My other scenes do not offer much pictorial possibility. I have just destroyed the second part of the story & am doing it over again—so I hope you can get the two illustrations from the 1st page of this letter..." Fitzgerald proceeds to furnish five suggestions for possible illustrations by Brown. On the lower portion of the concluding leaf, Fitzgerald makes a suggestion for a third illustration, adding a crude original drawing indicating the characters on the golf course and suggestions for caption, depiction of the characters, color of attire, etc. In lower-right corner, he has penned in conclusion: "Don't be jealous because I draw so well. F.S.F." Blank margins of all three leaves considerably frayed and chipped, affecting a few words of text, but in very satisfactory condition. An important and unusually interesting Fitzgerald letter. .... (850.00)
(See Full-Page Illustration)

111 FITZGERALD, F. SCOTT and OTHERS. Lot of three A.Ls.S. and nine Ls.S. Comprises: FITZGERALD, A.L.S., about 3/4 page, 4to, Gateway Drive, Great Neck, L.I., undated but 1922, to illustrator Arthur W. Brown, "The pictures arrived and now decorate the walls of my den together with W.E. Hill's cover for *This Side of Paradise* [published in 1920]. They seem marvellously done to me—and the whole household (including the baby) have inspected them admiringly...I remember your illustrations to *Seventeen*—the big fat lummox singing for instance and the two little girls 'walking with their stomachs out.' They were marvellous. I shall certainly specify you for my next stuff. I don't know about The Winter Club—it would be a perpetual Sunday night temptation & I have enough already..." (blank margins chipped and with a long marginal tear slightly affecting two words of text, otherwise good) □ with other letters, mostly to Brown, of: BOOTH TARKINGTON (about Brown's illustrations for Tarkington's *Girl, Girl, Girl*), CLARENCE BUDINGTON KELLAND (three, one lengthy and philosophical), BRUCE BARTON (two), MRS. THEODORE ROOSEVELT, JR., KATHARINE BRUSH, J. EDGAR HOOVER, ARTHUR TRAIN, and RUSSELL PATTERSON (art contents); some defects, but mostly very satisfactory to good. Together, 12 pieces. .... (400.00)

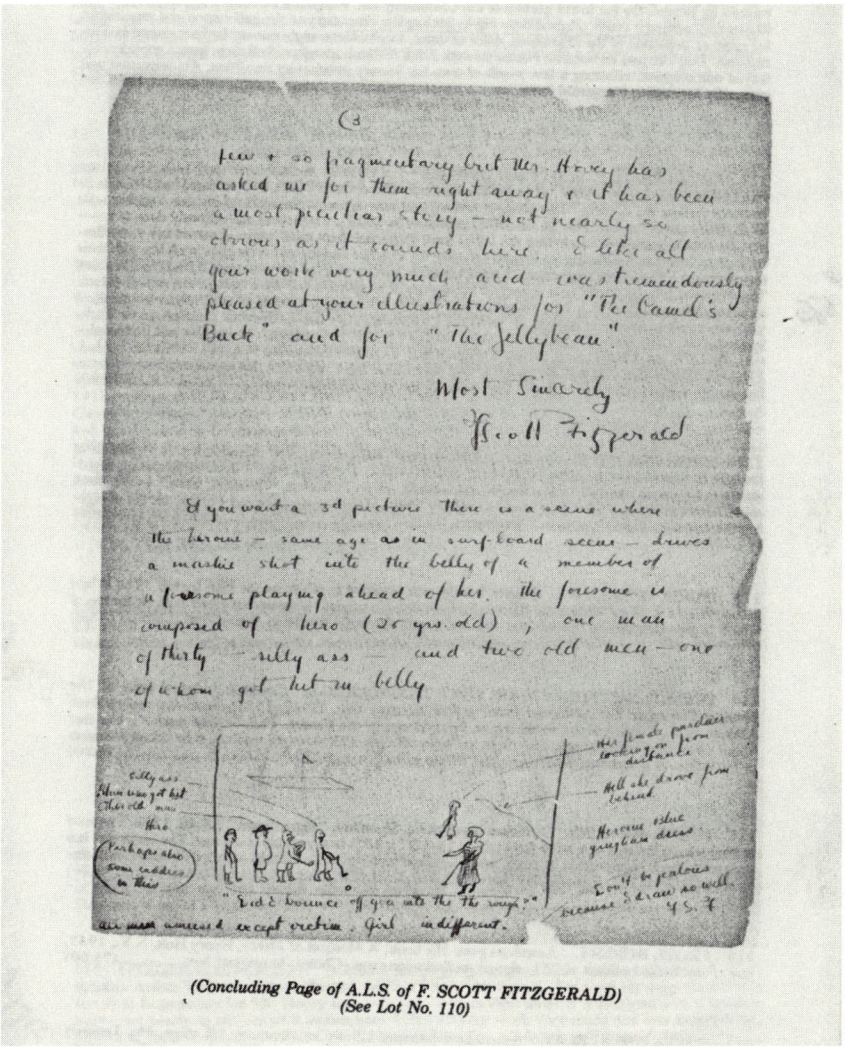

(Concluding Page of A.L.S. of F. SCOTT FITZGERALD)
(See Lot No. 110)

Charles Hamilton Auction Number 111

57. Sotheby Parke Bernet, New York, Sale Number 4128 (23 May 1978)

Item 299 is the only known advance copy of *The Great Gatsby*. It was subsequently catalogued three times by Rebecca Desmarais—in 1979, in 1981, and 1982—at $500 each time. It should have been recognized as a great copy. Now unlocated.

Item 301 was recatalogued in M. Taylor Bowie Catalogue 3 [November 1981] for $3,500.

56 F. Scott Fitzgerald in the Marketplace

Other Properties

■ 296 FAULKNER, WILLIAM. The Town
New York [1957]
8vo. Original cloth, with the acetate dust jacket (soiled)
First edition, one of 450 copies signed by the author

■ 297 FITZGERALD, F. SCOTT. This Side of Paradise   New York, 1920
8vo. Original green cloth; front endpaper discolored
Third printing of the author's first book, prepared for distribution to the American Booksellers Association by tipping in a glossy leaf with "The Author's Apology" signed by Fitzgerald

■ 298 FITZGERALD, F. SCOTT. The Vegetable
New York, 1923
8vo. Original cloth, with the very scarce pictorial dust jacket (worn)
First edition. Inscribed by the author during his first trip to Hollywood: "From one Vegetable to another/F. Scott Fitzgerald to Gilbert Brown/Los Angeles 1927"

■ 299 FITZGERALD, F. SCOTT. The Great Gatsby   New York, 1925
8vo. Original cloth; inner hinges tender
First edition, first printing. With the publisher's rubber stamp on the endpapers "Advance Copy/Not for Sale." Rare in this form. Connolly, The Modern Movement, 48

■ 300 FITZGERALD, F. SCOTT. John Jackson's Arcady   Boston, [1928]
8vo. Original printed wrappers
First edition. A fine copy, and very scarce

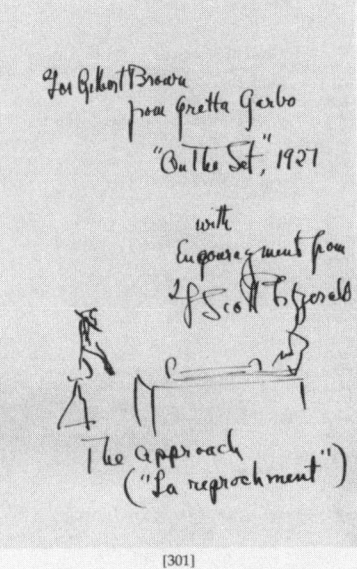

[301]

■ 301 FITZGERALD, F. SCOTT. All the Sad Young Men   New York, 1926
8vo. Original cloth; with the pictorial dust jacket
First edition. With a fine inscription by the author during his first trip to Hollywood: "For Gilbert Brown/from Gretta Garbo/'On the Set,' 1927/with/encouragement from/F. Scott Fitzgerald [this is followed by a small drawing by Fitzgerald]/The approach/('La reprochment')"
[SEE ILLUSTRATION]

58. Sotheby Parke Bernet, New York, Sale Number 4184 (28 November 1978)

Inscribed for the wife of David Silvette, who painted the portrait of Fitzgerald now in the National Portrait Gallery.

■ 100 FITZGERALD, F. SCOTT. The Great Gatsby   New York, Modern Library, [1934]
8vo. Original cloth; spine darkeded
Inscribed and signed on the half-title in verse: 'For Helen Silvette/(I'm all wet/ when it comes to/ dedications/ So I'll just confess/ This is for your dress/ my supreme/ felicitations!)/ May, 1935'

[SEE ILLUSTRATION]

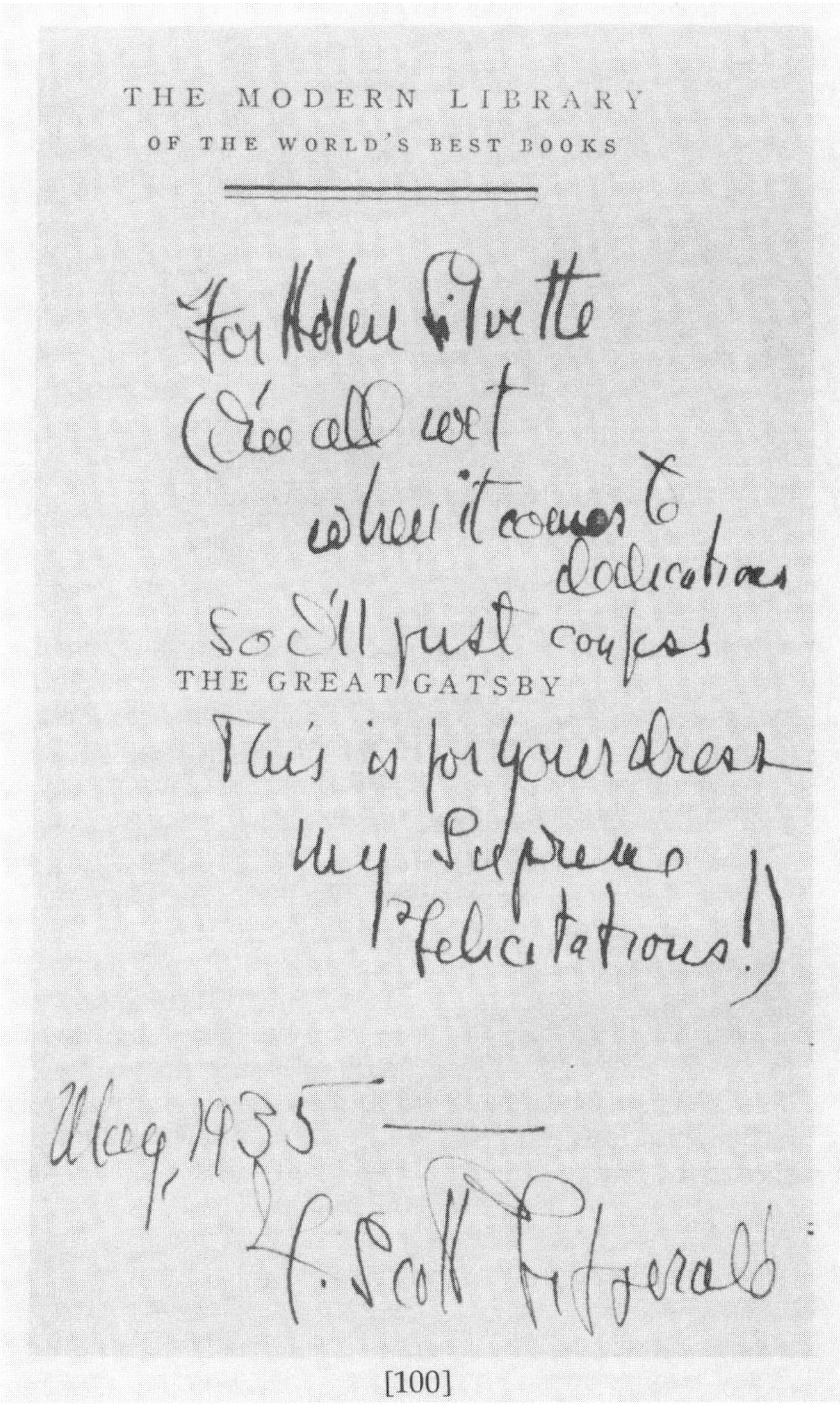

THE MODERN LIBRARY
OF THE WORLD'S BEST BOOKS

*For Helen Silvette
(I'm all wet
when it comes to
dedications
so I'll just confess*

THE GREAT GATSBY

*This is for your dress
my supreme
felicitations!)

May, 1935
F. Scott Fitzgerald*

59. Bradford Morrow Bookseller Catalogue 1 (1978)

The nineteen-page revised carbon copy of "That Kind of Party"—a Basil Duke Lee story that Fitzgerald was unable to sell—is inaccurately described as a manuscript. This story, which treats an early episode in Basil's life, was written after the series had begun in the *Saturday Evening Post*.

ONLY SURVIVING MANUSCRIPT OF FITZGERALD'S FIRST BASIL AND JOSEPHINE STORY

138. ———. We are pleased to offer the only surviving prepublication draft of what is now generally regarded the first of F. Scott Fitzgerald's important *Basil and Josephine* stories, "That Kind of Party." This important manuscript, discussed at length in *The Basil and Josephine Stories*, ed. Jackson Bryer and John

BRADFORD MORROW • BOOKSELLER (805) 687-9877

Kuehl (New York: Scribner's, 1973), pp. vii-viii, xii, xx, xxviii, was not published during Fitzgerald's lifetime. The manuscript consists of 19 carbon typescript pages, with 14 corrections in Fitzgerald's holograph, as well as several editorial corrections in another, unidentified hand. Some of the corrections are quite significant, adding whole phrases, and one correction of great importance occurs when Fitzgerald alters the name "Basil" to read "Terrence," establishing "That Kind of Party" as part of the Basil Duke Lee series which he published exclusively in *The Saturday Evening Post* in 1928-1929.

The Basil stories trace the growth to maturity of Basil Duke Lee, a young hero based on Fitzgerald himself from the ages of 11 to 17. "That Kind of Party," which deals with adolescent kissing games played by Basil and his friends at their parties, was rejected by the *Post* because, according to Arthur Mizener, "its editors did not care to believe that children of ten and eleven played kissing games." In effort to market the story elsewhere, Fitzgerald changed the protagonist's name from Basil Duke Lee to "Terrence R. Tipton," but all attempts to sell the story were unsuccessful, presumably because of the story's theme. Mizener published the story in 1951 in the *Princeton University Library Chronicle* proposing that it belongs second, chronologically, in the Basil series. However, Bryer and Kuehl place it first: "A comparison of details in the story with notes in Fitzgerald's autobiographical *Ledger* . . . unmistakably locates it as describing events of 1907, thus putting it first" (viii).

The manuscript is in very fine condition, 19 leaves typed on rectos only, preserved in half morocco slipcase with morocco label stamped in gilt on front. An interesting and important early Fitzgerald document. $3500.00

60. Samuel T. Freeman Auction Catalogue (29 June 1979)

This letter about his intentions for his novel was written shortly before Fitzgerald went to France where he completed *The Great Gatsby*.

IMPORTANT FITZGERALD LETTER

41. FITZGERALD (F. Scott) *Autograph letter, signed* "F. Scott Fitzgerald". 1 page, large 4to. Great Neck, postmarked April 11, 1924. To Moran Tudury, Adventure Magazine. "I am so anxious for people to see my new novel which is a new thinking out of the idea of illusion (an idea which I suppose will dominate my more serious stuff) much more mature and much more romantic than This Side of Paradise. The B & D was a better book than the first but it was a false lead . . . a concession to Mencken . . . The business of creating illusion is much more to my taste and my talent". With envelope in Fitzgerald's hand.

Two pieces

1980s

61. Walter Reuben Catalogue 37 (1980)

PRESENTATION COPY, WITH A CHARMING FITZGERALD SELF-PORTRAIT

87b. Fitzgerald, F. Scott. **The Beautiful and Damned.** Very fine in cloth (spine lightly used at edges). First edition, A MARVELOUS PRESENTATION COPY: "For Fred A. Rathje/from/F. Scott Fitzgerald/(recognized behind two days growth of beard)/The Blackstone/April 4th 1922." At the left of the date, Fitzgerald draws a crude and charming little picture of himself, and writes the word "Trade mark" on either side of his beard stubble. From only a month after the book was first published. $3000.

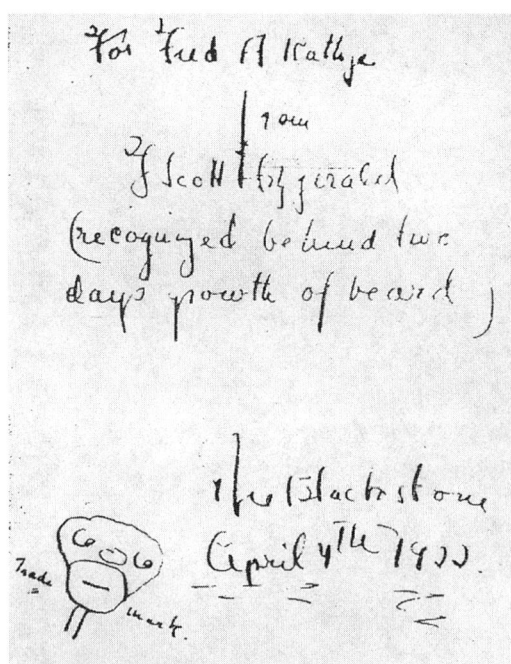

62. Goodspeed's Catalogue 592 (December 1980)

Subsequently offered in Jenkins Company Catalogue 139 [January 1982], Catalogue 144 [July 1982], Catalogue 155 [1983], and Catalogue 160 [November 1983]—each time at $3,500.

Goodspeed's Catalogue 592.

"IT'S GOING TO BE A LULU"

57 FITZGERALD, F. Scott. (1896-1940). A.L.S., "F. Scott Fitzgerald", one page, quarto. Great Neck, Long Island, April 19, 1923. [See illustration, p. 14.] $1,350.00

Fitzgerald forwards a copy of "the book", presumably *This Side of Paradise*—(". . . but I forgot to wrap it in the carbuncle paper and I autographed the wrong page.")—to Oliver Jenkins of Danvers, Mass., editor of the short-lived poetry magazine *Tempo*. He adds: "I thought I wrote and thanked you for the Winter *Tempo* with its notice of *The Jazz Age*. Perhaps I didn't. In all events much obliged for sending it. *The Vegetable* is a play written in the Lennox Robinson manner. I hope it sells like a novel. . . . I begin my new novel [*The Great Gatsby*] in three days. God help me! Eight months of the most laborious work in the world—perhaps a year. But it's going to be a lulu."

The Vegetable, which Fitzgerald described as "a brilliantly funny, political satire," closed after its Atlantic City tryout in the fall of 1923, and fewer than 8000 copies were sold in book form. Financially and emotionally ruined, the Fitzgeralds left for Europe the following spring, where *The Great Gatsby* was finished by year's end. Although a critical success, it too was a financial disaster.

The letter is not published in Bruccoli and Duggan, *Correspondence of F. Scott Fitzgerald*, 1980.

> Great Neck, Long Island
> April 19th 1923
>
> Dear Jenkins:
>
> I sent you the book — but I forgot I owed it on the carbuncle paper and I autographed the wrong page. I'm sorry. Hope it reaches you in good shape.
>
> Glad you liked the poems. I'm returning them to you as Elizabeth Thigpen would be delighted for you to use them. I'm enclosing your letter to her.
>
> I thought I wrote and thanked you for the Contempo with its notice of the "Jazz Age". Perhaps I didn't. In all events much obliged for sending it.
>
> The "Vegetable" is a play written in the Sinclair Robinson manner. I hope it sells like a novel.
>
> I hope your book comes out beautifully — I'm glad you changed the title as I didn't care much for the other. I begin my new novel in three days. God help me! Eight months of the most laborious work in the world — perhaps a year. But it's going to be a lulu.
>
> Faithfully yours,
> F Scott Fitzgerald

No. 57. F. SCOTT FITZGERALD.

63. Sotheby Parke Bernet, New York, Sale Number 4355 (9 April 1980)

Lot 153 sold for $2,500.

> **From a North Carolina Private Collection**
>
> ■ 153 FITZGERALD, F. SCOTT. Tender is the Night. *New York, 1934* ☆ FITZGERALD, ZELDA. Save me the Waltz. *New York, 1932*
>
> Together 2 vols., 8vo. Flyleaf of the first torn at inner margin. Original cloth, dust-jackets slightly torn. With an autograph letter signed by Fitzgerald and a collection of 19 flower sketches by Zelda Fitzgerald [see below]
>
> *First edition of the second work only. Presentation copy of the first, with a fine long inscription by the author to the psychiatrist Dr. [Robert S.] Carroll, director of the Highland Hospital, Asheville, North Carolina, dated April, 1936, the month in which Zelda was transferred to the Highland from the Sheppard-Pratt Hospital in Baltimore.*
>
> Fitzgerald refers to the publication of *Tender is the Night* and its *"pronounced critical success . . . several psychiatrists have reassured me that the technical layout is convincing."* Fitzgerald also confesses that *"there is a good deal of my wife in it though of course I transposed everything factual into a world of fiction . . . the book . . . is true symbolicly* [sic] *to the long tragic story of the last seven years."*
>
> Loosely inserted is an autograph letter signed, 2 pages, 8vo, Grove Park Inn, Asheville [n.d., but April 1936], continuing: *"Also, here is my wife's book . . . It is thinly disguised autobiography with a great deal left out . . . there is a great deal of felicitous description, perhaps too much, too cloying. It is an oddly tasteless book, seeming to be oriented to nothing. Parts of it made me angry—at the time of my quarrel (this seems to be a P.S.. . . .) with her French friend I could have annialated* [sic] *him in two minutes. I boxed for some months with Tommy and Mike Gibbons as a young man & this kid didn't know his left hand from his right. This is vain statement but the truth."*
>
> The presentation of the two books dates from Fitzgerald's first short visit to the Highland Hospital, at which time he placed Zelda in Dr. Carroll's care and on his instructions returned to Baltimore. Zelda was to remain at Highland four years, during which Fitzgerald and Dr. Carroll corresponded regularly. Some of the flower drawings were probably executed during her stay at the hospital; others date from her years at her mother's home in Montgomery. One is inscribed *"Wishing you a Merry Christmas"*, two others *"Easter"*, and all but two are signed *"Z.S.F."*.

[handwritten: Not sold?]

The prices for the following revised typescripts were bargains, even in 1980. Fitzgerald's working typescripts are textually important because of his heavy holograph revisions.

■ 208 FITZGERALD, F. SCOTT. Typescript of the short story "The Freshest Boy," 47 pages 4to, double-spaced, with autograph revisions by the author, and with his name typed at head of first page.
   The original title "The Fresh Boy" has been crossed out at head of page 1 and "The Freshest Boy" substituted in Fitzgerald's hand. His corrections and revisions include the alteration of several characters' names and the addition of a lengthy section at the conclusion. First published in the *Saturday Evening post* on 28 July 1928 and later collected in *Taps at Reveille*, New York, 1935. *Bruccoli C177* $8000 —
   See Illustration

[208]

■ 209 FITZGERALD, F. SCOTT. Typescript of the short story "At Your Age," 30 pages folio, double-spaced, with extensive autograph revisions by the author, and with his name typed at head of first page
> Beneath the pencilled title "At Your Age" the original erased title "The Old Beau" is clearly visible. Other erasures throughout the text are in many cases readable, due to the soft paper. Fitzgerald's autograph emendations are quite considerable; much of the extensive dialogue between characters is rewritten. On page 16, Fitzgerald has initialled an instruction to the editor concerning emphasis. "At Your Age" was first published in the *Saturday Evening Post* on 13 July 1929 and was later collected in *Great Modern Stories*, New York, 1930. Bruccoli C93.

■ 210 FITZGERALD, F. SCOTT. Typescript of the short story "Basil and Cleopatra," 47 pages 4to, double-spaced, with extensive autograph revisions by the author, with his name typed at head of first page and an autograph note signed [Scott Fitz] at head of penultimate page
> The original title "The Freshman's Tragedy," has been changed to "Basil and Cleopatra" at the head of the first page. The numerous emendations by Fitzgerald range from word substitutions and rearrangements of phrase and paragraph order to the complete rewriting of lengthy passages. The two final pages (numbered 29 and 30) are clean carbons of the final typescript, presenting a substantially altered version of the ending as it appears in the corrected typescript (at pages 42-43). The head of page 29 bears an autograph note to Harold Ober, Fitzgerald's literary agent: "Dear Harold, This is for your information. I forwarded the original [i.e. the fair typescript] directly to the Post to save time."
> The story first appeared in the *Saturday Evening Post* on 27 April 1929 and was collected in *The Afternoon of an Author*, Princeton 1957. Bruccoli C186.

See Illustration

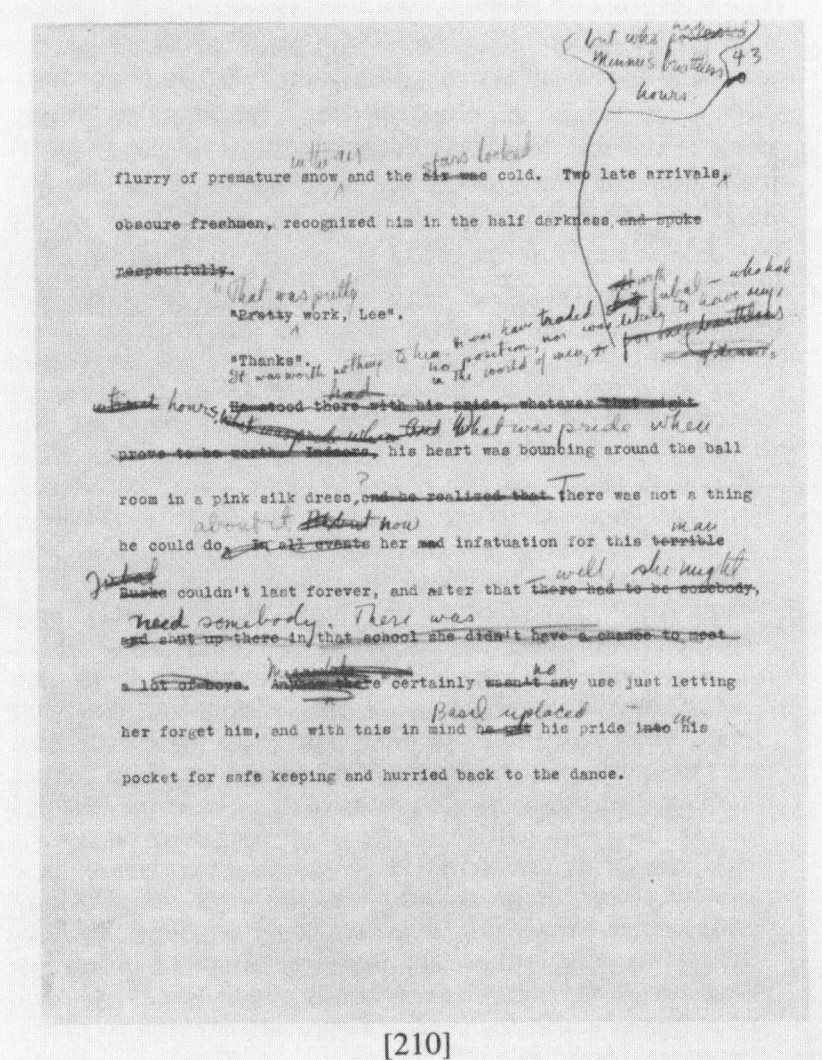

[210]

Item 208 was resold in the 13 April 2004 Sotheby's Neville auction for $90,000: see entry 135, item 63.

Item 209 subsequently brought $63,000 BP in Christie's, New York, Sale Number 9178 (9 June 1999) and then was offered "price upon request" in Kenneth W. Rendell Catalogue 298 (ca. 2003): see entry 134.

Item 210 was resold in the 16 November 2004 Sotheby's Neville auction for $84,000: see entry 135, item 304.

64. Charles Hamilton Auction Number 131 (18 September 1980)

110 FITZGERALD, F. SCOTT. American novelist. Original A.Ms.S., about ¾ page, oblong narrow 16mo, undated. Poem, originally contained in a birthday book, written by Fitzgerald for author ANITA LOOS. "This book tells that Anita Loos/Is a friend of Caesar, a friend of Zeus/Of Samuel Goldwyn and Mother Goose/Of Tillie the Viennese papoose [Tillie Lasch]/Of Charlie MacArthur on the loose/Of shanks, chiropodist[s]—what's the use?/Of actors who have escaped the noose/Lots of Hollywood beach refuse/Comics covered with Charlotte Russe/Wretched victims of self abuse/Big producers all obtuse/This is my birthday but what the deuce/Is that sad fact to Anita Loos." Probably unpublished and in fine condition. .... (600/800)

[See Full-Page Illustration]

[Original Poem by F. SCOTT FITZGERALD]
[See Lot No. 110]

65. Johnson & O'Donnell Catalogue (November 1980)

This copy of *Tender Is the Night* inscribed to literary historian Matthew Josephson was first offered by Johnson & O'Donnell at $4,500 and listed again in their Catalogue 4 (1981) and Catalogue 5 (1981) at the same price. It was catalogued in Waverly Auction Sale 17 (10 March 1982) with a pre-sale estimate of $3,000/$4,000; sale price undetermined. This copy was then offered in Reese Catalogue 14 (June 1982) and Catalogue 16 [1982] at $3,500. It also appeared in Pepper & Stern Catalogue 22 [ca. 1985] at $3,500.

202. *Association Copy of a Connolly 100*

Fitzgerald, F. Scott: TENDER IS THE NIGHT. New York: Charles Scribner's Sons, 1934. Cloth. First edition, first printing. Presentation copy, inscribed and signed by Fitzgerald. About fine in dust jacket, which is modestly worn at the extremities, and backed on the verso. Enclosed in a half morocco case.

Inscribed by Fitzgerald: "Dear Mathew Josephson . . . Save for the swell organization of Lola "Zola" + your reproduction of it this would never have reached the stalls—I'll skip the obvious remarks with best wishes and high hopes for you, Scott Fitzgerald." Josephson was contributing editor for *transition*, and associate editor for *Broom*, which he tried to revive when he returned to New York from Paris in 1929. He served for a period as literary editor for Macaulay Co., inspiring the small number of distinguished literary works which that firm issued amongst its larger parcel of drivel, and was the author of a number of books, including the acclaimed work of economic history, *The Robber Barons*. ". . . A wonderful evocation of the second phase of American expatriates ensconced in glittering villas on the Riviera in contrast to the home-spun tipplers of *The Sun Also Rises* . . . described with flashes of genius by an expert in self-destruction . . ."— Connolly.

CONNOLLY, *Modern Movement* 79. BRUCCOLI A14.I.a. $3500.

Reese Catalogue 16

66. Sotheby Parke Bernet, New York, Sale Number 4482M (25 November 1980)

Item 13, Fitzgerald's imperfectly transcribed and incorrectly titled holograph copy of Kipling's poem "The Way through the Wood," sold for $400.

> ■ 13   FITZGERALD, F. SCOTT. Autograph transcript of Kipling's poem "The Way through the Woods", 25 lines, written in the back of a copy of Kipling's Departmental Ditties and Ballads and Barrack Room Ballads; in pencil
> It appears that Fitzgerald transcribed the poem from memory; the title is given as "The Lost Road" and several lines are incorrectly recalled. The book is a curious testimony to Fitzgerald's interest in Kipling. On the rear endpapers he has also listed 25 of the poems appearing in the volume

The item was later creatively catalogued in Butterfields Auction Catalogue (14 November 2002) with an estimated price of $3,000–$5,000.

> 3162
> FITZGERALD, FRANCIS SCOTT KEY.
> Kipling, Rudyard. *Departmental Ditties and Barrack-Room Ballads.* NY: 1916. Orig. red cloth. Pages toned, hinges worn. Spine sunned, wear at head and tail.
>
> *Fitzgerald's copy, with his annotations in pencil.* On the last two leaves of this book is written a poem in Fitzgerald's hand entitled "The Lost Road." On the verso of the last leaf and endpaper appears a list of Kipling poems, some with check marks next to them.
> This book dates from Fitzgerald's later Princeton years, when he neglected his studies in favor of literary pursuits. Fitzgerald wrote many poems for the student paper, as well as lyrics for student reviews, and it is possible that "The Lost Road" falls into one of those two categories. The quality of the poem, however, lags far behind other Fitzgerald works. In part: *"They enclosed the road thru the wood / Seventy years ago / Weather & rain have undone it again / And now you would never know / There was once a road thru the woods / Before they planted the trees / It is underneath the coppice & heath / And thru the aenemones [sic / Only the keeper sees / That where the ring dove broods / And the budgy [sic] roles at east / There was once a road thru the woods."*
> Estimate 3,000/5,000

The Bruccoli Collection acquired it from R. A. Gekoski in September 2003 for $12,500.

70   F. Scott Fitzgerald in the Marketplace

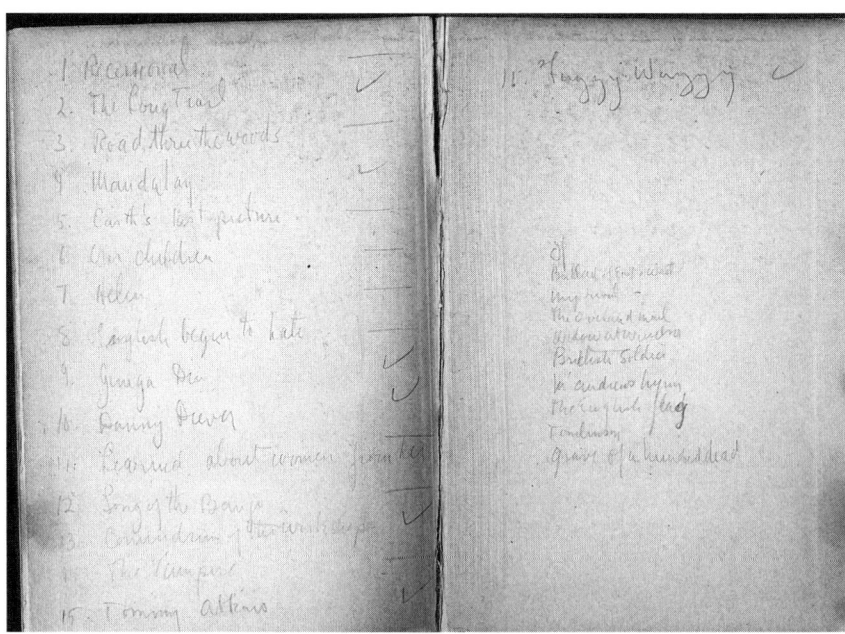

On rear blank pages

Rear endpapers

67. Letters about Spelling Errors in *Tender Is the Night*

The *Scribner's Magazine* serialization of *Tender Is the Night* and the book text were pock-marked with errors in the spellings of foreign words. Three letters in which Fitzgerald acknowledged offers of editorial help have been catalogued:

1. Christie's, London, Sale (29 April 1981). Stephen Vincent Benét was not a Book-of-the-Month Club judge, but William Rose Benét was.

[177]

177 FITZGERALD (F. SCOTT, 1896-1940): Nice T.L.S. to Mrs. Arthur J. Harris, 1307 *Park Avenue, Baltimore, 8 February* 1934, DISCUSSING THE FIRST FLUSH OF CRITICAL REACTION TO 'TENDER IS THE NIGHT' ('I am getting some responses from the book from writers but I am still pretty much alone with it and I'm grateful'), and appreciatively accepting her offer to correct his French and German in the novel: 'I am a simply hopeless linguist. I have a few corrections, but I am rushed for time because publication was begun on an unrevised manuscript and I have had to do my revisions in a hand to mouth fashion', 2 *pp.*, 4*to* (*tears in margins, one affecting two words of text*)

£380

Aiming for early book publication, Fitzgerald feverishly revised *Tender is the Night* during serialization in the winter of 1934, keeping one eye on his critics. He thanks Mrs. Harris for directing him to a surprisingly unfavourable comment on the novel by Stephen Vincent Benet: "Something tells me he did not finish the second installment or he'd have seen that the novel does really deal with deep dark matters, screaming girls tied to the railroad tracks. To tell the truth I don't rate his opinion very highly, but I do rate his vote in the Book of the Month Club'. In a second postscript to this attractively forthcoming letter he wonders, 'Who are you? Or is it none of my business?'

Not in *Letters*, ed. A. Turnbull (1964)

2. Robert F. Batchelder Catalogue 58 (1986).

FASCINATING F. SCOTT FITZGERALD LETTER CONCERNING HIS
MISUSE AND ERRATIC SPELLING OF FRENCH WORDS WHICH HE
USED IN THE WRITING OF HIS BOOK "TENDER IS THE NIGHT"
179. FITZGERALD, F. SCOTT. American author. Typed Letter Signed, 1 1/2 separate pages 4to, Baltimore, Feb. 3, 1934, to Miss Pauline Reinsch of Madison, Wisconsin, in reply to her letter to Fitzgerald asking if she could make some corrections in the French words and locales for his book "Tender is the Night" which, as a college student, she noticed in the book she just read. Fitzgerald replies "I am tremendously obligded to you for your letter of January 21. Though I lived in France for many years and studied French, and previous to that had studied French in America for 8 years, I have never been able to speak anything but pigeon-French, having absolutely no capacity as a linguist save in my own language. Even there I am an erratic speller and often misuse words. I shall, of course, incorporate your corrections in the proof and I am further emboldened by your interest to have advance copies mailed to you of the other two installments of my book, in hope that you might be good enough to note any more terrible errors that you might come across. So as not to trespass too much on your time and patience I am enclosing two self addressed envelopes. I am glad you liked the story and am sorry it is marred for you by these inaccuracies. Of course even after leaving me it goes through the hands of a typist and a printer, who do not speak French, so I do not take complete blame for every mislaid 'e.' However, that can't be explained to the public and the guilt will fall on me." Excellent condition. An important letter of this great author, with one holograph addition in his hand, showing his ability to accept criticism gracefully, and his desire to perfect his books more when necessary. The book "Tender is the Night" published in 1934 as indicated, is somewhat auto-biographical, reflecting his wife, Zelda's mental illness and his own eventual breakdown. 1200.00

F Scott Fitzgerald

THE ORIGINAL MANUSCRIPT OF A MUSICAL PLAY BASED
ON FITZGERALD'S NOVEL "THIS SIDE OF PARADISE,"
PRESENTED ON THE U.S. STEEL HOUR IN 1951
180. (THIS SIDE OF PARADISE). The original manuscript by noted playwright and lyricist Daley Paskman of a musical version of the F.Scott Fitzgerald novel, This Side of Paradise, 87 pages 4to, circa 1951. Included is a printed script of the show, and a program of the famous U.S. Steel Hour radio show describing the performance of the musical on April 8, 1951 starring Richard Widmark as Amory and Nina Foch as Rosalind. A fascinating grouping. 150.00

3. Butterfields Catalogue (14 November 2002).

> 3167
> FITZGERALD, FRANCIS SCOTT KEY.
> Autograph Note Signed ("F. Scott Fitzgerald"), 1 page, oblong octavo, n.p., n.d., to Madame White, leaf creased, toned, cut to lower right corner, offset from signature.
>
> In full: "*Dear Mme White: / Can you manage to get those French translations (or rather corrections) back to me through Mrs. Owens Thursday or Friday? Even if incomplete I should have them back. / With Best Wishes / F. Scott Fitzgerald.*" In addition to providing translations for Fitzgerald (perhaps for *Tender is the Night*, set on the French Riviera), Madame White was also involved in the care of Fitzgerald's daughter, Scotty.
> Estimate 1,000/2,000

68. Swann Galleries Sale Number 1245 (28 January 1982)

The pre-auction estimate for item 129 was $700–$1,000.

> **WITH A FULL-PAGE INSCRIPTION**
> 129 • FITZGERALD, F. SCOTT. The Great Gatsby. 8vo, green ribbed cloth, spine faded; fragments of the dust jacket present, but crudely repaired with cellotape. New York, 1925
> FIRST EDITION, Second Printing, with the 6 variants cited in Bruccoli (11.1a).
> INSCRIBED *on the front free endpaper:* "*For Maud Suman from hers sincerely F. Scott Fitzgerald 'Ellerslee' Edgemoor, Delaware, June 1927.*
> "*If it weren't for librarys [sic] how would 100,000 women like my mother ever get to sleep?*
> "*There was no answer—only the squeaky rustle of paper as 100,000 women turned another page.*"
> *Miss Suman was a librarian in Washington, D.C. and the aunt of the present consignor.*

69. Maurice F. Neville Catalogue 8 (1982)

> 145 FITZGERALD, F. SCOTT. Flappers and Philosophers. New York: Charles Scribner's Sons, 1921. $750.00
> LATER PRINTING. Signed presentation copy beneath which Fitzgerald has drawn a beer mug with a cross through it and written "yours in Xt. [Christianity]." Near fine.

Fitzgerald's "Xt." means "Christ."

> 148 FITZGERALD, F. SCOTT. Taps at Reveille. New York: Charles Scribner's Sons, 1935. $2500.00
> FIRST EDITION, SECOND ISSUE. Signed presentation copy inscribed: "For Marguerite Kennedy, the only inspiration of these stories—as indeed of all my writings—from her devoted chattel Scott Fitzgerald 'Fair youth beneath the trees thou canst not ever—' Hollywood 1939." Near fine in a chipped and internally repaired dust jacket.

This is the second state of *Taps at Reveille*, not the second issue.

70. Charles Hamilton Auction Number 148 (12 August 1982)

The copy of *Taps at Reveille* was resold in the Sotheby's Neville auction (16 November 2004): see entry 135, item 307.

> 66 FITZGERALD, F. SCOTT. American novelist. Two of his books. Comprises: FITZGERALD, *Taps at Reveille*, Chas. Scribner's Sons, N.Y., 1935, marked "A" on copyright page; inscribed in black ink on front flyleaf: "For John and Anita/this little sheaf of woodland/pipings/ from F. Scott ('Strangler') Fitzgerald/Hollywood-on-the-Binge, 1937"; the Anita Loos bookplate mounted on front endpaper (about fine, in worn and repaired dust wrapper) ☐ FITZGERALD, *The Vegetable*, Chas. Scribner's, N.Y., April, 1923, not signed by Fitzgerald but signed on front flyleaf by actress MABEL NORMAND; Anita Loos bookplate mounted on front endpaper (some stains and minor defects, but very good). Two books.⊗ ....(1000/1100)

Hamilton Auction Number 148

71. Bauman Rare Books (1983)

See Item 204: Presentation Copy of Fitzgerald's *Tender is the Night*.

SIGNED AND INSCRIBED BY FITZGERALD

204. FITZGERALD, F(rancis) Scott (Key). Tender is the Night. New York, 1934. Octavo, original green cloth. $1500.

First Edition. Signed and inscribed by Fitzgerald on the front free endpaper: "From one who wishes he could be at 1917's 20th." Very slight wear, good condition. Bruccoli A14.1.c.

72. Waverly Auctions at Quill & Brush, Sale Number 23 (15 May 1983)

Fitzgerald's revised galleys for "The Night at Chancellorsville"; also proof for the rejected foreword to *Taps at Reveille*, revised by Fitzgerald and killed by Maxwell Perkins. Sale prices undetermined.

> Fitzgerald, F. Scott. THE NIGHT AT CHANCELLORSVILLE. 2 Sheets of Galley Proofs, the complete story, to be included by Fitzgerald at the last minute in "Taps At Reveille.", when the book was in proof. Both sheets have extensive corrections in Fitzgerald's hand, in pencil. Sheet one has 30 one-word corrections, and at the bottom, 2 sentences added: "Maybe I'd be more pretty for you if I hadn't lost an eye at Gaine's Mill'. Then we notice he had lost an eye. He kept it sort of closed so we hadn't (word crossed out) remembered it before. Pretty". Second sheet has about 14 one-word corrections, and 3 nearly complete-sentence additions amounting to some 50 words. There are as well many proof reader marks. Both sheets have several folds (few tears in folds), and one chip out of fold (present). The proofs are, in part, in fragile condition. (See Mizener's biography for brief discussion of Fitzgerald's struggle with the proofs for "Taps". Included is an 8½ x 11 sheet of "Author's Foreword" to "Fitzgerald's Stories" which has corrections and the word "Kill" boldly written across the text, possibly by Fitzgerald as well. Rare for any galleys with holograph Fitzgerald corrections to appear at auction. (2500/3500)

76 F. Scott Fitzgerald in the Marketplace

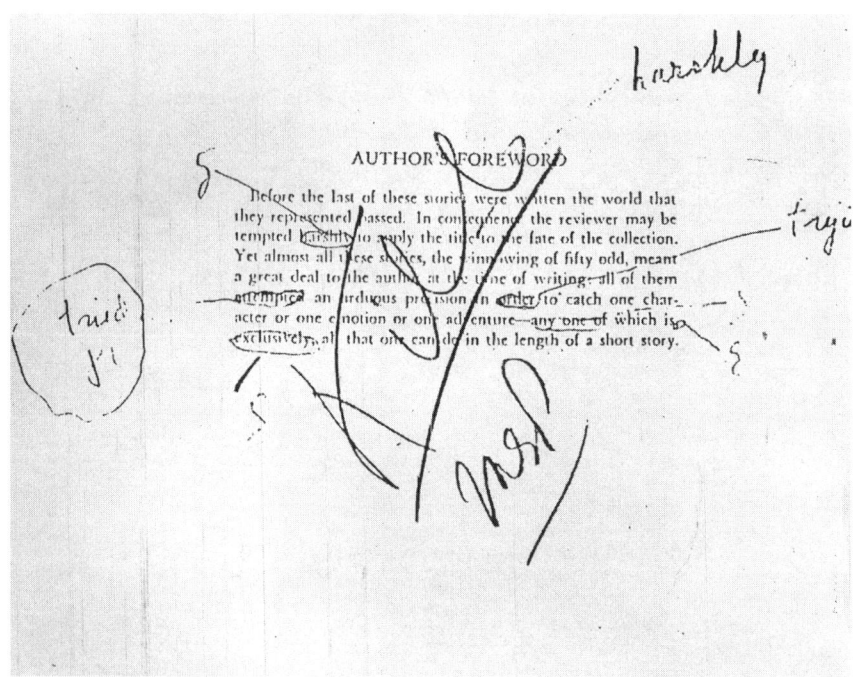

73. Charles Hamilton Auction Number 155 (26 May 1983)

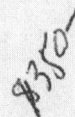

68 FITZGERALD, F. SCOTT. American author. Pencil A.Ms. (unsigned), about 1 full page, 4to, original working draft of an amusing poem consisting of three quatrains. In part: "As for me, well, I am handsome/I'm as clever as can be/I can dance, my voice is pretty/I'm a wonder you can see/Kindly catalogue your virtues/Eyes, features, face & figure too/If everything shall please me/Then perhaps I'll marry you." Some smudging and other defects, but very satisfactory. .... (300/350)

Five months later the poem was sold for a substantially higher price: see entry 74.

74. Phillips, New York, Sale Number 510 (20 October 1983)

• 35   FITZGERALD, F. Scott
   AUTOGRAPH POEM, 1p., 4to., n.p., n.d., (circa 1914), extensive deletions, etc.

   Robert says she's pretty
   Robert says she's sweet   } deleted
   Though she may be { } witty,
   has she got big feet?

   I've heard so much about you
   That I often quite regret
   That I can not judge your beauty
   You're a girl I haven'{t} met.

   As for me, well, I am handsome
   I'm as clever as can be,
   I can dance, my voice is pretty
   I'm a wonder you can see.

   Kindly catalogue your virtues
   -Eyes, features, face & figure too.
   {- - - - - -}
   Then perhaps I'll marry you..:
   (And if everything shall please me)

   Typed accross the top: *These lines below were written by F. Scott Fitzgerald in 1914. Apparently unpublished.*

   Fitzgerald wrote numerous verses and lyrics in his first year at Princeton for Triangle Club musicals and college newspapers.

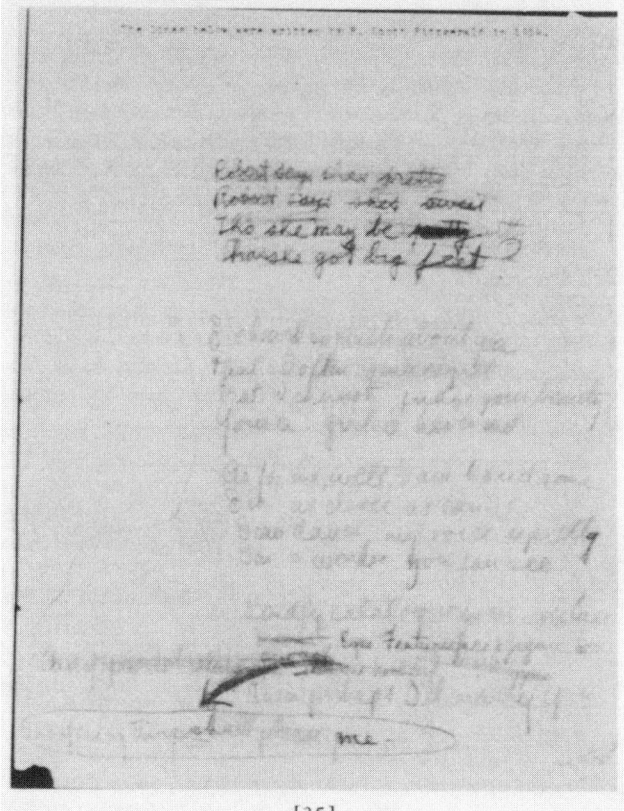

[35]

75. Charles Hamilton Auction Number 159 (10 November 1983)

FITZGERALD TO HIS MOTHER-IN-LAW

82 FITZGERALD, F. SCOTT. His book, *The Vegetable*, Chas. Scribner's Sons, N.Y., April, 1923. Inscribed on front flyleaf: "For Mrs. A. D. Sayre, with love/from/F. Scott Fitzgerald." Mrs. Sayre was Fitzgerald's mother-in-law, the mother of Zelda. Foxed and somewhat shaken, with corners crushed, but otherwise very good. A desirable association item. ....(600/800)

76. Sotheby's, New York, Sale Number 5114 (14 December 1983)

■ 100 FITZGERALD, F. SCOTT. Autograph letter signed ("F. Scott Fitzgerald"), 1 page 4to, St. Paul, Minn., 10 February 1922, to David Wallace, the Broadway producer and manager for the Schuberts and Ziegfeld. Some small nicks and paper losses at margins

Fitzgerald responds to an enquiry about the play [*The Vegetable*] he is writing: "It *is* about flappers in part but it is *not* in collaboration with Stewart". He will probably send the completed work to Wallace first but he has a friend in Frohman's (another important production company) office who is anxious to see it. He concludes by announcing the birth of his daughter [Scottie]

$900- $700/900

77. Christie's, New York, Sale Number 5474 (16–17 December 1983)

$660 BP • 413 FITZGERALD, F. SCOTT. This Side of Paradise, New York: Scribner's 1931, *8vo, original green cloth, spots on front cover, free end-papers a bit browned,* Later printing (290 copies) within the first edition of the author's first book, INSCRIBED BY FITZGERALD on front free endpaper: "For Dorothy Bissell, This little sheaf of wayward woodland pipings from F. Scott ("Bachus") Fitzgerald, Arcadia, 1937." At the time the book in this and the following two lots were inscribed, Fitzgerald was living at the Oak Hall Hotel in Tyron, North Carolina, prior to going to Hollywood in June, 1937. Bruccoli A5.I.p $300-400

$715 BP • 414 FITZGERALD, F.S. The Beautiful and Damned, New York: Scribner's 1922, *8vo, original green cloth, spine dull, slight foxing to endpapers,* FIRST EDITION, Third Printing. INSCRIBED BY FITZGERALD on front free endpaper: "For Dorothy Bissell from F. Scott ("Killer") Fitzgerald, The hide-out, Tyron, 1937." Bruccoli A8.I.c $300-400

$2,420 BP • 415 FITZGERALD, F.S. The Great Gatsby, New York: Charles Scribner's 1925, *8vo, original green cloth, a few small stains on spine, a few pages at end lightly foxed,* FIRST EDITION, Second Printing. INSCRIBED BY FITZGERALD on front free endpaper: "For Dorothy Bissell, April 1937, F. Scott Fitzgerald, in memory of hot arguments over the Supreme Court and the autonomy of Barcelona." Bruccoli A11.I.b; Connolly, *The Modern Movement,* 48 $400-600

Dorothy Bissell has not been identified. The copy of *The Beautiful and Damned* inscribed to her was offered again in a 1984 Bauman catalogue for $1,600. The same catalogue also offered the Bissell *This Side of Paradise.*

80 F. Scott Fitzgerald in the Marketplace

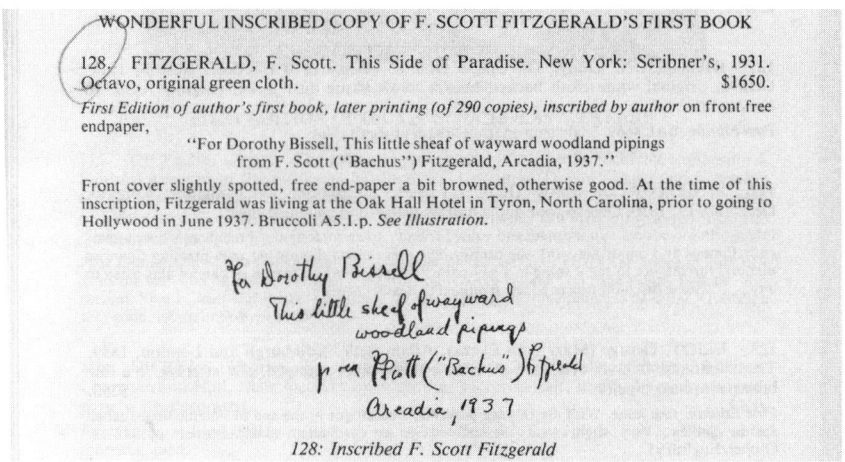

128: Inscribed F. Scott Fitzgerald

In 1986 Bauman twice recatalogued the Bissell *This Side of Paradise* for $1,650. *The Great Gatsby* inscribed to Bissell—which fetched $2,200 in the December 1983 Christie's sale—was resold by Christie's on 7 October 1994 for $4,000.

78. Maurice F. Neville Catalogue 12 [ca. 1985]

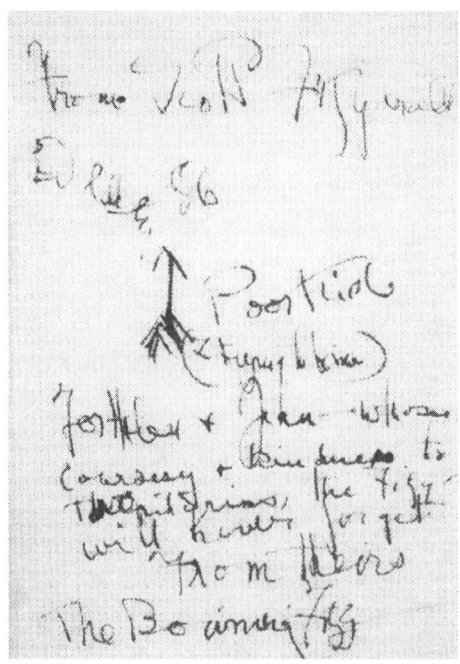

Item 497; Bruccoli Collection

INSCRIBED F. SCOTT FITZGERALDS

497. FITZGERALD, F. SCOTT. This Side of Paradise. New York: Charles Scribner's Sons, 1922. $750.00

    LATER PRINTING. Inscribed in an inebriated hand: "From Scott Fitzgerald [date and a few words illegible] For Helen and Jean [sic]—whose courtesy and kindness to the pilgrims, the Fitz will never forget. From theirs, The Bowing Fitz." Gene Buck was a neighbor of Fitzgerald's at Great Neck, Long Island, and was Florenz Ziegfeld's right-hand man. Andrew Turnbull, in his biography *Scott Fitzgerald* speculates that Buck's lavish parties might have been models for the festivities described in *The Great Gatsby*. Front endsheet removed, else a very good clean and tight copy.

498. FITZGERALD, F. SCOTT. This Side of Paradise. New York: Charles Scribner's Sons, 1920. $600.00

    AUTHOR'S APOLOGY EDITION. Signed by Fitzgerald on special tipped-in leaf. One of an unknown number of copies of the third printing prepared for a meeting of the American Booksellers Association. Very good.

499. FITZGERALD, F. SCOTT. This Side of Paradise. New York: Charles Scribner's Sons, 1920. $350.00

    LATER PRINTING. Signed "With Best Regards from F. Scott Fitzgerald" on front endpaper. Hinges loose, a good only copy.

500. FITZGERALD, F. SCOTT. Flappers and Philosophers. New York: Charles Scribner's Sons, 1921. $750.00

    LATER PRINTING. Inscribed on endpaper: "For Jean [sic] Buck from his most admiring friend F. Scott Fitzgerald." Very good.

501. FITZGERALD, F. SCOTT. Flappers and Philosophers. New York: Charles Scribner's Sons, [1920]. $375.00

    LATER PRINTING. Signed by Fitzgerald and dated "January 1926 or 7." Front endsheet removed, else very good.

502. FITZGERALD, F. SCOTT. The Beautiful and the Damned. New York: Charles Scribner's Sons, 1922. $800.00

    LATER PRINTING. Inscribed on endpaper: "For Helen (Buck)—not of Troy but of Great Neck—a lovely girl who is so sweet as to sing for us, now and then—F. Scott Fitzgerald." Very good.

503. FITZGERALD, F. SCOTT. The Vegetable. New York: Charles Scribner's Sons, 1923. $1750.00

    FIRST EDITION. Contemporary presentation copy inscribed: "For ―― from hers invisibly F. Scott Fitzgerald Aug 7th 1923." Very good in dust jacket missing a few chips.

79. George Robert Minkoff Catalogue 85-B [ca. April 1985]

49. FITZGERALD, F. SCOTT. This Side of Paradise. 8vo. Original grey cloth, head of spine chipped. New York, A.L. Burt Co. (1920). Later Edition of Fitzgerald's first book. Presentation copy inscribed, "For Carmel Myersin, Memory of that happy night in the bathroom. 'Oi bring back them happy hours' (Raquello). Georgetown Univ Aug. 1891". The recipient was actually Carmel Myers, an actress the Fitzgeralds met in Rome in 1924 while Myers was making the film "Ben Hur". Myers became a close friend of the Fitzgeralds, and there is even some evidence that her relation with Scott was a lot closer than friendship. $850.00

Bruccoli Collection

80. Harris Auction Galleries Sale Number 238 (22 November 1985)

WITH POSSIBLE HOLOGRAPH TEXT CORRECTIONS

215A. _____. Taps at Reveille. N.Y.: Scribner's, 1935. FIRST EDITION, First State, inscribed and signed by Fitzgerald in ink, 1935, at front endpaper. 8vo, dark green cloth, gilt lettering. Covers clean, gilt bright, text very clean and tight, first text leaf roughly opened, few leaves unopened. Bruccoli A.17.I.a.1.

In full: "For Ed Northam / a good fellow (when / not engaged in subluxating / the quota club at Old / Point Comfort) / from his Friend / F. Scott Fitzgerald / Baltimore / April Fool's Day / 1935". Bruccoli states the book was published only 11 days earlier. Northam was a Baltimore chiropractor who lived on Linden Avenue, a block or two from Fitzgerald's house on Park Avenue.

Fitzgerald has apparently made a few pencil text corrections at precisely the text lines on pages 350-351 which were altered in the Second State of the First Edition. But they are not precisely identical to the alterations in the Second State version.

On page 350, lines 5-7 are corrected to "-- he need not base himself on this adding machine-St. Francis of Assisi any longer." The simple deletion is consistent at line 15 of page 351, while line 29 is simply deleted until the final word "she", which is capitalized.

The deletions are wavy line, straight line, and straight double-line, respectively. Actual new lettering occurs twice on page 350, and the capitalization on page 351. The structure of these letters bears strong similarities to Fitzgerald's own handwriting; that the changes are in pencil while the inscription is in ink, and are different from any published format, encourages an interesting interpretation:

This could be one of the initial copies given to Fitzgerald by Scribner's, with intermediate corrections made by the author some time before he presented it to his neighbor. Quite a different circumstance than the usual inscription in a copy thrust before a famous author. [Estimate $500/800].

INSCRIBED TO CHILDHOOD FRIEND OF SCOTTY

216. _____. Tender Is the Night: a Romance. N.Y.: Scribner's, 1934. FIRST EDITION, signed and inscribed by Fitzgerald in ink at front blank. 8vo, dark green cloth, gilt spine lettering. Covers moderately worn with fraying and small snags at spine tips, gilt lettering partly lacking, small spots at front cover, contents very good, inscription clear and clean. Bruccoli A.14 I.a.

In black ink at front blank: "For the unknown, unmet / parents of / Clare / Knowing her, I / hope you'll find / something to like / in this / Best Wishes from / F. Scott Fitzgerald."

Clare is Claire (sic) Eager Matthai, descendant of John Eager Howard, and a classmate of Fitzgerald's daughter Scottie at Bryn Mawr School in Baltimore in the mid-1930s.

As Mrs. Matthai recently related, when this book was presented to her parents, her father sat down and read a good portion of it, after which he tossed the book into a cold fireplace, announcing to one and all that the text was trash, and that no book such as this would remain in his house, to be read by members of his family.

The nurse for Claire's grandmother retrieved the book from the ash pile and took it home; the story then has a long interlude, before the book was purchased at a rummage sale in southern Pennsylvania about ten years ago by the current consignor. [Estimate $600/800].

216A. _____. Tender Is the Night: a Romance. N.Y.: Scribner's, 1934. FIRST EDITION, signed and inscribed by Fitzgerald in ink, 1934, at front endpaper. 8vo, dark green cloth, gilt spine lettering. Very clean, bright copy, inscription fine, in somewhat unsteady hand. Bruccoli A.14.I.a.

In full: "For Edgar H. Northam / from his friend / F. Scott Fitzgerald / April 23d 1934." Northam was a Baltimore Bolton Hill neighbor of Fitzgerald (see Lot #215A). The writing is irregular not only in style, but Fitzgerald's pen was balky, resulting in some thin strokes and some duplications. Inscribed but 11 days after publication. [Estimate $400/600].

Item 215 A: Fitzgerald's emendations for "One Interne" were published on a tipped-in leaf, thereby creating the second state of *Taps at Reveille*. This copy of *Taps at Reveille* was recatalogued in Superior Galleries Auction Catalogue (6 November 1993), item 244.

> **244**
> **FITZGERALD, F. SCOTT**
> Taps At Reveille (NY, 1935).
> First edition, 5100 published. First state with pages 349-352 uncancelled. First dustjacket with printed price on rear flap and rubber-stamped price on front flap. A contemporary signed and inscribed presentation copy, in black ink, *"April Fools Day, 1935.* "The errors on pages 350 and 351 are corrected in pencil, probably by the author, though it's scary to buy into pencil unless there's a lot of it. One page opened a bit rashly but the cloth is brilliant and the dustjacket has only a single ³/₄" tear. Eighteen of Fitzgerald's greatest stories including eight about Basil and Josephine and his phenomenal Babylon Revisited, but he was already headed to Hollywood, his career in a bomb shelter without a can opener. "Show me a hero and I'll write you a tragedy," said he. "Don't love the one who helped you become unhappy," says we.
> Estimated Value.. $ 6000-9000

Superior Galleries Auction Catalogue (6 November 1993)

Harris Auction Galleries item 216 was recatalogued in Maurice F. Neville Catalogue 13 [1986] for $1,300.

81. Alphabet Bookshop Catalogue 14 [1986]

Billy de Beck was the cartoonist who drew the Barney Google strip. He and Fitzgerald met in Asheville.

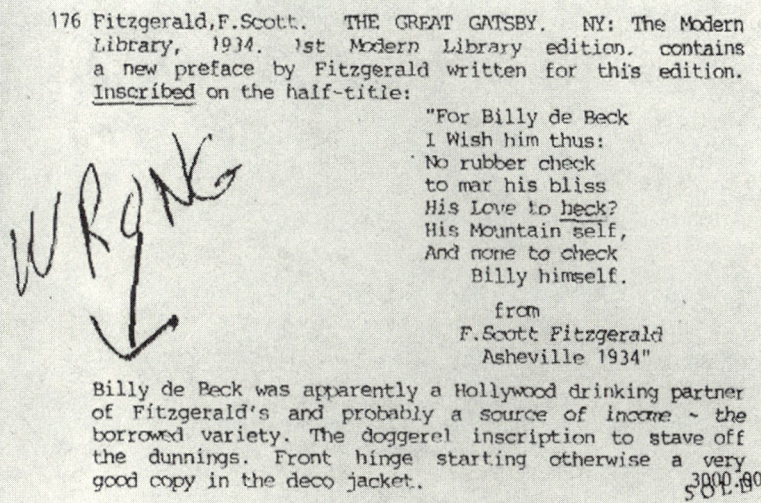

The Bruccoli Collection includes a page of de Beck's Barney Google drawings inscribed in Asheville to Fitzgerald and his nurse, Dorothy Richardson.

82. The George Cukor Collection. George Houle, Los Angeles (1986)

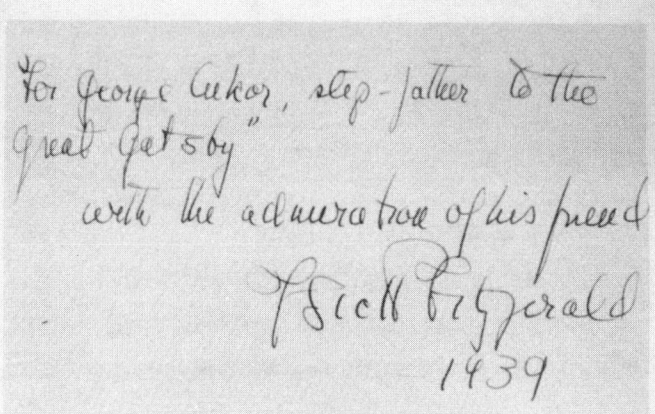

442. FITZGERALD

Step-Father of the 'Great Gatsby'

442. FITZGERALD, F. SCOTT
Taps at Reveille. N.Y., Scribner, 1935.
First edition, first issue. 8vo. Gilt stamped dark green cloth (small nick at head of spine), else fine.
$2,500.00

Inscribed by the author: "For George Cukor, step-father to the 'Great Gatsby' with the admiration of . . . F. Scott Fitzgerald. 1939." In addition Fitzgerald has drawn a line through line 29 on page 351, adding "misprint," and he had written above the chapter head of "One Interne," on page 349 — "A lot of pictures have grown out of this story. . . . 1931."

In 1939 Fitzgerald was in Hollywood working with Cukor on the screen version of "The Women;" he had also worked with Cukor on the screenplay of "Gone With the Wind."

Cukor directed the Broadway production of "The Great Gatsby," in 1926.

83. Profiles in History Catalogue 1. Joseph M. Maddalena [1987]

Pratt's review has not been identified.

> 11. FITZGERALD, FRANCIS SCOTT. 1896-1940. American fiction writer. Author of This Side of Paradise, The Great Gatsby, Taps at Reveille, etc. Autograph Letter Signed, One page, Quarto, Paris, Not dated. Written to Mr. Pratt (apparently a literary reviewer). Fitzgerald writes: *"Thanks for your flattering review, and for sending it to me. I undoubtedly owe many of my sales in California to such excellent publicity as you have given Gatsby. Thank you most of all for liking it."* A great letter mentioning Fitzgerald's most important work, The Great Gatsby. 1500.00

84. Robert F. Batchelder Catalogue 62 (1987)

> 228. FITZGERALD, F. SCOTT. American author. Typed Letter Signed, 1 page 4to, Baltimore, Oct. 2, 1934 to a lieutenant with whom he had served about their regiment. "It was fine hearing from you again after all these years. Winchell's report that I was sick was some of his hot air. I've seen only too little of the men of our regiment though whenever I take lunch at the Harvard Club in New York there is a waiter who rushes up to me and reminds me of the old days. His name escapes me now but it was one of the unpronounceable ones." Very good, a repaired tear in a blank portion. Actually Fitzgerald was not well at this time. He had finished his last great book, Tender is the Night, but was fighting a losing battle against Zelda's insanity and his own drinking problem. 550.00

85. Swann Galleries Sale Number 1450 (12 November 1987)

Recatalogued in Glenn Horowitz Catalogue 15 [1988] at $3,500.

> 84 • FITZGERALD, F. SCOTT. "The Light of Heart." Screenplay by F. Scott Fitzgerald. From the Play by Emlyn Williams. 1st Draft Continuity; October 14, 1940. 143 mimeographed pages, rectos only. 4to, gilt-stamped full calf, somewhat worn. See Bruccoli, pages 323, 325. Np, 1940 [400/600]

Swann Galleries Sale Number 1450

86. Black Sun Books Catalogue 78 (1988)

Recatalogued in George Robert Minkoff List 89–C (June 1989) at $2,750.

Fitzgerald used his observations of the *Ben-Hur* production in *Tender Is the Night*.

> 114. FITZGERALD, F. Scott. Tender Is The Night. New York, 1934. 8vo, cloth. First edition, second printing. Presentation copy from Fitzgerald, inscribed "For Carmel from one always faithful, & sometimes even tight, Scott." $3,000.00
> *The recipient was Carmel Myers, an actress that Fitzgerald met in Rome in 1924, while Myers was making the film 'Ben Hur'. Myers and Fitzgerald became close friends, and their friendship lasted until Scott Fitzgerald's death.*

Black Sun Catalogue 78

This book was acquired for the Bruccoli Collection from Seven Gables in the 1960s and returned to Myers when she claimed it had been stolen from her. She subsequently sold it.

87. R. A. Gekoski Catalogue 10 (Spring 1988)

> **INSCRIBED FIRST BOOK**
>
> 91. FITZGERALD, F. SCOTT. *This Side of Paradise*, New York, 1920. His first book, reprinted in year of publication. Author's presentation copy, inscribed on the front free endpaper, "For Kenneth Brightbill with the regards of F. Scott Fitzgerald April 15th 1921". The recipient was a fellow student with Fitzgerald. It is uncommon to find this title with a contemporary inscription. Front hinge tender but still a very good copy. £1,250

88. Sotheby's, New York, Sale Number 5729 (7 June 1988)

> ☐ 20
> FITZGERALD, F. SCOTT. Autograph letter signed ("F. Scott Fitzgerald"), 1 page 8vo, New York, 28 December 1920, to Mr. Wallace, discussing "Head and Shoulders"; traces of previous mounting on verso of integral blank
>
> A POSSIBLE STAGE PRODUCTION? In this letter, Fitzgerald responds to his correspondent's proposal of dramatizing "Head and Shoulders," a story which first appeared in *Flappers and Philosophers*, 1920. He writes, ". . . Considering that Head & Shoulders has been done in the movies I'm not inclined to think it'd be financially worth while dramatizing it. And, honestly, I'm not awfully fond of it. . . ." Fitzgerald closes his letter by noting that he is working on his novel; a novel he does not identify by name. At the time of this letter Fitzgerald was probably writing *The Beautiful and Damned*, 1922
>
> $700-900
>
> $1,000=

89. Profiles in History Catalogue 7. Joseph M. Maddalena [1989]

The Fitzgerald story that was cut by the *Saturday Evening Post* was "The Hotel Child" (31 January 1931).

F. SCOTT FITZGERALD COMMENTS: "YOUR SECTION HAS CERTAINLY PRODUCED A BIG BOY IN THIS MAN FAULKNER. HE'S FINE!"

FITZGERALD, F. SCOTT. 1896-1940. American novelist and short-story writer. Best known for his novels and stories of the 1920s, the "Jazz Age", including the classics, The Great Gatsby (1925), Tender Is The Night (1934), and The Last Tycoon (1941).

164. Excellent Autograph Letter Signed, on imprinted Grand Hotel De La Paix, Lausanne, Switzerland, letterhead, One page, Quarto, June 15, 1931. Written to Paul Eldridge, University of Oklahoma, Norman, Oklahoma. Fitzgerald writes (in full):

"Thank you for the open, pleasant tone of your letter. Frankly the English have long been on my nerves (those were real people & the Post cut the best scene when they kept feeding hashish to the pekenese.) I didn't write The Millionaire's Girl - not a line of it. My wife did it. We used my name for

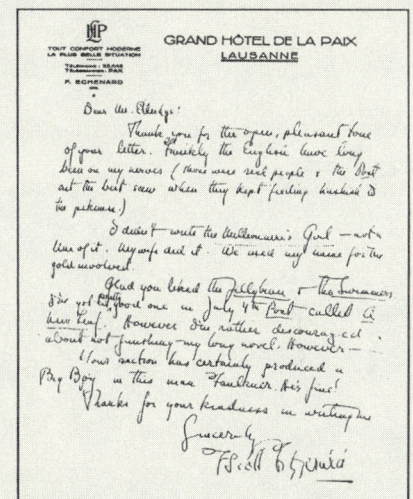

the gold involved. Glad you liked The Jellybean & The Swimmers. I've got a pretty good one in July 4th Post called A New Leaf. However, I'm rather discouraged about not finishing my long novel. However -. Your section has certainly produced a Big Boy in this man Faulkner. He's fine! Thanks for your kindness in writing me. Sincerely, F. Scott Fitzgerald".

A wonderful letter with fine literary content. Fitzgerald letters from this time period are very desireable.
$ 3,500.00

90. Christie's, London, Sale Number 4059 (24 May 1989)

Recatalogued in Paul Rassam Catalogue 12 [1989] for £4,000.

213 FITZGERALD (F. SCOTT): THIS SIDE OF PARADISE, FIRST EDITION, FIRST PRINTING, PRESENTATION COPY FROM THE AUTHOR, *original dark green cloth*, 8vo, New York, Charles Scribner's Sons [April] 1920

Bruccoli A5.1.a. Fitzgerald's first novel, dedicated to Sigourney Fay, with inscription on fly leaf 'Here you are Stephen [Parrot]—Dedicated to the best friend either of us ever had—F. Scott Fitzgerald March 20th 1920'. The inscription is dated the day his engagement to Zelda Sayre was announced, and this must be one of the earliest copies from the press. The first printing of 3,000 copies was published on 26 March 1920
£1,000-1,500

Christie's Sale Number 4059

This copy of the novel accompanied the incomplete carbon TS of *This Side of Paradise* sent to Stephan Parrott by Fitzgerald. San Francisco dealer Warren Howell bought both the TS and the inscribed book from the

Duchess of Argyll—reputedly Parrott's illegitimate daughter—and sold them to Bruccoli. The Duchess refused to deliver the book but kept the payment for it. Paul Rassam acquired it at the Christie's auction and included it in his 1989 Catalogue 12. He reported that it was bought by dealer David Mayou who sold it to dealer Mark Hime.

1990s

91. Pepper & Stern Catalogue 26 (1990)

ITEM 155

155 FITZGERALD, F. SCOTT. Tales of the Jazz Age. New York: Scribner, 1922. First Edition. Presentation copy, inscribed to his nurse: "For Anne Wilson from her chattell, F. Scott Fitzgerald. 'We were happy in Switzerland—will be ever be so happy again?' 1939." Bookplate. A very good to fine copy. $4,500.00

92. Glenn Horowitz Catalogue 19 [ca. 1990]

The description seems fanciful.

> 24 GLENN HOROWITZ, BOOKSELLER, INC.
>
> 63 Fitzgerald, F. Scott. *TAPS AT REVEILLE*. New York: Charles Scribner's Sons, 1935.
>
> 8vo., original green cloth, stamped in gilt; spine stamping almost completely flaked away; covers lightly rubbed; tight and sound. $3500
>
> First edition, first state, pp.349-352 uncancelled. 5100 copies printed in all. Bruccoli A17.I.a. A presentation copy, inscribed "For Ree Bayne, who would like "to see the whole picture" & miss the company of her friend F. Scott Fitzgerald June 1936 Baltimore." Two months earlier Zelda had been institutionalized in the Highland Hospital in Asheville, North Carolina and Fitzgerald noted in his Ledger: "Me caring about no one and nothing." But his troubles didn't lessen and soon after Fitzgerald was forced to return to Baltimore, where his mother was dying. Apparently Rebecca "Ree" Bayne was hired to try and keep Fitzgerald out of Baltimore's bars and lounges, or at least to monitor the quantity of alcohol he consumed. Fitzgerald's mother died in August 1936 and soon after the novelist left Baltimore, never to return. This inscription commemorates one of the saddest times in Fitzgerald's hard life.

93. James Cummins Catalogue 23 [1990]

Cummins priced the copy of *This Side of Paradise* inscribed to Mrs. Sayre at $11,000 in this catalogue. He raised the price for the book in his Catalogue 32 (Fall 1991), item 187.

> *Inscribed to Zelda's Mother*
>
> 187 FITZGERALD, F. SCOTT. *This Side of Paradise*. 8vo, New York: Scribners, 1920. First Edition, Second printing. Original cloth, a trifle rubbed, heel of spine frayed, covers slightly bowed, but overall a sound copy of an extraordinary association copy of one of the literary landmarks of the 20th century. $12,500
>
> Presentation copy to Zelda's mother, inscribed two days after Zelda and Scott's marriage: "For Mrs. A.D. Sayre. You've always been awfully darned encouraging about my writings - often when nobody else much was, and I suppose that['s] what keeps writers going - F. Scott Fitzgerald, New York City, April 5th, 1920." A stunning presentation, all the more intriguing when one considers the Sayres' not altogether happy acceptance of their daughter Zelda's romance with an unknown writer. The book (Fitzgerald's first) came out on March 26th in a printing of 3000 copies. Within a week the first printing had sold out, during which time Fitzgerald took rooms at the Biltmore Hotel to await Zelda's arrival from Montgomery and to see how the book would fair. They had postponed their marriage for a number of reasons, not the least of which being Zelda's parents. They were originally to have been married on the 5th, the date of this presentation; on the 30th Fitzgerald wired her, saying: "We will be awfully nervous until its over and would get no rest by waiting until Monday [a reference to the wedding day] First Edition of the book sold out." (Quoted in Zelda, A Biography, by Nancy Mitford.) It is not unlikely that this presentation of the book in its second printing was to serve as a notice to Mrs. Sayre of her new son-in-law's success, for it is unlikely that the writer himself could not have procured a first edition for his new mother-in-law. It goes without saying, an amazing association copy, inscribed at one of the most important moments in the young writer's life.
>
> *(See illustration over)*

For Mrs. A. D. Sayre

You've always been awfully darned encouraging about my writings — often when nobody else much was — — And I suppose that what keeps writers going —

F Scott Fitzgerald
New York City
April 5th, 1920

Item 187 - Fitzgerald

94. Glenn Horowitz Catalogue 24 [1991]

55 (Fitzgerald, F(rancis). Scott). [Cover title:] *Nassau Literary Magazine*, Volume LXXII, Number 6. January 1917.

8vo., brown printed wrappers; lightly frayed, some edge wear. $750

Princeton University's literary magazine containing the first appearances of Fitzgerald's play "The Debutante," (pp. 241-252) and his unsigned review of Booth Tarkington's *Penrod and Sam* (pp.291-292). Bruccoli C35, C36. "The Debutante," like many of the pieces Fitzgerald contributed to *The Nassau Literary Magazine*, was incorporated into *This Side of Paradise*, his fictionalized account of the Princeton years. It was revised for *The Smart Set*, LX, September 1919 (Bruccoli C75); the revised state was later collected in *The Smart Set: A History and Anthology*, 1966 (Bruccoli B62). The text as it appeared in *The Nassau Literary Magazine* was reprinted in *The Apprentice Fiction of F. Scott Fitzgerald*, 1965 (Bruccoli A27). The untitled review of *Penrod and Sam* was reprinted in *F. Scott Fitzgerald In His Own Time*, 1971 (Bruccoli A32).

It took Fitzgerald two years to break into the pages of "The Lit," as the *Nassau Literary Review* was affectionately called by the undergraduates; starting in 1915, Fitzgerald was a regular contributor to the publication and began a life long friendship with its editor, Edmund Wilson. In 1917 when Wilson enlisted in the army and was shipped off to France, he left Fitzgerald at the helm: "The Lit is prosperous," Fitzgerald reported to his mentor. "Biggs and I do the prose - Creese and Keller (a junior who'll be chairman) and I do the poetry..." (Andre LeVot, *F. Scott Fitzgerald*, New York, 1983, p.55).

56 (Fitzgerald, F(rancis). Scott). [Cover title:] *Nassau Literary Magazine*, Volume LXXIII, Number 2. May 1917.

8vo., brown printed wrappers, lightly soiled: some edge wear, rear cover lightly chipped. $750

Princeton's literary magazine, containing the first appearances of Fitzgerald's short story "Babes in the Woods," (pp. 55-64), his poem "Princeton -- The Last Day," (p.95), and his unsigned review of *The Celt and The World* by Shane Leslie (pp. 104-105). Bruccoli C56, C57, C58. Fitzgerald incorporated parts of "Babes in the Woods" into *This Side of Paradise*. It was revised for *The Smart Set*, LX, September 1919 (Bruccoli C74); and later reprinted in *The Apprentice Fiction of F. Scott Fitzgerald*, 1965 (Bruccoli A27). "Princeton -- The Last Day" and the untitled review of *The Celt and the World* were both reprinted in *F. Scott Fitzgerald In His Own Time*, 1971 (Bruccoli A32).

57 Fitzgerald, F(rancis). Scott. *This Side of Paradise*. London...W. Collins Sons... (1921).

8vo., preliminaries foxed; hinges starting; blue cloth, lettered in red on spine and front; spine worn, small loss of cloth; sound copy. $8,500

First English edition, first printing (of two) of Fitzgerald's first novel; number of copies printed unknown: Bruccoli A5.2.a, who notes: "The first English printing...varies unauthoritatively from the first Scribner's printing...in some 850 readings...Of the 850 variants, 32 are substantive." A presentation copy, inscribed: "For Mr. F.R. Henderson from F. Scott Fitzgerald -- June 1921 -- London." Fitzgerald has glued a contemporary magazine photo of himself to the front pastedown, beneath which he has noted: "The World's Work, June, 1921." Also pasted in, below and beneath the inscription, are typescript slips which quote Sinclair Lewis and Mencken's opinions of this work. We know of but one other copy of the first English edition of this title inscribed by Fitzgerald.

INSCRIBED TO O'HENRY'S "YIDDISH DESCENDENT"

58 Fitzgerald, F(rancis). Scott. *The Vegetable* or From President to Postman. New York: Charles Scribner's Sons, 1923.

8vo., dark green cloth; spine faded; covers slightly used; a good, sound copy.
$5,500

First edition of Fitzgerald's first commercially published play, preceded by undergraduate publications of undergraduate plays. 7650 copies published on April 27: Bruccoli A10.I.a. Not reprinted until a pirated edition was issued in 1971 in a fascimile of this edition. A presentation copy, inscribed: "For Fanny Hurst from hers admiringly F. Scott Fitzgerald May 4th, 1923." With Hurst's bookplate on the front pastedown.

In her later years Hurst's work would be characterized by more than one person as "a glorified *True Confessions* story," but in her prime -- at the time of this presentation to her -- her work not only earned critical acclaim but sold like hotcakes. In one of his first letters to Maxwell Perkins Fitzgerald lumped Hurst together with Edna Ferber as "the Yiddish descendants of O'Henry -- Fanny and Edna..."

59 Fitzgerald, F(rancis). Scott. *The Great Gatsby*. London: Chatto & Windus, 1926.

8vo., blue cloth, lightly rubbed; covers faintly soiled; spine cocked and lighty frayed. $22,500

First English edition, printed from American plates (first American edition, third printing), number of copies unknown. Bruccoli (All.I.C.) did not examine a copy in dust jacket. A presentation copy, inscribed: "For Allen [sic] Campbell from his friend F. Scott Fitzgerald ("The Furies" at Ellerslie, 1928)."

Alan Campbell (1904-1963), Broadway actor, Hollywood screenwriter, was twice married to Dorothy Parker. In 1927 he made one of his first successful stage appearances in Zoe Atkin's *The Furies,* in which he played opposite Laurette Taylor. Most likely Fitzgerald presented this book to him at a cast party for that play hosted by the Fitzgeralds at Ellerslie, their sprawling, rented home in Wilmington, Delaware. The raucous weekend parties held there were legends of the twenties -- one was the source for Edmund Wilson's 1928 vignette *A Weekend at Ellerslie.*

Parker and Fitzgerald met in 1919 and remained close for 20 years, even engaging in a brief extra-marital affair in the mid-1930's. At the time of this inscription, Parker was a constant companion of Fitzgerald and Zelda; she had not yet met Campbell. After Parker's 1934 marriage, the Campbells and Fitzgeralds frequently socialized together -- their last encounter (minus Zelda) occuring at Nathaniel West's house in December 1940, a week before Fitzgerald's death, two weeks before West's.

Although they ran in the same circles, Parker and Campbell did not meet until 1934: "Benchley introduced them...Alan Campbell was a personable young actor, who had published a few short stories in *The New Yorker* and whom Benchley knew only well enough to say hello and how are you. A few months later, Dorothy ran into him again...and was surprised to learn they had other mutual friends. She was immediately impressed by Alan's golden good looks...He resembled Scott Fitzgerald when Scott had been young and healthy, before he began drinking heavily, and some people thought him far better looking...His looks projected the image of a stunning man clad in a blazer carrying a raquet, bursting through the doors of a stage drawing room, asking, 'Tennis anyone?'" (Marion Meade, *Dorothy Parker. What Fresh Hell Is This?*, New York, 1988, p. 228).

After the marriage the duo moved to Hollywood, where they became a sought-after screenwriting team responsible for, among other triumphs, *A Star Is Born.* Although Dorothy initially described her honeymoon days as "a coma of happiness" (Meade, p. 239), the union was troubled; soon Dorothy, who all of her life battled a problem with liquor, publicly intimated that her husband was a homosexual who couldn't fulfill his conjugal responsibilities. Whatever his propensities, Campbell truly loved Parker and their 1947 divorce devastated him. In 1950 he proposed that they remarry and to his surprise, she accepted. ("What are you going to do when you love the son of a bitch?," she said at the ceremony -- Meade, p. 339). Alas, the second union lasted less than a year, and the two parted bitterly. In June 1963, aged 59, Campbell died of a barbiturate overdose; Parker lived for 4 more years, dying of a heart attack in 1967.

95. Cohasco Auction Catalogue 32 (31 October 1991)

Sale price undetermined.

> 597. F. SCOTT FITZGERALD. A.N.S., ON ALBUM LEAF. VERY FINE AND SCARCE IN HANDWRITTEN MATERIAL OF THE AMERICAN AUTHOR OF "GREAT GATSBY", "THIS SIDE OF PARADISE", & OTHER WORKS. E $300-400
>
> For Gultra Farrar in memory of those days of gladness on Mount Everest
>
> F Scott Fitzgerald
> Cannes, A—M—
> July 1929

96. Joseph the Provider Catalogue 46 [November 1991]

Numbers 294 and 295 were offered again in Joseph the Provider Catalogue 51 (1993) at $1,750 and $7,500 respectively. Number 295 was recatalogued for the Rechler sale at Christie's, New York, Sale Number 1098 (11 October 2002) at $21,510: see entry 128, item 92. For comment on the Fitzgerald-Warren connection, see entry 124.

294. Fitzgerald, F[rancis] Scott. **THIS SIDE OF PARADISE.** New York: Scribner's, 1931. First edition, later printing, of the author's first book. 8vo. According to the bibliographer, this printing comprised just 290 copies -- Bruccoli A5.1.p. This copy is inscribed (in pencil) by Fitzgerald to his protégé and "godson," Charles "Bill" Marquis Warren: "For Bill Warren from F. Scott Fitzgerald." Warren collaborated with Fitzgerald on a screenplay for Tender Is The Night and (see Crazy Sundays by Aaron Latham) was the author's amanuensis on the novel itself. Interestingly, the name of Nicole Diver's father, given as "Charles Marquis Warren" in the first and second printings of the novel, was inexplicably changed to "Devereux Warren" in the third printing and all subsequent editions. With the recipient's pictorial bookplate on the front pastedown. Some wear at spinal extremities, else about fine. A notable Fitzgerald association copy from his Hollywood years.   5,000.

295. Fitzgerald, F[rancis] Scott. **TAPS AT REVEILLE.** New York: Scribner's, 1935. First edition, first state (with pages 349-352 integral and unrevised). 8vo. This copy bears the author's contemporary presentation inscription to his protégé and "godson", Charles "Bill" Marquis Warren: "For Bill in Highest Hopes from his friend & collaborator, F. Scott Fitzgerald. The 'Winter of Discontent' 1935."

Fitzgerald's relationship with Warren is detailed at length in Aaron Latham's Crazy Sundays: F. Scott Fitzgerald In Hollywood. The two met in Baltimore when Fitzgerald came to rehearsals of a play for which Warren, who was in his late teens, had written both the text and music. The older writer was much impressed with the young man (in 1934 he wrote to Samuel Marx, story editor at M-G-M, saying "I haven't believed in anybody so strongly since Ernest Hemingway") and they soon were collaborating on a screenplay of Tender Is The Night (hence Fitzgerald's invocation of "collaborator" in the inscription). According to Warren's account, Fitzgerald woke him one morning at 2:00 am, took him to a nearby church, roused the priest, and had Warren baptized with Fitzgerald himself standing as godfather. Warren stayed with Fitzgerald and Sheilah Graham at their Malibu house when he first came out to Hollywood, where he later made a name for himself as a movie director ("Streets of Laredo," "Springfield Rifle," "Pony Express") and television producer ("Gunsmoke" and "Rawhide").

With the recipient's pictorial bookplate on the front pastedown. Dampstaining at foot of spine, very good in a likewise dampstained dust jacket with a few chips and tears.   12,500.

Joseph the Provider Catalogue 46

97. Between the Covers Catalogue 26 (July 1992)

Item 127 is one of two located books inscribed by both Fitzgeralds: see entry 123, item 295.

> INSCRIBED BY ZELDA AND F. SCOTT FITZGERALD
> TO HER PSYCHIATRIST
>
> 127. (FITZGERALD, F. Scott and Zelda). *THE MIND AND FAITH OF BOLSHEVISM* by Rene Fulop-Miller. NY:Knopf 1929. Some fading and moderate chipping to the head of the spine, as well as some light dampspotting lacking the DJ. A good plus copy. **Inscribed** to Zelda's psychiatrist: "To Tom Rennie:/ With the deepest devotion/ of/ Zelda and" (in her hand, and following in Scott's hand): "Adolf Meyer/ M. Bleuler/ Sigmund Freeud/ Mr. Jung/ and, [modestly]/ Adolph Forel/ F. Scott Fitzgerald/ 19233 (sic)".
>
> Rennie was Zelda's, as well as Thomas Wolfe's, principle psychiatrist at the Phipps Clinic. His lively and important relationship with both of the Fitzgerald's is well documented. Scott's facetious inscription refers to several psychiatrists, some of whom treated Zelda.
>
> Scott and Zelda Fitzgerald probably more than any other couple symbolize the romance, tragedy and excess of the "Lost Generation". While Scott's signature is avidly sought after, Zelda's is much less common. Books signed by both together are practically unobtainable. $7,500.00

The title of the book is *The Mind and Face of Bolshevism*. Rennie was not Wolfe's psychiatrist.

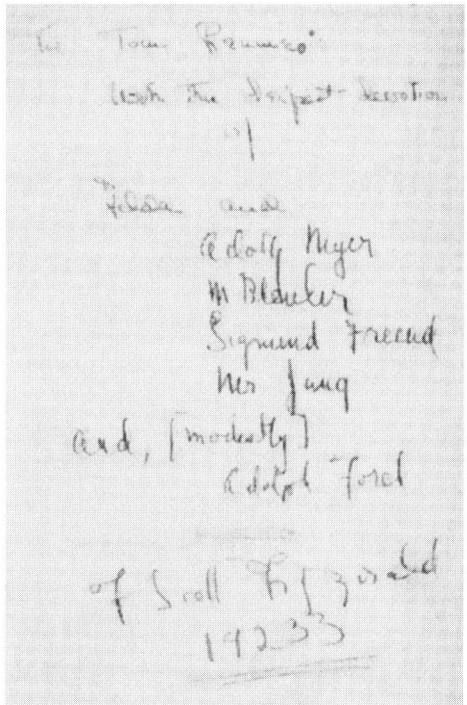

The Bruccoli Collection acquired this item for $4,000 from the Caliban Bookshop in 1992.

98. Christie's, New York, Sale Number 7574 (20 November 1992)

The galleys were acquired by a bidder from Italy and have not been traced. See the introduction (p. xvii).

> • 183 FITZGERALD, F. SCOTT. [Tender Is the Night. New York: Scribner's 1934]. *Thick 8vo, unpaginated, printed on rectos only, leaves measuring 7⅜ × 5 in. (185 × 128mm.), original plain tan wrappers, typed label pasted to front cover, spine worn, light marginal dampstaining on some leaves.* AN APPARENTLY UNIQUE SET OF PROOFS consisting of the unrevised *Scribner's Magazine* text of the novel reset in book-page format (without preliminary leaves, running heads, or pagination). *Tender Is the Night* first appeared in *Scribner's Magazine* in four installments from January to April 1934. Probably in order to expedite book publication—the book was issued on 12 April 1934—someone at the publishing firm decided to reset the serial installments in book line-width gallerys. Fitzgerald, however, virtually rewrote the novel on his set of galleys for the book, making the standing type in the galley trays useless and rendering galleys of the resetting of the unrevised periodical text obsolete.
>
> Possibly while Scribner's was waiting for Fitzgerald's revised set of galleys—while they still thought that they could use the galleys set from the serial text—someone made up one or more sets of these galleys in book-page format (as this copy), perhaps for promotional use. But Fitzgerald's extensive reworking of the text on his galleys made these copies (or copy) useless and discardable. Conjecturally, it is possible that someone at Scribner's kept these pages as a souvenir and had them handbound. *Tender Is the Night* is Connolly *The Modern Movement* 79.
>
> Christie's wishes to thank Matthew J. Bruccoli, Fitzgerald bibliographer and biographer, and Jefferies Professor of English at the University of South Carolina, for his invaluable assistance in the cataloging of this item (indeed much of our description is taken almost verbatim from his report to us on this copy). $2,500-3,500

99. Any Amount of Books Catalogue 16 (1993)

Relisted in this dealer's Catalogue 17 (1994) at £550.

> 136. **FITZGERALD, Scott.** The Beautiful and the Damned. Scribners, NY, 1922. Dedicatee's copy signed by Shane Leslie on the dedication page with the words 'Neither beautiful nor damned'. Leslie, one of the three dedicatees ("in appreciation of much literary help and encouragement") was a close friend through SF's early spiritual mentor Father Sigourney Fay. Leslie had hoped Fitzgerald would become a poet but on seeing the manuscript of This Side of Paradise (which he corrected) he sent it straight to his publisher Scribner. Loosely inserted is a long letter dated 1948 from Arthur Mizener about Shane Leslie's letters to Fitzgerald, with a letter from Mathew J Bruccoli and a letter from Fitzgerald copied out in Shane Leslie's hand (about Fitzgerald's projected book of poems in 1917). Reasonable copy VG/VG+. £1200

100. Swann Auction Galleries Catalogue (4 November 1993)

Sold for $660. Recatalogued in James Cummins Catalogue 41 (December 1993) at $4,000. Offered again in R. A Gekoski Catalogue 30 [2004], item 39.

> 39. **FITZGERALD, F. SCOTT.** *The Great Gatsby*, The Modern Library, New York, 1934. First Modern Library Edition, inscribed on the title page: "For Lovilla Bush with Best Wishes of the Author. F. Scott Fitzgerald. A Hot Sunday in June 1935." Lovilla Bush, or "Bushy", as she was known, was the telephone operator at the Algonquin Hotel, a haunt of the literati. For this edition, the only printing of the Modern Library edition, published September 13, 1934, Fitzgerald wrote a new preface.
> £20000

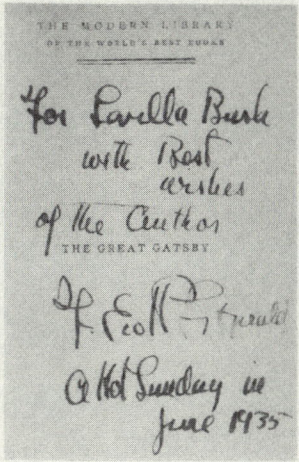

R. A. Gekoski Catalogue 30

101. Lame Duck Books Catalogue 19 (1994)

USC library dean George Terry later acquired this item for the Bruccoli Collection from bookseller Jeffrey Marks for $9,000.

> 191. **FITZGERALD, F. Scott.** *Tender is the Night.* Long galleys of the first installment of *Tender is the Night*, as serialized in Scribner's Magazine before its publication in book form. The book appeared in April of 1934 and the serialization in four parts began in January. Fitzgerald revised the work extensively from serial proofs between its submission to Scribner's in October 1933 and publication. Part one consisted of what would become the first 18 chapters of the published book. This set of galleys was retained by Fitzgerald. The sheets bear questions and comments directed to him from the proofreader. There are a few words and marks in Fitzgerald's hand, including the notation, "see other for queries," which suggests that he returned another set with corrections to Scribner's, from which the type was set. These galleys were in the possession of one of Fitzgerald's Baltimore secretaries until the mid 1980's. No other copy is known to have survived. A unique artifact from the Lost Generation. $17,500.00

102. David Schulson Autographs Catalogue 73 (March 1994)
The recipient has not been identified.

> 62. FITZGERALD, FRANCIS SCOTT. (1896-1940). American fiction writer best known for *This Side of Paradise* and *The Great Gatsby*.
>
> Unusual A.L.S., 4to, n.p., n.d.
>
> A wonderful, most attractive letter to an aspiring author on what inspires and teaches one to write. Fitzgerald writes, "There's only one way; read the books of stories of Kipling, O'Henry, Guy de Maupassant, Chekov, Sherwood Anderson, Hemmingway [sic]. Then read them again. Then write." This handsomely penned letter is surprisingly concise, but superb. Note that Fitzgerald spelled "Hemmingway" incorrectly. Signed, "F. Scott Fitzgerald." Uncommon. $4,250.00

> Dear Ernest:
> There's only one way: read the books of stories of
> Kipling
> O. Henry
> Guy de Maupassant
> Chekov
> Sherwood Anderson
> Hemmingway
> Then read them again. Then write
> Yours
> F Scott Fitzgerald

103. Pepper & Stern Catalogue J3 (April 1994)

257 FITZGERALD, F. SCOTT. This Side of Paradise. New York: Scribner, 1920. First Edition of Fitzgerald's first book. Presentation copy, inscribed by the author, "For Florence Griffiths from F. Scott Fitzgerald. Thanksgiving, 1920." A very good copy. $7,500.00

REMARKABLE FITZGERALD PRESENTATION COPY

258 FITZGERALD, F. SCOTT. Flappers and Philosophers. New York: Scribners, 1920. First Edition. Signed presentation copy to author Shane Leslie inscribed: "For Shane Leslie from his most grateful friend, F. Scott Fitzgerald." It was Leslie that recommended the manuscript of Fitzgerald's first book, *This Side of Paradise,* to Scribners and pushed for its publication. Fitzgerald originally intended to dedicate *This Side of Paradise* to Leslie but later admitted that he changed his mind at the last moment. Fitzgerald co-dedicated his second novel, *The Beautiful and the Damned,* to Leslie. Spine lettering rubbed and a few moisture spots to the front cover else a very good, tight copy of an historic volume. $7,500.00

104. Quill & Brush Catalogue 100 [ca. 1995]

1174. Fitzgerald, F. Scott TENDER IS THE NIGHT *A Romance* 2,750.00
Scribner's Sons New York 1934 Later edition; not in great condition but with GREAT CONTEMPORARY INSCRIPTION: "For Ivia ('Lupe') Waterman / Pride of Florida / with me three / sheets to the wind / and her six sheets / to the laundry pile / with Best Wishes / F. Scott Fitzgerald / Marb erg 1934." Perhaps read at the beach (or too close to the laundry) with fore edges damp stained throughout and Waterman's bookplate on pastedown; in tattered remains of dustwrapper lacking top 1 1/2 inches of spine (title partially present).

105. *Frost and Fire: 50 Depressive and Manic Depressive Writers of Genius . . . A Celebration.* Lakin & Morley Catalogue 3 (1995)

This letter was published in *F. Scott Fitzgerald: A Life in Letters* (New York: Scribners, 1994).

PAGE 8   LAKIN & MARLEY RARE BOOKS   415.388.4545

PERFECT LETTER

12.
Fitzgerald, F. Scott
AUTOGRAPH LETTER, SIGNED (SCOTT), one page, 4to., 14 Rue de Tilsill, Paris, France [n.d. but c. 1926] to Gilbert Seldes (author of *The Seven Lively Arts*, editor of *The Waste Land*, and man of letters):

Dear Gilbert:
    Thank you a thousand times for your enthusiasm about *Gatsby*. I believe I'd rather stir your discriminating enthusiasms than anyone's in America (did I tell you this before?) and to be really believed in again -- to feel "exciting," is tremendously satisfactory. My new novel may well be my last for ten years or so -- that is if it sells no better than *Gatsby* (which has only gone a little over 20,000 copies) for I may go to Hollywood & try to learn the moving picture business from the bottom up.
    We leave for Antibes on August 4th -- Zelda and I in our car (the same one) and Nurse and baby by train. There we shall spend one month growing brown and healthy -- then return here for the fall. Beyond January our plans are vague. Nice followed by Oxford or Cambridge for the summer perhaps. Don Stewart has been here -- he seemed horribly pretentious to me and more than usually wrong -- in fact it was rather a shock to see the change in him. I see Hemingway a great deal and before he left, something of Gerald -- both of them thoroughly charming.
    If you and Amanda come over in the Spring we may have a villa big enough for you to visit us in Nice. God, I'm wild about the Riviera!
    Love from us to you both,
                        Scott

This **unpublished** letter has some light wear and a few discolorations and chips, but otherwise it is in fine condition.

$15,000

Considering the tumultuous nature of Fitzgerald's life, it's a pleasure to offer an upbeat letter which touches on *The Great Gatsby* (his greatest critical success), his nascent enthusiasm for the movie business, his friendship with Hemingway, rare domestic harmony with Zelda, and Oh, God does he loves the Riviera! But by 1936, roughly ten years after this letter, Fitzgerald was reduced to sleeping 20 hours a day, making endless compulsive lists, suffering tremendous guilt and emotional pain. The lethargy, the drinking, the institutionalizations, the reclusive behavior: all so horribly symptomatic of his manic-depressive illness. Yet in the middle of everything, including the hack work to pay Zelda's hospital bills, he managed to reach inside and write his masterpiece *Tender Is the Night*. That's why courage never goes out of fashion.

Whitney Darrow came to regard publishing Fitzgerald as an extravagance.

13.
Fitzgerald, F. Scott
THIS SIDE OF PARADISE. New York: Charles Scribner's Sons, 1920.

First Edition, First Printing, with the dedicatee's name misspelled on page [v]. Original dark green cloth, a better-than-good copy, slightly discolored and dusty, without much wear but without much freshness either. Its charm lies in its wonderful **PRESENTATION INSCRIPTION:** "*Compliments and luck to Whitney Darrow from F. Scott Fitzgerald April 2nd 1920 New York City.*" Darrow worked for Scribner's as an executive in charge of sales and promotion and Fitzgerald is said to have appreciated his personal attention to this **first novel.** Thus not only is this one of the earlier inscribed copies, but it was given to a man whom Fitzgerald knew quite well, and who was intimately involved in the launching of Fitzgerald's career. The book is enclosed in a lovely black morocco box with marbled paper sides.

$8000

106. David Schulson Autographs Catalogue 80 (1995)

The recipient has not been identified.

> 41. FITZGERALD, F[RANCIS] SCOTT [KEY]. (1896-1940). American writer of novels and short stories that epitomized the mood and manners of the 1920s — the Jazz Age, as he called it; recognized as one of the twentieth century's most important authors.
>
> A.L.S. on a government postcard, Great Neck, Long Island, November 8, no year, but before the Fitzgeralds left their Long Island home in 1924 for France.
>
> He thanks his correspondent for the "London clipping — recognized your writing. We have moved to..." and he draws an arrow to "Great Neck, L.I." which he penned at the top of the postcard, with his telephone number circled under his new address. Signed, "F.Scott Fitzgerald." Fine in association to the North Shore Long Island location which figured so prominently in his *The Great Gatsby*. $1,500.00

107. Remember When Auctions Catalogue 34, Part I (7 January 1995)

Offered again with the same estimate in Remember When Auctions Catalogue 36, Part II (17 July 1995). Selling price undetermined. Jed Harris was a Broadway producer.

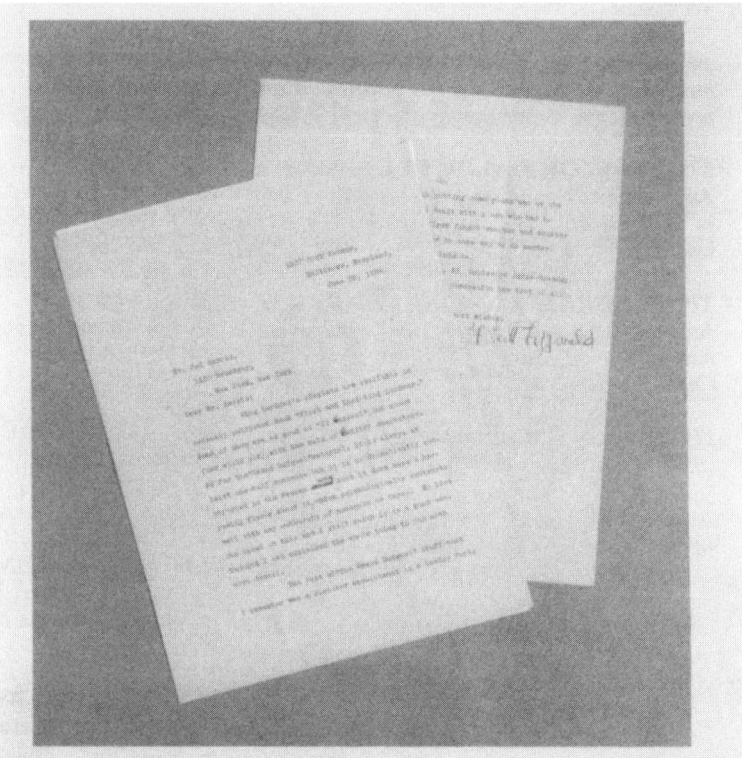

2789. **F SCOTT FITZGERALD** (1896-1940), legendary Am Author. TLS, 1 1/2 separate pages, June 22, 1934, 4to, Baltimore, to Jed Harris, excellent content re potential projects, written shortly after the commercial failure of his novel "Tender Is The Night." In part, *"...Ring Lardner's playlets are available in recently published book 'First and Last: Ring Lardner.' None of them are as good as 'Il Gaspari', but about four would play, with the help of Baliff characters. As for the 'Grand Guignol' material, it is always at least one-half nonsense but it is so dramatically constructed in the French way that it does have a harrowing flavor about it, which psychologically contrasts well with any outbursts of nonsense or farce...The best of 'The Grand Guignol' stuff that I remember was a sinister appointment in a tawdy Paris suburb...and another that dealt with a man who had to keep cutting off his first finger shorter and shorter because it had been used in some way to murder..."* VG. $2,000-3,000

108. Alexander Autographs (31 March 1995)

Lexicographer Vizetelly queried Fitzgerald about his use of "Bilphism" in *The Beautiful and Damned*. Acquired by the Bruccoli Collection for $1,000.

Belphism . . . is a euphemism for theosophy . . .

866. F. SCOTT FITZGERALD (1896 - 1940) American writer famed as the chronicler of the Jazz Age, author of *The Great Gatsby* and *Tender is the Night*. Important A.L.S. 1p. 4to., [n.p.,n.d.], to Dr. Vizetelly of Funk & Wagnalls. In full: "*Belphism is a coinage of my own. It is a euphemism for Theosophy - I wanted to take a crack at theosophy without hurting the feelings of a relative of mine. Several people have inquired about it. So I guess it will enter no dictionary. Sincerely, F. Scott Fitzgerald*" Very light toning at margins, top trimmed irregularly affecting only two letters of salutation, a few pinholes and short marginal tears carefully repaired on verso. $1,000-1,500

109. Christie's New York Auction Catalogue (19 May 1995)

Property from the Estate of
ANN R. COWAN

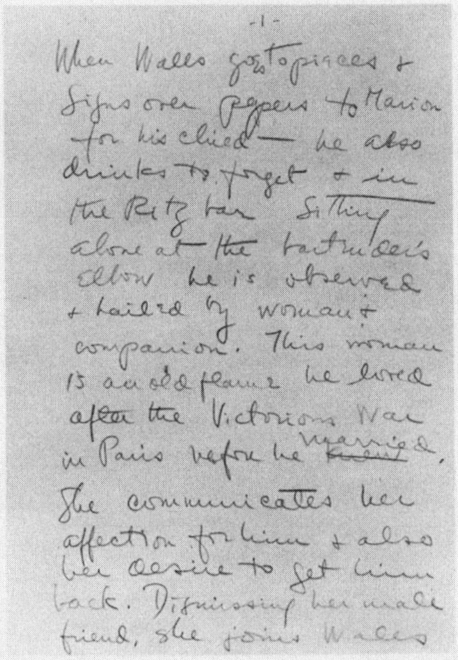

[handwritten manuscript page]

- 138 FITZGERALD, F. SCOTT. Autograph manuscript of his partial proposal (story idea, etc.) for the screenplay of the adaptation of his classic story "Babylon Revisited." [Santa Barbara or Los Angeles? c. Spring 1940]. *9 pages, 4to, in pencil on rectos of blue stationery of the Mar Monte Hotel in Santa Barbara, with one revision,* comprising 8 pages (paginated by Fitzgerald) dealing with the story line and one unnumbered page giving details on three characters. In fine condition.

FITZGERALD IN HOLLYWOOD: "BABYLON REVISITED" — FROM STORY TO MOVIE

In early 1940 Fitzgerald, hoping to complete his Hollywood novel *The Last Tycoon* by the end of the year, but fearing he was finished as a screen writer, was given an unexpected opportunity. "Independent producer Lester Cowan bought the movie rights to 'Babylon Revisited' (from *Taps at Reveille*, 1935) for $1,000 in March and hired Fitzgerald to write the screenplay . . . which brought him another $5,000 [see agreement for this in lot 142]. Cowan, who had made *My Little Chickadee* with W. C. Fields and Mae West, intended to produce 'Babylon Revisited' with the Columbia studios [perhaps with Shirley Temple in a starring role]. The price for the story was low, and the weekly salary was less than half Fitzgerald's studio rate; but he was to reveive a bonus if the movie was made. Fitzgerald needed the money and enjoyed working on one of his best stories at home . . . The movie was never made from Fitzgerald's screenplay [entitled *Cosmopolitan*]. Cowan later sold the rights to 'Babylon Revisited' to M-G-M for a reported $40,000, and it was made as *The Last Time I Saw Paris*" in 1954 from a new screenplay (Matthew J. Bruccoli, *Some Sort of Epic Grandeur: The Life of F. Scott Fitzgerald*, New York, 1993, pp. 574-575).

"*Cosmopolitan* has the reputation of being Fitzgerald's best screenplay. It is not a close adaption of 'Babylon Revisited,' for Fitzgerald invented a new plot which greatly enlarged the role of the child, Honoria. (In the screenplay the name of the child was changed to Victoria, in honor of Budd

Schulberg's baby daughter.) . . ." (Bruccoli, p. 575). In the manuscript — apparently unpublished — of Fitzgerald's partial proposal for the screenplay, he seems somewhat nearer the conception of the original story. The manuscript reads in part: "When [Charles] Wales goes to pieces & signs over papers to Marion [the sister of his deceased wife] for his child — he also drinks to forget & in the Ritz bar sitting alone at the bartender's elbow he is observed & hailed by woman & companion. This woman is an old flame he loved after the . . . war in Paris before he married . . . she joins Wales at the Bar & tries to evoke gay memories of the past by mentioning names & pulling out sweet memories to entice his interest.

One by one, figures fade into the scene peopling the bar with the hectic picture of What Used to Be. Wales & Woman become younger, gay, attractive in their romance . . . This love scene gives the film the background of romantic past which is so sadly lacking & adds character to Wales, who is to sublimate all his emotions later into that of devoted fatherhood . . .

"The Woman is Back Street. Her unrequited love, her pagan appeal, her desire to get Wales back as a playmate or lover . . . His sense of direction is defined all the more clearly as he gropes thru tragedy, frustration & circumstance toward the realization of his predominant reason for living — & that is his sole interest in his child. We don't know after the Ritz Bar scene whether he pursues drinking with the Woman or refuses to see her — until the scene where he takes Honoria alone to lunch & the circus . . . [The Woman] & friend burst into Marion's [house] just as his [Wales's] magical return to health & enjoyment of his afternoon with Honoria would make it obvious to the audience as well as to Marion that there is no reason now to keep father & daughter separated. But Marion's seeing the pleasure-loving Woman & Friend in *her* house is at once outraged to the point where Petrie [her husband] takes her hysteria as a plea for more time in this matter & Wales is frustrated now by circumstance.

"When he learns [of the] loss of the trust money, be tries to recoup his fortune in the scene where Honoria comes to read her birthday poem . . . When Marion & Petrie take the Child home at midnight they see at the hotel desk the Woman who is begging the clerk to tell Wales she is waiting for him. We know (1) she is hanging around still trying (2) Marion is now adamant against Wales getting the papers changed (3) Wales either doesn't want the Woman to come up or that he is too knocked out to answer his phone" (end of the eight-page story-line section of the manuscript). Fitzgerald manuscripts and letters of this final period of his life are very rare on the market.

$8,000-12,000

• 139 FITZGERALD, F. SCOTT. Two typed letters signed ("F. Scott Fitzgerald" and "Scott Fitz") to Lester Cowan, Encino and Hollywood ("1403 N. Laurel Ave."), 28 May and 14 June 1940. *Together 2 pages, 4to (one full and one half page), single-spaced, mild fold creases.*

"THE EAR OF HOLLYWOOD IS NOTORIOUSLY HUNGRY"

28 May 1940 (written just after completing the first draft of the script): ". . . The picture was fun to write. The only snag was in the final Swiss Sequence. I found out that there is no trace of winter sport in Switzerland *before the middle of December* and the stockmarket crash occurred very definitely the *last part of October* so, instead of a routine based on bob-sleds such as we talked about, I had to resort to an older device. I think this sequence carries the emotion of the others but it is the one with least originality of treatment, and audiences are more and more responding to originality after five years of double-feature warm-overs . . ." Fitzgerald discusses possible casting for the movie, and ends: ". . . There are so many new things in our script that I thought it best to deliver it to Bob [Cowan's assistant] under seal. So many of the scenes are easily repeated in the most innocent way, and the ear of Hollywood is notoriously hungry. I think you will like the title [*Honoria*, after the little girl in the story and script]. It is an unusual name with a peculiarly sonorous quality and so many of the more popular pieces — *Babbitt, Rebecca, David Copperfield* — have been only names . . . P.S. This of course, is the best and final version of the 1st draft . . ."

14 June 1940: "The enclosed picture tells its own story. The picture [movie] *All This and Heaven Too* [starring Charles Boyer and Bette Davis] is the old English tripe about the virtuous governess but it shows Virginia Wiedler well along in the awkward age with a face that now photographs exactly like an unripe pear . . ." The apparently enclosed photograph of Virginia Wiedler is not present. *Letters*, ed. M.J. Bruccoli & M.M. Duggan, pp. 599-600 (for the first letter, printed from a typed transcript or carbon copy at Princeton).   (2)

$3,500-4,500

> July 23 1940
>
> Dear Lester:
>
> I'm taking you at your word about your adjusting your schedule to mine for a couple days this week, so here would be the line-up: I'll start sending you the ms. by seven Wednesday evening (that'll be the first half)—follow with another batch Thursday noon—and finish by seven Thursday night, when the last quarter will reach you.
>
> I'll be ready for a conference any time Friday—say eleven A.M.—so if you'll really set aside enough of the previous thirty-six hours for digesting it with proper prayer and fasting, we could have a good conference Friday. This would give me Saturday, Monday and Tuesday to incorporate your final criticisms and suggestions.
>
> The veiled threat behind this is that after another week of work I know I'm going to be a cantankerous, uncivilized and unreasonable old man and will have to rest. So make hay while the sun shines and for the love of Shirley's father (old "Badminton" Temple) don't dare tell me Friday morning you haven't been able to get to it.
>
> Hell, why should I say this—you haven't stood me up yet.
>
> Your Friend,
>
> F. Scott ("High-Tension") Fitzgerald
>
> 1403 N. Laurel Avenue
> Hollywood, California

- 140 FITZGERALD, F. SCOTT. Two typed letters signed ("F. Scott ['High-Tension'] Fitzgerald" and "Scott") to Lester Cowan, 1403 N. Laurel Avenue, Hollywood, and n.p. (presumably same address), 23 July and 16 August 1940. *Together 2 pages, 4to, single-spaced, both signatures and 20-word holograph closing note on second letter in pencil, slight fold creases in first letter.*

"F. SCOTT ('HIGH-TENSION') FITZGERALD" AT WORK ON THE SECOND DRAFT

The first letter was written while working on the second draft of the screenplay, which was finished on 30 July. This second version was cut to 130 pages (from the previous 146) and apparently given the story's title *Babylon Revisited.* 23 July 1940: ". . . I'll start sending you the ms. by *seven* Wednesday evening (that'll be the *first* half) — to follow with another batch Thursday noon — and finish by seven Thursday night, when the last quarter will reach you. I'll be ready for a conference any time Friday . . . so if you'll *really* set aside enough of the previous thirty-six hours for digesting it with proper prayer and fasting, we could have a good conference Friday. This would give me Saturday, Monday and Tuesday to incorporate your final criticisms and suggestion. The veiled threat behind this is that after another week of work I know I'm going to be a cantankerous, uncivilized and unreasonable old man and *will have to rest.* So make hay while the sun shines and for the love of Shirley's father (old 'Badminton' Temple) don't dare tell me Friday morning you haven't been able to get to it . . ."

16 August 1940 (finishing revisions of a second draft, now apparently entitled *Cosmopolitan*): "Here you are — it's shorter, clearer and straighter and I breathe easier. Victoria's arrival [Honoria's name was changed] is *important* now but I can't make it crucial unless he's about to jump out the window, which weakens him again. I think it is *poignant* rather than *crucial* — remember, she was never to be Daddy's little helper in the conventional sense. You will see changes in 'E' that help along the situation also . . . P.S. I wasn't impressed with Ludwig's tandem suggestion. Do we want to begin the new Shirley Temple with a cast off musicomedy idea of Durbin's? . . . Have talked to you since writing this. I think it's [the screenplay] as close to right as I can make it now." Neither letter is in *Letters,* ed. M.J. Bruccoli & M.M. Duggan, and each is apparently unpublished. (2)

$3,500-4,500

• 141   FITZGERALD, F. SCOTT. Autograph letter signed ("Scott" at end, "F. Scott Fitzgerald" at top) to Lester Cowan, n.p. [Hollywood], n.d., "Mon Night" [c. August 1940]. *3 pages, 4to, on rectos, in pencil, slight, even offset from telegram paper on most of first page, two very slight edge tears,* headed at top of first page by Fitzgerald: "PRIVATE — from F. Scott Fitzgerald" (tops of a few letters in signature lost during writing but present at upper margin of second page).

"THE AUDIENCE . . . DESPERATELY TIRED OF SHIT PUT UP EVERY WEEK IN NEW CANS"

". . . I saw *The Great McGinty* [a Preston Sturges movie starring Brian Donlevy and Akim Tamiroff] and heard the crowd respond and I think your answer is there and not in this wretched star system. When you said you were not going to begin with the prologue and seemed to give credence to some director's wild statement that Petrie was the best character — I felt that you were discouraged about the venture and it was warping your judgment. If it is such a poor script that it can be so casually mutilated then how will it be improved with two slipping stars?

"The virtue of the *Great McGinty* was one and singular . . . it had only the virtue of being told to an audience as it was conceived. It was inferior in pace, it was an old story — the audience loved it because they are desperately tired of shit put up every week in new cans. It had not suffered from compromises, polish jobs, formulas and that familiarity which is so falsely consoling to producers . . . That scent of familiarity which seems to promise out here that old stuff has made money before, has become poison gas to those who have to take it as entertainment every night . . . The writing on the wall is that *anybody* this year who brings in a good story *intact* will make more reputation and even money, than those who struggle for a few stars. I would rather see new people in this picture than Gable and Temple . . ." *Letters*, ed. M.J. Bruccoli & M.M. Duggan, p. 605 (printed, with an omission and an error, from a typed transcript at Princeton). At the time Fitzgerald was possibly working again on his Hollywood novel, *The Last Tycoon*. He was to die four months later (on 21 December 1940).

$4,000-6,000

• 142   FITZGERALD, F. SCOTT. Document signed ("F. Scott Fitzgerald"), the agreement between him and the producer Lester Cowan for "the Writer to write, compose, and prepare a complete screenplay based upon the literary material or story entitled 'Babylon Revisited.' Los Angeles, 8 April 1940. *8 pages, folio, double-spaced, carbon copy, stapled to blue printed and typed law firm backing cover,* signed by Fitzgerald at end at space designated "Writer." The agreement, comprising nine terms, calls for Fitzgerald's "employment" to begin April 8 and to run for four weeks with payment of $2,500. If needed, an additional four weeks for rewriting and revisions would be paid for also at the $2,500 figure.

[*With:*]

FITZGERALD, F. S. Six telegrams from Fitzgerald to Lester Cowan (at Columbia Studios and in New York), Encino and Los Angeles, 1 May-14 August 1940, *together 6 pages, oblong 8vo,* arranging meetings with the producer, discussing casting, etc. 14 May: "More and more think [Shirley] Temple would be ill advised even as gift. Expect to see you drop from parachute any day now . . ." 23 May: "Believe that performer mentioned is much too frozen a character for script in public . . . also the sight of her with doll would be rather absurd . . ." [*And with*]. A typed copy of a 26 June 1940 Fitzgerald letter to Cowan, *2 pages, 4to,* labelled "*(COPY)*" at head, regarding rewriting the screenplay and casting for the movie. The text of this letter not in *Letters*, ed. M. J. Bruccoli & M. M. Duggan; A typed or carbon copy of a 6 May 1940 Cowan letter to Fitzgerald, *1 page, 8vo;* A TLS from John Biggs, Jr., Executor of the Estate of F. Scott Fitzgerald, to Cowan, Wilmington, Del., 14 March 1941, *1 p., 4to,* regarding the sums paid by Cowan to Fitzgerald, the inquiry made for tax purposes; A carbon copy of Cowan's reply to Biggs, 25 July 1941, *1 p., 4to:* "In response to your letter of March 14th . . . he received a total of $6,000 from me, which was divided as follows: $1,000 for the original story, and $5,000 for the screen play. The latter was covered by an employment contract dated April 8, 1940, between Mr. Fitzgerald and myself [see above] . . ."; A telegram to Cowan from his assistant Bob, Los Angeles, 17 May 1940, *1 p., oblong 8vo,* telling him to call Fitzgerald   (12)

$1,500-2,500

110. *American and English Literature from the Library of Mrs. Charles W. Engelhard*, Christie's, New York, Sale Number I-8314 (27 October 1995)

The most valuable group of Fitzgerald items auctioned in the Nineties. The eight lots totaled $91,225 with buyer's premiums.

Mrs. Engelhard's first husband, Fritz Mannheimer, was a German banker and art collector. Her second husband, Charles W. Engelhard, was a minerals industrialist; Ian Fleming's character Goldfinger was reputedly based on him.

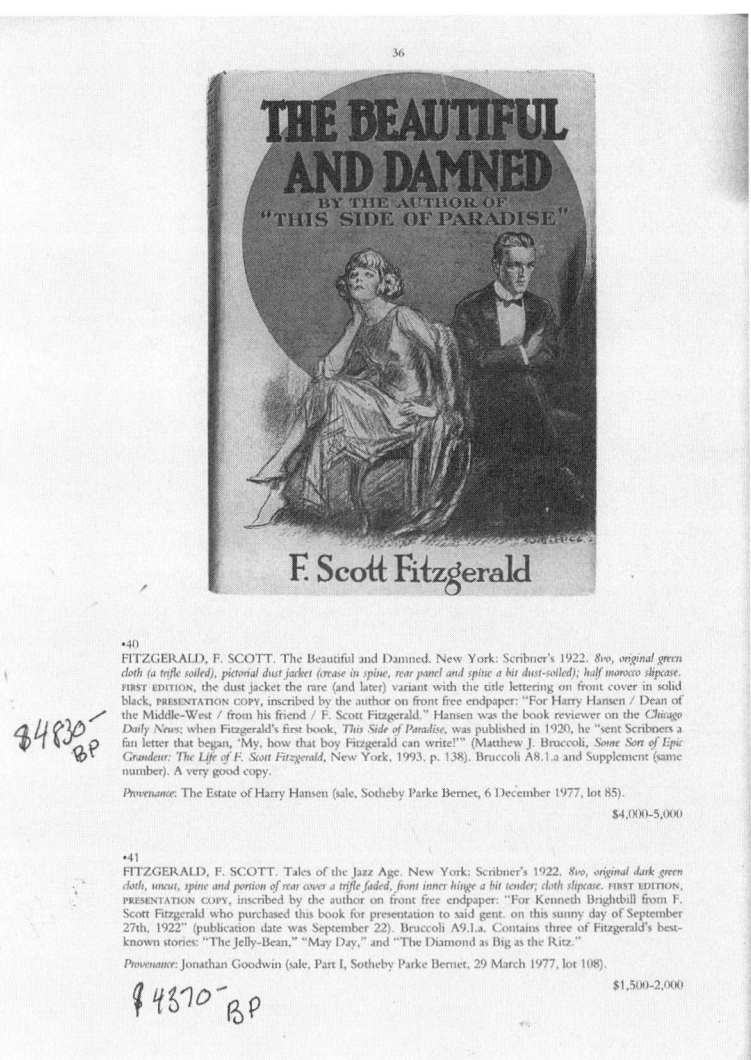

•40
FITZGERALD, F. SCOTT. The Beautiful and Damned. New York: Scribner's 1922. 8vo, *original green cloth (a trifle soiled), pictorial dust jacket (crease in spine, rear panel and spine a bit dust-soiled); half morocco slipcase.* FIRST EDITION, the dust jacket the rare (and later) variant with the title lettering on front cover in solid black, PRESENTATION COPY, inscribed by the author on front free endpaper: "For Harry Hansen / Dean of the Middle-West / from his friend / F. Scott Fitzgerald." Hansen was the book reviewer on the *Chicago Daily News*; when Fitzgerald's first book, *This Side of Paradise*, was published in 1920, he "sent Scribners a fan letter that began, 'My, how that boy Fitzgerald can write!'" (Matthew J. Bruccoli, *Some Sort of Epic Grandeur: The Life of F. Scott Fitzgerald*, New York, 1993, p. 138). Bruccoli A8.1.a and Supplement (same number). A very good copy.
Provenance: The Estate of Harry Hansen (sale, Sotheby Parke Bernet, 6 December 1977, lot 85).
$4,000-5,000

•41
FITZGERALD, F. SCOTT. Tales of the Jazz Age. New York: Scribner's 1922. 8vo, *original dark green cloth, uncut, spine and portion of rear cover a trifle faded, front inner hinge a bit tender; cloth slipcase.* FIRST EDITION, PRESENTATION COPY, inscribed by the author on front free endpaper: "For Kenneth Brightbill from F. Scott Fitzgerald who purchased this book for presentation to said gent. on this sunny day of September 27th, 1922" (publication date was September 22). Bruccoli A9.1.a. Contains three of Fitzgerald's best-known stories: "The Jelly-Bean," "May Day," and "The Diamond as Big as the Ritz."
Provenance: Jonathan Goodwin (sale, Part I, Sotheby Parke Bernet, 29 March 1977, lot 108).
$1,500-2,000

37

(actual size)

•42
FITZGERALD, F. SCOTT. The Great Gatsby. New York: Scribner's 1925. *8vo, original green cloth (front inner hinge a trifle tender, slight abrasion to inside front cover),* PICTORIAL DUST JACKET *after F. Cugat (frayed at ends of spine and a fore-corner, lightly worn); cloth slipcase.* FIRST EDITION, FIRST PRINTING of text and of dust jacket, PRESENTATION COPY TO ZELDA'S SISTER AND HER HUSBAND NEWMAN SMITH, inscribed by the author in blue-purple ink on front free endpaper: "For Rosalind and Capitan / with affection from / Scott and Zelda / June (May) 1925" ("Capitan" was their nickname for the brother-in-law). The Fitzgeralds, on their European stay, were at Capri when *The Great Gatsby* was published (on 10 April 1925), moving to Paris later that month; they stayed in Paris until August, when they left for the Riviera. While on Capri Fitzgerald sent Scribner's a number of inscriptions on slips of paper to be pasted in presentation copies sent to fellow writers: Sinclair Lewis, H.L. Mencken, Carl Van Doren, Van Wyck Brooks, etc. (see *Letters*, ed. Bruccoli, pp. 156-158). By the time of this inscription to Rosalind and Capitan, Fitzgerald had access to an actual copy of the first edition. Bruccoli A11.I.a; Connolly, *The Modern Movement* 48: "... one of the half-dozen best American novels ..." Exceedingly rare with a contemporary presentation inscription and in the dust jacket.

Provenance: Jonathan Goodwin (sale, Part I, Sotheby Parke Bernet, 29 March 1977, lot 110).

$25,000-35,000

$2,500-3,500

•44
FITZGERALD, F. SCOTT. Tender is the Night. A Romance. New York: Scribner's 1934. *8vo,* ORIGINAL PICTORIAL WRAPPERS MADE FROM THE DUST JACKET, *fore-edges uncut, spine slightly worn with some fraying at two of its corners; half morocco slipcase.* ADVANCE OR REVIEW COPY OF THE FIRST EDITION. Extremely rare: Bruccoli A14.I.a and Supplement (1980, same number) locating only three (other?) copies. Connolly, *The Modern Movement* 79: "The break-down of a marriage ... is described with flashes of genius by an expert in self-destruction ... and there is a haunting account ... of the predicament of 'grace under pressure' from too many parties and too much money." In very good condition.

See illustration opposite

$2,500-3,500

39

44   45

•45
FITZGERALD, F. SCOTT. Taps at Reveille. New York: Scribner's 1935. *8vo, original dark green cloth, pictorial dust jacket (one tiny abrasion near an edge on front cover); half morocco slipcase.* FIRST EDITION, FIRST STATE, price on front jacket flap 3/16in. high (no priority). Bruccoli A17.I.a1. Contains the classic stories "Crazy Sunday" and "Babylon Revisited." A particularly fine, bright copy.

Provenance: The Estate of Harry Hansen (sale, Sotheby Parke Bernet, 6 December 1977, lot 86).

$1,300–1,800

•46
FITZGERALD, F. SCOTT. Autograph letter signed ("F. Scott Fitzgerald") to his illustrator Arthur William Brown, n.p., n.d. [Fall 1922]. *3 pages, 4to, on two sheets,* WITH A SKETCH BY FITZGERALD OF A GOLF SCENE *in the text, marginal chipping and a few closed tears, half morocco slipcase.*

ILLUSTRATING "WINTER DREAMS"

Brown was the illustrator of one of Fitzgerald's finest stories, "Winter Dreams," for its appearance in *Metropolitan* (December 1922); he had illustrated many of Fitzgerald's stories for different magazines during the previous two years. Fitzgerald writes: "The story concerns a poor boy, his rise and his attempt to win a rich girl. He first sees her when he is a caddy about 14 years old and she is a little "*belle laide*" of 11. She comes on the golf course with her nurse carrying her clubs and tries to get a caddy. The sight of her stirs the poor boy to give up his job of caddying — He is too proud to caddy for a little girl as young as that — He rises in the world. At 25 he is a guest at the golf club where he has been a caddy. He swims out to a raft one moonlit night. She comes by in a motor boat … My other scenes do not offer much pictorial possibility. I have just destroyed the second part of the story & am doing it over again …"

Fitzgerald then suggests five scenes out of which he hopes Brown can get two illustrations. "If you want a 3d picture there is a scene where the heroine — same age as in the surf-board scene — drives a mashie-shot into the belly of a member of a foursome playing ahead of her. The foursome is composed of hero

continued

(25 yrs. old), one man of thirty — silly ass — and two old men — one of whom got hit in belly ... " To illustrate what he means Fitzgerald here (at bottom of third page) does a sketch of the golf scene with several labels and captions, adding playfully: "Don't be jealous because I draw so well. F.S.F."

"Winter Dreams," the only story Fitzgerald wrote in 1922 after the publication of his novel *The Beautiful and Damned* in March, was first collected in *All the Sad Young Men* (1926). As Matthew J. Bruccoli notes in *Some Sort of Epic Grandeur*, pp. 201-202: "'Winter Dreams' is virtually a preview of *The Great Gatsby* ... [It] clearly anticipates the major ideas and emotions in ... *Gatsby*: the ambitious boy whose dreams of success become blended with the image of a rich girl; her inconstancy; his faithfulness; and the inevitable sense of change and loss. Although Dexter Green does not match Jay Gatsby's romantic commitment, he is a preliminary sketch for Gatsby ..." Published (with the sketch reproduced) in *Letters*, ed. M.J. Bruccoli and M.M. Duggan, pp. 114-115.

Provenance: Unidentified owner (sale, Charles Hamilton Galleries, 23 March 1978, lot 110).

$3,500-4,500

•47
FITZGERALD, F. SCOTT. Autograph letter signed ("F Scott Fitzgerald") to "Dear Tom" (Thomas R. Smith, an editor at Boni & Liveright), Great Neck, L.I., n.d. [c. 1923]. *1 page, 4to, in brown ink, traces of tape on verso from previous mounting, show-through from verso of a long scratch; half morocco slipcase.*

FITZGERALD CHAMPIONS GERTRUDE STEIN, CASTIGATES WALDO FRANK

Smith, who hoped to woo Fitzgerald away from Scribner's, had sent him several new Boni & Liveright books. At the time Fitzgerald was living on the North Shore of Long Island, working on *The Great Gatsby*. "... The Waldo Frank novel is I'm afraid just his usual canned rubbish. He seems to be an ambitious but totally uninspired person under the delusion that by filching the most advanced methods from the writers who originated them *to express the moods of their definate* [sic] *personalities*, he can supply a substitute for his own lack of feeling and cover up the bogus 'arty-ness' of his work. He strains for a simile until his belly aches and brings up a mess of overworked words ... His horror of the cliche is entirely Freudian ... a man incapable of the disassociation of ideas can never think in any words except those that are immortally paired ... I'm afraid Horace [Liveright] has made a bad guess on him. I wish to God you'd republish Gertrude Stein's *Three Lives* and expose some of these jokers. Her book is utterly real. It's in her early manner before the attempt to transfer the technique of Mattisse [sic] & Picasso to prose made her coo-coo ..." (*Three Lives* was reissued in America in 1927 by Albert & Charles Boni.). Published in *Letters*, ed. M.J. Bruccoli and M.M. Duggan, p. 123.

$2,000-3,000

111. Sotheby's, London, Sale Number LN5749 (18 December 1995)
Sold on behalf of the Royal Society of Literature.

384 FITZGERALD (F. SCOTT) FINE AUTOGRAPH LETTER SIGNED ("F. SCOTT FITZGERALD"), TO THE PUBLISHERS CHATTO & WINDUS, ABOUT 'THE GREAT GATSBY':

Gentlemen:
It may have escaped your notice that a first and *very* enthusiastic review of my *The Great Gatsby* appeared in England about three weeks ago. It was in the December issue of *The* (London) *Criterion* leading off the American notes.
I call this to your attention because of the particularly favorable quality of the review. Hoping it may be of use to you...

1 page, 4to, publishers' receipt stamp (received 12 February 1926, answered 17 February), on blue paper, very light dust-staining and creasing at edges, but overall in fine fresh condition, c/o Guaranty Trust Co., Paris, no date (received 12 February 1926)

The English edition of *The Great Gatsby*, printed from the plates of the American first edition (second issue), was published by Chatto & Windus in February 1926 at 7s. The British Library copy bears a deposit stamp of 10 February, two days before the deposit stamp on this letter.
The publication of his novel in England meant a great deal to Fitzgerald. In the autumn of the year before, when he was in doubt whether Chatto would print it, he wrote to Maxwell Perkins: "Is there some reason why Chatto & Windus can't publish in the spring?... I hate to be a crabby old woman about this, Max, but it means a lot to me. *Gatsby* is just the sort of book which the English say that the Americans can't write... I know half a dozen influential people there who will go to bat for it right now and it seems to me that it should have a chance. I am further confused when your letter says 'Chatto & Windus and other publishers admired it but they thought it too American in its scene to be understood in England.' Does this mean Chatto & Windus aren't going to publish it? I'm disgruntled and up-in-the-air about the whole thing" (*Letters*, ed. Turnbull, p.192).

Presented by Chatto & Windus.

£1,000-1,500

112. Lion Heart Autographs Catalogue 33 (1996), $4,000

Adelaide Neall was a *Saturday Evening Post* editor. The story was probably "Too Cute for Words," published in the 18 April 1936 issue of the *Saturday Evening Post*.

FITZGERALD, F. SCOTT
(1896–1940)
American novelist; author of such classic novels as *This Side of Paradise*, *The Great Gatsby*, and *Tender is the Night*. ALS. ("F Scott Fitzgerald"). 1p. 4to. Baltimore, N.d. (ca. 1930–37).

"Could you do the unusual thing of wiring me a few hundred to the 1st National Bank?"

To Miss Neale of *The Saturday Evening Post*.

Here is the story. I am rushing it up to you in the hope of a decision before Xmas. If you do like it, it would be the most appreciated of Xmas presents to get a little money on it *before* Xmas as I've been sick again & my affairs are in poor shape . . . dare I to ask it & will it influence your judgment on the story?—could you do the unusual thing of wiring me a few hundred to the 1st National Bank in Baltimore? The balance to go thru [sic] Ober as usual. This request had best be kept from Mr. Lorimer until the story has been judged. If you don't like the story, of course simply disregard the matter . . .

Best known as a novelist, Fitzgerald also wrote numerous short stories, later collected in *Flappers and Philosophers*, *Tales of the Jazz Age*, *All the Sad Young Men*, and *Taps at Reveille*. Some, however, also appeared in *The Saturday Evening Post* which, under its editor-in-chief, GEORGE LORIMER (1867–1937), became an immensely successful and influential magazine, known for featuring the work of leading contemporary writers and thinkers. "Lorimer attracted writers to the *Post* by becoming the first editor to pay on acceptance and by returning decisions on manuscripts within seventy-two hours," (*DAB*) a practice which surely appealed to the financially-strapped Fitzgerald. Our letter was evidently written during one of these periods, during his seven years in Baltimore (1930–37). Fitzgerald's handwriting is shaky and labored, but clearly written. In fine condition, and uncommon in any form.
$4000

Bruccoli Collection

113. *James Joyce Books & Manuscripts* (New York: Glenn Horowitz, 1996)

FROM F. SCOTT FITZGERALD TO JOYCE

79] **Beerbohm, Max.** *A Christmas Garland.* London: William Heinemann, 1926.

8vo.; blue cloth, stamped in gilt; tips and edges lightly rubbed.

First edition, ninth printing. A terrific association copy, inscribed: "p. 133 et seg. James Joyce from the humblest but most devoted of his admirers F. Scott Fitzgerald Paris, June 28." Fitzgerald draws Joyce's attention to the story that begins on page 133, "A Recollection," Beerbohm's parodic description in the style of Edmund Gosse of a meeting between Browning and Ibsen in Venice, all of whom factored, with various degrees of significance, in Joyce's development. Until 1922, Fitzgerald perceived Joyce to be only "a common Irishman, outside the bonds of literary taste." When Edmund Wilson implored him to read *Ulysses*, however, Fitzgerald discovered that it made him feel "appallingly naked," and referred to it in a newspaper article as "the great novel of the future." He also listed *A Portrait of the Artist as a Young Man* among the "10 Best Books I Have Read."

At the invitation of Sylvia Beach, Fitzgerald dined with the Joyces in Paris in the spring of 1928. That dinner, the first of several meetings between Fitzgerald and Joyce, occurred on June 27, 1928, one day prior to the presentation of this gift. In honor of the meeting, Fitzgerald made a small sketch of himself kneeling in front of Joyce and titled it "Festival of St. James." According to one of his biographers, James Mellow, Fitzgerald—no doubt fortified by alcohol—heightened the drama of the evening by threatening to prove his admiration for Joyce's genius by jumping out of a fourth-floor window. Underwhelmed, Joyce later remarked "That young man must be mad. I'm afraid he'll do himself some injury."

The June 1928 inscription affords *A Christmas Garland* the status of the earliest of four extant books commemorating the "Festival of St. James." It is the only one left in private hands, the other three now preserved in the Sylvia Beach collection at Princeton University and the Matthew J. Bruccoli F. Scott Fitzgerald Collection at the University of South Carolina: *The Great Gatsby*, Beach's copy, with Fitzgerald's "Festival of St. James" drawing, dated July 1928; Fitzgerald's annotated first edition of *Ulysses*, with a Joyce letter, dated July 7, 1928, and a later printing of the Cape edition of *A Portrait of the Artist as a Young Man*, inscribed by Joyce to Fitzgerald on July 7, 1928.

* P.133 et seq.

James Joyce from
 the humblest but most devoted
   of his admirers
      F Scott Fitzgerald
       Paris, June 28

$27,500—

114. Metropolitan Book Auctions Catalogue (13 November 1996)
Probably sent to historian Carl Van Doren.

> 88 Fitzgerald, F. Scott TENDER IS THE NIGHT New York: Charles Scribner's Sons, 1934 First Edition, First Issue, Inscribed "Dear Van Doran glad as hell you liked the book Scott Fitz..." on front fly 8vo, cloth binding, tips and head and tail of spine lightly worn, slight wear to rear board, interior clean, a strong copy with agreat inscription
>
> 6,000
>
> 4,000-5,000

Lot #88

115. Sotheby's, New York, Sale Number 6925 (4 December 1996)
USC library dean George Terry attempted to buy all the Hurley items from the family for the Bruccoli Collection and made an opening offer of $40,000. The Hurleys were dazzled by the recent auction sale of Mrs. Onassis's property, and they decided to sell at auction. Three items were sold at Sotheby's for a total of $64,000—including the buyer's premium ($9,800). After the 20 percent seller's fee ($10,840) was deducted, the

Hurleys received $43,360. Items 90 and 91 were "bought in," meaning that the bids failed to reach the minimum prices set by Sotheby's and the Hurleys.

87
Fitzgerald, F. Scott
Autograph manuscript signed ("F Scott Fitzgerald") in pencil, 71 pages (size varies slightly, approximately 14 x 8½ in.; 356 x 216 mm), [Asheville, North Carolina, ca. summer of 1936], being the original manuscript draft with extensive additions, deletions and corrections of Fitzgerald's Civil War story, "The End of Hate," here entitled "The Tooth and the Thumb," the manuscript differing dramatically from the printed version; slight yellowing and slight marginal soiling.

A SUBSTANTIAL MANUSCRIPT BY F. SCOTT FITZGERALD. THIS LENGTHY FIRST VERSION OF "THE END OF HATE" DIFFERS TO SUCH AN EXTENT FROM THE PUBLISHED VERSION THAT IT ALMOST CONSTITUTES A SEPARATE UNPUBLISHED STORY.

"The End of Hate" is one of only two Civil War stories that Fitzgerald wrote during his professional career (the other was "The Night before Chancellorsville"). He had, however, a lifetime interest in the Civil War and his sympathies lay with the South. In the present story, Fitzgerald tried to weave together two unrelated events from his father's family—a gruesome incident in which his ancestor William George Robertson was hanged by the thumbs by Union soldiers and the story of a cousin of Napoleon III's being stricken with toothache behind Confederate lines. He struggled with this story and rewrote it a number of times over a three-year period. Fitzgerald titled this first version "The Tooth and the Thumb"; later it was retitled "Thumbs Up," "Dentist Appointment,""When the Cruel War—," and finally "The End of Hate." Under the title "Thumbs Up," the story was rejected by thirteen magazines, including *The Saturday Evening Post, Ladies' Home Journal, McCall's* and *Liberty*. The story was apparently not what editors expected from Fitzgerald and the graphic depiction of the thumb incident was considered too strong for women readers. Fitzgerald cut the story by about 3,500 words and sold it to *Collier's* in 1939. It was published in that magazine on 22 June 1940. It was first collected in *The Price Was High: the Last Uncollected Stories of F. Scott Fitzgerald*, edited by Matthew J. Bruccoli, New York, 1979.

With its many emendations, this first version of the story has the feel of a difficult work in progress. Fitzgerald's frustrations (and, presumably, his alcohol consumption) are reflected in his handwriting, which begins as a neat, tight, legible script and ends as a large, loose scrawl. On the final page of the manuscript, Fitzgerald creates an unsatisfactory, undeveloped ending for his story, which he crosses through with a large "X"; at the bottom of the page he writes the word "Nothing," which he crosses through several times. In this version, Fitzgerald gives close attention to describing the incident of the toothache, establishing the hero's credentials as a sensitive soul, and describing the heroine's life in France after the war. He minimizes the love story within in tale; and has his hero and heroine meet in unpleasant circumstances some years after the war. In the published piece, the love story is expanded and takes center stage, as the lovers meet in Georgetown on the night of Lincoln's assassination (the heroine having just returned home from Ford's Theater; the hero just come from his room at Mrs. Suratt's boarding house).

The manuscript is remarkably fresh and well-preserved. In 1936, James Hurley wrapped the present manuscript and the typescripts of "I Didn't Get Over" (see next lot) in a green paper dry-cleaning bag (labelled "Manuscripts: Thumbs Up, I Didn't Get Over") and stored them in a steamer trunk where they remained virtually undisturbed for the next sixty years.

$30,000–50,000

See illustration on preceding page

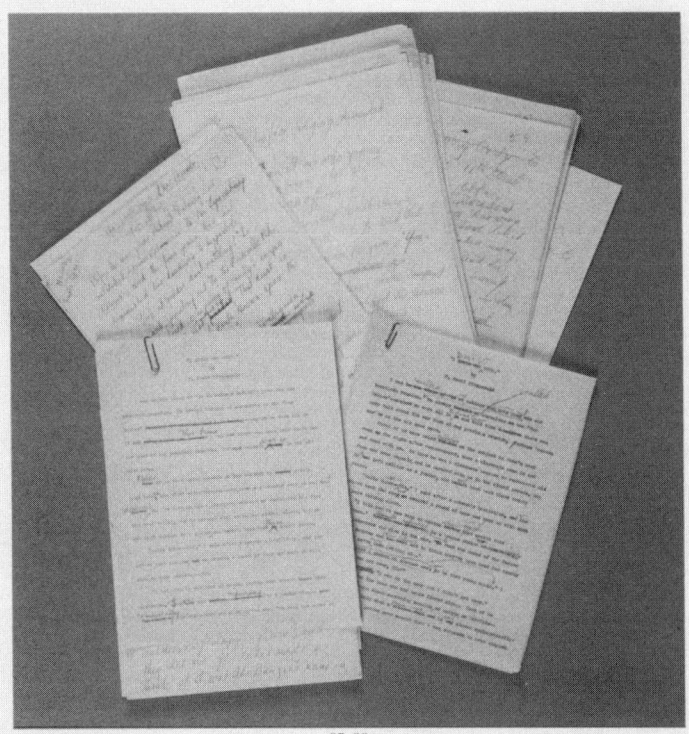

87, 88

Property from the Collection of the Late James B. Hurley

In 1936, James B. Hurley, who had just graduated from Brown University with a B. A. in English, left his hometown of Providence, R. I., and went to North Carolina in search of employment. As his son, James A. Hurley writes, "... the Great Depression was on and he found himself clerking at Asheville's Grove Park Inn for $2.00 a day. When he answered a classified ad to do some typing, he learned that he was in the employment of ... F. Scott Fitzgerald. Dad typed Fitzgerald's manuscripts, which were written in longhand, on a Remington portable designed for double-spaced work. Since Fitzgerald wanted his stories triple-spaced in order to edit between the lines, Dad turned the roller and carriage by hand to provide three spaces. Another duty Fitzgerald assigned my father was monitoring finances. When Dad would report the checking account was low, Fitzgerald would instruct him to wire The Saturday Evening Post that he had a story coming. After the check arrived, Fitzgerald would compose a short story ... My father worked for Fitzgerald for a period of nine months. When they parted company, the author inscribed three of his novels to my father and presented him with the manuscripts of two short stories ..."

continued

88
Fitzgerald, F. Scott
Two drafts for his short story "I Didn't Get Over," the first an autograph and typed draft, 20 pages (various sizes), [Asheville, North Carolina, ca. summer 1936], autograph insertions and corrections in pencil, being the first draft of the story, the second a typescript, 9 pages (11 x 8½ in.; 279 x 216 mm), [Asheville, North Carolina, ca. August 1936], autograph corrections in pencil, being a second typed draft of the story; slight marginal soiling.

TWO EXTENSIVELY REVISED DRAFTS OF A FITZGERALD SHORT STORY. THE SECOND DRAFT BEARS A PRESENTATION INSCRIPTION IN PENCIL ON THE VERSO OF THE LAST LEAF: "For James Hurley from F Scott Fitzgerald."

Fitzgerald based "I Didn't Get Over" on an incident which took place while he was stationed at Camp Sheridan, Alabama, during World War I. A ferry overloaded with troops was swamped in the Talapoosa River, and Fitzgerald was responsible for saving a number of lives in the rescue effort. In the story, the author confronts some of the inferiority he felt for not serving on the front in Europe during the war. The story was first published in *Esquire* in October 1936. It was first collected in *Afternoon of an Author; A Selection of Uncollected Stories and Essays*, edited by Arthur Mizener, Princeton, 1957.

The two drafts together present a vivid picture of Fitzgerald in the midst revisions. The first draft is heavily corrected and contains nine full sheets of holograph text in addition to a profusion of changes in pencil on the typed sheets. The second draft has fewer corrections, but a number of stylistic changes have been made in the first few paragraphs and the crucial thirty-five word ending of the story has been added in Fitzgerald's hand.

$10,000–15,000

See illustration on preceding page

89
Fitzgerald, F. Scott
Tender Is the Night. *New York: Scribner's, 1934*

In 8s (7⅜ x 5¼ in.; 187 x 133 mm). Text vignettes by Edward Shenton. Publisher's cloth, gilt-lettered spine; minor wear and soiling.

FIRST EDITION. PRESENTATION COPY, INSCRIBED BY FITZGERALD to James B. Hurley's mother, "For Margaret Hurley with much respect & regard from F Scott Fitzgerald. April 1936. Ashville [sic]."

References: A15.1.a

$2,000–3,000

90
Fitzgerald, F. Scott
The Great Gatsby. *New York: Modern Library, (1934)*

In 8s (6½ x 4¼ in.; 165 x 108 mm). Shaken, left margin of title-page repaired with cellotape. Publisher's red cloth flexible binding; some wear, spine faded.

First Modern Library edition, with the first publication of Fitzgerald's introduction. PRESENTATION COPY, INSCRIBED BY FITZGERALD, "For Jim Hurley from his friend F Scott Fitzgerald."

$2,000–2,500

91
Fitzgerald, F. Scott
Taps at Reveille. *New York: Scribner's, 1935*

In 8s (7½ x 5¼ in.; 190 x 133 mm). Publisher's cloth, gilt-lettered spine; minimal wear.

FIRST EDITION, second state. PRESENTATION COPY, INSCRIBED BY FITZGERALD for James B. Hurley, "For Jim Hurley, adhesive tape expert ('May every typewriter ribbon prove to be an adhesive tape' Dorothy Dix) from his friend F Scott Fitzgerald. Ashville [sic] 1936." Of this cryptic inscription, James A. Hurley writes, "The inscription … refers to an incident at the Grove Park Inn swimming pool where Fitzgerald dived in under the influence, fracturing his right collarbone. Since there was no tape of any sort in the vicinity, my father pulled the ribbon from his typewriter and bound Fitzgerald's limb to his side for the journey to the hospital. Fitzgerald wrote the remarks with his left hand."

References: Bruccoli A18.1.a$_2$

$3,000–4,000

116. Peter L. Stern Catalogue 28 [early 1997]

This item was again catalogued at $35,000 by Stern in his April 1997 list.

> *An Inscribed "Gatsby" in Dust Jacket*
> **100. FITZGERALD, F. SCOTT.** *The Great Gatsby.* New York: Scribner, 1925. First Edition, second printing in the second issue dust jacket with the "J" in "Jay Gatsby" corrected in type. Signed presentation copy to his friend, Hollywood screenwriter Hugo Butler, inscribed, "For Hugo Butler, with apologies that in writing this story of his life I had to leave out so much for which the public is not yet 'ready' - and feeling that in dedicating the proceeds to his speedy release I will make those days in St [San] Quentin pass more swiftly for him. From his old buddy in cell block 3. F. Scott Fitzgerald. Hollywood-on the-Square, August 1938." "Cell block 3" is a reference to the portion of the Irving Thalberg Building at the MGM studios where Butler and Fitzgerald were screenwriters together. Hugo Butler wrote such notable films as the Jean Renoir directed *The Southerner, Young Tom Edison, Lassie Come Home, The Adventures of Huckleberry Finn,* and *A Christmas Carol.* Front hinge professionally repaired. Near fine in a completely unrestored dust jacket with a few small chips at the extremeties and some tears. $35,000.00

117. Christie's East, New York, Sale Number 8001 (14 May 1997)

> THE PROPERTY OF
> A GENTLEMAN
>
> •101 FITZGERALD, F. SCOTT. Autograph letter signed ("F. Scott Fitzgerald") to the American novelist Cyril Hume, whose first book, *Wife of the Centaur,* had just appeared, Great Neck, Long Island, n.d. [1923]. *3 pages, 4to, on rectos of three leaves, usual fold creases.*
>
> FITZGERALD QUOTES CONRAD: "TO MAKE YOU HEAR, TO MAKE YOU FEEL, ABOVE ALL TO MAKE YOU SEE..."
>
> An excellent letter entirely devoted to a critique of *Wife of the Centaur* (Hume had sent Fitzgerald a copy): "...I read it with the greatest interest and it strikes me as an excellent and most amusing first novel...Now I'll tell you the things I was less enthusiastic about: 1st. The long polyphonic prose passages which seemed to me without true significance and which without doubt interupt [sic] the flow of the narrative. 2nd. The scenes at school...This 'history of a young man' business is intrinsicly [sic] an exhausted art form anyhow — because it always tends to a dumping of dozens of very youthful experiences and impressions in the reader's lap with a profound air of importance. My own novel [*This Side of Paradise*, 1920] & [Stephen Vincent] Benét's [*The Beginning of Wisdom*, 1921] suffered from this. Elliot Paul in *Indelible* and *Impromptu* [1922 & 1923] did a better job...The only really gorgeous novel of this type for years has, of course, been [James Joyce's] *The* [sic] *Portrait of the Artist as a Young Man* [1917] because it was done with the most rigid and austere sense of selection..."
>
> "...My objection to the polyphonic passages is that they often follow other pages from which you have not bothered to delete trite phrases and unmemorial clichés [Fitzgerald gives several examples]...I found these just now at random & it makes your high spots look mere 'fine writing' to find slovenly work in your narrative. But you have an abounding interest in things, a style that needs work on it, but seems sound at bottom & most of all an ability to convey feeling or, as [Joseph] Conrad says in his famous preface [to *The Nigger of the 'Narcissus'*] 'to make you hear, to make you feel, above all to make you see'..." Hume had been a fellow student of Fitzgerald's at the Newman School (1911-13); as a novelist he had a vogue in the 1920s. Not in *Letters,* ed. M.J. Bruccoli, and presumably unpublished.
>
> *$7,000* $3,500-4,500

128 *F. Scott Fitzgerald in the Marketplace*

118. Sotheby's, New York, Sale Number 7001 (3 June 1997)

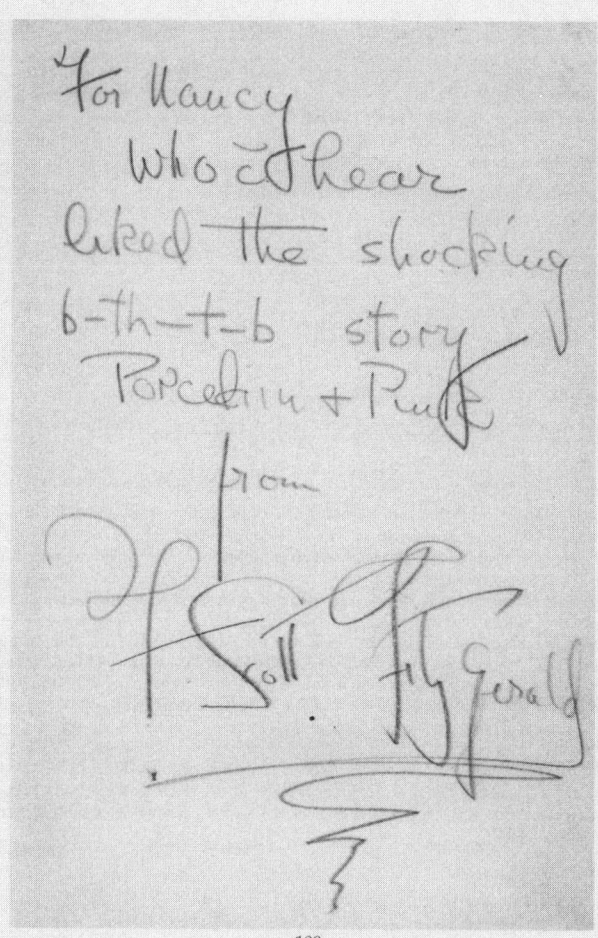

108

108
Fitzgerald, F. Scott
Flappers and Philosophers. *New York: Charles Scribner's Sons, 1920*

In 8s (7½ x 4⅞ in.; 190 x 124 mm). Two half-titles, dedication leaf to Zelda, contents leaf. Blue-green linen-like cloth, title an author's name blind-stamped on upper cover, gilt-lettered on spine, plain endpapers and edges; lacks dust-jacket, lightly rubbed, hinges a little weak.

PRESENTATION COPY OF THE FIRST EDITION, FIRST ISSUE. Written forcefully in pencil using large, bold characters, Fitzgerald writes: "For Nancy | who I hear liked the shocking b-th-t-b story Porcelain & Pink from F Scott Fitzgerald." *Porcelain and Pink* was first published January, 1920, in *The Smart Set* magazine and later in book form as one of *The Tales of the Jazz Age* (1922).

$13,000— $2,000–3,000

119. Peter L. Stern Catalogue 29 [1997]

USC library dean George Terry acquired this copy for the Bruccoli Collection; he paid $6,000. The inscription refers to Jay Gatsby's time at Oxford.

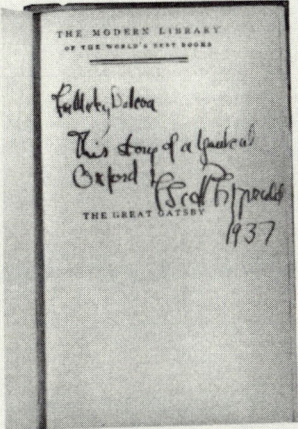

Fitzgerald In Hollywood
148. FITZGERALD, F. SCOTT. *The Great Gatsby*. New York: The Modern Library, 1934. First Modern Library Edition. With a new introduction by the author. An excellent association copy, inscribed by the author, "For Micky Balcon, This story of a Yank at Oxford, F. Scott Fitzgerald, 1937." Fitzgerald, along with many others, worked on the script for A Yank At Oxford, released in 1938. Balcon produced this film, and was head of production for MGM-British. Although uncredited, Fitzgerald worked on the script for three weeks, and is considered responsible for much of the better dialogue. An important edition, the introduction is partly a defense against his critics (after claiming that "...I have no cause to grumble about the 'press' of any book of mine..."), "...Because the pages weren't loaded with big names of big things and the subject not concerned with farmers (who were the heroes of the moment), there was easy judgment exercised that had nothing to do with criticism but was simply an attempt on the part of men who had few chances of self-expression to express themselves..." This is a near fine copy in a dust jacket with a one inch chip at the top of the spine. $7,500.00

120. Sotheby's, New York, Sale Number 7197 (15 December 1998)

The apparition in "The Devil" section of book 1, chapter 3, continues to puzzle readers.

> 63
>
> **Fitzgerald, F. Scott**
> Autograph letter signed, 1 page (11 x 8½ in.; 279 x 216 mm), New York, 16 November 1920, to Harvey C. Robert; lightly browned, faint mat burn to upper margin, one small tear at fold, with original stamped and postmarked envelope
>
> F. SCOTT CANDIDLY DESCRIBES A CHAPTER IN HIS FIRST NOVEL "... AS ONE OF ... NUMEROUS FLAWS ..." Seven months after publishing *This Side of Paradise*, Fitzgerald responds to an inquiry: "Several people have asked me about that chapter & I can only explain it by telling how it came to be written. It was part of my first draft of my novel [*This Side of Paradise*] begun three years ago when I was an ardent supernaturalist & believed that a `personal devil' could and often did materialize before humans. Since then as you can see thru [sic] the book I have become practically a materialist so the incident becomes incongruous & out of place. You are right in saying that it was only a delirious apparition conjured up in Amory's drunken mind. Tom would not have seen him. You'll just have to take it as one of the numerous flaws in the book."
>
> $3,500–5,000

2000S

121. Peter Harrington Catalogue (March 2000)

The Bruccoli Collection acquired this item from Glenn Horowitz for $14,000 in 2001.

> FINE INSCRIBED COPY
>
> 218 **FITZGERALD, F. Scott.** Tender is the Night A Romance *Charles Scribner's Sons, New York 1934*
>
> 8vo., original publishers ribbed green cloth, gilt lettering to the spine, in the colourful dustwrapper with a scene of the French Riviera. A very desirable copy with a personal inscription to the front free-end paper. Decorations throughout by Edward Shenton. A fine copy with only the slightest touches of foxing to the page edges, and a very good First Issue dust wrapper with the review blurbs by T.S.Eliot, Mencken and Rosen. The dustwrapper has some signs of wear with slight fading and some small nicks to the top and bottom of the spine. There are also some very small stains to the rear of the jacket. Although we are going into great detail over the condition of this d/w it is in overall very good condition. *[14422]* **£18,000**
>
> *FIRST EDITION. First Issue.*
>
> *The inscription on the front free-end paper reads:-*
> *"Dear Lady Florence / Willert / You were so kind to / write me about my book /that I think you deserve / a copy of the 1st American / edition. (The chief difference / is the illustrating / which rather catches the / Spirit of the older centuries) / With Best Wishes / to your husband, to / Paul & to yourself*
> *F. Scott Fitzgerald"*

122. Lion Heart Autographs Catalogue (April 2000)

Fitzgerald's poem to Carmel Myers was in her autograph album. He worked with Joseph Mankiewicz but not in vaudeville.

> **26 · FITZGERALD, F. SCOTT** (1896–1940)
> American novelist and short story writer; author of *The Great Gatsby*, *Tender is the Night*, and *This Side of Paradise*. AQS. ("*F. Scott Fitzgerald*"). 1p. 4to. N.p., 1931. To actress and vamp CARMEL MYERS (1899–1980).
>
> > Orange pajamas and heaven's guitars
> > Never, oh <u>never</u> the twain shall meet
> > Never mind, though; the advantage is ours
> > Reach for a Carmel instead of a sweet
>
> Zelda and F. Scott Fitzgerald met Myers in Rome in 1924 while she was making the movie-classic *Ben-Hur*. During their first trip to Hollywood in January and February of 1927, they shared a bungalow at the Ambassador Hotel with Myers, novelist and critic Carl Van Vechten, and the actor John Barrymore. Though Fitzgerald professed little interest in the movies as an art form, many of his short stories and novels found their way to the silver screen. Dabbling as a scriptwriter in the early 30s, Fitzgerald moved to Hollywood in 1937, making scriptwriting his primary source of income. It was here that he began his affair with Hollywood columnist Sheilah Graham, with whom he spent his final years. The last line, "*Reach for a Carmel*," is a light-hearted take-off on the cigarette advertisement, "Reach for a Camel." This quote shares the page with several autograph inscriptions, including film director and producer JOSEPH MANKIEWICZ (1909–1993) with whom Fitzgerald worked in Hollywood and Vaudeville, and Hollywood actor GEORGE E. STONE (1903–1967). Framed. $2500

123. Christie's East, New York, Sale Number 8363 (12 April 2000)

Item 295 is one of two located books inscribed by both Fitzgeralds: see entry 97, item 127. Recatalogued in Kenneth W. Rendell Catalogue 294 [ca. 2002] at $57,500. Item 296 was recatalogued in Kenneth W. Rendell Catalogues 289 [ca. 2001] and 294 [ca. 2002] at $47,500. Only one Fitzgerald-to-Perkins letter has been noted in an auction catalogue.

295

295 FITZGERALD, F. Scott. *Flappers and Philosophers.* New York, 1920. 8°. Original cloth (fine); front panel and flap of scarce dust jacket tipped in at rear (edges frayed). FIRST EDITION, RARE PRESENTATION BY SCOTT AND ZELDA FITZGERALD TO A FELLOW SCRIBNER'S AUTHOR. Inscribed on the flyleaf and dedication page respectively, with Zelda's inscription apparently dated on the novel's publication date. Scott Fitzgerald begins warmly, "To JW Rogers/ Wishing him a most/ amusing trip to a better land/ than this. (not double entendre)/ As Ever F. Scott Fitzgerald." Zelda's inscription, written along the top edge and around her printed name on the dedication page, is even more playful, "Wishing you a happy birth-/day- only it isn't, is it?" She then adds the novel's month and day of publication, "Sept. 10", but inexplicably records the year as "1912".

Books presented by both F. Scott and Zelda Fitzgerald are extremely scarce. Along with his debut novel, *This Side of Paradise*, this first collection of stories catapulted Fitzgerald to fame on campuses across America with its perfectly turned accounts of Jazz Age excesses among the young romantic set. Scott and Zelda worked hard to be the embodiment of the glamorous party couples that Fitzgerald portrayed in his prose, and having them both inscribe the book that set the aura of the Roaring Twenties is particularly emblematic. *Provenance:* John William Rogers, a Texan playwright ("Judge Lynch") and Scribner's author in the 20s (he edited a compilation of Robert Louis Stevenson's essays on writing) who was apparently one of the few writers that impressed Fitzgerald from the rather lacklustre stable of authors published by Scribner's at the time.

Estimate: $10,000-15,000

296 FITZGERALD, F. Scott. ALS to Maxwell Perkins, Westport CT, [ca. May 1920]. 1 page, oblong 4°, with 2 separate "notes" on either side. "I AM, THANK THE GOOD LAWDY GAWD, WRITING AGAIN." In an unpublished letter, Fitzgerald comments on the press notices for his first novel and thanks legendary Scribner's editor Maxwell Perkins for a contract (most probably for his first collection of short stories, *Flappers and Philosophers*, published in September 1920). Fitzgerald also remarks on the first appearance of one of his best stories, "The Ice Palace in this week's Post. I'm curious to know whether it'll take. I'll be in town this wk & will drop in." On the facing side and with a different pencil, which Fitzgerald has titled "Idea for a Literary Note", he records the number of quotes taken from his work used in the reviews for his first novel, *This Side of Paradise*. "In the first 3 dozen notices of Fitzgerald's book 360 different and distinct lines were quoted entire by various reviewers [This is indeed a quotable book full of epigrams, observations with every sentence pointed 7 finished oh what a line of bull!]." Fitzgerald letters to Perkins, especially from early in their association, are almost unknown on the market. *Provenance:* John William Rogers.

Estimate: $4,000-6,000

297 [FORE-EDGE PAINTING]. HORATII, Quinti. *Opera Omnia.* London, 1831. 8°. Contemporary black hard-grained morocco bound by Hayday, elaborately gilt, g.e. DOUBLE FORE-EDGE PAINTING OF A VENETIAN CANAL.

Estimate: $400-600

Christie's Sale Number 8363

124. James Cummins Catalogue 75 (May 2001)

Warren consistently lied about his association with Fitzgerald. He did not collaborate in the writing of *Tender Is the Night*; this inscription refers to his work on a scenario for an unproduced *Tender Is the Night* movie.

ADDENDUM

118. FITZGERALD, F. Scott. *Tender is the Night*. 8vo, New York: Scribner's, 1934. First Edition, first printing. Original green cloth, small tear at head of spine, worn. With the bookplate of Charles Marquis Warren and Anne Crawford Warren. In half morocco slipcase and chemise. Bruccoli A14.I.a.

$60,000

Inscribed on the front free-endpaper:

"For Charles (Bill) / Warren / With hopes that / our cooperation /will show us to / prosperity / F. Scott Fitzgerald / April 1st (Fools Day 1934)."

The book was published April 12, 1934, eleven days after this inscription.

A MATCHLESS ASSOCIATION COPY OF ENORMOUS SIGNIFICANCE, for Bill Warren (Charles Marquis Warren) was none other than Fitzgerald's collaborator on the film treatment of *Tender is the Night*, recruited by Fitzgerald when Warren was only a 17-year-old youth with a talent for writing musical theater. Warren began working with Fitzgerald even before the novel was finished, and according to Aaron Latham, in his book *F. Scott Fitzgerald in Hollywood*, (NY, 1970): "Warren worked with Fitzgerald on the final drafts of *Tender is the Night*, then they collaborated on a motion-picture treatment of the novel. Some days Bill simply acted as a kind of stenographer. Other days he would take pages covered with Scott's sprawling handwriting, sit down with a legal pad, and rewrite whole scenes. He remembers especially the shooting episode at the railroad station in Paris, which he reworked, trying to give it a more dramatic structure. In recognition of Bill's efforts, Scott put him in the book: the author named Nicole's father Charles Marquis Warren in the first edition of the novel, then changed it to Devereux Warren in later printings. 'It was our hidden symbol,' remembers the man who gave his name. 'If I tell you that I wrote part of *Tender is the Night*, then you'll tell me that you wrote *The Sun also Rises*,' says Warren. But when the novel was published, eight years after it was begun, Fitzgerald inscribed a copy to his 'godson' as follows: 'For Charles (Bill) Warren with the hope that our co-operation will show us to prosperity'..." (Latham, pp. 83-84). That copy, of course, is the one being offered here.

Fitzgerald's collaboration with Warren on *Tender is the Night* bore no fruit, and the author's high hopes expressed in the inscription to his partner in this presentation copy — written several days before the book's publication — came to nothing. Fitzgerald had orginally conceived the novle as the story of man who wanted to make movies, and, given the author's unhappy sojourn and ultimate failure in the land of make believe, the ironies contained in the inscription here abound. (For a full discussuion of Warren & Fitgerald's treatment of the novel, see Latham, pp.76-96.).

END OF CATALOGUE 75

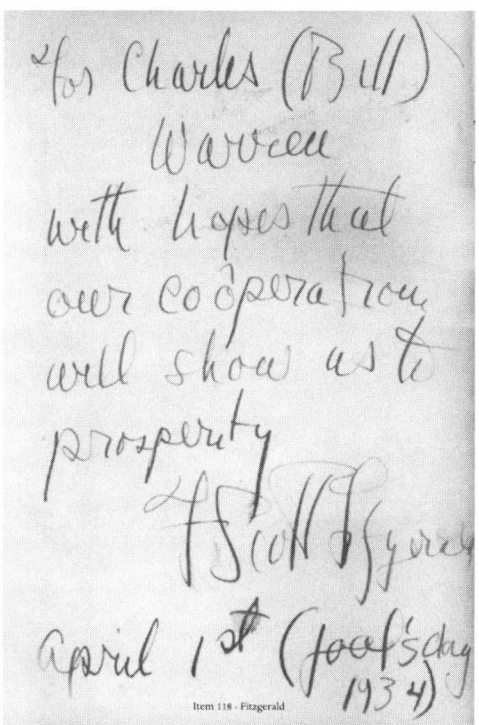

Item 118 - Fitzgerald

125. Christie's, New York, Sale Number 9652 (22 May 2001)

Item 232 was listed again in the 19th Century Shop Catalogues 85 (Fall 2001) and 87 (June 2002) for $18,000.

230
FITZGERALD, F. Scott (1896-1940). *The Beautiful and Damned.* New York: Charles Scribner's Sons, 1922.

8°. Original green cloth (spine dulled slightly).

FIRST EDITION, PRESENTATION COPY, INSCRIBED TWICE BY FITZGERALD on front free endpaper. The first inscription reads: "Sincerely FScott Fitzgerald," and later inscription continues below an arrow pointing to above inscription: "Believe it or not *this* was in this book when it came to me from the Tryon book shop. I must have autographed it for some book-seller years ago & it fell into a stock of remainders. Such is fame. / Tryon 1938 / I mean 1937." Bruccoli A8.1.a (a).

Estimate: $10,000-15,000 $15,275— BP

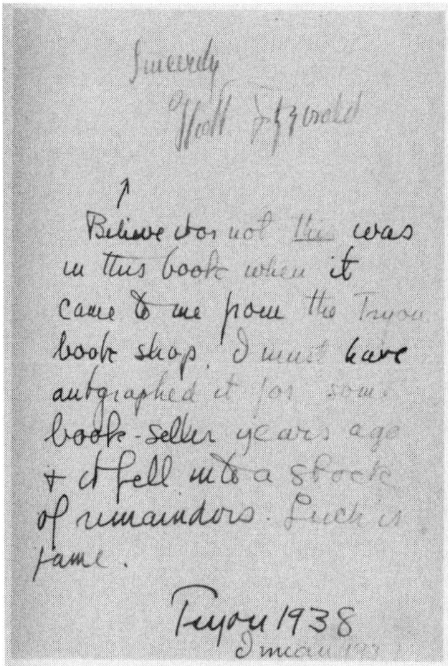

231

FITZGERALD, F. Scott. *The Great Gatsby*. New York: Charles Scribner's Sons, 1925.

8°. Original green cloth (gilt rubbed on spine; rectangular offset from newspaper clipping to inscription and signature on front endpaper).

FIRST EDITION, second state. PRESENTATION COPY, INSCRIBED BY FITZGERALD on the front free endpaper: "For Howard Ballantyne / (Agent 16 of the C.I.O.) / from comrade / Scott Fitzgerald / A story with criminals, crimes and a mystery, as ordered. 1937 [below Fitzgerald has drawn a sketch of a hammer and sickle]." Bruccoli A11.1.b.

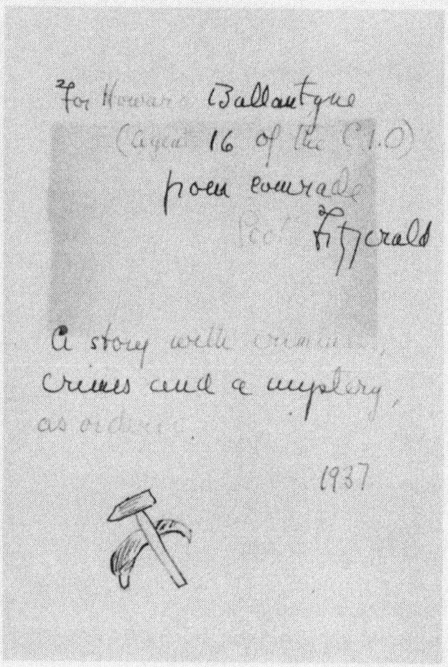

Estimate: $15,000–20,000

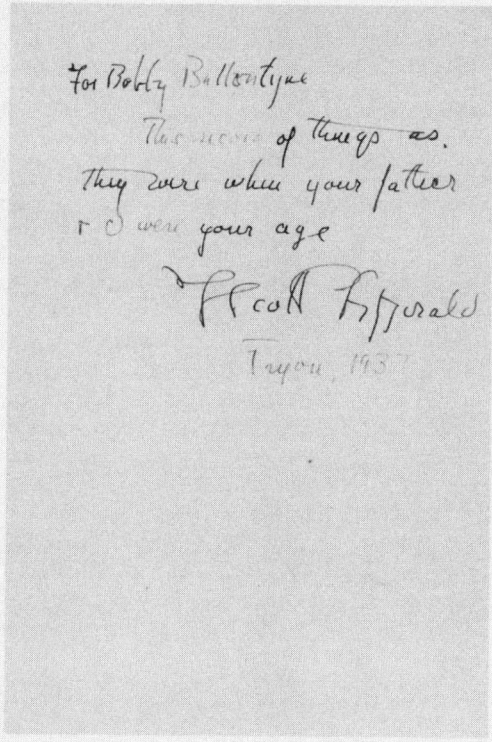

232

FITZGERALD, F. Scott. *This Side of Paradise*. New York: Charles Scribner's Sons, 1931.

8°. Original green cloth (spine slightly darkened with a few splits at ends).

Later printing, PRESENTATION COPY, INSCRIBED BY FITZGERALD on the front free endpaper: "For Bobby Ballantyne / This record of things as they were when your father & I were your age / F Scott Fitzgerald / Tryon, 1937."

Bobby Ballantyne was the son of fellow-Princetonian Howard Ballantyne. Additionally ANNOTATED BY FITZGERALD on p. 47, Spires and Gargoyles, where he has added in margin "named Howard Ballantyne-only it was President" with an arrow pointing to character referenced as "a Lawrenceville celebrity vice-president."

[With:]

FITZGERALD, F. Scott. *All the Sad Young Men*. New York: Charles Scribner's Sons, 1926. 8°. Original green cloth (front hinge cracked). FIRST EDITION. Bruccoli A13.1.a.

(2)

Estimate: $8,000-12,000 $9,988 — BP

> For Barbara Trigo
>   The scourge of Princeton
> This tale of days in the
> Austrailian Bush when
> you were the girl with
> two nose rings when the
> others had only one.
>   FScott ("Hotsy-Totsy") Fitzgerald
>   Tryon 1937

233
FITZGERALD, F. Scott. *Tender Is the Night*. New York: Charles Scribner's Sons, 1934.

8°. Original green cloth (light wear to head of spine).

FIRST EDITION, PRESENTATION-COPY, INSCRIBED BY FITZGERALD on the front free endpaper: "For Barbara Trigo ["i" changed to "e" in pencil, presumably by recipient] / The scourge of Princeton this tale of days in the Austrailian Bush when you were the girl with two nose rings when the others had only one / FScott ("Hotsy-Totsy") Fitzgerald / Tryon 1937." Barbara Trego Ballantyne was the wife of Fitzgerald's Princeton friend Howard Ballantyne. Bruccoli A15.1.a.

Estimate: $15,000-20,000 $35,250   BP

126. Kenneth W. Rendell Catalogue 289 [ca. 2001]

This catalogue includes a misattributed item purporting to be a drawing by Fitzgerald inscribed to his wife. Given the prices that Fitzgerald material brought in the Nineties and after, it is surprising that there have been so few questionable items on the market.

F. SCOTT FITZGERALD. American writer who defined the 1920's. (See Center Pages and Background of Cover.)

Typewritten Note Signed, on an original pen and ink drawing by Fitzgerald, created for his wife Zelda, one page, oblong legal folio, undated.

Fitzgerald has drawn a couple riding in a Stutz-Bearcat convertible, which is decorated with slogans of the Jazz Age: "23-Skidoo!" and "Oh — You Kid" as well as the words "Princeton or Bust!!." The driver wears a bright red hat firmly tied under her chin, an orange overcoat and yellow gauntlets; her companion wears a raccoon coat, beanie and goggles. Above the drawing Fitgerald types, "Dear Zelda / Thank you for that mad, mad drive in your open stutz-Bearcat!!!" and signs it boldly. Note that the typewriting is light.

Scott Fitzgerald attended, but did not graduate from, Princeton. He and Zelda were married in April 1920. Their wild and well-publicized pranks sometimes made them seem like characters in Fitzgerald's novels, and stories, and constantly provided him with fresh material for his writing. They had many escapades in cars, usually involving mechanical breakdowns, absurd mishaps, and fast driving. Framed dimensions: 17 3/8 inches wide by 15 1/4 inches high.

$65,000

F. SCOTT FITZGERALD. American writer who defined the 1920's.

Flappers and Philosophers, inscribed to his literary agent at the top of the front free endleaf, "For Harold Ober who chaperoned these debutantes / with best wishes from / F. Scott Fitzgerald." New York: Scribner's, 1920. First edition. Original green cloth. With some annotations and markings in pencil on the contents page, presumably by Ober.

Flappers and Philosophers is Fitzgerald's second book and first collection of stories. His inscription refers to Ober's marketing of four of these first Fitzgerald stories to magazines. Ober's annotations concern sales of a few of the stories to movie studios. Among the eight stories are "The Ice Palace," "The Offshore Pirate," and "Bernice Bobs Her Hair."

An important association copy. Harold Ober was Fitzgerald's agent for his magazine stories and was instrumental in his financial success. (Maxwell Perkins was Fitzgerald's editor at Scribner's. He handled the books and Fitzgerald dealt with him directly.) Fitzgerald became Ober's client in November 1919 when the author was trying to sell his first stories (Scribner's had accepted the novel *This Side of Paradise*, which would be published in March 1920). Ober quickly placed these "debutante" stories with the *Saturday Evening Post*, etc. He would be the only agent Fitzgerald would ever have, handling magazine and movie sales and always providing guidance to the marketplace. He was as uncommonly generous with advice and money, and always behaved with old-fashioned courtesy and extreme reserve. During his twenty-one-year association with Fitzgerald he served as his agent, accountant, banker, confidante, friend, and surrogate parent to Fitzgerald's young daughter, Scottie. Housed in a custom designed clamshell box.

$75,000

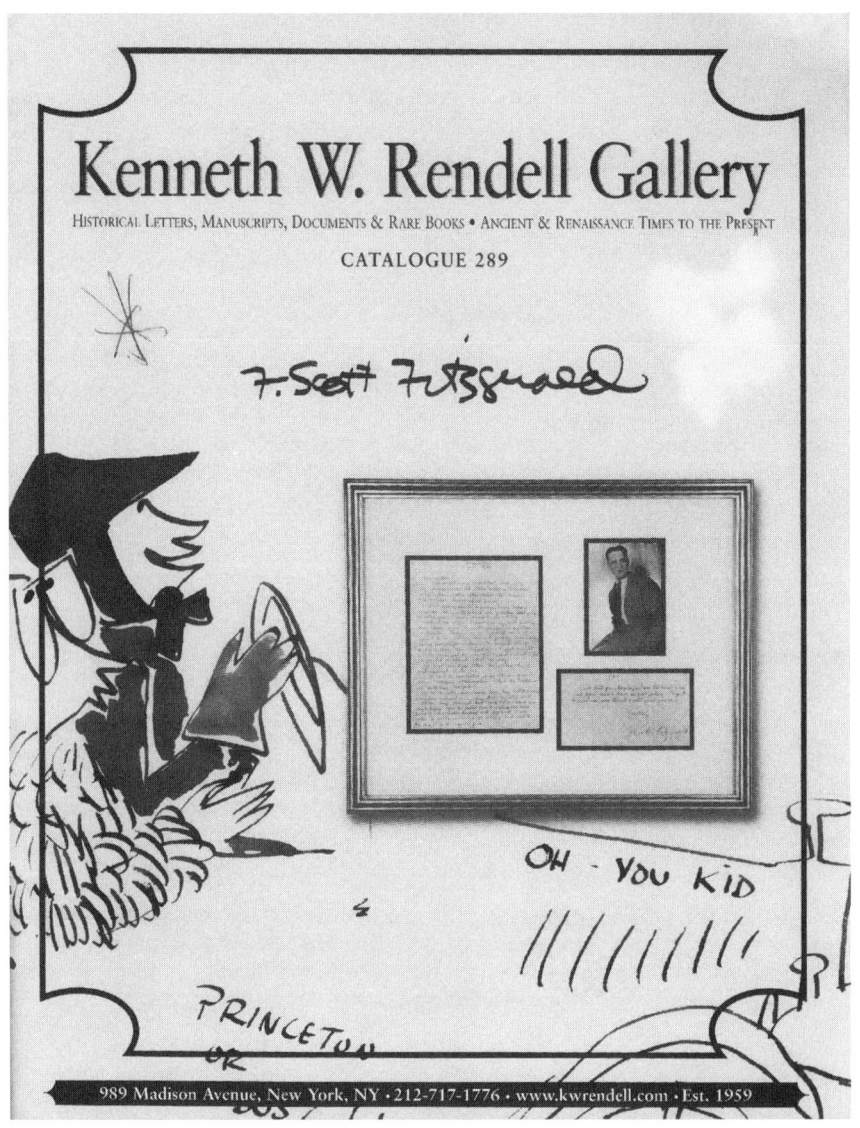

Catalogue cover

127. Kenneth W. Rendell Catalogue 292 [ca. July 2002]

Recipient unidentified; possibly John Peale Bishop or John Biggs, Jr.

> "...IT'S NOT CLEAR. I CAN'T FOLLOW IT."
>
> **F. SCOTT FITZGERALD.** American author.
>
> Autograph Letter Signed, *Scott*, one page, quarto, undated. To *"Dear John"*.
>
> *"Your story came just after I had left for N. Y. and during the past three weeks I've been intending to get at it every day but I've been swamped with work. The Bezoar stone is too slight a thread on which to hang together so much diverse incident. I sympathize with your instinct to make use of so much excellent stuff from your novel but it is wasted here. And it's not clear. I can't follow it. Yrs in awful haste"*
>
> Aged appearance with two file holes in left margin away from the writing. We can frame this piece quickly and in accordance with your desires. $12,500

128. *Masterpieces of Modern Literature: The Library of Roger Rechler.* Christie's, New York, Sale Number 1098 (11 October 2002)

The 375 lots included five books—four of them inscribed—totaling $378,600. Item 88: For Fitzgerald's relationship with Gauss, see appendix 3. Item 90: This was the record price to date for *The Great Gatsby*. An uninscribed copy in a good but creased jacket brought $71,700 in the 8 April 2003 Lackritz sale at Christie's. A copy inscribed to Tatnall Brown brought $130,000 in the 13 April 2004 Neville sale at Sotheby's: see entry 135, item 61.

Rechler's foreword explained that his collecting rationale was to restrict himself to "modernist texts with significant literary or biographical associations." There were twenty dedication copies. He did not provide reasons for disposing of his books. The sale total was $6,928,911.

88
FITZGERALD, F. Scott (1896-1940). *This Side of Paradise*. New York: Charles Scribner's Sons, 1920.

8°. Original dark green cloth, spine lettered in gilt (a little wear to extremities, hinges shaken). *Provenance*: Christian Gauss (1878-1951), Princeton professor, friend and mentor to Fitzgerald (presentation inscription).

FIRST EDITION of the author's first book. AN IMPORTANT ASSOCIATION COPY, INSCRIBED BY FITZGERALD TO HIS MOST SIGNIFICANT PROFESSIONAL INFLUENCE WHILE AT PRINCETON, on the front free endpaper: "Dear Mr. Gauss, Behold the famous American 'novel about flappers written for philosophers.' 'Read 'em an' weep!' / F. Scott Fitzgerald / March 20th, 1920."

Fitzgerald entered Princeton in the fall of 1913, where he was conditionally admitted to the Class of 1917. With his energy primarily devoted to extra-curricular social and literary pursuits, his grades suffered miserably there. After repeated failed attempts to make-up for missed classes or failing grades, he would eventually drop-out and join the army rather than complete his degree.

Although he did not impress the faculty at Princeton, he did form an important friendship with a professor of French Romantic poetry, Christian Gauss (later Dean Gauss). Serving as a mentor, Gauss discouraged Fitzgerald from attempting to publish an early draft of the novel, and read parts of Fitzgerald's revision while the author was in the Army. He was instrumental in Scott's ultimately contacting Charles Scribner offering the manuscript for "The Romantic Egoist," as the novel was originally titled.

"Fitzgerald had known Charles Scribner at Princeton; and Christian Gauss suggested that Scott send 'The Romantic Egoist' to the venerable firm that published his own works as well as those of such eminent authors as Meredith, James, Stevenson, Barrie, Wharton and Galsworthy ... Fitzgerald used [Rupert] Brooke's poem 'Tiare Tahiti' for the title, epigraph and theme (age has nothing to tell the young in this world) of 'The Romantic Egoist,' which was published as *This Side of Paradise*" (Jeffrey Meyers, *Scott Fitzgerald*, New York, 1994, p. 36).

Fitzgerald was in residence at Princeton for the publication of *This Side of Paradise*, on March 26, 1920. He inscribed this copy to Gauss seven days before publication. The autobiographical Princeton set novel was an immediate success, and secured Fitzgerald's reputation as the voice of his generation.

"The novel's defiant tone had the same powerful impact on rebellious postwar youth as Salinger's *Catcher in the Rye* did in 1951, and it became a bible and guidebook as the Twenties began to roar. Like Eliot's *Poems*, Owen's *Poems*, Huxley's *Limbo* and Lawrence's *Women in Love* (all of which appeared in 1920), Fitzgerald's novel captures the spirit of disillusionment that followed the Great War" (Meyers, p.56).

Fitzgerald and Gauss maintained their friendship for years. When Gauss was in Paris in 1925 Fitzgerald took considerable satisfaction in arranging "seminar-lunches" for Gauss, Hemingway, and himself. As perhaps a tribute, joke, or gesture of affection, Fitzgerald named a minor character after him in *Tender is the Night*, with the slightly changed spelling to "Gausse." Bruccoli A5.1.a.

Estimate: $30,000-40,000

$35,850

89

FITZGERALD, F. Scott. *The Beautiful and Damned.* New York: Charles Scribner's Sons, 1922.

8°. Original dark green cloth, gilt-lettered on spine; pictorial dust jacket (some very minor wear at edges, otherwise very fine). *Provenance*: F.J. Warner, Hollywood film producer (presentation inscription).

FIRST EDITION, second printing. PRESENTATION COPY, HUMOROUSLY INSCRIBED BY FITZGERALD TO JACK WARNER on the front free endpaper: "For F.J. Warner / producer of this forgotten tragedy of the 'beautiful but dumb' / from / F. Scott Fitzgerald / 1937." The pre-publication serialization of the complete text appeared in *Metropolitan Magazine* (September 1921-March 1922), and contained a two-paragraph conclusion Fitzgerald ultimately omitted when he revised it for book publication.

Despite his long residence in Hollywood, and close relation with numerous people in the film industry, Fitzgerald and Jack Warner never became close. This may have been due in part to the failure in 1922 of Warner's silent version of *The Beautiful and Damned*, the rights for which his studio purchased soon after publication for $2,250. Apparently, even fifteen years later Fitzgerald could not resist taking a poke at the disaster Warner made of his novel. A FINE ASSOCIATION COPY, IN A VERY FINE DUST JACKET. Bruccoli A8.1.b.

Estimate: $20,000-30,000

90

FITZGERALD, F. Scott. *The Great Gatsby*. New York: Charles Scribner's Sons, 1925.

8°. Original green cloth, spine lettered in gilt, very bright; pictorial dust jacket by F. Cugat depicting a woman's face above an amusement park at night (a few tiny chips at head of spine panel and corners, some minor wear at edges, front panel very lightly rubbed).

A FINE COPY OF FITZGERALD'S MASTERPIECE

FIRST EDITION, FIRST PRINTING, in a first state just jacket, with a lowercase "j" in "Jay Gatsby" on the rear panel hand-corrected in ink. "*The Great Gatsby*, as both [Maxwell] Perkins and [Ring] Lardner perceived, is Fitzgerald's most perfectly realized work of art. The novel reveals a new and confident mastery of his material, a fascinating if sensational plot, a Keatsian ability to evoke a romantic atmosphere, a set of memorable and deeply interesting characters, a witty and incisive social satire, a surprisingly effective use of allusions, an ambitious theme and a silken style that seeems as fresh today as it did seventy years ago" (Meyers, p. 122).

Set on the North Shore of Long Island and Manhattan, and inspired by the extravagant social scene Fitzgerald observed during his eighteen-month residence in Great Neck over 1922-24, *The Great Gatsby* tells the tragic story of the American Dream gone awry as seen through the eyes of a midwestern narrator. The novel went through several failed starts prior to 1924, but it was not until he and Zelda had escaped the New York social scene to the Riviera in May 1924, that he seriously set himself to work on what would become his masterpiece. Although the finished work was admired by virtually all the eminent literary figures of his day, sales did not meet his expectations and only barely paid off his advance from Scribner's.

"In 1925—the year Dreiser published *An American Tragedy*, Dos Passos *Manhattan Transfer* and Hemingway *In Our Time*—Fitzgerald made an impressive leap from his deeply flawed early novels to his first masterpiece" (Meyers, p. 122). A BRILLIANT COPY IN A FINE UNSOPHISTICATED DUST JACKET of what may be 'The Great American Novel.' The striking dust jacket, designed by Cugat, ranks among the most original and attractive American dust jackets ever produced. Bruccoli A11.1.a; Connolly, *The Modern Movement* 48.

Estimate: $60,000-80,000

$163,500

The record price.

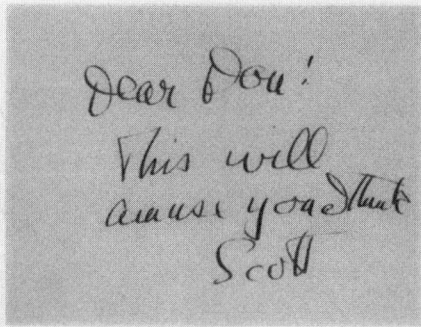

(detail)

91
FITZGERALD, F. Scott. *Tender is the Night.* New York: Charles Scribner's Sons, 1934.

8°. Original green cloth, gilt-lettered on spine; dust jacket (slightest edgewear, otherwise particularly fine and bright). *Provenance*: DONALD OGDEN STEWART (1894-1980), actor, humorist, film writer (presentation inscription).

FIRST EDITION, FIRST PRINTING. A VERY FINE ASSOCIATION COPY, INSCRIBED BY FITZGERALD TO DONALD OGDEN STEWART on the front free endpaper: "Dear Don: / This will amuse you I think / Scott." Fitzgerald met Stewart in 1919, in Fitzgerald's home town of St. Paul, Minnesota, where Stewart was working for AT&T after graduating from Yale. In his autobiography years later, he described the early days of their friendship:

"And then, as though on cue, there arrived shortly after a young, blond, good-looking Princeton graduate named Francis Scott Fitzgerald. Kay Tighe had said 'You'll like Scott'—and I did. He had just come up from Montgomery, Alabama, where he had been unsuccessfully trying to get Zelda Sayre to marry him. I told him about Diana and we became commiserating 'rejects' under the skin. He still had hopes, however, of getting somewhere with his girl... I got him to lend me his cardboard box full of *This Side of Paradise* [the manuscript], written in pencil. I approved of it, with my Yale reservations. I didn't know enough to appreciate his style and form, but the content was exciting.

"...I was lucky with Scott, because I first knew him intimately in that comparatively calm period before he sky-rocketed as a novelist to somewhat unapproachable heights. He and I had one thing in common: we were both impoverished and ambitious 'outsiders.' I think that he was almost as obsessed as I with the magic of great names, both in Finance and Society. We were both products of Eastern upper class universities, and both insecure and unprepared for sudden success. My 1920s and 1930s were, on a smaller scale, the Fitzgerald 1920s and 1930s..." (*By a Stroke of Luck! An Autobiography*, London, 1975, pp. 86-88).

Stewart was a member of the entourage that made the famous journey of 'The Lost Generation'—the trip in 1924 to Pamplona for the festival of the running of the bulls organized by Ernest Hemingway. Hemingway incorporated Stewart into *The Sun Also Rises* as the character Bill Groton. In 1935, Fitzgerald was instrumental in launching Stewart's literary career by introducing him to his Princeton classmates Edmund Wilson and John Peale Bishop at *Vanity Fair*.

Fitzgerald and Stewart remained in touch until Fitzgerald's final years, drifting apart in the late 1930s over Stewart's leftist leanings. At the time of Fitzgerald's death in 1940, Stewart was working in Hollywood, but after a hightly successful career (he won the Academy Award for his screenplay for *The Philadelphia Story*) he was blacklisted and driven into exile in London during the McCarthy hysteria. Bruccoli A15.1.a; Connolly, *The Modern Movement* 79.

Estimate: $30,000-40,000

92
FITZGERALD, F. Scott. *Taps at Reveille*. New York: Charles Scribner's Sons, 1935.

8°. Original green cloth, gilt-lettered on spine; pictorial dust jacket (some edgewear and darkening, a few closed tears at edges). *Provenance*: Charles "Bill" Marquis Warren (1868-1954), Fitzgerald's godson and protégé (presentation inscription and bookplate).

FIRST EDITION, FIRST STATE, with pp. 349-352 integral and unrevised. PRESENTATION COPY, INSCRIBED BY FITZGERALD TO HIS GODSON on the front free endpaper: " For Bill in Highest Hopes from his friend & collaborator, F.Scott Fitzgerald / The 'Winter of Discontent' 1935." Fitzgerald met Warren in Baltimore, when he attended rehearsals for a play in which the young Warren had written the text and music. Fitzgerald was greatly impressed by the teen's accomplishment and shortly after wrote to Samuel Marx, story editor at MGM: "I haven't believed in anybody so strongly since Ernest Hemingway." Before long, they embarked on a screenplay of *Tender is the Night*, hence the "collaborator" reference in the inscription in this copy.

Their collaboration grew into a close friendship, with Fitzgerald serving as a supporting father-figure to the young talent. According to Warren's account, Fitzgerald woke him at 2:00 a.m. one morning and took him to a nearby church, where he a roused a local priest to have him baptized with Fitzgerald standing as his godfather. Warren stayed with Fitzgerald and Sheilah Graham at their Malibu house when he first visited Hollywood. He would later make a name for himself there as a movie director ("Steets of Laredo," "Springfield Rifle," and "Pony Express" among some of his films) and television producer ("Gunsmoke" and "Rawhide"). Their friendship is detailed at length in Aaron Latham's *Crazy Sundays: F.Scott Fitzgerald in Hollywood* (New York, 1971).

This collection of eighteen stories would be the last book published in Fitzgerald's lifetime. A VERY FINE ASSOCIATION COPY. Bruccoli A18.1.a1.

Estimate: $10,000-15,000

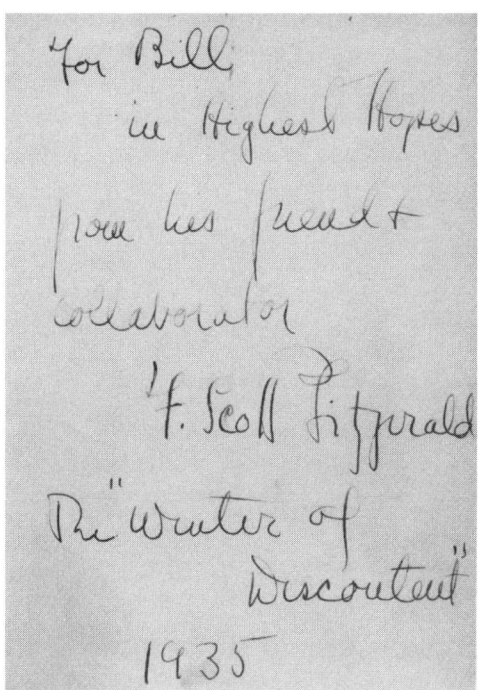

129. Butterfields Auction Catalogue (14 November 2002)
Recatalogued by Heritage Book Shop (April 2003) at $12,500.

3163
FITZGERALD, FRANCIS SCOTT KEY.
Autograph Letter Signed ("F. Scott Fitzgerald"), 3 pages recto and verso, octavo, Asheville, N.C., n.d., to Madame White, on letterhead of Grove Park Inn, light creasing, thumbing, tracing impression to signature.

This letter was most likely written during 1936-37 when Zelda Fitzgerald was confined in Highland Hospital and F. Scott Fitzgerald lived nearby in a series of Asheville hotels. By this time their daughter Scotty lived almost exclusively in boarding schools or with family friends, though Fitzgerald still attempted to parent by mail. He writes this letter to a woman who is helping to care for Scotty. In part: "*I know how kind you have been to Scotty and I am grateful for your patience in helping out the disordered situation in which she is in, perforce. Some of the hardness in her which you may find unsympathetic comes from this never knowing where her house is, being, in effect, what we call a 'hotel child.' Except for her white Persian in the country I don't think she has been able to fix her affections solidly on anything for four years. All the rest has been flux and make-the-best-of-it. The best of it has been the childish dazzle of being popular! I've made the usual masculine mistake of either bullying her or spoiling her.*"
Estimate 3,000/5,000

148 *F. Scott Fitzgerald in the Marketplace*

130. Sotheby's, New York, Sale Number 1744 (13 December 2002)

Myron Selznick was a Hollywood agent; Fitzgerald worked briefly for his brother David O. Selznick on *Gone with the Wind*.

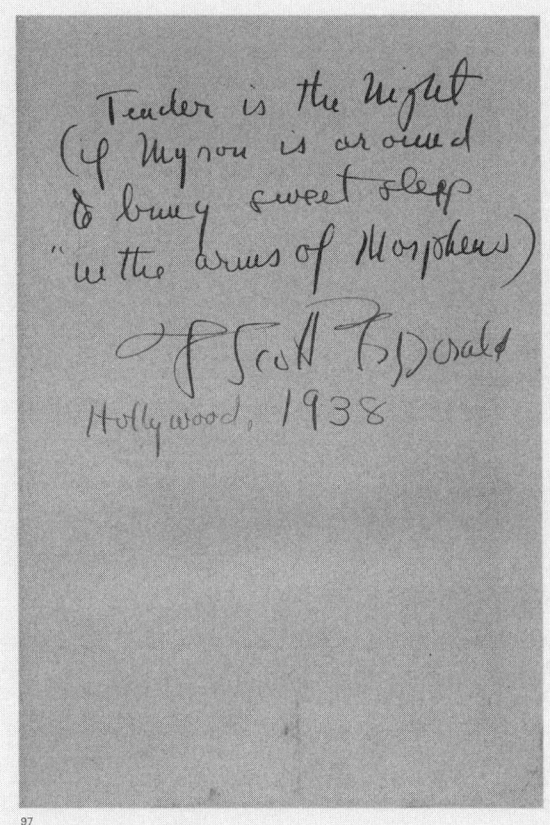

97

97 FITZGERALD, F. SCOTT

Tender is the Night. *New York: Scribner's, 1934*

In 8s (7⅜ x 5¼ in.; 187 x 133 mm). Text decorations and vignettes by Edward Shenton; preliminaries lightly stained along lower margin. Publisher's blue cloth, gilt-lettered spine; boards scuffed, light wear to extremities.

FIRST EDITION. PRESENTATION COPY INSCRIBED BY FITZGERALD, "Tender is the Night (if Myron is around to bring sweet sleep in the arms of Morpheus) F Scott Fitzgerald. Hollywood, 1938". The inscription dates from Fitzgerald's time in Hollywood during the late 1930s, when he was engaged as a script writer for Metro-Goldwyn-Mayer. In 1938 Fitzgerald was working on the script for *Gone with the Wind*. However, as with most of his Hollywood endeavors, Fitzgerald received no screen credit. "Myron" is undoubtedly David O. Selznick's brother Myron Selznick, who had invested heavily in Selznick International and worked with Fitzgerald on *Gone with the Wind*.

REFERENCE: Bruccoli A15.1.a

$12,000–18,000

131. *Literature Including the Detective Fiction Library of Richard M. Lackritz, M.D., Part III.* Christie's, New York, Sale Number 1216 (8 April 2003)

ANOTHER PROPERTY

146
FITZGERALD, F. Scott. 3 Typed Letters Signed ("Scott Fitz" and "Scott") to Nathan Kroll. [Hollywood, California], May 6, August 23 and December 19, 1940. *Together 3 pages, 4to, two mounted on pastedown and front free endpaper of a copy of the volume described below, the second letter with signature traced in ink and with some separation along fold, the second with signature partially smudged, a little browning along top edge of third letter.*

Nathan Kroll was a musician and brother of Fitzgerald's Hollywood secretary, Frances Kroll (Ring). Frances Kroll (b. 1918) worked for Fitzgerald from April 1939 until his death late in the following year. These letters were written during the final months of his life, while Fitzgerald was working on his last novel, "The Love of the last Tycoon: A Western." The work was left unfinished at the time of his fatal heart attack on December 21, 1940.

The letter dated May 6, refers to Nathan's attempt to adapt Fitzgerald's Pat Hobby character to a play. According to Frances Kroll (a copy of her letter dated 1 January 2003 is included), Fitzgerald did not feel Nathan's approach caught the essence of Pat, and in his letter he describes the bitter humor essential to Pat's person:

"...the series is characterized by a really bitter humor and only the explosive situations and the fact that Pat is a figure almost incapable of real tragedy or damage saves it from downright unpleasantness. The play should attempt to preserve some of this flavor. It is the only thing actually new about the original conception." See *Correspondence*, Eds. M.J. Bruccoli and M.M. Duggan (New York, 1980), p. 595.

The letters of August 23, and December 19 (the latter written TWO DAYS BEFORE HIS DEATH) "concern music lists Fitzgerald was preparing for study courses he designed for Sheilah Graham's College of One. He wanted suggestions of recording that would parallel her courses in literature and the arts." His final letter reads: "Would you give Frances the name of a piece which would be an approximate equivalent to Mozart's Hunting Quartet which is out of press...That's what I want—something preferably by Mozart that has a popular phrase or so in it and something that would be on two or three records." He congratulates Kroll on his successful concert, and concludes the letter on a reflective note: "It must be a grand feeling to have made such a beginning out here. Sincerely, Scott."

In late November, Fitzgerald had his first heart attack in Schwab's drugstore. "He almost fainted, and said that 'everything started to fade.' After this attack he could no longer climb the stairs to his third floor apartment on Laurel Avenue and moved into Sheilah's [Graham] first-floor flat at 1443 North Hayworth Avenue, on the next street... On December 20, after seeing a film with Sheilah, he had a second heart attack and just managed with her help to stagger out of the Pantages Theater. The following day, Saturday, December 21, at three o'clock in the afternoon, Fitzgerald suffered his third—and this time fatal—heart attack" (Meyers, p. 333).

[With:] FITZGERALD, F. Scott. *The Last Tycoon*. New York: Scribner's, 1941. 8°, original cloth (hinges cracked); dust jacket (chipped). *Provenance*: Nathan Kroll. FIRST EDITION. Bruccoli A19.I.a.

(3)

Estimate: $5,000-7,000

Not sold

December 19 1940

Dear Nathan:

I'm crashing in on your success to ask you one more piece of information in a musical line. Would you give Frances the name of a piece which would be an approximate equivalent to Mozart's Hunting Quartet which is out of press. Originally you suggested Haydn's "Lark", which is out of press and I tried for Mozart's Hunting Quartet instead as I heard it had a strong melodic line. That's what I want--something preferably by Mozart that has a popular phrase or so in it and something that would be on two or three records. Isn't it funny that they would let two such popular pieces go out of print?

Again congratulations on your concert. It must be a grand feeling to have made such a beginning out here.

Sincerely,

Scott

132. Peter L Stern Catalogue 30 (2003)

The inscribed *Tender Is the Night* was recatalogued in Between the Covers Catalogue 124 (May 2006), again for $65,000.

> A Refugee From Malibu
> 87. FITZGERALD, F. SCOTT. **Tender Is The Night.** New York: Scribner's, 1934. First Edition. Very good in a first issue dust jacket with a fingernail-sized chip at the bottom of the front panel and some creases and interior archival mends where tape has been removed, but the spine is much less faded than usual.Presentation copy; inscribed, "For Edward Everett Horton, Page 74 et sequitor may interest you to dip into if you like cathedral tours - and my daughters evidence is that you do. F. Scott Fitzgerald. Encino, 1939." Fitzgerald moved for the winter from Malibu into Horton's Encino estate in November, 1938. Horton's long film career spanned nearly fifty years; many of us fondly remember him as the narrator of "Fractured Fairy Tales" in *Rocky and Bullwinkle*. $65,000.00

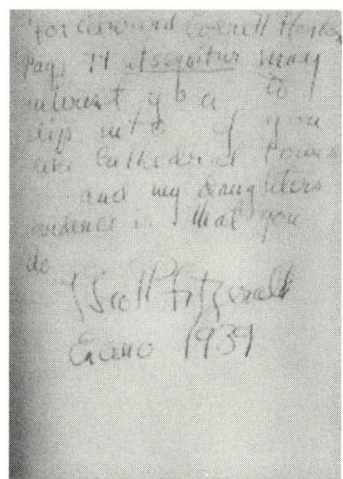

133. George Robert Minkoff Catalogue A2 (April 2004)

> 44. **FITZGERALD, F. SCOTT**. 1 holograph postcard, N.D. postmarked Paris, France, Mai 16th. "Thanks for your kind letter thinking you might like to know what I looked like. I am sending you some pictures (on the other side) that I had taken. Sincerely & Gratefully F. Scott Fitzgerald / the resemblance is said to be excellent." On the verso of the postcard are two black and white images published by "Ligue Nationale Contre L'Alcoolism." The image on the left depicts the stomach of an alcoholic and on the right a normal stomach. Fitzgerald has drawn an arrow pointing to the normal stomach and has written "at 22." Another arrow points to the alcoholic's stomach, with the notation "at 32." A delightful postcard from Fitzgerald when he and Zelda were living in Paris, ca. 1920. Fine. Rare. $1500.00

134. Kenneth W. Rendell Catalogue 298 [ca. 2003]

See appendix 1.

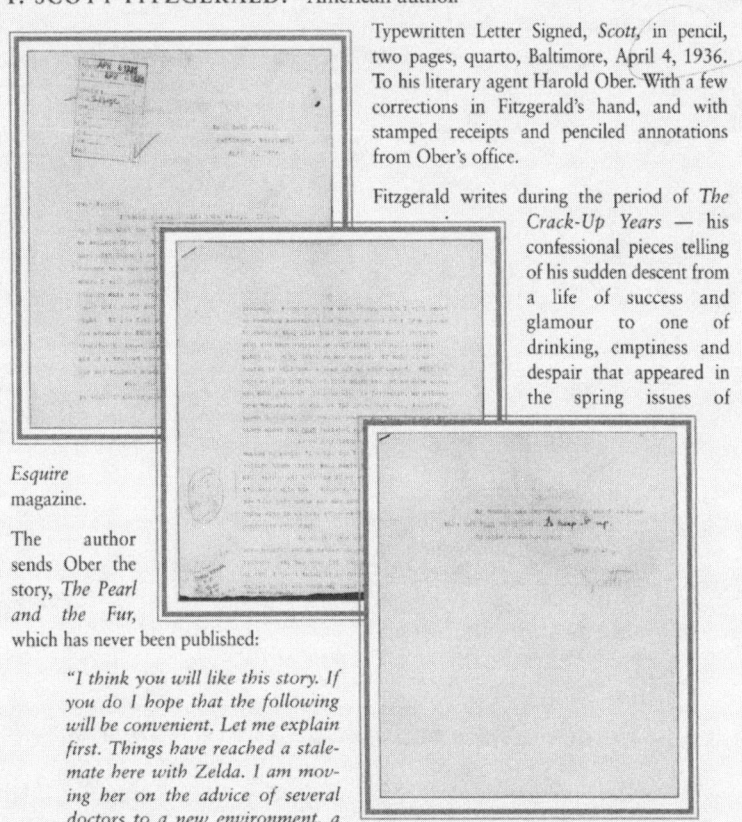

"MY MORALE HAS IMPROVED LATELY AND I DO HOPE THIS NEW POST STORY SELLS TO KEEP IT UP."

F. SCOTT FITZGERALD. American author.

Typewritten Letter Signed, *Scott,* in pencil, two pages, quarto, Baltimore, April 4, 1936. To his literary agent Harold Ober. With a few corrections in Fitzgerald's hand, and with stamped receipts and penciled annotations from Ober's office.

Fitzgerald writes during the period of *The Crack-Up Years* — his confessional pieces telling of his sudden descent from a life of success and glamour to one of drinking, emptiness and despair that appeared in the spring issues of *Esquire* magazine.

The author sends Ober the story, *The Pearl and the Fur,* which has never been published:

> "I think you will like this story. If you do I hope that the following will be convenient. Let me explain first. Things have reached a stalemate here with Zelda. I am moving her on the advice of several doctors to a new environment, a sanitarium in Asheville, where I will probably again have to pass the summer. I plan to make the trip immediately now that I have finished this story and am planning to leave on Tuesday night. If you feel pretty confident of this story can you advance me $200 which will enable me to make the transfer to Asheville? It will have to be done with the aid of a trained nurse as she is still in a most dangerous and violent condition.

"When the story sells, and I feel confident it will, I should also like to count on $2000 of the proceeds. Perhaps on the next story, which I will start on reaching Asheville (or rather when I hear from you as to whether they like this one and want me to continue with the Gwen stories or quit them) you could deduct $1500 per story until we are square. If this is accepted it will take a load off my mind indeed. Will you wire me your opinion of this story and let me know about the $200 advance....

"As to the Gwen story for the [Saturday Evening] Post I felt more hopeful and am rather surprised that you had no bidders. Who has seen it? Can you get me any opinions on it? I don't think it is first rate but it has good things in it and somebody ought to like it. My morale has improved lately and I do hope this new Post story sells to keep it up. Scottie sends her best...."

The Pearl and the Fur was one of four stories Fitzgerald wrote about Gwen, a "series about a father and his daughter.... The girl, Gwen, was based on [his daughter] Scottie, and Fitzgerald hoped his feelings as a sole parent would make the Gwen stories as successful as the Basil and Josephine stories. In 1935 and 1936 he wrote four stories about Gwen. The *Post* took...[two of the stories] but declined the other two and recommended that Fitzgerald discontinue the series. The material was thin because Fitzgerald did not respond intensely to Scottie's interests, but the main difficulty with the Gwen stories was that they were hastily written. They were freighted with too many incidents and the plots were labored. By this point Ober was functioning as editor and even collaborator because the versions Fitzgerald sent him weren't in salable form. For one of the Gwen stories, *The Pearl and the Fur*, Ober sent Fitzgerald a list of twenty-nine recommendations for revisions. The two Gwen stories rejected by the *Post* — *The Pearl and the Fur* and *Make Yourself at Home* — were sold for $2,500 and $1,000 to the *Pictorial Review* with the names of the characters changed, but they were not published there...."

As for Zelda, Fitzgerald's wife, she "did not improve at Sheppard-Pratt and was experiencing a religious mania. On 8 April 1936 Fitzgerald transferred her to Highland Hospital at Asheville, where the minimum monthly fee was $240.... Zelda responded to the course of treatment at Highland. There were no further suicide attempts; her religious mania became less intense, although she still prayed a great deal...." [Matthew J. Bruccoli, *Some Sort of Epic Grandeur: The Life of F. Scott Fitzgerald*].

During this period, Fitzgerald's financial situation was desperate. "By the summer of 1936 Fitzgerald owed Scribners $9,000, and his debt to Ober had reached $11,000. Ober's business, like most others, was suffering from the Depression. He had two sons to educate and was concerned about the mounting total. It did no good to explain that he could not keep advancing money; Fitzgerald continued to wire desperate pleas for $50 or $100 when his bank account was overdrawn" [Bruccoli].

We can frame this piece quickly and in accordance with your desires. $25,000

ORIGINAL WORKING MANUSCRIPT OF HIS SHORT STORY, *AT YOUR AGE*
FOR WHICH HE WAS PAID THE HIGHEST PRICE HE EVER RECEIVED

F. SCOTT FITZGERALD. American writer. (See Center Pages.)
Typewritten Manuscript, Signed, thirty pages, legal folio, [Paris, June 1929]. A working draft entitled *At Your Age*, with the original title *The Old Beau* visible beneath the new. The title and extensive revisions in pencil, in Fitzgerald's hand.

See Center Pages for full description. Price upon request

...AND ALL THAT JAZZ

The Great Gatsby was published in 1925, while the Fitzgeralds were living in Europe where they had gone to escape their madcap life and give Scott the tranquility he needed to write. Gatsby received critical praise, but sales were disappointing. Scott set about writing another (his fourth) novel which, when it was published in 1934, would be called Tender Is the Night.

Meanwhile, to support their "jazz age" lifestyle, even as he was defining it in his books, Fitzgerald wrote short stories, principally for The Saturday Evening Post. One of them, "At Your Age," so thrilled his agent Harold Ober that he called it "the finest story you have ever written — and the finest I have ever read." His enthusiasm was matched by the price he got for it — $4,000, the highest price Fitzgerald ever received for a story.

We are offering the working draft of "At Your Age". Fitzgerald manuscripts — outside institutional libraries — are very rare. This typewritten manuscript is thirty pages long, with extensive revisions, in pencil [here in italics], in Fitzgerald's hand. It is true to Fitzgerald's themes of aspiration (the idealism he regarded as defining American character), and mutability or loss.

The story, set in Minneapolis, is about a man of fifty attempting to recapture his lost youth in a romance (and a planned marriage) with a young woman, and his discovery that while he has lost the battle against youth, "Conflict itself has a value beyond victory and defeat". In the passage that follows, Fitzgerald introduces Tom Squires, the hero. Note that the cross-outs and italics are the author's revisions.

"He was tall, lean and handsome with the ruddy, bronzed face of a sportsman and a just faintly greying moustache. Until his marriage, undertaken late in his thirties, and quickly, tragically over, Once he had been one of among the city's best beaux, organizer of cotillions and charity balls, popular among with with both sexes men and women and with several generations of them. Left with Sonny, After the war he had decided he wasn't rich enough, suddenly felt poor, gone into business and so in twelve ten years he had accumulated nearly a million dollars. Tom Squires was not introspective, but he perceived now that the wheel of his life had revolved again, bringing up forgotten, yet familiar dreams and yearnings. Entering his house he turned suddenly to a pile of unanswered disregarded invitations to see if whether or not he had been invited bid to a dance tonight.

"Throughout his dinner, which he ate alone at the Downtown Club, his eyes were half-closed, and on his face was a faint smile. It was a self-protective expression, for he wanted to be ready to laugh at himself painlessly, if he proved to have embarked upon a spiritual wild goose chase. He was practising so that he would be able to laugh at himself painlessly if necessary. 'I don't even know what they talk about,' he admitted. 'They pet — prominent broker goes to petting party with

debutante. What is a petting party? Do they serve refreshments? Will I have to learn to play a saxophone?'

"These matters, lately as remote as China in a news-reel, came alive to him. They were serious questions. At ten o'clock he walked up the steps of the College Club to a private dance with the same sense of entering a new world as when he had gone into a training camp back in nineteen seventeen. He spoke to a hostess of his generation and to her daughter, overwhelmingly of another, and sat down in a corner to acclimate himself. He was not alone long. A silly young man named Leland Jaques who lived across the street from Tom, and remarked him kindly and came over to brighten his life. He was such an exceedingly silly and fatuous young man that, for a moment, Tom was annoyed, but he perceived craftily that Mr. Jaques he might be of service.

"'Hello, Mr. Squires. How are you, sir?' 'Fine, thanks Leland. Quite a dance'. As one man of the world with another Mr. Jaques sat, or lay, down on the couch and lit — or so it seemed to Tom — three or four cigarettes at once. 'You should have of been here last night, Mr. Squires. Oh, boy, that was a party and a half!' The Caulkins. Half-past Hop past five!' 'Who's that girl who changes partners every minute?', Tom asked, 'No, the one in white passing the door'. 'That's Annie Lorry'. 'Arthur Lorry's daughter?' 'Yes'. 'She seems popular'. 'About the most popular girl in town, anyway at a dance'. 'Not popular except at dances?' 'Oh, sure, but she hangs around with Randy Cambell all the time'. 'What Cam bell?' 'D.B.' There were new names in town in the last decade.

"'It's a boy and girl affair'. Pleased with this phrase Jaques tried to repeat it. 'One of those boy and girls affair — boys and girl affairs'. He gave it up and lit several more cigarettes, crushing out the first series on Tom's lap. 'Does she drink?' 'Not especially. At least I never saw her passed out — that's Randy Cambell just out in on her now'. They were a nice couple. He dark-haired, bright-cheeked beauty sparkled bright against his strong, tall form, and they floated hoveringly, delicately, like two people in a nice, amusing dream. They came near and Tom admired the faint dust of powder over her freshness, the guarded sweetness of her smile, the fragility of her body calculated by nature to a millimeter to suggest a bud and yet guarantee a flower. Her innocent, passionate eyes were brown perhaps but almost violet in the silver light. 'Is she out this year?' 'Who?' 'Mrs Lorry'. 'Yes'.

"Although the girl's beauty loveliness interested Tom, he was unable to picture himself as one of the attentive, grateful little queue that pursued her about around the room. Better to meet her when the holidays were over and when most of these young men would be were back in college 'where they belonged'. Tom Squires was old enough to wait. (See also page 21.)"

Rendell Catalogue 298, center page 24

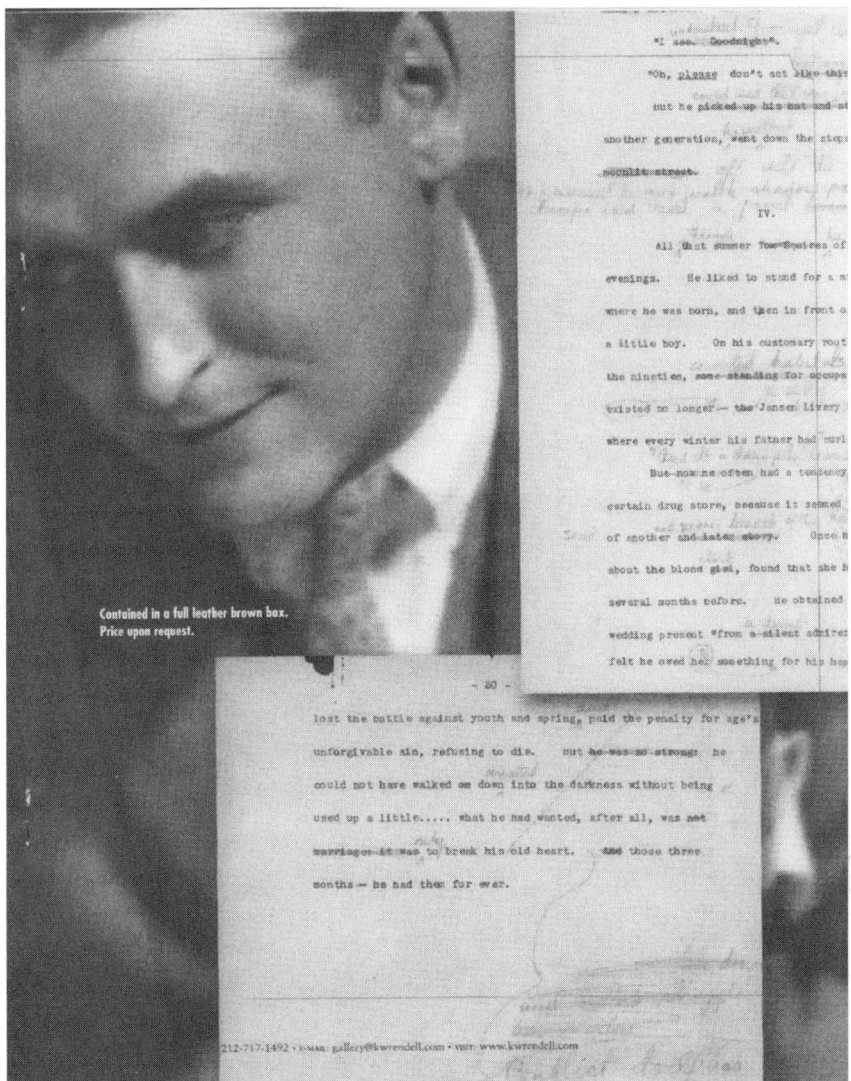

Rendell Catalogue 298, center page 25

135. *The Maurice F. Neville Collection of Modern Literature*, Sotheby's, New York, Sale Number 7980 (13 April 2004), and *The Maurice F. Neville Collection of Modern Literature (Part II)*, Sotheby's, New York, Sale Number 8012 (16 November 2004)

The collection of Santa Barbara book dealer Maurice F. Neville was sold in two parts at Sotheby's in April and November 2004. The twenty Fitzgerald items—seventeen F. Scott Fitzgerald and three Zelda Fitzgerald—were offered in two sales in expectation of increasing the take. The most valuable assemblage of Fitzgerald material sold at auction, it brough a total of $794,400 (including the 20 percent buyer's premium).

The star items were the revised typescripts of two Basil Duke Lee stories in separate sales. "The Freshest Boy" brought $108,000, and "Basil and Cleopatra" brought $84,000. A top price of $120,000 was realized by the copy of *Flappers and Philosophers* inscribed to Fitzgerald's mother. It was not much of an inscription; but there are collectors who specialize in books inscribed to authors' mothers. Fitzgerald's two-and-one-half-page ALS to Marya Mannes brought $90,000—apparently the record price for a Fitzgerald letter. One of Fitzgerald's engraved pocket flasks reached $42,000.

April sale: Holograph prices on items do not include buyer's premium

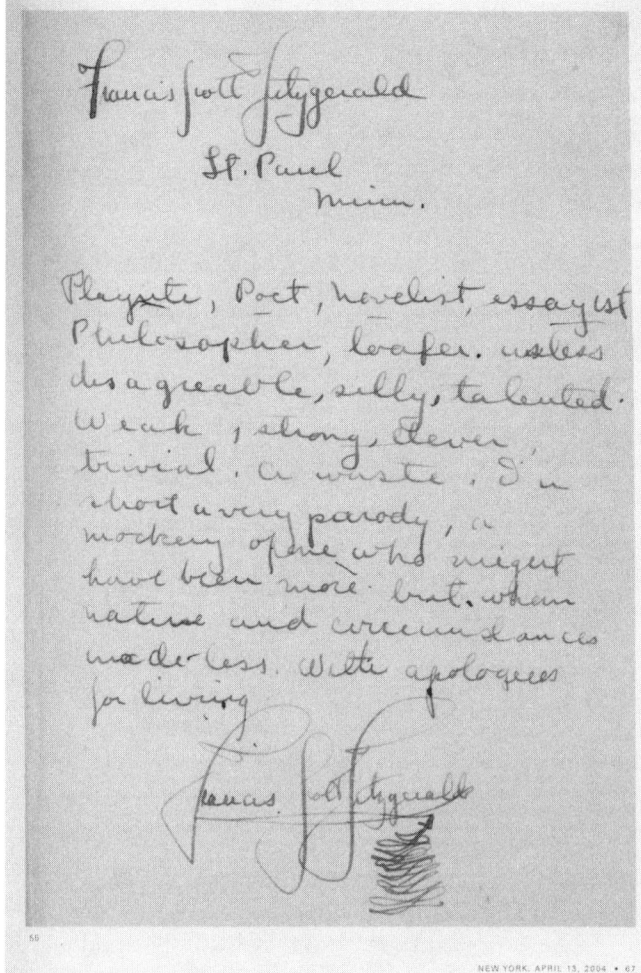

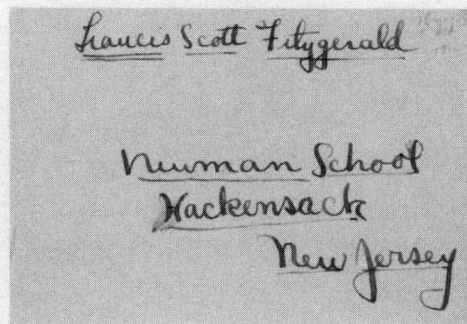

55 DETAIL

55 [FITZGERALD, F. SCOTT]

The Farewell Address of George Washington. Edited by Frank W. Pine. [And] The First Bunker Hill Oration of Daniel Webster. Edited by ... Pine. *New York: American Book Company, [cop. 1911]*

2 volumes-in-1, in 8s (6¼ x 4⅛in.; 159 x 105mm). Blank fore-corners of the majority of leaves torn or chipped away (presumably by Fitzgerald). Original red cloth; extremities slightly rubbed, a few tiny ink stains on rear cover. Red half morocco folding case.

FITZGERALD'S COPY OF THIS TEXTBOOK ON ORATORY USED AT THE NEWMAN SCHOOL, SIGNED FOUR TIMES, ANNOTATED, AND WITH A SELF-PROPHECY WRITTEN ON THE REAR ENDPAPER. The volume is in The Gateway Series of English Texts, Henry Van Dyke general editor. Fitzgerald's ink ownership inscription appears on the front free endpaper: "Francis Scott Fitzgerald / Newman School / Hackensack / New Jersey." On the inside rear cover, in a neat hand and with his fancier signatures, the young Fitzgerald has written his self-analysis and prophecy, again in ink: "Francis Scott Fitzgerald [,] St. Paul[,] Minn. Playrite [sic], Poet, Novelist, essayist [,] Philosopher, loafer. Useless, disagreable [sic], silly, talented. Weak, strong, clever, trivial. A waste. In short a very parody, a mockery of one who might have been more, but whom nature and circumstances made less. With apologies for living. Francis Scott Fitzgerald" (this last signature is more ornate). Some 15 of the book's 100 or so pages of text, plus a flyleaf at front, have ink or pencil markings (mostly underlinings) and/or words, etc., by Fitzgerald. Most of these occur in Washington's "Farewell Address" where Fitzgerald's roman numerals and capital letters divide or mark passages. At the top margin of p. 23 he has also pencilled the phrase: "Your most humblest & obedient servant Geo. Washington." In the bottom margin of p. 43 of the Washington he produces in ink his most florid signature yet: "Francis Scott Fitzgerald," which is preceded by a few practice "F"s. Only four pages in the Webster section show his attention: two have marginal doodling, another has an underlining, and the fourth has a small marginal ink sketch captioned "Little girl"; the same page also has 11 words listed in the margin.

Fitzgerald attended the Newman School, which aimed to be the Catholic equivalent of the prestigious Protestant prep schools in New England, from September 1911 (when he was 15) until he graduated in June 1913. That September he entered Princeton University in the Class of 1917. His prophetic statement on the rear endpaper was apparently written during the Newman School years when he was at home in St. Paul on vacation. "Fitzgerald was bossy, unpopular, and unhappy during his first year at Newman — an experience reflected in his 1928 Basil Duke Lee story 'The Freshest Boy' [see lot 63]; but his behavior and popularity improved in his second year. He did poorly academically, failing four courses in two years; but he won medals for elocution [using this textbook?] and tract" (Mary Jo Tate, *F. Scott Fitzgerald A to Z*, NY, 1998, p. 175).

$20,000-30,000   *Bought in.*

For Shane Leslie
with apologies that this is
not the 1st edition
F. Scott Fitzgerald

56 DETAIL

$16,000

56 FITZGERALD, F. SCOTT

This Side of Paradise. *New York: Scribner's, 1920*

In 8s (7 x 5⅛in.; 190 x 130mm). Original green cloth; inner hinges tender; spine dull. Pictorial dust jacket, "Seventh Large Printing" at top of front panel; lightly stained. Dark green half morocco slipcase.

Seventh printing (August 1920) within the first edition (first printing was March 26). AN EXCEPTIONAL PRESENTATION COPY OF FITZGERALD'S FIRST BOOK TO SHANE LESLIE, inscribed by the author on the front free endpaper and with an important letter to Leslie pastedin. In addition, on the dedication page Fitzgerald has identified Sigourney Fay, the dedicatee, as Mgr. Darcy in the book. *The inscription*: "For Shane Leslie with apologies that this is not the 1st edition, F. Scott Fitzgerald." *The letter*: an autograph letter signed ("F. Scott Fitzgerald"), 1 ½ pages (9½ x 7½in., 240 x190mm, for the first page; 5 x 6⅞in., 125 x 175mm), for the second), New York, 16 November 1920, pasted to a front blank page and the half-title, in brown ink, a minor tear cutting across a word. Fitzgerald writes to Leslie in England mainly about the Catholic priest Cyril Sigourney Webster Fay, the headmaster at the Newman School which Fitzgerald attended, who became his virtual surrogate father: "... It seems a pity that something even more exhaustive can't be written about Dr. Fay [who died in January 1919]. He always told me to save his letters and some day we'd all publish them anonymously in some form. I found, however, that he'd written me less that he thought so the three letters that occur in the book [*This Side of Paradise*] are largely pierced together and even considerably added to from memories of remarks he'd made to me plus even a few things I thought he might have said. The entire funeral description you quoted [of Monsignor Darcy's funeral in *This Side of Paradise*] was culled from your letter except that 'he would have enjoyed his own funeral' and 'making all religion a thing of lights and shadows, etc.' I apologize most humbly. I think the influences of your style on me are traceable in various other portions of the book...Do you know that the story 'Benediction' [published in *The Smart Set*, February 1920; collected in *Flappers and Philosophers*, published 10 September 1920] that I sent you and that also received the imprimatur of the most intelligent priest I know has come in for the most terrible lashing from the American Catholic intelligentsia. It's too much for me. It seems that an Englishman like [Robert Hugh] Benson can write anything but an American had better have his works either pious tracts for nuns or else disassociate them from the church as a living issue ..."

Shane Leslie (1885–1871) was an Irish writer and lecturer whom Fitzgerald met at the home of Father Fay in Washington in November 1912. Leslie was instrumental in getting *This Side of Paradise* published: he corrected the typescript of "The Romantic Egoist," an early form of the novel, for grammar and spelling and then forwarded it to Scribner's with a letter recommending its publication. He was one of three dedicatees of Fitzgerald next novel, *The Beautiful and*

continued

Damned (1922). This copy is inscribed by Leslie below Fitzgerald's inscription to him: "This book I present to my hostess Mrs. [Margaret] Turnbull of La Paix Lane, Towson [Maryland] in memory of her kindness to Scott Fitzgerald and to myself — Shane Leslie, 1958." Margaret Turnbull and her husband were the couple from whom Fitzgerald rented "La Paix," a house on their estate outside Baltimore from May 1932 to December 1933. Their son Andrew became Fitzgerald's second biographer and the first editor of his letters. Laid in is an autograph letter signed from Leslie to Mrs. Turnbull (2 pages, 4to), Ireland, 21 July 1958, regarding this copy and his and Father Fay's friendship with Fitzgerald: "... I add this volume of Scott Fitzgerald to your library, a book he sent me with apologies it was not a 1st edition. I have pasted in a letter he wrote about the beloved Mgr Fay and my part of midwifery in delivering the book to the publisher Andrew will find in my letters to S. F. at Princeton. Mgr Fay was the decisive figure in his life ... When Fay died he appeared to Fitzgerald who told me how certain he was of seeing him, move in the curtains of a room in Atlantic City at the hour of death. This was the exciting Catholic atmosphere against which the crude boyish Fitzgerald impinged. Betwixt myself and Fay he had no chance of escape and became the kind of literary Liturgical Catholic we made him ... Whatever he became before his own death his best character was what we made of him. When Fay went and I had passed him on to Zelda — it was *facilis descensus* to the end."

REFERENCE: Bruccoli A5.1.g; the letter is printed in *The Letters of F. Scott Fitzgerald*, ed. Andrew Turnbull, p. 378

PROVENANCE: Shane Leslie (bookplate, received from Fitzgerald) — Margaret Turnbull (received from Shane Leslie)

$15,000-25,000

57 FITZGERALD, F. SCOTT

Flappers and Philosophers. *New York: Scribner's, 1920*

In 8s (7½ x 5⅛in.; 189 x 130mm). Original green cloth. Pictorial dust jacket by W. E. Hill showing a girl getting her hair bobbed; jacket from a copy of a later printing (probably the sixth) of the book. Cloth slipcase.

FIRST EDITION of Fitzgerald's second book. PRESENTATION COPY FROM THE AUTHOR TO HIS MOTHER, inscribed by him on the front free endpaper: "Here's No 2 Mother. Hope / you like it / Love / Scott Fitz." Following on the big success of *This Side of Paradise*, which was published in March 1920 and which made Fitzgerald famous almost overnight, Scribner's issued *Flappers and Philosophers*, the author's first collection of short stories, some six months later. Five thousand copies were published on 10 September 1920, in a dust jacket inspired by "Bernice Bobs Her Hair," Fitzgerald's first story to capture national attention. The collection of eight stories, all culled from 1920 magazine appearances, also includes two of Fitzgerald's best: "The Ice Palace" and "The Offshore Pirate." Despite mixed reviews, the book sold well: by November 1922 there were six printings totalling 15, 325 copies.

Whether his mother "liked it" is another matter. The printed dedication in Fitzgerald's second story collection, *Tales of the Jazz Age* (1922) is telling: "QUITE INAPPROPRIATELY TO MY MOTHER." "Scott was embarrassed by his mother, who was considered eccentric, dressed carelessly, and read sentimental and religious books ... She discouraged his literary ambitions and destroyed most of his juvenilia ... [She] died in ... September [1936]; Fitzgerald, who had a broken shoulder, was unable to attend her funeral. Before her death he had written an obituary story, 'An Author's Mother'[published in *Esquire*, September 1936], about an old woman who doesn't understand the modern world or her son's books ... He later wrote about his mother: 'She was a defiant old woman, defiant in her love for me in spite of my neglect of her, and it would have been quite within her character to have died that I might live'" (leaving the "cracked-up" and financially desperate Fitzgerald money from her estate) – Mary Joe Tate, *F. Scott Fitzgerald A to Z*, 85. A fine copy, despite the later jacket, and a remarkable association.

REFERENCE: Bruccoli A6.I.a

$40,000-60,000 $100,000—

> Here's no. 2 Mother. Hope you like it
>
> For
>
> Scott Fitz.

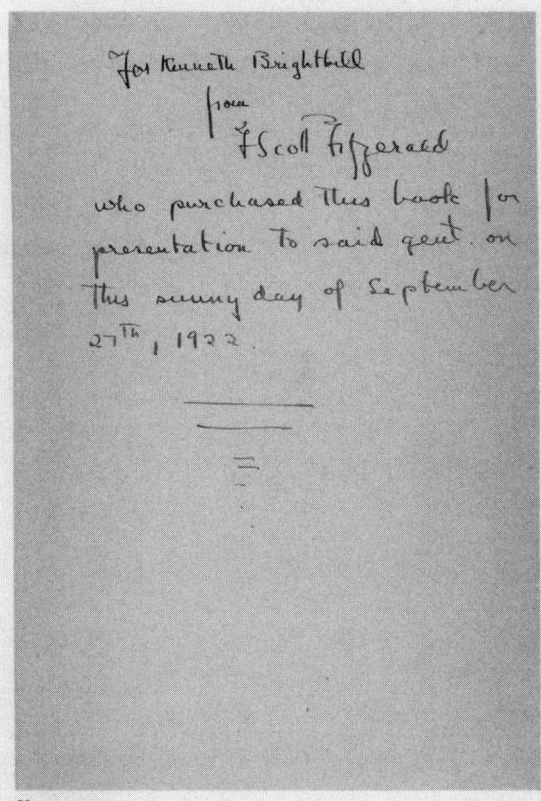

58

58 FITZGERALD, F. SCOTT

Tales of the Jazz Age. *New York: Scribner's, 1922*

In 8s (7⅜ x 5¼in.; 188 x 133mm). Original dark green cloth; front inner hinge a bit tender, spine and portion of rear cover a trifle faded. Pictorial dust jacket by John Held, Jr.; jacket from another copy, soiled, worn at ends of spine, corners, and one fore-edge. Cloth slipcase.

FIRST EDITION. PRESENTATION COPY, inscribed by the author on the front free endpaper: "For Kenneth Brightbill from F. Scott Fitzgerald who purchased this book for presentation to said gent. On this sunny day of September 27th, 1922" (publication date was 22 September). At the time of this inscription the Fitzgeralds were living at the White Bear Lake Yacht Club near St. Paul; they would move back east, settling in Great Neck, Long Island, in October. This is Fitzgerald's second collection of stories, containing three of his best-known: "The Jelly-Bean," "May Day," and "The Diamond as Big as the Ritz." A difficult Fitzgerald title to find inscribed, and in any sort of dust jacket.

REFERENCE: Bruccoli A9.I.a

PROVENANCE: Jonathan Goodwin (sale, Sotheby Parke Bernet, Part I, 29 March 1977, lot 108) — Mrs. Charles W. Engelhard (sale, Christie's, 27 October 1995, lot 41)

$8,000-12,000

59 FITZGERALD, F. SCOTT

The Vegetable or from President to Postman. *New York: Scribner's, 1923*

In 8s (7⅜ x 5⅛in.; 188 x 131mm). Original dark green cloth. Pictorial dust jacket by John Held, Jr.; slight wear. Tan half morocco slipcase.

FIRST EDITION. Signed by Ernest Truex, the actor who played the leading role in the play, in purple ink at top of the front free endpaper. INSCRIBED BY FITZGERALD TO HIM ON OPENING DAY; also in purple ink, just below: "'The best postman in the world' / F. Scott Fitzgerald / Atlantic City / Nov 19th 1923." The quotation is a line from the ending of the play referring to Truex's role, Jerry the postman. Fitzgerald's early interest in the theatre, from his St. Paul schooldays through his Triangle Club shows at Princeton, led to *The Vegetable*, his only professional play. Fitzgerald expected that it would be a great financial success. Scribner's published the play in book form in April 1923. "It was widely reviewed but regarded as a minor effort, and there was only one printing" (Tate, *F. Scott Fitzgerald A to Z*, p. 265). A producer was found and the play began an Atlantic City one-week tryout on 19 November. But opening night was disastrous and *The Vegetable* never made it out of Atlantic City. After this dismal flop, which left him in debt, Fitzgerald never seriously contemplated another play.

Fitzgerald himself suggested the idea for the dust jacket on *The Vegetable*, adding to its desirability. In a January 1923 letter to Max Perkins he wrote: "Cover something like the Jazz Age [the jacket on *Tales of the Jazz Age*, 1922, also designed by John Held], with a different color background and little figures [from the play] — Dada, Jerry, Doris, Charlotte, Fish, Snooks and Gen Pershing scattered over it" (*Scott/Max*, p. 65). Two other copies of *The Vegetable* with the same Fitzgerald inscription beneath the Truex signature are known: one is in The Matthew J. & Arlyn Bruccoli Collection, The Thomas Cooper Library, University of South Carolina (*F. Scott Fitzgerald Centenary Exhibition* 5); the other was sold at auction in 1980 (Christie's 22 May 1980, lot 110). This Neville copy is in fine condition with a bright dust jacket.

REFERENCE: Bruccoli A10.I.a

PROVENANCE: Thomas A. McGraw (bookplate) *$11,000 —*

$7,000-10,000

60 FITZGERALD, F. SCOTT

Autograph letter signed ("F Scott Fitzgerald"), 2½ pages (10½ x 8in.; 265 x 205mm), 14 Rue de Tilsitt, Paris, the envelope postmarked 21 October 1925, to Marya Mannes in New York; in light blue ink on the rectos of three sheets pale green paper with deckle edges, a small, closed tear at the bottom of each sheet, cutting across three letters on the first two pages, a tiny fold hole at the center of each page, with the original stamped envelope addressed in Fitzgerald's hand. In very good condition.

"AMERICA IS THE STORY OF THE MOON THAT NEVER ROSE." A superlative letter about the American scene and its artists and commenting on *The Great Gatsby* and Gerald and Sara Murphy. Marya Mannes, later a journalist, was the daughter of the conductor and violinist David Mannes; Fitzgerald had met them on the Riviera. "Thank you for writing me about *Gatsby* [published in April] — I especially appreciate your letter because women, and even intelligent women, haven't generally cared much for it. They do not like women to be presented as EMOTIONALLY passive — as a matter of fact I think most women are, that their minds are taken up with a sort of second rate and inessential bookkeeping which their apologists call 'practicallity' — like the French are centime-savers in the business of magic ... You are thrilled by New York ... I carry the place around the world in my heart but sometimes I try to shake it off in my dreams. America's greatest promise is that something is going to happen, and after awhile you get tired of waiting because nothing happens to people except that they grow old and nothing happens to American art because America is the story of the moon that never rose. Nor does the 'minute itself' ever come in life either, the minute not of unrest & hope but of a glowing peace — such as when the moon rose that night on Gerald & Sara's garden & you said you were happy to be there. No one ever makes things in America with that vast, magnificent, cynical disillusion with which Gerald & Sara make things like their parties ..."

continued

60

"My new novel [the ur-version of what would become *Tender Is the Night*, published in 1934] is marvellous. I'm in the first chapter. You may recognize certain things and people in it. The young people in America are brilliant with 2nd hand sophistication inherited from their betters of the war generation who to some extent worked things out for themselves. They are brave, shallow, cynical, impatient, turbulent and empty ... My God, Marya, where are your eyes — Or are they too fresh and strong to see anything but their own color & contour in the glass. America is so decadent that its brilliant children are damned almost before they are born — Can you name a single American artist except [Henry] James & Whistler (who lived in England) who didn't die of drink? If it is fresh & strong to be unable to endure or tolerate things-as-they-are, to shut our eyes or to distort and lie — then you're right Marya Mannes and no one has ever so misinterpreted the flowers of civilization, the Greek & Gallic idea, as Your Sincere Admirer F Scott Fitzgerald."

THE FINEST FITZGERALD LETTER TO APPEAR AT AUCTION SINCE THIS VERY LETTER WAS SOLD IN 1970.

REFERENCE: *Letters*, ed. A. Turnbull, 488–89, and in *F. Scott Fitzgerald: A Life in Letters*, ed. M. J. Bruccoli and J. S. Baughman, 129–30

PROVENANCE: "An Auction of Literary and Artistic Materials for the benefit of antiwar Congressional candidates...at the Gotham Book Mart Gallery ... Sponsored by Publishers for Peace," 8 October 1970, lot 44 (donated by Marya Mannes)

$25,000-35,000 $75,000—

74 • THE MAURICE F. NEVILLE COLLECTION OF MODERN LITERATURE

164   F. Scott Fitzgerald in the Marketplace

61   FITZGERALD, F. SCOTT

The Great Gatsby. *New York: Scribner's, 1925*

In 8s (7½ x 5⅛in.; 188 x 130mm). Original green cloth; faint small spot on rear cover, spine a trifle faded. Pictorial dust jacket after Francis Cugat; top of spine and three fore-corners frayed, some other wear.

FIRST EDITION, FIRST PRINTING; second printing of the dust jacket. WITH A POIGNANT INSCRIPTION BY FITZGERALD ON THE FRONT FREE ENDPAPER: "For Tatnall Brown from one, who is flattered at being remembered [,] F. Scott Fitzgerald [,] Hollywood, 1939." "Tat" Brown (1900–1983) was Dean of Haverford College from 1929–1942, a close friend of Christopher Morley's, co-author of a Morley bibliography, and a noted book collector. The inscription is reflective of Fitzgerald's feeling that he had been forgotten as a writer. His books were virtually out of print — most copies of the second printing of *Gatsby* were still in the Scribner's warehouse when he died in December 1940 — and magazines were no longer buying his stories. His contract with MGM, which brought him to Hollywood in July 1937, was not renewed and it expired in January 1939. The next month saw the Dartmouth *Winter Carnival* movie fiasco when he was fired for drunkenness. In a 24 December 1938 letter to Max Perkins, urging the re-publication of some of his works, Fitzgerald had written: "I have come to feel somewhat neglected. Isn't my reputation being allowed to slip away? I mean what's left of it. I am still a figure to many people ... [I have] a deep feeling that something could be done if it is done at once, about my literary standing — always admitting that I have any at all" (*A Life in Letters*, pp. 373–75).

continued

NEW YORK, APRIL 13, 2004 • 75

Item 61 sold for $130,000.

The dust jacket on *The Great Gatsby* — a depiction of a woman's face (Daisy's?) brooding over an amusement park version of New York at night — has achieved iconic status. The design by Francis Cugat (the brother, incidentally, of bandleader Xavier Cugat) is certainly more surreal than those for the jackets on Fitzgerald's previous five books. "Fitzgerald's comment to Perkins, 'For Christs sake don't give anyone that jacket you're saving for me. I've written it into the book' (*A Life in Letters*, p. 79), has not been fully explained, but it may refer to Nick Carraway's statement [at the end of] Chapter IV: 'Unlike Gatsby and Tom Buchanan, I had no girl whose disembodied face floated along the dark cornices and blinding signs ...'" (Bruccoli/*Fitzgerald Centenary Exhibition* 21). The first printing of the jacket has a lower case "j" in Gatsby's name in line 14 on the rear panel. This was corrected by hand, forming the second state (apparently no copies of the first state, i.e., uncorrected, are known). With the second printing of the jacket, the "J" was in the correct upper case.

A very good copy — with a touching inscription — of a prime candidate for the title "the great American novel." Fitzgerald, in a letter to Perkins of ca. 25 August 1924, made a similar claim: "I think my novel is about the best American novel ever written" (*Letters*, ed. Turnbull, p. 166). For Cyril Connolly, *The Great Gatsby* is "one of the half-dozen best American novels." He adds: "... it remains a prose poem of delight and sadness which has by now introduced two generations to the romance of America, as *Huckleberry Finn* and *Leaves of Grass* introduced those before it."

REFERENCE: Henry Tatnall Brown, Jr. (bookplate)

$60,000-90,000

62 FITZGERALD, F. SCOTT

All the Sad Young Men. *New York: Scribner's, 1926*

In 8s (7½ x 5in.; 188 x 130mm). Original dark green cloth; endpaper cracked at rear inner hinge. Pictorial dust jacket by Cleonike; slightly frayed at top of spine, faint stain on front.

FIRST EDITION. PRESENTATION COPY, inscribed facetiously by the author in blue ink on the front free endpaper: "For Bob Ingalls, In memory of a summer on the Baltic Sea from His Faithfully, F. Scott Fitzgerald, Juan-les-Pins 1926." The Fitzgeralds stayed at Juan-les-Pins on the Riviera from March until December 1926; *All the Sad Young Men* was published at the end of February. It was his third collection of stories (containing nine), including several of his finest: "The Rich Boy," "Winter Dreams," "The Baby Party," "Absolution," and "The Sensible Thing."

REFERENCE: Bruccoli A13.I.a

PROVENANCE: R. J. Ingalls, Jr. (signature at top on half-title)

$8,000-12,000 $27,000—

He stopped— realizing that Tresdway was in the company of Brick Wales, a boy he had had a fight with and one of his bitterest enemies. He looking from one to the other, Basil saw a look of impatience in Tresdway's face and a far away expression in Brick Wales' and he realized what must have been happening. Tresdway, making his way into the life of the school, had just been enlightened as to the status of his room-mate; like Fat Gaspar, rather than acknowledge himself eligible to such an intimate request he preferred to cut their friendly relations short.

"Not on your life," he said briefly. "So long." The two walked past him into the candy kitchen.

Had these slights, so much the bitterer for their lack of passion, been visited upon Basil in September, they would have been unbearable. But since then he had developed a shell of hardness which, while it did not add to his attractiveness, spared him certain delicacies of torture. He went the other way along the street in misery enough and despair and self-pity for a little distance until he could control the violent contortions of his face — then, taking a round about route, he started back to school.

-22-

63 FITZGERALD, F. SCOTT

Heavily revised typescript of the short story "The Freshest Boy," 47 pages (11 x 8½in.; 280 x 215mm), [Paris, April 1928], ribbon copy, double-spaced on paper watermarked "Smith Co. Bond," author's name typed under the title, minor rust marks from clip at upper left corner of first page, a few small marginal tears in last leaf; in very good condition.

BASIL DUKE LEE AT PREP SCHOOL. The original typed title, "The Fresh Boy," has been crossed by Fitzgerald at the top of page 1 and "The Freshest Boy" substituted in his pencilled holograph. There are extensive corrections and revisions by Fitzgerald in pencil throughout this working draft, ranging from punctuation changes and repagination, through numerous deletions (the crossed out words are easily readable) and the insertion of phrases and sentences, to the ending of the story (four-and-a-half sentences of the printed text) being supplied in the author's handwriting. Important emendations include the alteration of the names of few characters. In total, there are more than 1,000 words in Fitzgerald's holograph.

"The Freshest Boy," one of Fitzgerald's most anthologized short stories, was first published in *The Saturday Evening Post*, 28 July 1928 issue; it was collected in *Taps at Reveille* (1935) along with four other Basil stories and three Josephine (Perry) tales. It is the second in the series of nine stories centering on young Basil Duke Lee, really Fitzgerald himself, which he wrote for *The Saturday Evening Post* between March 1928 and February 1929. All of the stories in the two series were gathered in *The Basil and Joseph Stories* (1973), edited by Jackson R. Bryer and John Kuehl. Malcolm Cowley notes, in his edition of *The Stories of F. Scott Fitzgerald* (New York, 1986, p. 307): "... the Basil stories ... written in 1928 ... tell us nothing about Fitzgerald's emotions at the time, except that he was unhappy about himself and in a mood for retrospection. He relived his boyhood in the stories and made little effort to disguise the fact that he was writing autobiography. Almost every incident happened in life and almost every character can be identified ... St. Regis School, where Basil was 'The Freshest Boy' [the most unpopular boy], was of course the Newman School; during his first year at Newman [which he entered in September 1911], Fitzgerald was just as miserable as his hero." In the story Basil Duke Lee, age fifteen, overhears an unhappy conversation between Ted Fay, the Yale football captain and his girlfriend, and "he realizes that life is difficult even for apparently successful people. He thus forgoes a trip to Europe, which would have removed him from his painful school experience, because he is unwilling to give up his dream of 'the conquest of the successive worlds of school, college and New York'" (Tate, *F. Scott Fitzgerald A to Z*, p. 92). In his spring term things improve a bit for Basil, though he "was snubbed and slighted a good deal for his real and imaginary sins, and he was very much alone. But on the other hand, there was Ted Fay [the Yale captain], and 'Rose of the Night' on the phonograph — 'All my life whenever I hear that waltz' — and the remembered lights of New York, and the thought of what he was going to do in football next autumn and the glamorous mirage of Yale and the hope of spring in the air ... There would be new fresh boys in September; he would have a clean start next year."

A WORKING DRAFT OF AN IMPORTANT FITZGERALD STORY; VIRTUALLY ALL OF HIS MANUSCRIPTS ARE IN INSTITUTIONAL LIBRARIES.

PROVENANCE: Unnamed consignor (sale, Sotheby Parke Bernet, 9 April 1980, lot 208)

$60,000-90,000   *890,000 —*

64

64 (FITZGERALD, SCOTT F.)

A sterling silver pocket flask, with marks of R. Blackinton & Co., North Attleboro, Massachusetts, ca. 1920, with a hinged pull-off cap opening to the right, overall, 4⅞ x 3⅛ x ⅝in., engraved, upper left F. SCOTT FITZGERALD.

AN UNFORTUNATELY EMBLEMATIC ARTIFACT OF SCOTT FITZGERALD'S LIFE—AND DEATH. While alcohol has been too often the muse of American letters, it has seldom taken a more tragic toll than in the life, career, and marriage of Scott Fitzgerald.

The present is one of at least three flasks that Fitzgerald owned, the two others being in the Matthew J. and Arlyn Bruccoli Collection, Thomas Cooper Library, University of South Carolina. Though not of Tiffany manufacture, the flask was evidently engraved with Fitzgerald's name by Tiffany's. It is accompanied by a signed affidavit by Stuart A. Washborn, a previous owner, 20 November 1979: "This Scott Fitzgerald stirling [sic] flask came to me as a gift from Mrs. June Stern. late of Othica, N.Y. She told me that she had received it from Ernest Hemingway while on a visit to Cuba. Mr. Hemingway, she said, had received it from Mr. Fitzgerald in Paris. Regardless of the above, however, when the flask was taken to Tiffany's to have the cap cork replaced, the flask was recognized as belonging to Mr. Fitzgerald and places where dents had been removed were pointed out to me. Further, Mr. Alfred Van Duym of Scribner's also recognized the flask as having been Mr. Fitzgerald's."

$10,000-15,000   *$35,000-*

65 FITZGERALD, ZELDA

Autograph letter signed ("Zelda"), 4 pages (10⅝ x 8⅛in.; 268 x 208mm), [Paris, The American Hospital, envelope postmarked 2 July 1926], to Madeleine Boyd, wife of the critic Ernest Boyd, in New York; in pencil on two sheets of gray paper, fold creases; with stamped envelope envelope addressed by Zelda.

"SCOTT'S WRITING AN AMAZING GOOD NOVEL." A very rare Zelda-in-the-Twenties letter, written from the hospital where she just had her appendix removed, rambling and chatty, giving news of the Paris and Riviera scenes and telling of Scott's writing: "Scott and I have not been in Paris since Jan. until now ... We had a wild week before I came here — but Paris in June is too much a question of headwaiters to be pleasant. Personally, I have never believed that all people in livery are enigmatic — nor do I believe that all American bartenders in France are great characters — nor do I believe that all famous harlots know a lot about human nature ... So I was very bored with our gala week and am longing for the splendour of our Louis XV drawing room in Juan-les-Pins ... the generations never seem to change in the Ritz bar. I think a seat there is probably hereditary and no new people can come till their fathers die ... We are having a divine time tanning our stomachs on the beach at Antibes. I swim all day and enjoy tremendously a vague nostalgia that comes from living in a perfect place and wishing there was somewhere to go ... We are coming home in Nov. or Dec. — neither Scott nor I quite know why [the expatriates did return in December, with Scott making his first trip to Hollywood in January] ... Scott is writing an amazingly good novel [an abortive, early version of what became *Tender Is the Night*, 1934] which goes so slow it ought to be serialized in the Encyclopedia Britannica ... Dorothy Parker is here showing her wounds — and Dorothy Gish looking like the fancy radiator on a lesser-make car tho she is very attractive – but we have not seen anybody interesting. Scott's last book [*The Great Gatsby*] has been translated by Victor Llona and is coming out in Oct. — over here — we won't be able to read the criticisms so it doesn't matter how it goes ... give my love to Ernest and Lewey Collins is a bitch even if sick and everybody *hates* the [Louis] Bromfields and life is, after all, very complicated."

Later letters of Zelda Fitzgerald are occasionally seen, but early vintage letters like this one about herself and Scott are simply unobtainable: in fact, none have appeared since this last sold at auction (see provenance).

PROVENANCE: Jonathan Goodwin (sale, Sotheby Parke Bernet, Part I, 29 March 1977, lot 117)

$6,000-9,000 $10,000—

66 FITZGERALD, ZELDA

Save Me the Waltz. New York: Scribner's, 1932

In 8s (7⅜ x 5⅜in.; 188 x 136). Original light green cloth; a trifle faded, free endpapers with natural discoloration. Pictorial dust jacket by Cleonike depicting an idealized young couple dancing among flowers against a pink sky, photograph of Zelda on rear panel; light wear at ends of spine and edges of front panel. Cloth slipcase.

FIRST EDITION. "Zelda Fitzgerald's only novel is heavily autobiographical, and Fitzgerald was upset by her appropriation of material he intended to develop in *Tender Is the Night*. After she made revisions, Scribner's published the novel on October 7. It was not well received; readers and critics had difficulty with Zelda Fitzgerald's idiosyncratic prose style" (Bruccoli Collecion, *F. Scott Fitzgerald Centenary Exhibition* 169). Zelda wrote the novel mainly during a six-week period while at the Phipps Psychiatric Clinic at John Hopkins University Hospital in Baltimore (she was there from February to June 1932 following her second breakdown). Copies of *Save Me the Waltz* inscribed by her are exceedingly rare, as evidenced by the absence of one in this collection after all the years of searching. Cleonike also designed the dust jackets for Hemingway's *The Sun Also Rises*, *A Farewell to Arms*, the 1930 *In Our Time*, and for Fitzgerald's *All the Sad Young Men*; the one on *Save Me the Waltz* is his most delightful. A very good copy.

REFERENCE: Bruccoli I1

$4,000-6,000 $4,500—

67 FITZGERALD, ZELDA

Original pastel drawing of a group of brightly colored tropical flowers in an Art-Deco-style vase (23½ x 18½in.; 595 x 470mm), unsigned, [Maryland, circa 1934]; on light brown art board with faint ribbed pattern, matted, framed and glazed.

Probably drawn by Zelda Fitzgerald while she was under psychiatric treatment at the Sheppard-Pratt Hospital just outside Baltimore. In April 1934 an exhibition of Zelda's art work was held in New York (her husband helped to arrange the event). Many of her drawings and paintings have been lost — most destroyed by a fire — and only about 100 have survived. This pastel (in orange, blue, red, yellow, brown, and purple chalks) is unusual in that it lacks any background, unlike most of her reproduced work of the period. The flowers drape over the front of the vase, which is a blend of curves and diagonals. The flowers also emphasize curves and jutting lines and their petals have a spear-like configuration, similar to those of Bird of Paradise flower. In fine condition.

REFERENCE: Exhibited in a show of Zelda Fitzgerald's work at the Montgomery (Alabama) Museum of in the 1970s

PROVENANCE: Direct descendant of Mr. and Mrs. Paul T. MacKie, Jr., close Baltimore friends of the Fitzgeralds (sale, Harris Auction Galleries in Baltimore, 10 May 1985, lot 207)

$4,000-6,000 $4500-

November sale: Holograph prices on items include buyer's premium

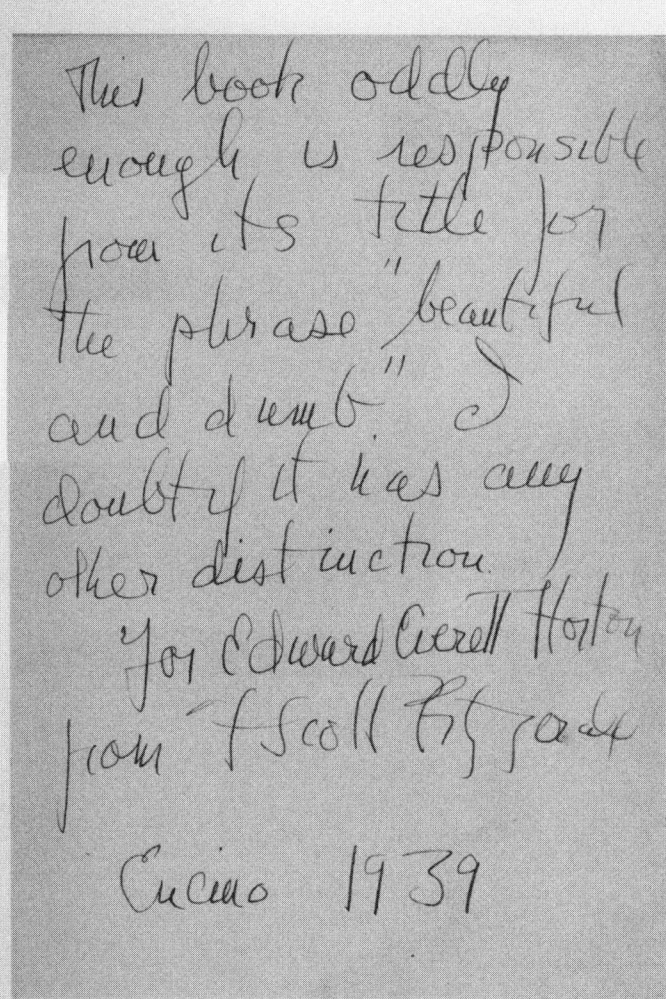

302

302 FITZGERALD, F. SCOTT

The Beautiful and Damned. *New York: Scribner's,* 1922

In 8s (7½ x 5⅛ in.; 188 x 130 mm). Original dark green cloth; a waterstain (1 x 3 inches) on front cover, a smaller one on rear. Pictorial dust jacket from an A. L. Burt reprint of 1922 or 1924 (modeled after the original dust jacket); worn. Dark green half morocco slipcase.

FIRST EDITION, third printing. PRESENTATION COPY TO THE ACTOR EDWARD EVERETT HORTON, HIS LANDLORD AT THE TIME, inscribed by the author on the front free endpaper: "This book oddly enough is responsible for the phrase 'beautiful and dumb.' I doubt if it has any other distinction. For Edward Everett Horton from F. Scott Fitzgerald, Encino 1939." From October 1938, when he left Malibu (because of it's winter dampness) until May 1940, when he moved to Hollywood, Fitzgerald lived in a guest cottage on the Edward Everett Horton estate – named "Belly Acres" by the actor (a pun the writer loathed) – at 5521 Amestoy Avenue, Encino, in the San Fernando Valley. "In 1938 Encino was mostly ranch land and citrus groves, one of the driest and warmest parts of Los Angeles County...The house that Sheilah [Graham, his mistress] had rented for Scott [at $200 a month] was one of three white clapboard cottages on Horton's sprawling estate...Horton, the landlord, was a comic actor with a trademark prissy voice, famous for his exaggerated double takes..." (Robert Westbrook, *Intimate Lies: F. Scott Fitzgerald and Sheilah Graham. Her Son's Story*, 1995, p. 273). In February 1940 Horton approached Fitzgerald with the proposal of turning the Pat Hobby stories into a theatrical vehicle for him, but nothing developed from it.

The Beautiful and Damned, Fitzgerald's second novel, the story of the dissolute life style and the deterioration of a wealthy, glamorous young couple ('The victor belongs to the spoils'), was published on 4 March 1922 in a first printing of 20,600 copies. A second printing of 19,750 copies was done in March and a third printing of 10,000 copies followed in April. But the popular and critical response was disappointing and *The Beautiful and Damned* has long been judged the weakest of Fitzgerald's five novels (reflected in his self-deprecating inscription). A copy of the second printing of the novel in the Roger Rechler sale (Christie's, 11 October 2002, lot 89) had a 1937 inscription to the Hollywood producer Jack Warner which included the phrase "this forgotten tragedy of the 'beautiful but dumb.'"

REFERENCE: Bruccoli A8.I.c

$10,000-15,000   *Not sold*

303 FITZGERALD, F. SCOTT

Autograph letter signed ("Scott Fitzg-"), 1 page (10⅝ x 8 in.; 270 x 205 mm), 14 Rue de Tilsitt, Paris, n.d. [late May 1925], to Thomas R. Smith, an editor at Boni & Liveright; in dark brown ink on mauve paper, professionally backed with some repairs touching several letters, three light and mostly marginal stains.

MENTIONING *THE GREAT GATSBY* AND ERNEST HEMINGWAY. A letter of excellent content to an editor who was trying to lure Fitzgerald from Scribner's: "Thank you many times for your kind letter about *Gatsby* [published on 10 April]. I'm afraid it's not going to sell like the others but I'm delighted at the response from the people who care about writing. Now as to the publishing business. Max Perkins is one of my closest friends & my relations with the Scribners in general have always been so cordial and so pleasant that I couldn't imagine breaking them. But as I told you once before if anything should happen to make our relations impossible I should certainly come to your firm and I know we'd get along. But it would be a monopoly in restraint of trade. You already have the only other two Americans under thirty who promise a great deal – Hemmingway [sic] & Cummings. I hope the former's book [*In Our Time*, which would be published by Boni & Liveright on 5 October] succeeds & will be glad to review it for any paper you might select. We'll be here in Paris the rest of 1925 and, we sometimes hope, forever..." At the bottom of the page Fitzgerald adds, referring to the sentence above naming Hemingway and E. E. Cummings: "But please don't quote about them; I don't want to step on the toes of two other particular friends." Fitzgerald and Hemingway had met for the first time that April. Oddly, Fitzgerald was constantly misspelling Hemingway's name in his letters: either "Hemminway" as here, or "Hemmingway." Rather than Fitzgerald going to the rival publishing house, it was Hemingway (with Fitzgerald's help) who moved to Scribner's: he signed with that firm in February 1926 after Boni & Liveright refused to publish *The Torrent of Spring*, a send-up of Sherwood Anderson, their star author.

REFERENCE: *F. Scott Fitzgerald: A Life in Letters*, ed. M. J. Bruccoli and J. S. Baughman, p. 114

$15,000-20,000   *18,000*

flurry of premature snow ^(in the air) and the ~~air was~~ ^(stars looked) cold. Two late arrivals, (but who ^^possessed^^ Minnie's breathless hours) obscure freshmen, recognized him in the half darkness, ~~and spoke respectfully.~~

"^("That was pretty) ~~Pretty~~ work, Lee".

"Thanks". ^(It was worth nothing to him. It was how traded ^(with) Jubal — who had no position, nor was likely to have any, ^(for one of Minnie's breathless hours)) ~~first hours, He stood there~~ ^(had) ~~with his pride, whatever that might prove to be worth. Indoors,~~ ^(And what was pride when ?) his heart was bouncing around the ball room in a pink silk dress, ~~and he realized that~~ There was not a thing he could do ^(about it ~~without~~ now). ~~In all events~~ her ~~mad~~ infatuation for this ~~terrible~~ ^(man) ~~Burke~~ ^(Jubal) couldn't last forever, and after that ~~there had to be somebody,~~ ^(well, she might need somebody. There was) ~~and shut up there in~~ that school she didn't have ~~a chance to meet a lot of boys. Anyhow there~~ ^(Meanwhile) certainly ~~wasn't any~~ ^(no) use just letting her forget him, and with this in mind ~~he put~~ ^(Basil replaced) his pride ~~into~~ ^(in) his pocket for safe keeping and hurried back to the dance.

304 FITZGERALD, F. SCOTT

Very heavily revised typescript of the short story "Basil and Cleopatra," 47 pages (10⅞ x 8⅜ in.; 276 x 212 mm), [Paris, February 1929]; ribbon copy, double-spaced, of the first 45 pages, with very extensive revisions by Fitzgerald; clean carbon copy of the last two pages from a later draft, double-spaced, with a marginal autograph note signed by him at head of penultimate page; all on paper watermarked "Whiting's Mutual Bond," author's name typed under the title; the first page a trifle darkened and with a few nicks at top edge, next-to-last page with some slight soiling; in very good condition.

BASIL DUKE LEE IN LOVE. The original typed title, "The Freshmen's [sic] Tragedy," has been crossed through by Fitzgerald at the top of page 1 and "Basil and Cleopatra" substituted in his penciled holograph. There is a multitude of corrections and revisions by Fitzgerald in pencil throughout the first 45 pages of this working draft, ranging from punctuation changes and repagination, through extensive deletions (the crossed out words are easily readable) to the virtual re-writing of entire pages (in which the names of a few characters are also altered). There are approximately *1,800 words of emendations in Fitzgerald's holograph*. In fact, the deletions, insertions, and other revisions are so heavy (there are also several words on two of the versos) that the typescript has been almost re-written by Fitzgerald in pencil. (The heavily revised typescript of "The Freshest Boy" in Neville Part I, lot 63, had 1,000 words in Fitzgerald's handwriting.) The final two pages (numbered 29 and 30) are clean carbons from the final typescript, presenting a substantially altered version of the ending of the story as it appears in the revised ribbon typescript, at pages 42-43. (Fitzgerald also has two half pages in his pagination, thus bring the page count of the ribbon typescript to 45.). Fitzgerald's note at the head of page 29 (the penultimate page) is to his literary agent Harold Ober and reads: "Dear Harold: This is for your information. I forwarded the original [i.e., the ribbon copy] directly to the Post to save time. Scott Fitz."

"Basil and Cleopatra," which first appeared in the *Saturday Evening Post* (27 April 1929) "was the final story in the Basil Duke Lee series. Fitzgerald did not include it in *Taps at Reveille* although it is one of the strongest of the Basils. Perhaps he felt that it wraps up Basil's youth too neatly; at the end of the story Basil, unlike Mark Antony, chooses discipline over love" (Matthew J. Bruccoli in *The Short Stories of F. Scott Fitzgerald*, ed. by Bruccoli, 1995, p. 431). It was first collected in *Afternoon of an Author* (Princeton, 1957). All of the nine stories centering on the young Basil Duke Lee, a persona of Fitzgerald himself, which he wrote for the *Saturday Evening Post* between March 1928 and February 1929, were gathered, together with the five Josephine tales, in *The Basil and Josephine Stories* (1973), edited by Jackson R. Bryer and John Kuehl.

In the story, Basil Duke Lee, age 17, realizes that his great love, Minnie Bibble, has fallen for a rival. Shortly after, Basil enters Yale, where he makes the freshman football team. During the Yale-Princeton game (superbly described by Fitzgerald), Basil learns from his rival (now on the Princeton team) that Minnie has left him for one of Basil's Yale classmates. At a dance, "when Minnie is once again attracted to Basil, he resists the urge to return to her, because he wishes to concentrate on his ambitions" (Tate, *F. Scott Fitzgerald A to Z*, p. 12). The story ends with Basil reaching this significant point in his maturation: he left the dance floor and "walked out on the veranda. There was a flurry of premature snow in the air and the stars looked cold. Staring up at them he saw that they were his stars as always – symbols of ambition, struggle and glory. The wind blew them through, trumpeting that high white note for which he always listened, and the thin-blown clouds, stripped for battle, passed in review. The scene was of an unparalleled brightness and magnificence, and only the practiced eye of the commander saw that one star was no longer there."

AN EXTENSIVELY REVISED WORKING DRAFT OF AN IMPORTANT FITZGERALD STORY; VIRTUALLY ALL OF HIS MANUSCRIPTS ARE IN INSTITUTIONAL LIBRARIES.

PROVENANCE: Unnamed consignor (sale, Sotheby Parke Bernet, 9 April 1980, lot 210)

$70,000-90,000

[handwritten annotations: 84,000 / USC did NOT bid. But on 19 million / Now USC hired Football coach for 5]

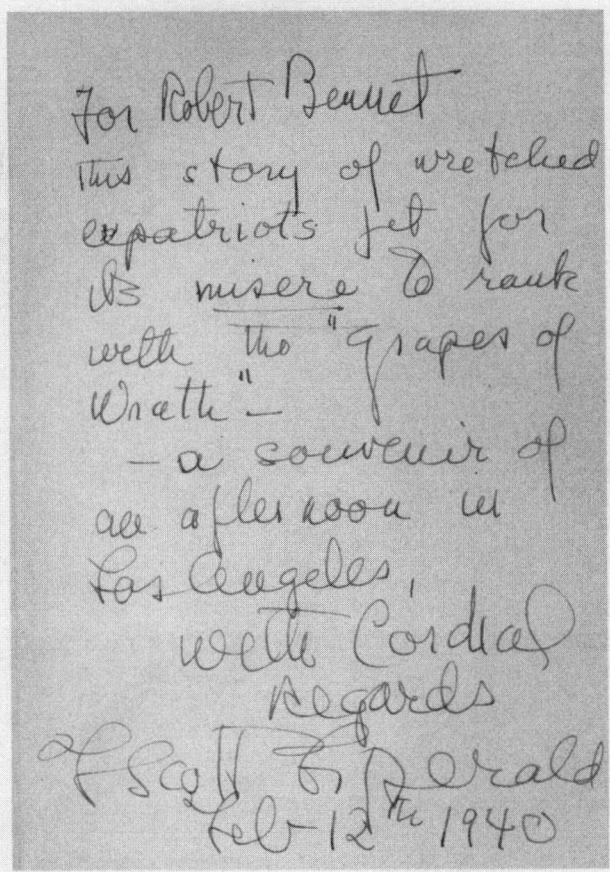

306

305 FITZGERALD, F. SCOTT

Typed contract signed ("F Scott Fitzgerald") between the author and Warner Bros. Pictures, Inc., for movie rights to *The Beautiful and Damned*, 10 pages, 11 x 8⅜ in.; 278 x 215 mm); New York, 29 June 1929; original ribbon copy, double-spaced, stapled in blue wrappers (stained) with studio typing on front; also signed by Albert Warner, a notary public as witness for his signature, and a Vice-Consul at the American Embassy in Paris as witness for Fitzgerald's signature.

THE BEAUTIFUL AND DAMNED IN HOLLYWOOD. Fitzgerald had originally sold the movie rights to the novel to Warner Bros. for $2,500 in 1922, the same year it was published. He was very disappointed in the result, writing to a friend after seeing the film in December 1922: "...its by *far* the worst movie I've ever seen in my life – cheap, vulgar, ill-constructed and shoddy. We were utterly ashamed by it" (*Correspondence*, ed. M. J. Bruccoli and M. M. Duggan, p. 119). Warner Bros. did not make another movie version this time around, nor has *The Beautiful and Damned* been filmed since then.

$2,500-3,500

306 FITZGERALD, F. SCOTT

Tender Is the Night. A Romance. *New York: Scribner's, 1934*

In 8s (7¼ x 5¼ in.; 185 x 132 mm). Decorations by Edward Shenton. First two text leaves opened a bit roughly. Original dark green cloth; front inner hinge slightly tender, very light rubbing at some edges. Pictorial dust jacket with a scene of the Riviera on front, blurbs by T. S. Eliot and H. L. Mencken on front flap; small piece chipped from top front edge partially injuring four letters in "Fitzgerald," other light wear. Dark green half morocco slipcase.

FIRST EDITION, first state of the dust jacket. WITH A MORDANT INSCRIPTION BY FITZGERALD on the front free endpaper: "For Robert Bennett this story of wretched expatriates set for its *misere* to rank with the 'Grapes of Wrath' – a souvenir of an afternoon in Los Angeles, With Cordial Regards F. Scott Fitzgerald, Feb. 12th 1940." The recipient was part of the noted Los Angeles bookselling firm of Bennett and Marshall; the year before he had authored an early essay on Steinbeck, *The Wrath of John Steinbeck or St. John Goes to Church* (Los Angeles, 1939). Fitzgerald himself had a poor opinion of the California novelist, commenting scathingly in a letter written in spring 1939: "...this Steinbeck...is a cheap blatant imitation of D. H. Lawrence. A book club return of the public to its own vomit...he's a phoney..." (Fitzgerald, *A Life in Letters*, ed. M. J. Bruccoli, p. 389). *The Grapes of Wrath* had been published in April 1939 and saw 430,000 copies printed in its first year. In contrast, the first three printings of *Tender Is the Night* – Fitzgerald's other masterwork and a novel in polar opposition to Steinbeck's – comprised only some 15,000 copies (the fourth printing was not until 1951) and royalties from the novel failed to pay off Fitzgerald's debts to Scribner's. At the time of this inscription, although he had started work on what would become *The Last Tycoon*, Fitzgerald felt that he had been forgotten as a writer. His books were virtually out of print – most copies of the second printing of *The Great Gatsby* were still in the Scribner's warehouse when he died in December 1940 – and only his Pat Hobby stories and a few others had starting selling (to *Esquire* at $250 each, down from his $4,000 high for a story in 1929).

"The beginning [of *Tender Is the Night*]...is a wonderful evocation of the second phase of American expatriates ensconced in glittering villas on the Riviera in contrast to the home-spun tipplers of *The Sun Also Rises*. The break-down of a marriage in which the doctor-husband [Dick Diver], having fulfilled his healing role, makes it inevitable that his wife [Nicole] should leave him, is described with flashes of genius by an expert in self-destruction, and there is a haunting account of Fitzgerald's own pet drunk, the story-teller Ring Lardner (Abe North) and of the predicament of 'grace under pressure' from too many parties and too much money"(Connolly).

REFERENCE: Bruccoli A15.I.a; Connolly, *The Modern Movement* 79

PROVENANCE: Ruth Etting (popular singing star of Broadway and early talkies, signature on front paste-down)

$30,000-45,000   *28,800*

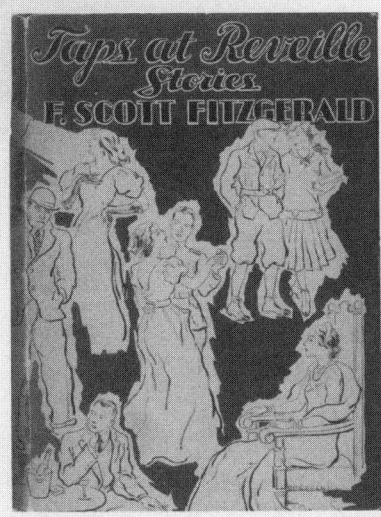
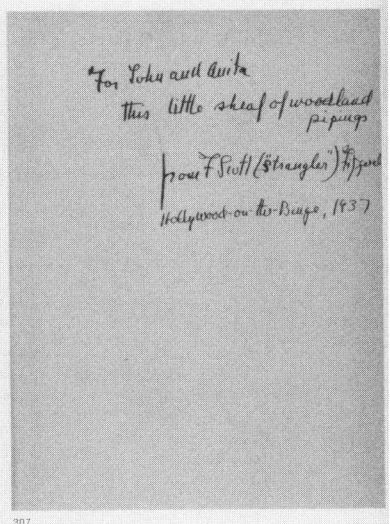

307

307 FITZGERALD, F. SCOTT

Taps at Reveille. New York: Scribner's, 1935

In 8s (7⅜ x 5⅛ in.; 187 x 130 mm). Original dark green cloth; two small abrasions on front cover, top of spine slightly nicked. Pictorial dust jacket; some light edge wear, spine and rear panel a bit darkened.

FIRST EDITION, FIRST STATE, with pages 349-352 integral and unrevised. PRESENTATION COPY TO THE AUTHOR OF GENTLEMEN PREFER BLONDES, inscribed by Fitzgerald on the front free endpaper to Anita Loos and her husband: "For John [Emerson] and Anita this little sheaf of woodland pipings from F. Scott ("Strangler") Fitzgerald, Hollywood-on-the-Binge, 1937." Fitzgerald had returned to "Hollywood-on-the-Binge" in July 1937 for the third and last time, with a six-month MGM contract at $1,000 a week. He lived at The Garden of Allah (moving to Malibu in April 1938), met Sheila Graham, and from September 1937 through January 1938 worked on the script for There Comrades, his only screen credit. Fitzgerald had known Loos in the Twenties – she was an old friend – and he sometimes lunched with her and other writers at the MGM commissary. During a previous stay in Hollywood, in 1931, Fitzgerald wrote a screenplay for the MGM movie Red-Headed Woman, but the studio replaced it with one written by Loos. She also would replace him on a movie during this final stay when MGM decided that the screenplay for The Women, on which Fitzgerald worked in 1938, needed female screenwriters. Of Fitzgerald at this time Sheilah Graham's son writes: "Despite his determination in 1937 to do well in his new Hollywood venture, Scott's confidence was gone. He had been out of sight for too many years. It was painful to remeet old friends both at Metro and The Garden of Allah – friends such as Anita Loos, Dorothy Parker, Robert Benchley, and John O'Hara whom he had known in better days...'Scott had that unhealthy humility of the reformed alcoholic,' Anita Loos said later" (Robert Westbrook, Intimate Lies: F. Scott Fitzgerald and Sheilah Graham. Her Son's Story, 1995, pp. 35-36).

Fitzgerald's "little sheaf of woodland pipings" is the fourth and largest collection of his short stories and the last book to be publish in his lifetime. *Taps at Reveille* was issued in March 1935 in an edition of 5,100 copies; there was no second printing. The volume contains eighteen stories: eight Basil and Josephine tales, plus ten others, including two of his very finest – "Crazy Sunday" (set in Hollywood) and "Babylon Revisited."

REFERENCE: Bruccoli A18.I.a1

PROVENANCE: Anita Loos (presentation inscription, pictorial bookplate)

$15,000-25,000

308 FITZGERALD, F. SCOTT

The Crack-Up: With Other Uncollected Pieces, Note-Books and Unpublished Letters. *[New York]*: New Directions, [1945]

In 8s (8⅞ x 5½ in.; 225 x 128 mm). Original beige cloth, spine lettered vertically in brown; covers rather soiled. Dust jacket from another copy.

FIRST EDITION, second or third printing. INSCRIBED BY ZELDA FITZGERALD on the front free endpaper: "Best wishes to a fellow literary aspirant – in reflected glory. Sincerely Zelda Fitzgerald. May 18-46." The recipient, Paul C. McLenden, Jr., was a young Alabamian who wanted to be a writer and who had first met Zelda in 1941. They became friends and he would often visit her; a correspondence began, with McLenden sending her manuscripts of his work for criticism. (A group of nine letters from Zelda to him was sold at Christie's, 14 December 2000, lot 68.) This copy was inscribed by Zelda while she was living with her mother in Montgomery; she would return to Highland Hospital in Asheville, North Carolina, in November 1947 and would die in a fire there the following March. Inscriptions by Zelda in her own book, *Save Me the Waltz* (1932), are exceeding rare; those in books by her husband are no less so. The publication of *The Crack-Up*, edited by Edmund Wilson, was a major event in bringing about the Fitzgerald revival.

REFERENCE: Bruccoli A20.I.b or c; Nancy Milford, *Zelda* (New York: Avon, 1971, pp. 445-48)

PROVENANCE: Paul C. McLenden, Jr. (signature on front free endpaper)

$1,000-1,500   *1200*

136. Sotheby's, New York, Sale Number 8006 (18 June 2004)
Recatalogued in Heritage Bookshop Catalogue (2006) for $60,000.

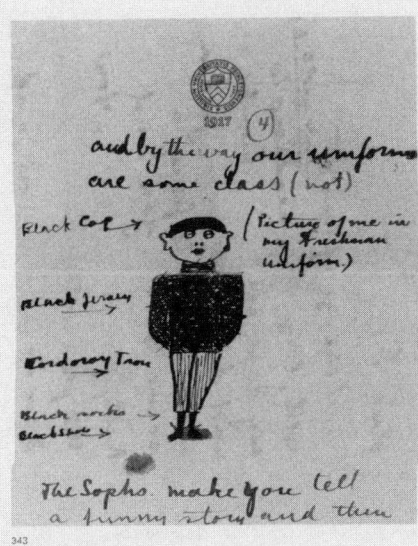

343

343 FITZGERALD, F. SCOTT

A group of three autograph letters signed ("Francis Scott Fitzgerald"), together 10 pages, Princeton, New Jersey, 26 September 1913–7 December 1916, all to Elizabeth Craig Clarkson; with two original drawings (one of Fitzgerald in his freshman uniform, the other showing one sober sitck-figure supporting an inebriated stick-figure), with two postscripts signed ("F.S.F." and "Scott"), with three original envelopes in Fitzgerald's hand, one letter on Princeton University stationery, one letter on mourning stationery, minor separations at folds, very light browning.

"I AM NOW A PRINCETONIAN." Three charming letters from collegian F. Scott Fitzgerald to Elizabeth Craig Clarkson, a girl he met at a swimming party in his hometown of St. Paul, Minnesota. The first letter, written the day after F. Scott was accepted by Princeton, is a self-pitying missive, with an attempt at rhyme. *[15 September 1913:]* "I write to tell you how very sorry I was that I couldn't accept your 'invite' yesterday. But bronchitis interposed its highly annoying hand and spoiled it ... I am in a particularly despondent and dissipated mood. Outside the sun is shining but I am perfectly positive it is only doing it out of spite. In the church across the way they are singing ... My mind is all a-tumble, And the letter seems a jumble, For the words they seem to mumble, And my pen's about to stumble, And the papers made to fumble, So I sign myself your humble ...." Two weeks later, a much cheerier Fitzgerald gives a detailed description of his freshman experiences at Princeton University, complete with a self-portrait caricature of F. Scott in his freshman uniform. *26 September 1913:* "... I am now a Princetonian. Its great. I'm crazy about it. Today we had the rushes. The Sophs mass in a body in front of the gym and the Freshmen try to rush their way in. You can imagine it. Four hundred Freshman, among them yours truly, against 380 Sophs. Everything was ruined. Shirts, jerseys, shoes, socks, trou[sers], hats, &ct. were strewn over the battle & field. I was in the front row and a soph and I almost killed each other. I am a mass of bruises from head to foot ... When we came out

continued

again the sophs. tried to bust our line. We beat H— out of them. Then we paraded around the campus, yelling 'Whoop it up for seventeen,' which is a wonderful song. Lip!!! This is SOME place. I have a big piece of some soph's shirt. Somebody has a big piece of my jersey. (Lord only knows who.) Tonight is the cannon rush so if you never hear of me again you'll know I died a freshman ... I could fill up a lot of writing paper telling you about the place, it is wonderful ... Well, Elizabeth, needless to say I am still your humble and devoted. Harry Jackson and I are trying to fix up a sc[h]eme to bring you and Kitty down ... How the plan will work I don't know, I am crazy to see you and sure hope you enjoy 'Miss Hartridge's School for Goils ..."

"... AS USUAL I WROTE THE LYRICS AND THEY'RE USING THE SAME OLD 'SHOW GIRL PICTURE' FOR ADVERTISING IN THE PAPERS ..." After nearly three years, Fitzgerald writes Elizabeth again, gossiping about old friends and making plans to meet. *[7 December 1916:]* "Is this the second letter I've ever written you or the third? Idea is this—you and Marie come down here Saturday afternoon—ine with us at The Princeton Inn ... Then we will proceed to the [Triangle] show at the Casino. This is not a gala occasion and you two will very conceivable *[sic]* be the only out of town girls down here but as the [Triangle] isn't coming to St. Paul we thought you might like to see the faculty performance ... [O]n Sunday we will amuse you to the best of our ability though I haven't the slightest idea how as Sunday here is desolate ... Of course I've got my same old chemistry condition and for the fourth time can't go on the trip or be in the show [produced by the Triangle Club]. As usual I wrote the lyrics and they're using the same old 'show girl picture' for advertising in the papers ..." During the second semester of his freshman year, Fitzgerald joined Princeton's theater group, the Triangle Club, as well as the university's humor magazine, *The Princeton Tiger.* He remained affiliated with these extra-curricular clubs when his grades allowed: Fitzgerald unfortunately had a difficult time with the academics at Princeton, failing many of his courses, repeating his entire Junior year, and eventually being forced to leave without a receiving his diploma.

$30,000-40,000

137. *From F. Scott Fitzgerald to a Nurse Unknown to His Biographers: Two Letters, Two Telegrams and Eight Inscribed Books.* Quill & Brush Catalogue (2004)

A separate catalogue for twelve Fitzgerald-Brownell items. The lot, which was offered at $275,000, was broken up.

Q&B
Quill & Brush
(301) 874-3200

Fax: (301)874-0824   E-mail: firsts@qbbooks.com
Home Page: http://www.qbbooks.com

The Quill & Brush has acquired a remarkable collection of eight inscribed books, together with two letters and two telegrams from F. Scott Fitzgerald to Pauline Phillips Brownell and/or her husband, George.

According to a brief, unpublished biography written by her daughter, Brownell was born in 1907 on a farm near Spruce Pine, North Carolina, and named Ruth Pauline Phillips by her adoptive family. She attended nursing school in Statesville, NC, where, by school tradition, she was nicknamed "Phil." She was working as a registered nurse in Asheville, NC, when she met Fitzgerald.

> *A significant event in her life was her experience as the private nurse of novelist F. Scott Fitzgerald. He had come to Asheville to be near his wife, Zelda, who was a patient in a near by sanitarium. While he was in Asheville, living in the lovely Grove Park Inn, he made the drunken mistake of diving into an empty swimming pool, and broke his collar bone; hence his need for private nursing care. One of her duties was to keep him away from the gin--not easy to do. During his recuperation, they spent many hours talking . . . They became good friends, and George and Phil [Pauline Brownell] showed Scott, and sometimes Zelda, much of the mountain area he wouldn't otherwise have seen. Scott enjoyed the Phillips farm and meeting the Phillips family.*
>
> — excerpt from "My Mother"

We are unable to locate mention of Pauline Phillips Brownell in Fitzgerald biographies, although it seems clear she was employed as his nurse after his diving accident in July 1936. References to private nurses employed during that period include mention of Dorothy Richardson (whose handwritten list of reading recommended by Fitzgerald is in the Matthew J Bruccoli Collection of Fitzgerald at the University of South Carolina) and a "Ms. Williamson." Neither Bruccoli, a Fitzgerald bibliographer, nor Jackson Bryer, the President of the Fitzgerald Society, has heard of Brownell. Andrew Turnbull, in his biography of Fitzgerald notes, "In periods of depression Fitzgerald was used to hiring a registered nurse to keep him company and help control his drinking." (Scott Fitzgerald, p. 275.) An observation that certainly fits the description of the terms of Brownell's employment, described by her daughter above. **It is our opinion that the fact that Brownell is unknown makes the contents of this collection all the more interesting, and valuable.**

$275,000. for the entire collection *—

* We would prefer to sell the collection in total because we feel the books should remain together. Therefore, we will hold the collection until July 9th. After that date, we will sell the books individually at the prices indicated herein. Please let us know as soon as possible if you are interested in any of the individual books, as we will give preference to the first order received.

Patricia and Allen Ahearn
1137 Sugarloaf Mountain Road, Dickerson, MD 20842

Q&B
Quill & Brush
(301) 874-3200

Fax: (301)874-0824   E-mail: firsts@qbbooks.com
Home Page: http://www.qbbooks.com

The relationship between Scott and Pauline seems to have been fairly close and warm, based on the letters in the collection. Unfortunately, only two letters survived. It is assumed that there were others but that Pauline threw them away.

Autograph Letter 1 (to be sold with *This Side of Paradise*): *a 202-word, Undated, Autograph Letter Signed in Pencil, Written on One Side of a Legal-size Sheet, It Reads in Part*:

Oak Hill Tryon, N.C.

Pauline:

I wrote you a month ago but it seemed a silly letter. I've had a strange two months trying to pull together the fragments of a lost year and I wonder if life will ever again make much sense...

I wonder if you are happier – somehow you seemed so when I saw you, even to my alcoholic eye. God, I hope so – it was sad to see anyone so young and with so much stuff in such a state of depression.* I wish I could have helped you as you tried to help me.

Anyhow I want to see you ... and talk to you and hear your adventures.

Best to George

Always affily Scott

* According to her daughter, Pauline was raised by her grandparents as one of their own but nonetheless suffered insecurities stemming from the stigma of being an illegitimate child. Her daughter writes: "We tried, but none of us–husband, children, friends–could ever unburden her of this sad, secret, unreasoning conviction of her own unworth—the curse of a tainted birth..." Presumably this is the state of depression that Fitzgerald speaks of in his letter to her.

Autograph Letter 2 (to be sold with *Tender Is the* **Night**): *a 277-word, Undated, Autograph Letter Signed in Pencil, Written on Both Sides of a Legal-size Sheet, It Reads in Part*:

Pauline:

Last night, tossing into the wastebasket the tattered shreds of a sweater once brought back to life by you—remember?—It occurred to me that you took with you some shirts & things you said ought to be mended...will you stick it in a box & give it to the bus driver?...

I still come to Ashville [sic] once a month but simply pick up Zelda & take her out...She is much better...

Even tho you don't answer letters I think of you and wonder about you... We did have a lot of good times mixed in with the bad.

Write me if only to tell me where you are.

Scott F

The phone book is out of date here & I don't have your address so I'm sending this to Appallachian [sic].

Pauline Brownell, circa 1930s

 Patricia and Allen Ahearn
1137 Sugarloaf Mountain Road, Dickerson, MD 20842

Q&B
Quill & Brush
(301) 874-3200

Fax: (301)874-0824   E-mail: firsts@qbbooks.com
Home Page: http://www.qbbooks.com

Telegram 1 (to be sold with *The Beautiful and The Damned*)
Western Union telegram dated November 27, 1936, with envelope:

Mrs George Brownell

Mountain Sanitarium Fletcher NCAR

Sorry we couldn't spend the evening together took Zelda out for two hours and felt rather unhappy that our thanksgiving midday dinner wasn't as successful as it might have been STOP Please stick it out STOP Affection always Scott

Telegram 2
(to be sold with *Flappers and Philosophers*)
Western Union telegram dated December 24, 1936, with envelope:

Mr and Mrs George Brownell Ashville NCAR

Thinking of you both tonight and tomorrow.
Scott

George Brownell, circa 1930s

EIGHT INSCRIBED BOOKS, AS FOLLOWS:

Patricia and Allen Ahearn
1137 Sugarloaf Mountain Road, Dickerson, MD 20842

Q&B
Quill & Brush
(301) 874-3200

Fax: (301)874-0824 E-mail: firsts@qbbooks.com
Home Page: http://www.qbbooks.com

This Side of Paradise - New York, 1931. His first book, originally published in 1920, this is the 17th printing (290 copies). About fine, lacking dustwrapper.

> For Pauline
> I could see her today
> as a child, bare-headed,
> bare-footed – and
> on bare-back, and
> it was touching
> to think of her so
> Scott

— $22,500., together with Autograph Letter 1 —

Patricia and Allen Ahearn
1137 Sugarloaf Mountain Road, Dickerson, MD 20842

Q&B
Quill & Brush
(301) 874-3200

Fax: (301)874-0824   E-mail: firsts@qbbooks.com
Home Page: http://www.qbbooks.com

Tales of the Jazz Age - New York, 1922. First edition, with "an" for "and" in line 6 on page 232. Minor cover wear and spine lettering fading, otherwise very good, in very nice, bright dustwrapper.

> For two people who lived
> after the Jazz age
> + had neither its
> wild pleasures nor
> its terrible hangover
> — in hopes that
> They never will
>   F Scott Fitzgerald

— $45,000. —

Patricia and Allen Ahearn
1137 Sugarloaf Mountain Road, Dickerson, MD 20842

Q&B
Quill & Brush
(301) 874-3200

Fax: (301)874-0824 E-mail: firsts@qbbooks.com
Home Page: http://www.qbbooks.com

*Patton Memorial Library
(Their property —
not to be filched or
stolen)*

The Beautiful and the Damned - New York, 1922. First edition, third printing, published one month after the first printing. Although there was a Patton Memorial Hospital nearby (in Henderson, NC), we could not determine whether it actually had a Library. As this book was with the other books inscribed to Pauline and/or her husband, we assume it is a joking inscription to the Brownells, perhaps in reference to Fizgerald's treatment there after his accident (although there is no evidence of such).

F Scott Fitzgerald

— $7,500., together with Telegram 1 —

Patricia and Allen Ahearn
1137 Sugarloaf Mountain Road, Dickerson, MD 20842

Q&B
Quill & Brush
(301) 874-3200

Fax: (301)874-0824   E-mail: firsts@qbbooks.com
Home Page: http://www.qbbooks.com

Flappers and Philosophers - New York, 1922. Originally published in 1920, this is the 6th printing. Tiny tear at head of spine, otherwise fine and bright.

For George & Pauline from the bookseller (F Scott Fitzgerald told me to send you this. I will bill you 1st of the month)

— $17,500., together with Telegram 2 —

Patricia and Allen Ahearn
1137 Sugarloaf Mountain Road, Dickerson, MD 20842

Q&B
Quill & Brush
(301) 874-3200

Fax: (301)874-0824 E-mail: firsts@qbbooks.com
Home Page: http://www.qbbooks.com

The Great Gatsby - New York, 1925. First edition, second printing with the textual corrections. Minor cover wear but still very good or better, lacking dustwrapper.

For George Brownell with best wishes for the new house, from one of its well-wishers

Scott Fitzgerald

— $90,000. —

Patricia and Allen Ahearn
1137 Sugarloaf Mountain Road, Dickerson, MD 20842

Q&B

Quill & Brush

(301) 874-3200

Fax: (301)874-0824 E-mail: firsts@qbbooks.com
Home Page: http://www.qbbooks.com

All the Sad Young Men - New York, 1926. First edition. The type on page 38 is perfect, whereas the page number 90 and the type on page 248 are battered. There is a tiny tear at head of spine and a few pages have some finger marks, otherwise a bright fine copy in dustwrapper with one hinge split and repaired on verso with archival tape, spine a little darkened and minor chipping on spine ends.

*For George & Pauline
with affectionate regards
from
Scott*

— $27,500. —

Patricia and Allen Ahearn
1137 Sugarloaf Mountain Road, Dickerson, MD 20842

Q&B
Quill & Brush
(301) 874-3200

Fax: (301)874-0824 E-mail: firsts@qbbooks.com
Home Page: http://www.qbbooks.com

Tender is the Night - New York, 1934. First edition, third printing with "Devereux" for "Charles" in line 17 on page 320. Not sure which shoulder he broke but he may have written this with his left hand. Some finger smudging in the text otherwise internally good or better with cover worn on edges and spine.

> For Pauline Brownell
> from a broken
> shouldered
> veteran of the
> pools
> in much gratitude
> F Scott Fitzgerald
> 1936

— $20,000., together with Autograph Letter 2 —

Patricia and Allen Ahearn
1137 Sugarloaf Mountain Road, Dickerson, MD 20842

Q&B
Quill & Brush
(301) 874-3200

Fax: (301)874-0824　　E-mail: firsts@qbbooks.com
Home Page: http://www.qbbooks.com

Taps at Reveille - New York, 1935. First edition, first issue with **misprints on pages 350 and 351 hand-corrected by Fitzgerald and with "Repeat from <u>Tender</u>" in margin on page 407.** *[please see next page].* Three small spots on top edge and cover shows minor edgewear, otherwise very good or better in worn dustwrapper with split at front spine hinge neatly repaired with archival tape on verso.

*For George & Pauline
in memory of
another amusing and
unforgettable trip
Asheville - Spruce Pine
1936
F Scott Fitzgerald*

— $45,000. *(please see next page)* —

 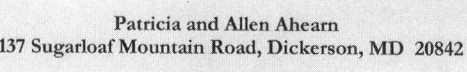

Patricia and Allen Ahearn
1137 Sugarloaf Mountain Road, Dickerson, MD 20842

Q&B
Quill & Brush
(301) 874-3200

Fax: (301)874-0824   E-mail: firsts@qbbooks.com
Home Page: http://www.qbbooks.com

HAND-CORRECTIONS IN THE SHORT STORY "ONE INTERNE," IN *TAPS AT REVEILLE*

be right and Doctor Norton's would be wrong. In that moment he would emancipate himself—he need not base himself on the adding machine-calculating machine-probability machine-St. Francis of Assis machine any longer.

Bill Tulliver had not arrived unprovoked at this pitch of egotism. He was the fifth in an unbroken series of Dr.

[Page 350]

"Oh, yes." She was still breathing hard; her bosom rose, putting out its eternal promises, as if the breath she had taken in were the last breath left in the world.

[Page 351] "Oh, catch it—oh, catch it and take it—oh, catch it," she sighed. "I realized right away that they were students. I shouldn't have gone by there tonight."

SIGNIFICANT NOTATION IN FITZGERALD'S HAND IN "BABYLON REVISITED," THE FINAL STORY IN *TAPS AT REVEILLE*, PAGE 407, LAST PARAGRAPH

In the final paragraph of "Babylon Revisited," (see below) Fitzgerald expressed Charlie Wales' frustration with the words "He wasn't young any more, with a lot of nice thoughts and dreams to have by himself." He used very similar phrasing to express Dick Diver's thoughts at the end of *Tender Is the Night*: "He was not young any more with a lot of nice thoughts and dreams to have about himself ...".

He would come back some day; they couldn't make him pay forever. But he wanted his child, and nothing was much good now, beside that fact. He wasn't young any more, with a lot of nice thoughts and dreams to have by himself. He was absolutely sure Helen wouldn't have wanted him to be so alone.

F. Scott Fitzgerald wrote "Babylon Revisited" in December 1930, and the short story was published in The Saturday Evening Post *on February 21, 1931. Fitzgerald revised the story for* Taps at Reveille, *a collection of his short fiction published in 1935 . . . Fitzgerald would not hesitate to lift passages from his magazine work for use in his novels. This necessitated his rewriting the stories . . . Thus Fitzgerald revised "Babylon Revisited" for* Taps at Reveille *. . . Nearly a hundred revisions were incorporated; of those, only five passages were revised because of their incorporation into his novel* Tender Is the Night, *one of which, nevertheless, would appear in* Taps, *much to Fitzgerald's chagrin.*

— Thomas A. Larson, "F. Scott Fitzgerald's 'Babylon Revisited':
A Long Expostulation and Explanation"

Patricia and Allen Ahearn
1137 Sugarloaf Mountain Road, Dickerson, MD 20842

138. Peter Harrington Catalogue (April–May 2005)

MacLeish was not the "founding editor of *Fortune*." The statement about "the outrages Fitzgerald had written" is baffling.

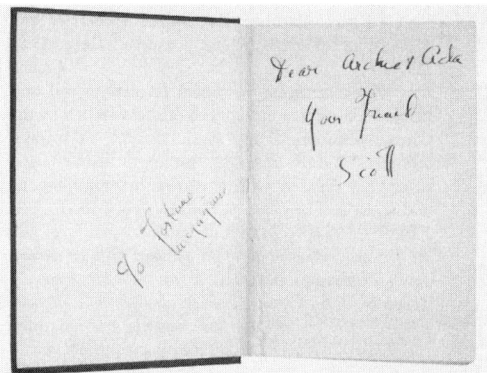

45.   **FITZGERALD, F. Scott.** Tender Is the Night. A Romance. *New York, Scribner's, 1934* [27003]   £30,000
8vo. Original green cloth, titles to spine gilt. With the remains of the dustjacket. Margins very lightly age toned, front free endpaper excised - almost certainly by the author (see below), spine somewhat dull and a trifle marked a very good copy in the remains of the dustjacket lacking the tell-tale front flap and large pieces from the front panel and elsewhere.

FIRST EDITION First Printing. With the author's signed presentation inscription to the first extant blank, "Dear Archie & Ada / Your Friend / Scott". And with Fitzgerald's further holograph admonition to the front pastedown, "c/o Fortune / magazine". The recipients were Archibald and Ada MacLeish. "Archie" was the founding editor of Fortune and a key figure in the lives of Scott and Zelda during their French years. Even closer friends to the Murphy's - on whom, of course the novel's central characters were based - it fell to MacLeish to write one of the earliest letters of "apology" to the couple for what they perceived to be the outrages Fitzgerald had written.
"The beginning [of Tender Is the Night]...is a wonderful evocation of the second phase of American expatriates ensconced in glittering villas on the Riviera in contrast to the home-spun tipplers of The Sun Also Rises. The break-down of a marriage in which the doctor-husband [Dick Diver], having fulfilled his healing role, makes it inevitable that his wife [Nicole] should leave him, is described with flashes of genius by an expert in self-destruction, and there is a haunting account of Fitzgerald's own pet drunk, the story-teller Ring Lardner (Abe North) and of the predicament of 'grace under pressure' from too many parties and too much money"(Connolly).
Bruccoli A15.1.a; Connolly, The Modern Movement 79

139. *The Library of George Cosmatos: Part 2.* Sotheby's, New York, Sale Number 8145 (17 June 2005)

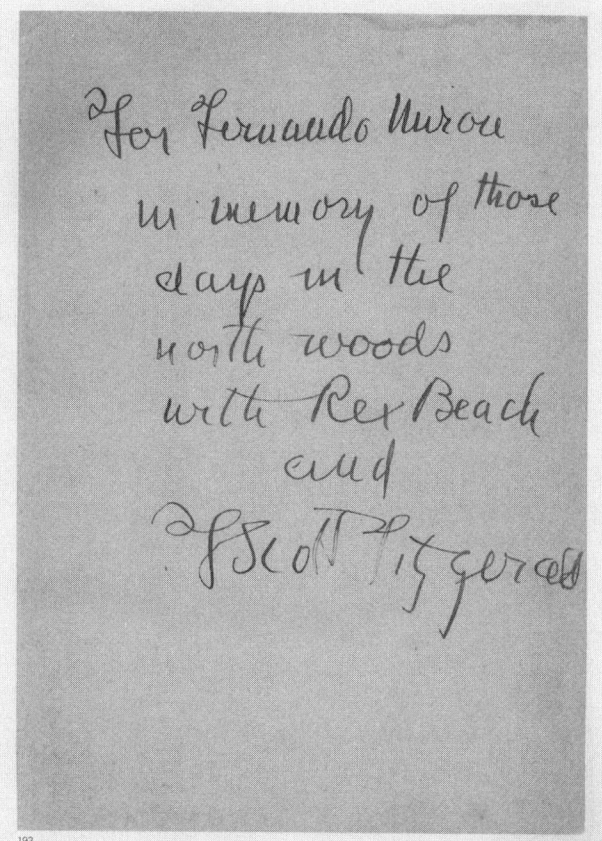

193 **FITZGERALD, F. SCOTT.** *This Side of Paradise. New York: Charles Scribner's Sons, 1920*

FIRST EDITION, sixth printing, PRESENTATION COPY INSCRIBED BY THE AUTHOR on front endpaper ("For Fernando Miron | in memory of those | days in the | north woods | with Rex Beach | and | F Scott Fitzgerald"), 8vo (7½ x 5⅛in.; 190 x 130mm.), original dark green cloth, collector's cloth folding box, *light browning, worming to corners of last few gatherings, some wear to covers, small loss to head of spine*

REFERENCES: Bruccoli A 5.I.f

$10,000-15,000

$5,100 w̄ premium

140. *The Donald G. Drapkin Library*. Christie's, New York, Sale Number 1631 (29 June 2005)

130
FITZGERALD, F. Scott. *The Great Gatsby*. New York: Charles Scribner's Sons, 1925.

8°. Original green cloth, spine lettered in gilt (slight wear to extremities); quarter morocco folding case with onlaid cloth design based on dust jacket. *Provenance*: Margaret Turnbull, see note below (presentation inscription from the author on front free endpaper).

FIRST EDITION, second printing. PRESENTATION COPY, INSCRIBED BY FITZGERALD on the front free endpaper: "With the pleasant memories of La Paix behind me, alas and alack! Souvenir of 1932-1933 for M.T. from her—at least from one who was almost made to feel like—guest. / F. Scott Fitzgerald." The inscription refers to the time Scott and Zelda Fitzgerald spent with the Turnbull's at "La Paix," a fifteen-room Victorian frame house on the 28-acre Turnbull estate in Rodgers Forge, near Towson, just north of Baltimore. The Fitzgerald's lived in the house during a period when Zelda was having bouts with her mental illness. It was during this important, and somewhat sober, period in his career that Fitzgerald completed his second masterpiece *Tender Is the Night*, as well as some short stories.

"The Fitzgerald's retreat to the quiet, isolated La Paix was, as Zelda remarked, a notable contrast to the wild weekend parties at Ellerslie. In the fall of 1933 Fitzgerald said they had dined out only four times in the last two years. Zelda remained near Phipps for frequent consultations with her doctors, and the Turnbull family, who owned the property and lived in the main house on the estate, provided another stabilizing influence. Bayard Turnbull, a wealthy architect and graduate of Johns Hopkins, was (according to his younger daughter) a rather distant Victorian gentleman who did not drink and was careful about money. He disapproved of Fitzgerald. But his wife, Margaret, a proper but cultured woman, shared Scott's interest in literature and became a good friend. The Turnbulls had three children—Eleanor, Frances and the eleven-year-old Andrew, who was the same age as Scottie" (Myers, pp. 224-25). It was Margaret Turnbull who introduced Fitzgerald to T.S. Eliot when he was lecturing on the Metaphysical poets at Johns Hopkins University.

A VERY FINE ASSOCIATION COPY OF FITZGERALD'S MASTERPIECE. Bruccoli A11.1.b; Connolly, *The Modern Movement* 48.

Estimate: $40,000-60,000

$40,000

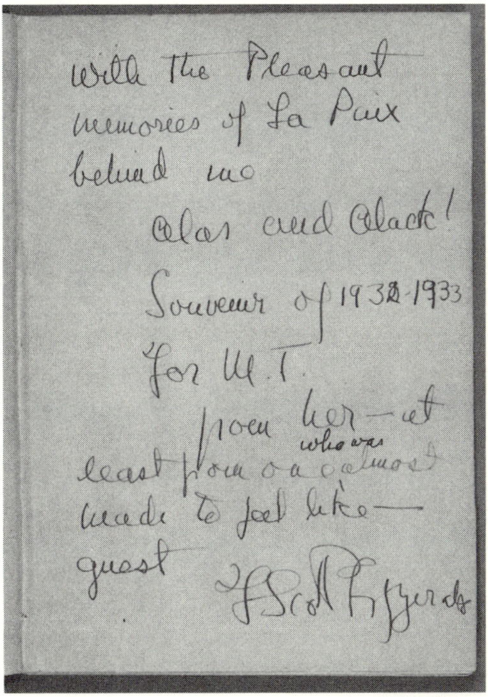

With the Pleasant
memories of La Paix
behind me
    Alas and Black!
Souvenir of 1932-1933
For M.T.
    from her — at
least from one who was almost
made to feel like —
guest
            F Scott Fitzgerald

Item 130

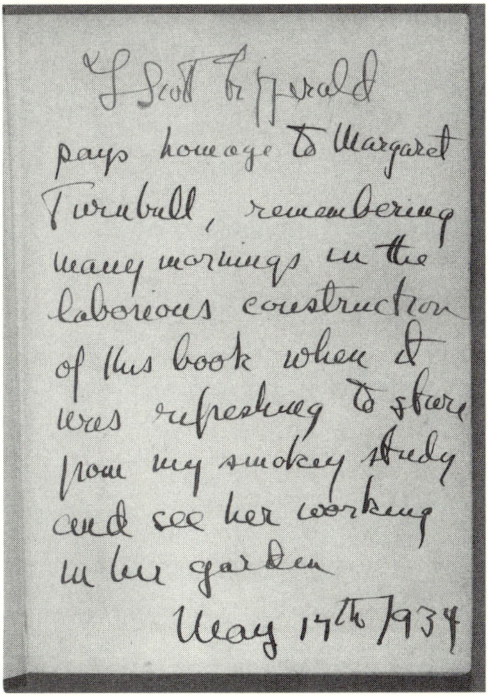

F Scott Fitzgerald
pays homage to Margaret
Turnbull, remembering
many mornings in the
laborious construction
of this book when it
was refreshing to stare
from my smokey study
and see her working
in her garden
        May 14th 1934

Item 131

131
FITZGERALD, F. Scott. *Tender is the Night.* New York: Charles Scribner's Sons, 1934.

8". Original green cloth, gilt-lettered on spine (minor wear to spine ends and extremities); dust jacket (minor edgewear, spine panel slightly dulled). Provenance: Margaret Turnbull, see previous lot.

FIRST EDITION, FIRST PRINTING, IN FIRST STATE DUST JACKET. PRESENTATION COPY, INSCRIBED BY FITZGERALD TO MARGARET TURNBULL on the front free endpaper: "F. Scott Fitzgerald pays homage to Margaret Turnbull, remembering many mornings in the laborious construction of this book when it was refreshing to stare from my smokey study and see her working in her garden. May 17th 1934."

The Fitzgeralds stayed at La Paix from May 1932 to November 1933, and its solitude offered Scott a more condusive environment to work than their previous residence at Ellerslie. Zelda split her day between La Paix and the Phipps Clinic, where she was undergoing treatment for her mental illness. It was during this important period at La Paix that Fitzgerald was able to complete his second masterpiece, *Tender is the Night*—making this inscription all the more poignant. The smoke reference may refer to the fire at La Paix in August 1933, which was accidentally started by Zelda while burning some things in an unused fireplace there. The fire damaged the second story and roof at La Paix, but Fitzgerald rescued his manuscripts from destruction, and managed to convince Bayard Turnbull to leave the reconstruction until he completed work on *Tender Is the Night*. A VERY FINE ASSOCIATION COPY. Bruccoli A15.1.a; Connolly, *The Modern Movement* 79.

Estimate: $40,000-60,000

$40,000

141. David Schulson Autographs Catalogue 126 (July 2005)

'Stupidest tax collector since Louis XV'

39. **FITZGERALD, F. SCOTT** (1896-1940). American author regarded as the literary spokesman of the Jazz Age.

Intriguing Autograph Letter Signed, folio, Hotel Rennert, Baltimore, MD, April 6, 1931.

To Miss Silcox, possibly an accountant. Fitzgerald lengthily discusses tax exemptions for writers. "I hate to call on you once again even before I have had a chance to thank you for your past favor, but I am embroiled with the stupidest tax collector since Louis XV. He refuses to allow me one cent of deductions for typing (though I can't type a word myself); office rent ect [sic] because I have not kept expense books! However the immediate matter is the moot question of earned income. Can you tell me if any writers pay taxes on magazine stories as unearned income? Do not all writers that you know of list their stories as earned income and are they ever questioned? Is not the ruling vague and in practice haven't the authorities in Washington recognized the money earned by a writer as earned income? Can you write me about this? I believe I am merely up against the stupidity of one man but will be glad to know if you are Cognizant of the general precedent and any variants thereupon that may have reached your ears." In a postscript Fitzgerald continues, "P.S. needless to say he did not allow the movie gift as a charity." A beautifully penned letter, signed "Sincerely and gratefully, F. Scott Fitzgerald."

During the 1920's his income from all sources averaged under $25,000, which was not considered a fortune. Scott and Zelda did spend money faster than he earned it, and, Fitzgerald did write so eloquently about the effects of money on character and managing one's finances. Therefore, this most provocative letter dealing with his struggles with money is quite fascinating. The Fitzgeralds returned to America in the fall of 1931 and rented a house in Montgomery, later making a second unsuccessful trip to Hollywood. Zelda suffered a relapse of mental instability in February, 1932 and entered Johns Hopkins Hospital in Baltimore. She spent the rest of her life as a resident or outpatient of sanatoriums. This letter, beautiful in appearance, is most significant for his battle with a tax collector to help him navigate his financial existence. $14,500.00

142. Bonhams & Butterfields Auction Catalogue (19 February 2006)

H. N. Swanson was one of Fitzgerald's agents for his movie work. "Swannie" represented important writers including William Faulkner, Raymond Chandler, and Elmore Leonard. As editor of *College Humor* he had offered $10,000 for prepublication serial rights to *The Great Gatsby* in 1925.

The fourteen Fitzgerald items brought a total of $73,494 with buyers' premiums. Item 1128 was recatalogued twice in 2006 by Stuart Lutz Historic Documents for $4,000.

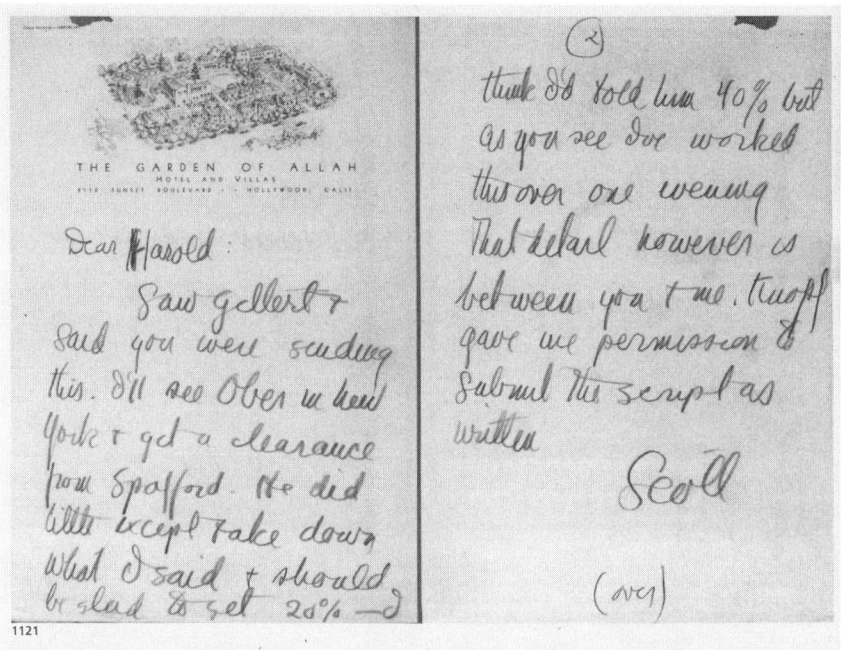

1121

1121
FITZGERALD, FRANCIS SCOTT KEY. 1896-1940.
Autograph Letter Signed ("Scott"), in pencil, 2pp recto and verso, 4to, Hollywood, n.d. [but 1937-1938], to Harold, on Garden of Allah letterhead, pinholes and chip at upper left corner, leaf lightly creased and toned.

This letter most likely accompanied a script submission by Fitzgerald. In full: *"Dear Harold: Saw Gellert & said you were sending this. I'll see Ober in New York & get a clearance from Spofford. He did little except take down what I said & should be glad to get 20%—I think I'd told him 40% but as you see I've worked this over one evening. That detail however is between you & me. Knopf gave me permission to submit the script as written. / Scott."* "Ober in New York" is Fitzgerald's agent Harold Ober, who probably must deal with the sticky issue of co-authorship with the mysterious Mr. Spofford. "Knopf" is M-G-M producer Edwin Knopf, brother of publisher Alfred, who frequently worked with Fitzgerald during his Hollywood tenure.
See illustration.
$4,000 - 6,000

$3,585 - BP

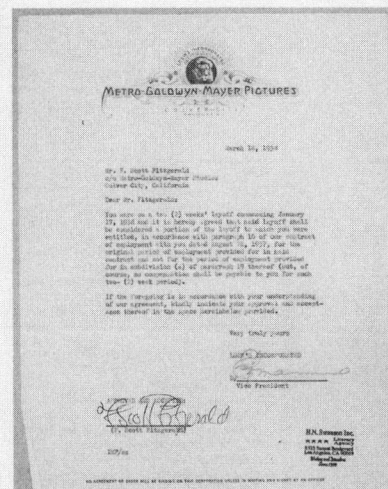
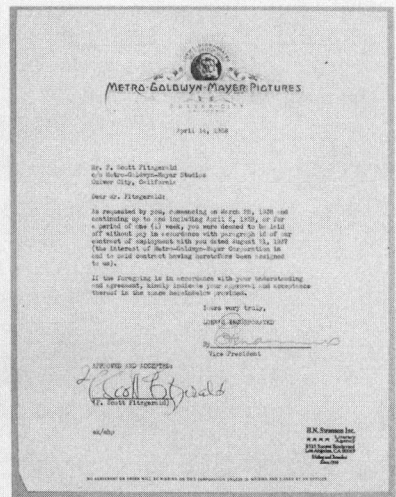

1122
FITZGERALD, FRANCIS SCOTT KEY.
Document Signed ("F. Scott Fitzgerald"), 1 p, 4to, Culver City, March 18, 1938, on M-G-M letterhead, being a typed carbon of an agreement between Metro-Goldwyn-Mayer and the author regarding a period of two weeks layoff without pay, with Swanson Agency stamp to lower left corner, leaf with creasing and war, lower left corner creased, some toning overall.

Scott Fitzgerald first went in Hollywood in 1927, when he was hired to write an original flapper comedy for United Artists. He returned in 1931 to work for Irving Thalberg on the Jean Harlow classic, *Red-Headed Woman*. His third sojourn in Hollywood lasted from 1937 until his death in December of 1940. Normally the studios owned or had a proprietary interest in all creative works produced by staff writers while under contract, but agent H.N. Swanson was careful to obtain "layoff periods"—gaps of a few weeks during which Fitzgerald could work on his own projects while in Hollywood. This contract refers to a brief two-week period during which M-G-M respects Fitzgerald's right to work on his own material (without, however, collecting a salary from the studio). In part: *"Dear Mr. Fitzgerald: / You were on a two (2) weeks' layoff commencing January 17, 1938 and it is hereby agreed that said layoff shall be considered a portion of the layoff to which you were entitled, in accordance with paragraph 16 of our contract of employment with you dated August 21, 1937, for the original period of employment provided for in said contract and not for the period of employment provided for in subdivision (a) of paragraph 19 thereof (but, of course, no compensation shall be payable to you for such two (2) week period)."*
See illustration.
$1,500 - 2,000

1123
FITZGERALD, FRANCIS SCOTT KEY.
Document Signed ("F. Scott Fitzgerald"), 1 p, 4to, Culver City, April 14, 1938, on M-G-M letterhead, being a typed carbon of an agreement between the studio and Fitzgerald regarding a layoff period, with Swanson Agency stamp to lower right corner, very light creasing and toning, lower left corner creased.

In part: *"As requested by you, commencing on March 28, 1938 and continuing up to and including April 3, 1938, or for a period of one (1) week, you were deemed to be laid off without pay in accordance with paragraph 16 of our contract of employment with you dated August 21, 1937 (the interest of Metro-Goldwyn-Mayer Corporation in and to said contract having heretofore been assigned to us)."*
See illustration.
$1,500 - 2,000

March 25, 1939

Mr. F. Scott Fitzgerald
Hollywood, California

Dear Mr. Fitzgerald:

Please take notice that your employment agreement with the undersigned corporation, dated March 1, 1939, is hereby terminated as of March 25, 1939, at the end of said day.

Yours very truly,

PARAMOUNT PICTURES INC.

By: _____
    Vice President

Form O.K. _____

ACCEPTED:

F. Scott Fitzgerald

ms

1125

1124
FITZGERALD, FRANCIS SCOTT KEY.
M-G-M FIRES FITZGERALD.
Document Signed ("F. Scott Fitzgerald"), 2 pp, 4to, Culver City, January 16, 1939, on M-G-M letterhead, being a typed carbon regarding Fitzgerald's release from his studio contract, with Swanson Agency stamp at center right of page 2, staple perforations to upper margins of both leaves, ink smudge to lower right corner of 1st leaf, light creasing and toning.

After a year and a half under contract to Metro—with only one earned screen credit during that time—Fitzgerald was released by the studio. This document confirms his departure, with the studio retaining the right to use the author's name and likeness to promote the results of his services. In part: "*Dear Mr. Fitzgerald: / This will confirm the following agreement between us: / 1. Your employment under any and all previous agreements between us and particularly under that certain contract of employment between us dated August 21, 1937, as amended, is hereby cancelled and terminated as of January 20, 1939. Each of us hereby releases the other and from all further liability and obligations under said contract from and after that date, and of and from all claims and demands of every kind which either of us ever had or now has or may hereafter have or claim to have against the other, arising out of or based upon, directly or indirectly, all such contracts and agreements and particularly said contract of August 21, 1937. / 2. Nothing herein contained, however, shall be construed to constitute a waiver or release by us of any rights which, we may have in and to the results and proceeds of services rendered by you*

for us under all such contracts and agreements and particularly said contract of August 21, 1937, or of the right to use your name, voice, and/or likeness in connection with the advertising and exploitation relating to such results and proceeds of your services, it being agreed that we reserve all of said rights."
$2,000 - 3,000

1125
FITZGERALD, FRANCIS SCOTT KEY.
FITZGERALD'S PARAMOUNT CONTRACTS.
This lot features three documents bound together in off-white wraps reading "Paramount Pictures Inc. and F. Scott Fitzgerald / Agreement / Dated March 1, 1939, bound at left margin with staples:
1. Mimeographed Document Signed ("F. Scott Fitzgerald"), 4 pp, 4to, Hollywood, CA, March 1, 1939, being an employment agreement between the author and Paramount Pictures for a salary of $1,500 per week, also signed by two unidentified Paramount executives, pages creased and lightly toned.
2. Typed Document Signed ("F. Scott Fitzgerald"), 1 p, 4to, [Hollywood, CA], March 25, 1939, being a carbon copy of notice to Fitzgerald terminating his employment by Paramount, also signed by two Paramount executives, page lightly creased.
3. Typed Letter Signed ("Scott"), 1 p, 4to, Encino, CA, May 12, 1939, to H.N. Swanson asking for revisions to a new Paramount contract, page creased and toned.

After being dropped by M-G-M, Fitzgerald worked a number of freelance writing jobs. The first was the disastrous *Winter Carnival* for United Artists, where Fitzgerald was fired after a two-week drunk at Dartmouth College. Soon after returning to Hollywood, Swanson got Fitzgerald work at Paramount on *Air Raid*, a film ultimately never produced.
See illustration.
$5,000 - 7,000

1126
FITZGERALD, FRANCIS SCOTT KEY.
Document Signed ("F. Scott Fitzgerald"), 1 p, 4to, Hollywood, April 13, 1939, being a typed carbon of an agreement between Fitzgerald and Paramount Pictures, Inc., with Swanson Agency stamp at lower right corner, page lightly creased and toned.

This contract, written six weeks after he was originally hired by Paramount, refers to the rewrites he was additionally commissioned to do—and also confirms that the finished product has been delivered. In part: "*Dear Mr. Fitzgerald: / This will confirm our agreement as follows: / 1. That after the termination of your employment agreement with the undersigned corporation dated March 1, 1939, you and the undersigned corporation agreed that you would render your services as an employee of the undersigned corporation, to write certain additional material in connection with the screen play of the motion picture photoplay tentatively entitled*

> April 13, 1939.
>
> Mr. F. Scott Fitzgerald
> Hollywood, California
>
> Dear Mr. Fitzgerald:
>
> This will confirm our agreement as follows:
>
> 1. That after the termination of your employment agreement with the undersigned corporation dated March 1, 1939, you and the undersigned corporation agreed that you would render your services as an employee of the undersigned corporation, to write certain additional material in connection with the screen play of the motion picture photoplay tentatively entitled AIR RAID for a total compensation of One Thousand Two Hundred Dollars ($1,200.00).
>
> 2. That all other provisions of your employment agreement with the undersigned corporation dated March 1, 1939 will be applicable to the employment referred to in Paragraph 1 hereof, and to the material written by you pursuant thereto.
>
> 3. That you have completed and delivered to the undersigned corporation said additional material.
>
> 4. That you do hereby acknowledge receipt of the sum of One Thousand Two Hundred Dollars ($1,200.00) as payment in full in accordance with the employment agreement referred to in Paragraph 1 hereof.
>
> If the foregoing correctly sets forth our understanding, please signify your acceptance at the place indicated below.
>
> Very truly yours,
>
> PARAMOUNT PICTURES INC.
>
> By _____
> Vice President
>
> ACCEPTED:
> F Scott Fitzgerald

1126

AIR RAID for a total compensation of One Thousand Two Hundred Dollars ($1,200.00). / 2. That all other provisions of your employment agreement with the undersigned corporation dated March 1, 1939 will be applicable to the employment referred to in Paragraph 1 hereof, and to the material written by you pursuant thereto. / 3. That you have completed and delivered to the undersigned corporation said additional material. / 4. That you do hereby acknowledge receipt of the sum of One Thousand Two Hundred Dollars ($1,200.00) as payment in full in accordance with the employment agreement referred to in Paragraph 1 hereof." See illustration.
$1,500 - 2,000

1127
FITZGERALD, FRANCIS SCOTT KEY.
Document Signed ("F. Scott Fitzgerald"), 1 p, 4to, Hollywood, April 13, 1939, being an agreement between Fitzgerald and Paramount Pictures, Inc., Fitzgerald signature crossed through, text also crossed through, page lightly creased and toned.

"This is obviously an earlier draft of the previous contract, signed by Scott perhaps before Swanson realized the document should include reference to the fact that Fitzgerald has in fact concluded the work he was originally hired to do.
$800 - 1,200

1128
FITZGERALD, FRANCIS SCOTT KEY.
Typed Letter Signed ("Scott"), 1 p, 4to, Encino, CA, June 19, 1939, to H.N. Swanson, on typing paper, two small perforations to lower margin not affecting text, ¼ inch closed tear at upper margin, light creasing and toning.

Fitzgerald sends this note along with an unknown short story manuscript submitted to Swanson in the hopes he can make a sale to one of the studios. In part: "Dear Swanie:- / Though this story was actually commenced before 'Gone With the Wind' was published, the Collier's man told me it probably wouldn't be scheduled before a couple of months so it had best be referred to as a new story, which in part it is. / I have looked over the list of story needs you sent me and it doesn't seem particularly to apply to any of them but perhaps will suggest something to you."
$1,500 - 2,000

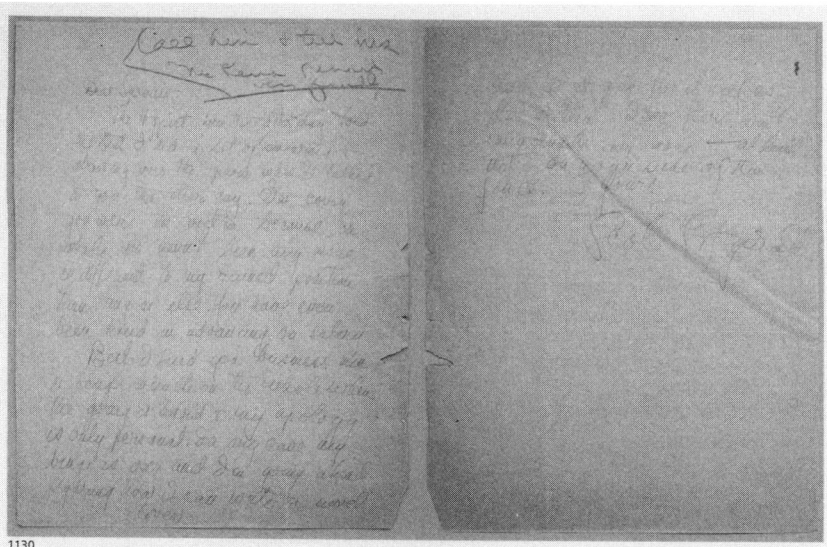

1130

1129
FITZGERALD, FRANCIS SCOTT KEY.
Document Signed ("F. Scott Fitzgerald"), 3 pp, 4to, Los Angeles, September 8, 1939, on Samuel Goldwyn Inc. letterhead, being an employment agreement between the studio and Fitzgerald to work on the film *Raffles*, also signed by JAMES ROOSEVELT, perforations at upper right corner, very light creasing and toning, otherwise fine. Together with unsigned "exhibit A" form and TLS from the Goldwyn studios transmitting the contract to the Swanson agency.

In late 1939 Fitzgerald landed a job working at the Goldwyn studio on the remake of *Raffles*, the story of an aristocratic jewel thief with a penchant for returning the property he has stolen. The length of employment is left open in this contract, and Fitzgerald wound up working for only one week on the film at a salary of $1500. Incidentally, the executive signing on behalf of the Goldwyn Studios is James Roosevelt, eldest son of Franklin and Eleanor Roosevelt who, after a stint in his father's administration and as a representative for the insurance and wheat industries, went to work for Sam Goldwyn.
$2,500 - 3,500

1130
FITZGERALD, FRANCIS SCOTT KEY.
FITZGERALD APOLOGIZES FOR HIS BEHAVIOR WHILE ON A BINGE.
Autograph Letter Signed ("Scott Fitzgerald"), in pencil, 2 pp recto and verso, 4to, n.p., n.d., to H.N. Swanson, on typing paper, with annotation by Swanson to upper right corner, page creased horizontally and vertically, chips at right margin and lower right corner, leaf significantly toned.

This letter was most likely written in 1939 after Fitzgerald was let go by M-G-M and was struggling to succeed as a freelance writer. He writes this note to apologize to Swanson after an unpleasant phone call. In full: "The typist here the other day told me that I did a lot of swearing & shouting over the phone when I talked to you the other day. I'm sorry you were the victim because on [the] whole you haven't been any more indifferent to my ruined position than anyone else. You have even been kind in advancing me salary. / But I find you business men a tough bunch on the whole when the going is hard & my apology is only personal. In any case my binge is over and I'm going ahead figuring how I can write a novel (over) and let it pay for itself as it's written. I see there aren't any angles any more—at feast not on your side of the fence." In late 1939 Fitzgerald hatched the idea of serializing his novel-in-progress, *The Last Tycoon*, in one of the popular magazines that had regularly published his short fiction. *Collier's* was interested, but Fitzgerald felt their offer was too low; the *Saturday Evening Post* passed altogether.
See illustration.
$5,000 - 7,000

Bonhams & Butterfields

1131
FITZGERALD, FRANCIS SCOTT KEY.
Typed Letter Signed ("F. Scott Fitzgerald"), 1 p, 4to, Encino, CA, April 1, 1940, to H.N. Swanson, on typing paper, page creased and toned, minor chipping at right margin. Together with typed carbon (unsigned) of H.N. Swanson's response to Fitzgerald's letter dated April 2, 1940 and a Typed Note Initialed ("H.O") of Harold Ober, 1 p, 8vo, New York, January 12, 1940, to H.N. Swanson, regarding Fitzgerald's break with his agent.

New York literary agent Harold Ober had long been one of Fitzgerald's biggest supporters, providing encouragement and even loans when the author fell on hard times. Ober even served as a surrogate parent to Scottie Fitzgerald, Scott and Zelda's only daughter, paying her tuition at Vassar after Fitzgerald's death. In late 1939 Ober abruptly and without explanation stopped advancing Fitzgerald money against future sales. (It appears that Ober was suffering his own financial crisis, but never shared this information with Fitzgerald.) Fitzgerald was angry and hurt, and, after a period of time, broke off his relationship with Ober—and by extension, H.N. Swanson. He sends this letter to Swanson in April of 1940: "*Have you or Carter, or Mollson, or Lewis by any chance got a cope [sic] of my story 'The Intimate Strangers', the McCall story. It seems to have disappeared and it is so hard to dig up this stuff from magazine files.*" Swanie filed this note with a carbon of his letter written the next day sending along the story, and with Harold Ober's memo from January 12, 1940 regarding Fitzgerald's defection. In full: "*I am very sorry about Scott Fitzgerald. I hope that after he has fooled around for a while with Leland Heyward he will realize what we have done for him and come back to us. I never imagined that Scott could act as he has acted. I am afraid it is the effect of Hollywood.*"
See illustration.
$1,500 - 2,000

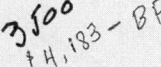

1132
FITZGERALD, FRANCIS SCOTT KEY.
"*FAR FROM BEING SICK, I'VE DONE TWENTY ESQUIRE STORIES AND SIX CHAPTERS OF A NOVEL....*"
Typed Letter Signed ("Scott"), 1 p, 4to, Encino, CA, May 20, 1940, to H.N. Swanson, on typing paper, leaf creased and lightly toned, minor wear at right margin, with typed memo initialed of Harold Ober dated July 3, 1940 and a second unsigned typed carbon from Harold Ober dated August 2, 1940.

Fitzgerald writes a sharply worded note to his former agent responding to gossip about his health that has gotten back to him. In part: "*Dear Swanie:- / Daughter writes me that Mrs. Ober told her that you said I was ill again. It worried Scottie. Swanie, that was last year, remember? I was sick and I told you about it. Now, far from being sick, I've done twenty Esquire stories and six chapters from a novel beside the picture job I am now doing. / Of course, Mrs. Ober might have gotten the news some time ago but I simply want to correct any impression you may have that I'm ill at present.*" Fitzgerald's tone is petulant: he doesn't want his spurned agent to bad-mouth him, and at the same time, he wants the office to know just how productive he's been since the split. The novel Fitzgerald refers to in this note is his unfinished masterpiece, *The Last Tycoon*.
See illustration.
$2,000 - 3,000

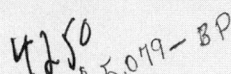

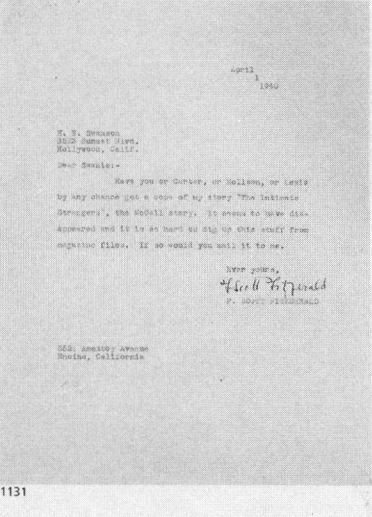

1131

1132

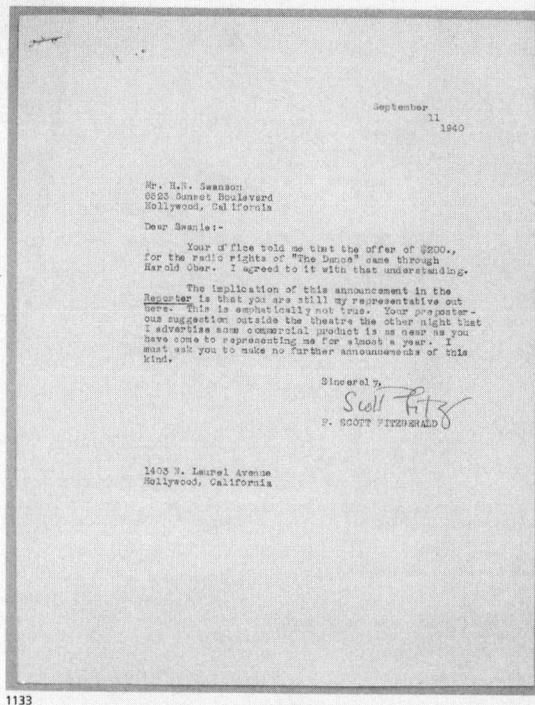

1133

to get a portion of the commission. / I, like to think that if our radio lads could bring you an offer for the rights of some of your published stories that you would still want us to negotiate for you. / At all events, Scott, I wish you would answer this last question for me. I feel I have known you for a long time and worked for you for a long time just as Harold Ober has. The fact that you are no longer with us as a client shouldn't mean that you misunderstand or mistrust our motives. I will always be a booster of yours."
See illustration.
$2,000 - 3,000

1134
[FITZGERALD, FRANCIS SCOTT KEY.]
This lot features two binders of correspondence between Fitzgerald's east coast literary agent, Harold Ober, and his Hollywood agent, H.N. Swanson, November 20, 1934 to April 4, 1956, regarding attempts to sell new Fitzgerald stories to the studios, land Fitzgerald a writing job in Hollywood, and license his works for radio, television and film after his death. Ober and Swanson also try to keep tabs on Scott, and send on reports of whether he has been drinking or not. After his death they consider Zelda's hospital expenses when negotiating sales of Scott's works. The two agents negotiate options and sales for A COURSE IN LANGUAGES, HEAD AND SHOULDERS, OFF-SHORE PIRATE, TROUBLE, WHAT YOU DON'T KNOW WON'T HURT YOU, ZONE OF ACCIDENT, BERNICE BOBS HER HAIR, THE CRACK-UP, ESQUIMO BOY, MAJESTY, and the JOSEPHINE stories, as well as *Tender is the Night* and *The Last Tycoon*. Present also is a 7 pp typed manuscript, n.p., n.d., a suggested treatment for *Tender is the Night* by Sanderson MacGown, a 5 pp extract from Fitzgerald's 1937 contract with M-G-M, and several Western Union telegrams sent by Fitzgerald to Swanson.
$2,500 - 3,500

1133
FITZGERALD, FRANCIS SCOTT KEY.
Typed Letter Signed ("Scott Fitzg"), 1 p, 4to, Hollywood, September 11, 1940, to H.N. Swanson, regarding the recent sale of radio rights for a short story, on typing paper, perforations at upper left corner, small chip at upper margin, page creased and toned. With unsigned typed carbon of Swanson's response, dated September 17, 1940.

Even after Fitzgerald broke with the Ober Agency, Harold Ober continued to try to make sales based on the author's previous work. Agency memos present in this collection reveal that Ober had a difficult time trying to make the sale for the radio rights of "The Dance," largely because no one could find Fitzgerald in the summer of 1940. Once the sale went through, however, Fitzgerald took offense at publicity that insinuated Ober and Swanson were still representing him. In part: "*Dear Swanie:- / Your office told me that the offer of $200., for the radio rights of 'The Dance' came through Harold Ober. I agreed to it with that understanding. / The implication of this announcement in the Reporter is that you are still my representative out here. This is emphatically not true. Your preposterous suggestion outside the theatre the other night that I advertise some commercial product is as near as you have come to representing me for almost a year. I must ask you to make no further announcements of this kind.*" In his response, Swanie explains that the notice in the *Reporter* was standard practice, as was the splitting of the commission between Ober and Swanson. He goes on: "*I hope your letter doesn't mean what it just possibly might mean: that you would not have accepted money from the sale if you had known we were*

143. Christie's, New York, Sale Number 1677 (14 June 2006)

Recatalogued by Peter Harrington in December 2006 at £15,000 ($29,250). Inscribed to Rita Swann, a Baltimore friend.

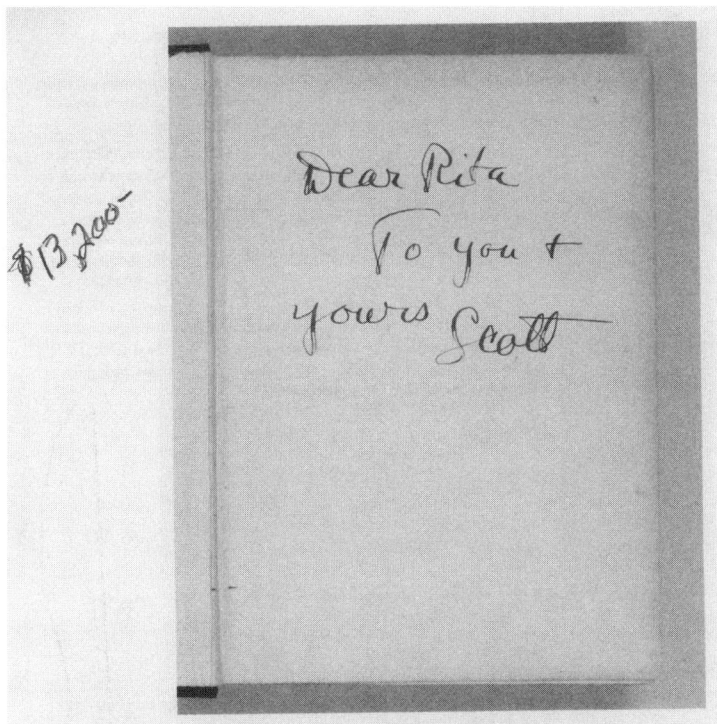

ANOTHER PROPERTY
273
FITZGERALD, F. Scott. *Tender is the Night*. New York: Charles Scribner's Sons, 1934.
8°. Original green cloth, gilt-lettered on spine (minor wear at extremities, short ink stain on fore edges of sheets).
FIRST EDITION, FIRST PRINTING. PRESENTATION COPY, INSCRIBED BY FITZGERALD on the front free endpaper: "Dear Rita / To you & yours Scott." "The beginning... is a wonderful evocation of the second phase of American expatriates ensconced in glittering villas on the Riviera in contrast to the home-spun tipplers of *The Sun Also Rises*. The breakdown of a marriage... is described with flashes of genius by an expert in self-destruction... and there is a haunting account... of the predicament of 'grace under pressure' from too many parties and too much money" (Connolly *The Modern Movement* 79). Bruccoli A15.1.a.
$10,000-15,000
PROPERTY FROM THE ESTATE OF GUY FAIRFAX CARY, JR.

144. R & R Enterprises Autograph Catalogue 313 (20 September 2006)

Uncertain about Gatsby onstage: *"Thanks for your letter about Gatsby. Have just had a wire... asking for dramatic rights and wired my agent asking him to see what... plans are"*

496. F. Scott Fitzgerald. Rare and significant ALS, one page, 8 x 10.5, no date [circa 1925–1926]. Fitzgerald writes from Paris to literary agent and editor William C. Lengel regarding plans for a stage adaptation of the Great Gatsby. In full: *"Thanks for your letter about Gatsby. Have just had a wire from Brady asking for dramatic rights and wired my agent asking him to see what Brady's plans are—all this before your letter came, as it went to Cannes & Homer Croy whom I've never met. As soon as I get any word I will let you know. Perhaps he has no one in mind for the dramatization & in that case it would much better [sic] if it were done by someone like who already has some plan in his head. With many thanks...."* After signing, Fitzgerald adds a postscript and signs again with his initials: *"Word has just come that Owen Davis is going to do it for Brady. Thanks many times for your interest."* Fitzgerald's most famous novel, widely regarded as one of the finest in the English language, was published in spring 1925 to a rather unremarkable reception. Still, with the public's ever-increasing appetite for entertainment, newly published fiction provided an instant source of material for the stage and screen. With its dramatic force and colorful characterizations, it was only a matter of time before Gatsby would attract the attention of stage and screen producers, and it first made the jump from page to stage in a semi-successful adaptation by dramatist Owen Davis that ran for 112 performances in 1926. Later that same year, Gatsby, as played by Warner Baxter, made his debut on the silver screen. The novel was filmed at least three more times—most notably in 1974, with an Oscar-winning script by Francis Ford Coppola. A new, well-received stage adaptation debuted at the Guthrie Theater in Minneapolis in July 2006, and the novel was even transformed into an acclaimed opera by Pulitzer Prize–winning composer John Harbison. Letters mentioning Gatsby occupy a singular niche at the pinnacle of Fitzgerald's autograph material, and, indeed, among literary autographs as a whole. The early date, excellent preservation, and spectacular visual appeal of the present example add up to a trophy that no serious collector will let pass without a spirited fight! In fine, bright condition, with faint intersecting mailing folds (one touching signature), small marginal tears (all well away from text; one expertly repaired), vertical filing notation in another hand (*"Fitzgerald"*) in right margin, and the subtlest suggestion of handling wear—all mentioned for the sake of strictest accuracy, for the item presents most beautifully, indeed. COA John Reznikoff/PSA/DNA and R&R COA. ....(MB $900)

145. R. M. Smythe Auction Number 267 (16 November 2006)

58 FITZGERALD, F. SCOTT *($700-Up)*

American writer (1896-1940); coined the term ``the Jazz Age'' and became the period's definitive chronicler with his tales of the

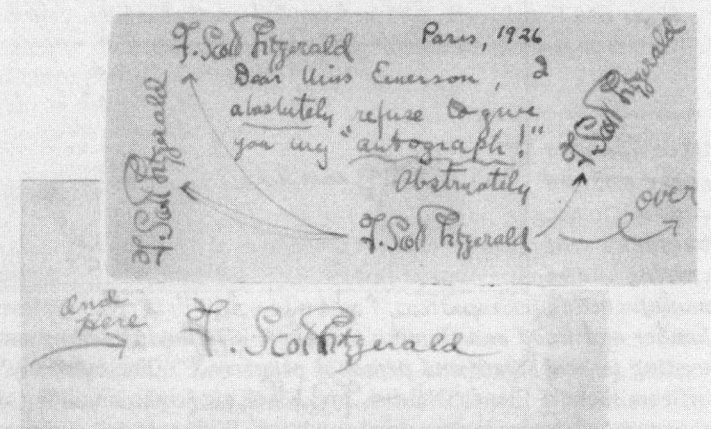

dissolute rich and the loneliness of the realized American dream; his classics include *The Great Gatsby* and *Tender is the Night;* his own life was plagued by alcoholism and debt, and he died in 1940 at just 44 years of age. Charming **Autograph Note Signed** five times, *"F. Scott Fitzgerald,"* 1 page and 1 line, narrow oblong 12mo [2-3/4" x 5-3/4"], *"Paris, 1926,"* no precise date. He writes comically: *"Miss Emerson, I absolutely refuse to give you my 'autograph!' Obstinately,"* and proceeds to sign the note below and in three other places on recto (indicated by arrows), as well as once on verso with the words *"And Here."* Irregular edges, especially at bottom, otherwise in fine condition. The previous year, Fitzgerald published his masterpiece, *The Great Gatsby,* and soon embarked for Europe, where he became part of the thriving group of American expatriates in Paris, which included Ernest Hemingway and Gertrude Stein. This note, from that time, shows the writer in high humor during that brief period of success - and excess.

Appendix 1
Fitzgerald–Harold Ober Correspondence and Inscribed Fitzgerald Books

Harold Ober, Fitzgerald's agent, had an influence on his career equal to that of Maxwell Perkins at Charles Scribner's Sons. Ober handled Fitzgerald's magazine work—especially the *Saturday Evening Post* short stories that provided most of Fitzgerald's income. He advanced Fitzgerald money against unsold—and, later, unwritten—stories. When Fitzgerald moved to Hollywood in 1937, the Obers took Scottie into their home. But there was no warmth between these men, as there was between Fitzgerald and Perkins.

The Fitzgerald-Ober correspondence from the Harold Ober Associates files published in *As Ever, Scott Fitz— : Letters between F. Scott Fitzgerald and His Literary Agent Harold Ober, 1919–1940* (New York: Lippincott, 1972) is now at the Lilly Library, Indiana University. Other Fitzgerald letters that leaked out of the Ober agency files have been sold. The Fitzgerald-Ober letters described in catalogues are from the "Crack-Up" period when Fitzgerald was unable to write his way out of debt with magazine stories.

Books Inscribed to the Obers*

Flappers and Philosophers

Christie's, New York, Sale Number 9548 (14 December 2000), $35,000.
Kenneth W. Rendell Catalogue 289 [ca. 2001], $75,000.
William Reese Catalogue 241 (October 2005), $55,000.

PROPERTY OF NATHANIEL AND RICHARD OBER

61
FITZGERALD, F. Scott (1896-1940). *Flappers and Philosophers.* New York: Scribner's, 1920. 8°. Original green cloth (ends of spine and rear outer-joint worn, inner hinges broken).

FIRST EDITION of Fitzgerald's second book and first collection of stories. PRESENTATION COPY TO HIS LITERARY AGENT HAROLD OBER, inscribed by the author at top of front free endpaper: "For Harold Ober who chaperoned these debutantes, with best wishes from F. Scott Fitzgerald" (referring to Ober's marketing of four of these first Fitzgerald stories to magazines). With some pencilled annotations and markings on the Contents page, presumably by Ober, regarding sales of a few of the stories to movie studios. Among the eight stories in *Flappers and Philosophers* are "The Ice Palace," "The Offshore Pirate," and "Bernice Bobs Her Hair." Bruccoli A.6.I.a.

This, and the inscribed copies in the following four lots, constitute an important series of five presentation copies from Fitzgerald to the man (or his wife) who was his literary agent (and more!) for some twenty-one years. Fitzgerald became the client of Harold Ober in November 1919 when the author was trying to sell his first stories (Scribner's had accepted the novel *This Side of Paradise*, which would be published in March 1920). Ober, with the Paul Reynolds agency at the time, quickly placed these "debutante" stories with the *Saturday Evening Post*, etc. He would be the only agent Fitzgerald would ever have, handling magazine and movie sales and always providing guidance to the marketplace. Fitzgerald would dedicate *Taps at Reveille* (1935), his fourth and final collection of stories to him. "During their twenty-one-year association Ober served as Fitzgerald's agent, accountant, banker, confidante, friend, and surrogate parent to his young daughter. In expectation of a magazine sale Ober often advanced Fitzgerald money on the receipt of a story. As Fitzgerald's stories became harder to place in the mid-1930s, Ober's advances became noninterest loans. By 1937 Fitzgerald owed Ober more than $12,000. While under contract to M-G-M, Fitzgerald repaid his debt within two years" (*F. Scott Fitzgerald Centenary Exhibition...The...Bruccoli Collection*, The Thomas Cooper Library, University of South Carolina Press, 1996, p. 53).

Estimate: $12,000-18,000

Christie's (14 December 2000)

[*The Vegetable* inscribed for the Obers and a copy of George Barton's *The Bell Haven Eight* (1914) jokingly inscribed to Ober are in the Bruccoli Collection.]

The Beautiful and Damned

Christie's, New York, Sale Number 9548 (14 December 2000), $11,000.

Peter L. Stern Supplementary List, "Mostly New Arrivals" (May 2003), $25,000.

Peter L. Stern Catalogue 30 (November 2003), $25,000.

62
FITZGERALD, F. Scott. *The Beautiful and Damned.* New York: Scribner's, 1922. 8°. Original green cloth (most of spine strip partially loose, ends of spine and fore-corners a bit worn, rear inner hinge broken, natural darkening to endpapers).

FIRST EDITION of Fitzgerald's second novel. PRESENTATION COPY TO HIS LITERARY AGENT HAROLD OBER, inscribed by the author on front free endpaper: "For Harold Ober from his friend F. Scott Fitzgerald, Feb. 6th, 1922. St. Paul, Minn." This is one of the 25 copies of *The Beautiful and Damned* that Fitzgerald requested be sent to him in his letter to Max Perkins at Scribner's of 30 January 1922: "My twenty five are all for family, authors who have sent books + personal friends" (*Letters*, ed. M.J. Bruccoli and M.M. Duggan, p. 94). February 6 was the earliest date on which he inscribed copies; the one presented to his mother also bears that date; publication day was not until March 4. Bruccoli A8.I.a.

Estimate: $10,000–15,000

Christie's (14 December 2000)

Tales of the Jazz Age

Christie's, New York, Sale Number 9548 (14 December 2000), $38,000.

> For Harold Ober
> who fathered
> The Camel's Back
> Benjamin Button
> The Diamond as Big as the Ritz
> The Jellybean
> The Lees of Happiness
> & The Russet Witch
> from his gratefully
> F Scott Fitzgerald
> (note the Table of contents)
> 1922

63
FITZGERALD, F. Scott. *Tales of the Jazz Age*. New York: Scribner's, 1922. 8°. Original green cloth (spine dull, front cover slightly soiled, front inner hinge tender).

FIRST EDITION of Fitzgerald's second book of stories. PRESENTATION COPY TO HIS LITERARY AGENT HAROLD OBER, inscribed by Fitzgerald covering most of front free endpaper: "For Harold Ober / who fathered / The Camel's Back / Benjamin Button / The Diamond as Big as the Ritz / The Jellybean / The Lees of Happiness / & / The Russet Witch / from his gratefully / F. Scott Fitzgerald / (note the Table of Contents)." The year "1922" is written at an angle below this, presumably in Fitzgerald's hand (publication day was September 22). The six stories in the inscription that Ober "fathered" were the ones sold to magazines through his agency. Among the other five "Tales of the Jazz Age" is the well-known "May Day." Bruccoli A9.I.a. Sold with a reading copy (covers spotted) of the first edition. (2)

Estimate: $12,000-18,000 $38,000

All the Sad Young Men (inscribed to Anne Ober)

Christie's, New York. Sale Number 9548 (14 December 2000), $16,000.
Kenneth W. Rendell Catalogue 290 [January 2002], $25,000.
Kenneth W. Rendell Catalogue 298 [ca. 2003], $25,000.
William Reese Catalogue 241 (October 2005), $35,000.

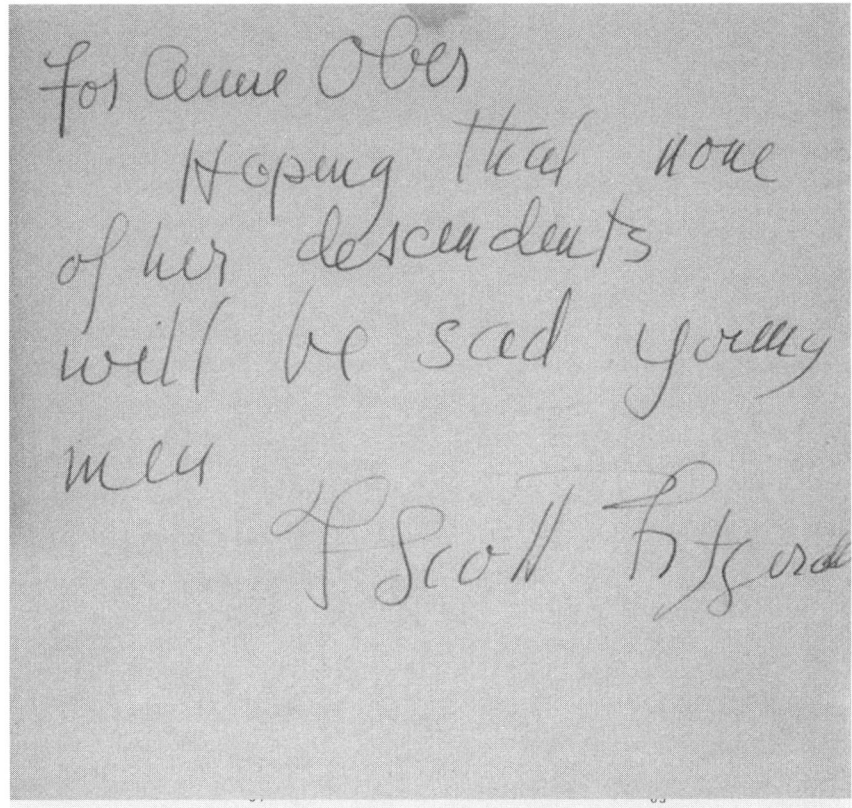

64
FITZGERALD, F. Scott. *All the Sad Young Men*. New York: Scribner's, 1926. 8°. Original green cloth (spine dull with fraying at ends, inner hinges broken).

FIRST EDITION. PRESENTATION COPY TO ANNE OBER, WIFE OF FITZGERALD'S LITERARY AGENT, inscribed by the author on front free endpaper: "For Anne Ober, Hoping that none of her descendants will be sad young men. F. Scott Fitzgerald" (echoing the book's title); with Harold Ober's signature on inside front cover. Fitzgerald's third collection of stories, including two of his finest: "The Rich Boy" and "Winter Dreams." When the Fitzgeralds' daughter Scottie was sent to boarding school in 1936 Anne Ober and her husband became her virtual foster parents. See Fitzgerald's grateful letters to Anne in *F. Scott Fitzgerald: A Life in Letters*, ed. M.J. Bruccoli, New York, 1995. Bruccoli A12.1.a.
Estimate: $8,000-12,000

Christie's (14 December 2000)

Tender Is the Night

Christie's, New York, Sale Number 9548 (14 December 2000), $26,000.

Peter L. Stern Supplementary List, "New Arrivals & Selections from Stock" (February 2001), $85,000.

Peter L. Stern Supplementary List, "New Arrivals" (January 2002), $85,000.

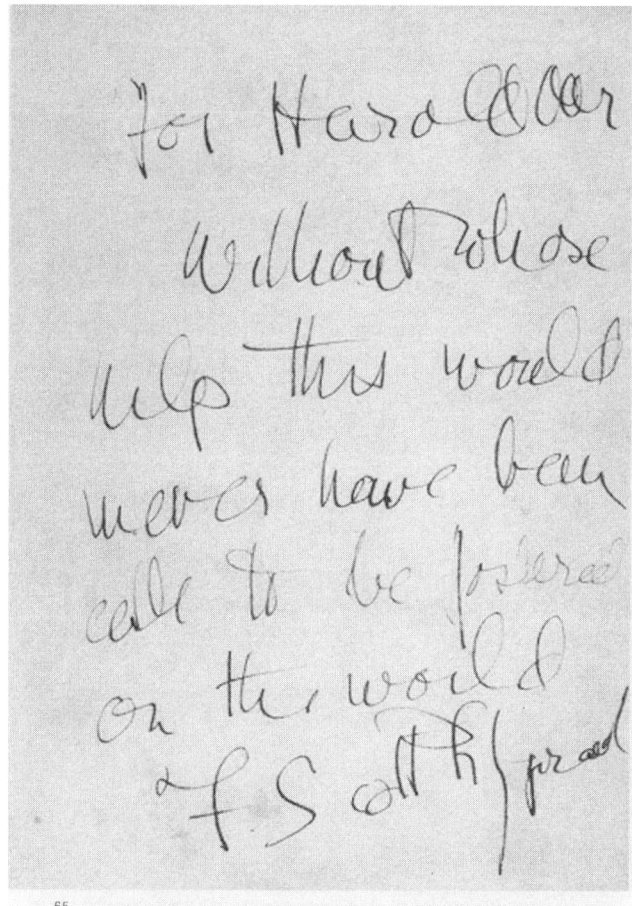

Christie's (14 December 2000)

Letters to Ober*

ALS, 1 p. (11 March 1936)

Sotheby's, New York, Sale Number 5114 (14 December 1983), $440.

> ■ 101 FITZGERALD, F. SCOTT. Autograph letter signed ("Scott"), in pencil, 1 page 4to, [Baltimore], no date [but with recipient's stamp 11 March 1936], to his literary agent Harold Ober. A single horizontal tear across half the page
>> Fitzgerald informs Ober that he has sent off a 600 word synopsis of a ballet story for a possible film by Goldwyn. He wishes it to be treated with respect ("To let this be around a Hollywood office, pored over by every script writer who came in would be fatal") but thinks that a continuity writer could work directly from the synopsis with few plot changes, "but of couse I would want to do a treatment for the sake of the dialogue and the ballet atmosphere that I know so well". Fitzgerald's knowledge of the ballet world came from Zelda's efforts to become a dancer, a struggle she fictionalized in *Save Me the Waltz*
>
> $600/900

ALS, 1 p. (12 March 1936)

Sotheby's, New York, Sale Number 5114 (14 December 1983), $165.
Pepper & Stern Catalogue 21 (1985), $600.
Pepper & Stern Catalogue 22 (1985), $750.
Pepper & Stern Catalogue 23 (1986), $750.
Pepper & Stern Catalogue 26 (1990), $850.

> ■ 102 FITZGERALD, F. SCOTT. Short autograph letter signed ("Scott"), in pencil, 1 page 4to, [Baltimore], no date [but with recipient's stamp 12 March 1936]. Small brown stains, lower margin ragged
>> Fitzgerald sends "the revision covering all your points & some others. It's much better". The letter bears a pencilled annotation "Outside the House", presumably Ober's note of the story to which the letter refers. Bruccoli's bibliography lists no story of that name
>
> $250/400

Sotheby's (14 December 1983)

[*None of these letters is in *As Ever, Scott Fitz—* : *Letters between F. Scott Fitzgerald and His Literary Agent Harold Ober, 1919-1940.*]

TLS, 3 pp. (4 April 1936)

Sotheby's, New York, Sale Number 4833Y (6 April 1982), $1,000.

Christie's, New York, Sale Number 9178 (9 June 1999); together with 31 May 1936 letter, $11,000.

Kenneth W. Rendell Catalogue 298 [ca. 2003], $25,000.

> ■ 41 FITZGERALD, F. SCOTT. Typed letter signed ("Scott"), 2½ pages 4to, Baltimore, 4 April 1936, to his agent Harold Ober, with stamped receipt and annotations from Ober's office; light staining, a few short tears, section torn away from bottom of second page but apparently without loss of text
> Fitzgerald sends Ober a story ["The Pearl and the Fur", never published in his lifetime] and asks for an advance of $200, giving the reason for his need of money: "... *Things have reached a stalemate here with Zelda I am moving her on the advice of several doctors to a new environment, a sanatarium {sic} in Asheville ... If you feel pretty confident of this story can you advance me $200 which will enable me to make the transfer to Asheville? It will have to be done with the aid of a trained nurse as she is still in a most dangerous and violent condition ...*" He writes of financial arrangements for the future, mentioning that he intends to start a new story "... *on reaching Asheville (or rather when I hear from you as to whether they like this one and want me to continue with the Gwen stories or quit them) ... I hadn't wanted to revise "I'd Die for You" because I suppose the suicide theme pretty well damns it ... As to the Gwen story for the Post I felt more hopeful and am rather surprised that you had no bidders ... I don't think it is first rate but it has good things in it ...*"

Sotheby's (6 April 1982)

ALS, 1 p. (22 April 1936)

Sotheby's, New York, Sale Number 5114 (14 December 1983), $1,100 BP.

> ■ 103 FITZGERALD, F. SCOTT. Autograph letter signed, ("Scott Fitg"), 1 page 4to, [Baltimore], no date [but with recipient's stamp 22 April 1936], to Harold Ober. Lower margin ragged ☆ MARX, GUMMO. Typed letter signed, 1 page 4to, New York, 17 April 1936, to Scott Fitzgerald
> Gummo Marx writes, on headed paper of the Zeppo Marx Agency, that he has heard from Groucho that Fitzgerald might go to Hollywood and offers the services of the agency: "We represent some of the finest writers in the country today, and I am sure we could arrange a swell deal for you". Clearly somewhat bewildered by this communication from the eldest Marx brother of whom he had never heard, Fitzgerald sends the letter on to Ober: "Who on God's earth is "Gummo" - a nephew? Is there anything in it for me? I might go to Hollywood on a specific set up but not as a gag man. Groucho might like my fantasies ... and I might enjoy doing something along those lines". He askes Ober to advise him and to let him know his opinion of "Pearl and Fur" [a story that was never published]
> $600/900

ALS, 3 pp. (ca. 7 May 1936)

Sotheby Parke Bernet, New York, Sale Number 4771E (24 November 1981), $2,970.

■ 141 FITZGERALD, F. SCOTT. Autograph letter signed ("Scott") with long postscript, 3 pages folio, [Baltimore, c. 7 May 1936], to his agent Harold Ober, written in pencil, with stamped receipt from Ober's office dated 9 May 1936; light staining to first sheet

A desperate and revealing letter in which Fitzgerald bemoans the affect of his financial problems on his morale, his health and his work. 1936 was perhaps the year in which his finances reached the lowest ebb and, encouraged by Ober who did his best to sell his stories, Fitzgerald struggled to produce work which he himself thought was of small merit. Here he sends Ober eleven stories for the *Pictorial,* all reworkings of already published pieces (". . . *Every single story since Phillipe I in the Spring of 1934 two years ago I'd had to write over . . .*") and complains that the pressure of debt prevents him resting: ". . . *This business of debt is awful. It has made me lose confidence to an appalling extent. I used to write for myself - now I write for editors because I never have time to really think what I do like or find anything to like. It's like a man drawing out water in drops because he's too thirsty to wait for the well to fill . . .*" He mentions some work he has sent to Paramount Pictures (". . . *Do they want to use The Gold Hat as a title*[?] *I thought of calling Gatsby that at first . . .*") The remainder of the letter is a crescendo of misery: ". . . *there are collecting agencies at the door every day . . . There seems to be too much to contend with to get any piece* [sic] *of mind . . . Just got word that I am being sued for debt by Zelda's last sanatorium . . . I realize that I am at the end of my resources physically & financially . . . I am cutting expenses to the bone, taking Scotty to Carolina instead of camp & going to a boarding house . . . I have got to do that to get a sense of proportion . . . Zelda & I did that twice when I was making more than I am now & had less expenses . . . This copy looks mixed but it really isn't. Its only my hand sticks to the paper its so hot here . . .*"

TLS, 3 pp. (31 May 1936)

Sotheby's, New York, Sale Number 4833Y (6 April 1982), $1,500.

Christie's, New York, Sale Number 9178 (9 June 1999), together with 4 April 1936 letter, $11,000.

> ■ 42   FITZGERALD, F. SCOTT. Typed letter signed ("Scott"), 3 page 4to, Baltimore, 31 May 1936, to Harold Ober, stamped receipt and annotations from Ober's office; light browning
>
> > He writes that *"When I finished that story* [identified in pencil at the head of the page as "Cyclone in Silent Land", never published in his lifetime] *I felt absolutely sure it was the best story I had written in a year. . . ."* If the [*Saturday Evening*] *Post* turn it down he feels that they should revise the arrangement by which the *Post* gets first choice of his stories: *". . . when they keep declining stories on such grounds as purely moral ones as in the case of "Intimate Strangers" and "Crazy Sunday" or because they are overbought with medieval stuff as in the case of the first Philippe story, or because the heroine is married in the first chapter as in the fortune telling story . . ."* Having work turned down by the *Post* is bad for his standing with other magazines. He describes his disastrous financial affairs and the effect it is having on his work: *". . . I can see that situation has got to stop. I'd rather put Zelda in a public insane asylum and live on* Esquire's *$200 a month because I can count on it and because he believes in me than see my morale being gradually sucked away by this struggle in the big time . . ."*

Sotheby's (6 April 1982)

TLS, 1 p. (19 June 1936)

Sotheby's, New York, Sale Number 5114 (14 December 1983), $495 BP.

>
>
> ■ 104 FITZGERALD, F. SCOTT. Typed letter signed ("Scott"), 1 page 4to, Baltimore, 19 June 1936, to Harold Ober. Light stains and marginal nicks, date-stamped by recipient
>
> > Fitzgerald sends a story (identified at the head of the page as "Thank You for the Light") and suggests it might do for the *New Yorker* ("It's an old idea I had hanging around in my head for a long time"). He rejects Ober's suggestion that he publish some of his other old stories, "Travel Together", "What to Do About It" and "On Your Own": "I've destroyed them here and while I still have "Nightmare" I've stripped the latter and used almost all of the best lines from it in "Tender is the Night" and I scarcely remember the plots of two of the stories now". None of the stories mentioned in this letter were ever published despite the fact that Fitzgerald was at this time desperate for money, with no regular income and burdened by the expense of Zelda's asylum
>
>
>
> $400/600

TLS, 1 p. (10 September 1936)

Sotheby Park Bernet, New York, Sale Number 4771E (24 November 1981), not sold.

Sotheby's, New York, Sale Number 4883Y (6 April 1982), $650.

> ■ 43   FITZGERALD, F. SCOTT. Typed letter signed ("F. Scott Fitzgerald") with five words added in autograph, 1 page 4to, Asheville, N.C., 10 September 1936, to Harold Ober, with stamped receipt from Ober's office; badly stained with slight paper losses at margins
>
> Writing when recovering from an attack of fever, testified by the shakiness of his signature, Fitzgerald sends Ober a story he has just revised and comments on his recent work: "... *Perhaps the Esquire articles were unfortunate. As you know they were emergency things, each one following a revision made on a Post story, helping to tide over the interval in between. Of course anybody would prefer to do the Post stories, in fact the longer a piece is the more I enjoy doing it — it is the all the result of this working under pressure business* ..." A pencilled note [?by Ober] at the head of the page states *"wrote Scott that story was here and that I liked it."*

The 1936 *Esquire* articles included "The Crack-Up," "Pasting It Together," and "Handle with Care." Sotheby's (6 April 1982)

Appendix 2
Fitzgerald-Owens Archive

Isabel Owens became Fitzgerald's secretary in 1932 when he was writing *Tender Is the Night* at "La Paix," Towson, Maryland. Her duties included typing, paying his bills, and helping him to care for Scottie and Zelda. She remained in his employment after Fitzgerald moved to Baltimore in December 1933, and he continued to rely on her to manage his finances during the "Crack-Up" period in 1935–1937 when he was in Tryon, Hendersonville, and Asheville, North Carolina. His letters from North Carolina provide a record of his money and career anxieties. Fitzgerald corresponded with Mrs. Owens after he went to Hollywood in July 1937. A total of twenty-four letters and six wires from Fitzgerald to Owens have been located in catalogues.

The largest group was sold for Mrs. Owens by the Harris Auction Galleries, Baltimore, in 1985 (sale number 234). This catalogue offered thirty-three Fitzgerald-related lots—including five letters and six wires from Fitzgerald to Owens. Twenty-five of these lots realized a total of $8,392.50; eight were unsold. The top price of $1,500 was brought by the inscribed *Tender Is the Night* (item 187); it was recatalogued in Joseph the Provider Catalogue 51 (1993) at $6,500 and by R. A. Gekoski Catalogue 30 [2004] at £45,000.

Harris Auction Galleries Sale Number 234 (10 May 1985)

The 1985 prices now seem absurdly low.

F. SCOTT FITZGERALD

F. Scott Fitzgerald is legend, a key figure in the literary history of this country during the "Jazz Age" of the 1920s and 1930s. His novels and short stories are in the pantheon of 20th Century American writing.

Harris Auction Galleries is pleased to offer an entirely unpublished trove of correspondence and related material dealing with Fitzgerald's years in Baltimore, the stretch which Fitzgerald himself termed his "Crack-Up" period. Retained for almost 50 years by Isabel W. Owens, who served as Fitzgerald's first full-time secretary from 1932-1936, all the correspondence listed below is being offered to the public for the first time.

The significance of the material cannot be underestimated. The Fitzgerald manuscript and correspondence which has come on the market in the past two decades has been concerned with Fitzgerald as renowned author and man-about-town. In contrast, we encounter here Fitzgerald as employer, father, and husband. Almost all the correspondence is directed to Mrs. Owens, who became an integral part of the Fitzgerald operations. She typed Fitzgerald's correspondence, maintained his accounts, typed and re-typed the drafts of "Tender Is the Night", ran errands, babysat for his daughter Scottie, dealt with creditors, and all the other typical tasks of a person with such a job.

Most of the material of the sort listed below is already institutionalized, primarily at Princeton University, or still belongs to family members. The text of many such letters have been included in the several volumes of Fitzgerald correspondence published in the last two decades, but availability of the actual letters for purchase by private collectors and dealers has been nearly impossible.

The correspondence included here is family material -- Fitzgerald concerned about Scottie's occasional rebelliousness, Zelda's confinements and the effect on her relatives: One fine 4-page ALS from Fitzgerald, several from Zelda, several from Scottie, and others from other family members, plus numerous original telegrams and typed letters, and the original account and address/telephone books kept by Mrs. Owens as secretary for Fitzgerald; further, signed presentation copies with choice inscriptions of "Tender Is the Night" and "Taps at Reveille", plus other First Editions in dust wrappers, and one original pastel drawing by Zelda.

Fitzgerald's four years in Baltimore were some of his most trying; family and financial problems were becoming a tremendous drain on his emotional resources, and getting published and staying in print was increasingly difficult. The picture of Fitzgerald in this material is not a romantic one, but completely honest, open and fraught with indecision, anxiety, and personal turmoil. Standard biographies and the extensive published correspondence have already allowed us an intimate view of Fitzgerald and his family, but there is nothing like the genuine items.

226   Appendix 2

179. BRUCCOLI, SMITH, and KERR, Editors. The Romantic Egoists. N.Y.: Scribner's, (1974). FIRST TRADE EDITION, signed presentation copy from Scottie Fitzgerald Smith to Isabel W. Owens, in orange felt-tip, January, 1975, at half-title. Tall wide 4to, black cloth, gilt and orange lettering, x and 246 pages, 100s facsimiles and reproductions throughout. Very clean, bright copy, in excellent dust wrapper.
  Inscription reads: "For 'Missy Owen', with infinite appreciation for her kindness always to the main characters in this book, and memories of many happy times despite the vicissitudes / Love from Scottie, January, 1975". In addition, laid in is small plain note card, in same orange felt-tip: "There's a nifty picture of you in here, I think; so glad I found it! Love (written as heart), Scottie / (See p. 188)".
  Further, Mrs. Owens has made several small pencil notations or corrections in the text, all entries clarifying or correcting errors. As well, laid in is 1-page TLS, June 24, 1974, to Mrs. Owens, from Matthew J. Bruccoli, one of the joint editors, on "Fitzgerald/Hemingway Annual" letterhead, text dealing with attempts to gather material for this title, and few queries for Mrs. Owens -- wondering if she still held any Fitzgerald manuscripts, or knew of location of any of Zelda's paintings. One sheet, 8vo, few wrinkles, very good over-all. [Estimate $150/300].

180. FITZGERALD, F. SCOTT. The Beautiful and Damned. N.Y.: Scribner's, 1922. FIRST EDITION, First State of 2d Printing, with ad leaf at rear. Small 8vo, dark green cloth, gilt and blind lettering. Covers sound with moderate rubbing and some wear, backstrip somewhat darkened, contents lightly shaken, front hinge cracked, bookplate removed.
  Together with sound reading copy of "Tender Is the Night" (N.Y., 1934), First Edition, original dark green cloth, covers spotted with wear, contents good, lightly shaken, bookplate removed. Bruccoli A.8.1.b and A.14.1.a. (Together, 2 volumes).   [Estimate $45/65].

SIGNED PRESENTATION COPY

181. _____. Flappers and Philosophers. N.Y.: Scribner's, 1920. FIRST EDITION, 3d Printing, Signed presentation copy from Fitzgerald to Beatrice Ecks, undated, in black ink script at front blank. Small 8vo, dark green cloth, gilt and blind lettering. Backstrip darkened with gilt lettering becoming dull, covers lightly worn with brief fraying at corners, contents solid and tight, inscription and signature very nice and clear. Bruccoli A.6.1.c.   [Estimate $750/1000].

182. _____. Gatsby le Magnifique. Traduction de Victor Llona. Paris: Simon Kra, (1926). FIRST FRENCH TRADE EDITION. 12mo, original printed buff wraps with blue and black lettering, 217 pages, untrimmed, gravure frontis portrait, 1 page of publisher's texts at rear (listing this title as "Ouvrage a Paraitre"), with additional 8-page stapled publisher's catalog laid in. Some chipping to spine ends, light wear and some aging to wraps which are still clean and intact, contents very nice, pencil ownership signature of Isabel W. Owens at front blank.
  The first French version also appeared in 415-copy limited edition, as detailed on reverse of title page. This volume issued as number 26 of "Collection Europeenne".
  Much of "The Great Gatsby" was written while the Fitzgeralds lived in France, and the French influences on the text have been grist for the thesis mill for many years. According to Andre Le Vot, this edition was translated "(atrociously) into French in 1926 and virtually unnoticed at the time".   [Estimate $300/500].

183. _____. The Great Gatsby. N.Y.: Scribner's, 1925. FIRST EDITION, Second Printing, with textual variations. Small 8vo, gilt and blind lettering. Covers clean and bright, text lightly foxed, front blank removed, pencil ownership signature of Isabel W. Owens at half-title, in original First State dust wrapper which is incomplete and in sections, lacking bottom half of spine and bottom right corner of rear panel, some other small chips, front panel with some creases, chips and short tears, end flaps listing works by Fitzgerald or Ring Lardner, rear panel with hand-inked capital "J". Bruccoli A.11.I.b.
   [Estimate $250/450].

184. FITZGERALD, F. SCOTT. Tales of the Jazz Age. N.Y.: Scribner's, 1922. FIRST EDITION, First or Second printing (indistinguishable). Small 8vo, dark green cloth, gilt and blind lettering. Very nice, clean copy, light aging, some foxing (mostly at endpapers), pencil ownership signature of Isabel W. Owens at front blank, in original dust wrapper which is now in sections, chipped at all edges, lacks portion of lettering of "Tales" on backstrip, as well as bottom third of spine; front panel illustrations by John Held complete (chipping to some lettering). Bruccoli A.9.I.a. [Estimate $350/500].

INSCRIBED TO HIS SECRETARY

185. _____. Taps at Reveille. N.Y.: Scribner's, 1935. FIRST EDITION, First State, without cancel at pages 349-352. Author's Presentation copy, inscribed and signed in ink to Isabel W. Owens by Fitzgerald at front blank. Thick small 8vo, dark green cloth, gilt spine lettering. Very clean, bright copy, light aging at endpapers, in rubbed and lightly chipped intact and complete dust wrapper. Bruccoli A.17.I.a.1.
  At front blank, in black ink: "For Isabel Owens / Hoping we'll both be able to look back to this winter as a bleak exception, in a business way / From F. Scott ("Old Scrooge") Fitzgerald." Few letters in author's signature slightly smudged. [Estimate $1500/2000].

186. _____. Taps at Reveille. N.Y.: Scribner's, 1935. FIRST EDITION, First State, without cancel at pages 349-352. Thick small 8vo, dark green cloth, gilt spine lettering. Quite clean, tight copy, front blank previously removed, pencil ownership signature of Isabel W. Owens at reverse of leaf opposing half-title, first page of text roughly opened with tear, aging to torn section of that leaf. Bruccoli A.17.I.a.1. [Estimate $100/150].

THE TYPIST'S REWARD

187. _____. Tender Is the Night: A Romance. N.Y.: Scribner's, 1934. FIRST EDITION, First Printing, with "A" at copyright page. Author's Presentation copy, inscribed and signed in ink to Isabel W. Owens by Fitzgerald at front blank. Thick small 8vo, dark green ribbed cloth, gilt spine lettering. Covers lightly worn with few light dents at bottom left of front cover, one small indistinct spot at rear cover, contents clean and tight with light aging, in mostly complete original dust wrapper which is now in sections, chipped at edges, lacking top half of spine. Bruccoli A.14.I.a.
  At front blank, in black ink: "For Isabel Owens ("I.W.O.") / with many memories of her patience & cooperation in the concoction of this / F. Scott Fitzgerald". Few characters slightly smudged, very clean and clear throughout.
  As Fitzgerald's secretary, Mrs. Owens typed (by her recollection at least three times) the original manuscript of "Tender Is the Night", which ran to over 700 double-spaced pages. [Estimate $2000/3000].

188. (FITZGERALD). The Nassau Herald -- Class of Nineteen Hundred and Seventeen -- Princeton University. Princeton: Princeton University Press, 1917. Tall 8vo, black cloth, gilt lettering, t.e.g., 363 pages, extensive reproduced photographs (2 folded). Mild wear at extremeties, very good copy over-all; personal copy of Walter H. Johnson, Jr., member of the class of 1917, with numerous ink or pencil marginal notations, plus his pencil signature and date at front pastedown.
  Contains entry on F. Scott Fitzgerald at pages 99-100, including photo portrait. Further, mention of "Fie! Fie! Fi-Fi" at page 329, and several other mentions of Fitzgerald's extra-curricular activities, all literary. [Estimate $75/100].

189. FITZGERALD, FRANCES SCOTT. Two-page ALS, (Simsbury, Connecticut), April 18, 1937, to Isabel W. Owens. 12mo, folded sheet with letterhead of Ethel Walker School, completely in blue ink script, center crease, in very fine condition.
  Written during Scottie's junior year, her first at the boarding school. Admission had been arranged before the September, 1936 death of her grandmother (her father's mother), but the grandmother's estate made financing much easier.
  Very friendly and chatty letter to "Missey Owen" of about 400 words. Much of the text covers school life and adolescent peeves. Near the end are some family comments: "Mama seems very much better & Daddy is really wonderful. He is going to Hollywood soon, at last. He sent you his best,

(Continued).

incidentally .. I know this letter is terribly boring ... someday I'll write something interesting."
On the first page is small self-portrait of Scottie as she writes the letter, with one ink splotch on text (done by Scottie -- reference in text to splotch).   [Estimate $75/100]

190. FITZGERALD, FRANCES S. ("SCOTTIE"). 4-page ALS, Vassar College, Thursday, (December 8, 1938), to Isabel W. Owens. 12mo, on all sides in blue ink script on single folded sheet with circular college seal at top of first page, one additional center fold, in fine condition, with original hand-addressed stamped cover (also fine).
Written during the first semester of Scottie's freshman year at Vassar. Text is general chit-chat, primarily interrogatories about old friends in Baltimore and memories of days gone by living with Mrs. Owens.
One interesting segment, however, concerns Scottie's father: "Vassar is marvelous & it's grand being a college girl although I want to go to Dramatic School next year instead because I dont feel I really ache for a diploma -- it is difficult to break the news to Daddy -- we have done nothing but fight since last spring, & it is very unpleasant."
F. Scott Fitzgerald was then living in California, and was constantly admonishing, encouraging, and instructing his daughter on how to adjust to college life, what he expected of her, and what she was to accomplish.
    [Estimate $75/125].

FROM SCOTTIE TO HER FATHER

191. _____. One-page ALS, October 7, 1939, to her father, F. Scott Fitzgerald. 4to, single sheet with two binder punch holes at left edge, completely in blue ink script, approximately 200 words, numerous old folds and wrinkles, in quite good condition considering, all text very clear and legible.
Written from Vassar, where Scottie was then a sophomore. Text covers family matters, schoolwork, and chit chat. In part:
"Dear Daddy -- I dont suppose you'd gotten my letter when you wrote me (no published text located) ... and by the way, thanks for wiring Mrs. Owens about what a heel I am - I appreciated that.
"I love my courses and my teachers & I work about nine hours a day -- and for the first time in my life I really love to work. If you once get started in a routine it isnt hard to keep going ... but if you have done 2 good things you hate to let the 3rd slip.
"Thanks for sending me money ... Mr. Ober said the story was awful, so I guess that's two weeks' effort gone to waste. It's very disappointing.
"Hope things are picking up with you. Love, Scottie."
Nice text, showing Scottie's reaction to the continual concerns Fitzgerald had for his daughter's extended earlier indifference to schoolwork, as documented in published correspondence.
The reference to Fitzgerald's telegrams to Mrs. Owens concern the three wires included in Lot #197. The comment about Mr. (Harold) Ober deals with the rejection letter sent by Ober to Scottie on October 3, 1939 (c.6, "As Ever, Scott Fitz--", pages 416-417); Scottie submitted a short story to her father's agent, who politely returned it, with comments and encouragement.   [Estimate $200/350].

FITZGERALD'S FRACTURED SHOULDER

192. FITZGERALD, F. SCOTT. One-page typed letter, Grove Park Inn, Asheville, August 4, 1936, to Isabel W. Owens, signed in type. Single 4to plain sheet, single spaced, approximately 275 words, few original folds, in fine condition.
In part: "When I fractured and dislocated my shoulder it seemed at first there would be no complication and after two or three days I worked right ahead on my story and then hell broke loose with a high fever which is only just now beginning to abate. I naturally had to stay in bed and was too woozy to pay any but the vaguest attention to (financial) obligations....
"If the improvement continues my story ["Thumbs Up"] should be off (it is in the middle of revision) by this weekend and I can raise money on it early next week. Till then I am practically living on the hotel here. There have been hospital and nursing expenses and I have to pay a portion of the operating charge which was $425 including the anesthesia. All in all it was a very expensive swimming trip.   (Continued).

"I thought at first there must be some morbid condition of the bones that I could crack and dislocate my shoulder in midair but the x-ray showed nothing like that and it is properly knitting and I remember that Archie McLiesh (sic), who is a crack swimmer, once dislocated his back doing a two and a half ...".
Probably dictated to Martha Marie Shank, his secretary in Asheville; Fitzgerald was then in a body cast with his right arm elevated. Additional evidence is the notation "Enclosure" at bottom left beneath text (professional secretary's routine addition). The enclosure is a short telegram of August 4, 1936 to Fitzgerald from Cecilia Delihant Taylor, Fitzgerald's cousin (and model for Clare in "This Side of Paradise"), concerning his mother's medical condition. Fitzgerald was laid up in North Carolina, and his cousin reported that she and Fitzgerald's sister, Annabel, would attend a medical hearing at the Chestnut Sanitorium, in Rockville, Maryland, that "everying (is) settled", and Fitzgerald need "not hurry back". On original Western Union form, normal folds, also very nice.
Fitzgerald also makes reference to this telegram in the text of the typed letter of August 4. His mother died the following month.
Fitzgerald used to claim he heard his shoulder crack before he hit the water; the doctors told him it broke because of his awkward position at entry, buy mythology always beats out dull fact to a romanticist. C.f., letter to Zelda Fitzgerald, July 27, 1936, in "Correspondence", pages 440-441.   [Estimate $500/750].

193. FITZGERALD, F. SCOTT. Short one-page TL, Grove Park Inn, Asheville, August 14, 1936, to Isabel W. Owens. On single plain 4to sheet, few intersecting folds, top left blank corner torn off and lacking, otherwise very good, signed in type, slight aging.
Approximately 100 words in 3 short paragraphs. Text probably dictated to Martha Marie Shank, whom he enlisted as business manager in Asheville. Miss Shank operated a secretarial service and did some court reporting, and handled almost all of Fitzgerald's typing during his recuperation from a broken right shoulder in a diving accident in July, 1936.
In part: "I am still flat on my back with this shoulder. I've gotten up a couple of times and succeeded in getting right up to the very last day's revision of the story ["Thumbs Up"] only to come down with a high fever ... you can imagine how depressed I am about all this. There is very little to do but tell Ellis and Shephard (sic) Pratt the situation and postpone everything another week.
"I am too sick to write any more today. The facts are simply as stated. They don't seem to think it is dangerous or they would transfer me back to the hospital."
Reference to Ellis (full name not determined) and Sheppard Pratt Hospital probably deals with outstanding debt; Zelda entered Highland Hospital in Asheville in April, 1936.   [Estimate $150/225].

FITZGERALD'S MOTHER'S DEATH, AND HIS INHERITANCE

194. _____. Original telegram, Asheville, North Carolina, September 2, 1936, to Isabel W. Owens: "Mother died at Chestnut Lodge Sanitorium Rockville (Maryland) tonight arriving north Friday or Saturday will communicate. Scott Fitzgerald." On standard Western Union oblong 8vo form, in fine condition, in original envelope.
Mrs. Owens was at Camp Perry, Ohio, on vacation at the time, and to which location the telegram is addressed. Fitzgerald had eliminated Baltimore as a residence by the time of his mother's death, but still left behind a maze of financial entanglements. Mrs. Owens was no longer actually working for him, but the relationship had become such a regular aspect of their lives that Fitzgerald considered her one of the first to whom the news should be passed, even when on vacation.
His mother's death (and his subsequent inheritance of just under $23,000) helped to temporarily put Fitzgerald on an even financial level. Accompanying the September 2, 1936 telegram in this lot is a 1-page TLS, September 17, 1936, to Mrs. Owens from Edgar A. Poe, Jr., Fitzgerald's Baltimore attorney, and acting as executor of Fitzgerald's mother's estate.
(Continued).

Approximately 225 words, single 4to sheet, law firm letterhead, original folds, signed in black ink, in very good condition, old paper clip rust mark at top center in letterhead. Text concerns Poe's estate role, and seeking information of Fitzgerald's unpaid loans from his mother, which were to be paid back to the estate from Fitzgerald's 50 per cent share.
In part: "Will you please be kind enough to send me, in detail, an accurate account of all money lent to Scott by his mother, giving the individual amounts with their dates ... Scott is particularly anxious to have the estate settled with the utmost speed, as he wishes to borrow on his prospects ..."
Text also includes quotation from September 5, 1936 letter from Fitzgerald to Poe, in which Fitzgerald outlines his recollection of the maternal loans. (Together, 2 items). [Estimate $250/400].

195. FITZGERALD, F. SCOTT. One-page typed letter, Asheville, October 28, 1936, to Isabel W. Owens, signed in ink for Fitzgerald by Martha Marie Shank, with her initials beneath signature. 4to, single plain sheet, original folds, in very nice condition.
Together with this letter are two original telegrams from Fitzgerald to Mrs. Owens, October 26 and 30, 1936, on original forms, both very nice.
As a unit the three items tell a small chapter in the lengthy resolution of Fitzgerald's financial debt to Mrs. Owens, highlighted by a serio-comic crossing of correspondence in the mails. In sequence:
October 26 wire: "Will arrange to send balance tomorrow ... What you mean about 'other things be taken care of immediately'? What other things? Five thousand has been apportioned much as you would have suggested. Fitzgerald."
October 28 letter: "... if you have gone into any debt or inconvenience because of the money I have owed you, I certainly hold myself responsible for any interest you may have had to pay. When you answer this, will you figure out what that might be plus any interest on the money I owed you this summer.
"... will you find out what I do owe (Monumental Storage) and also tell me about what they would be satisfied with, because I have pretty well exhausted this present borrowing ... Zelda wants both pairs of ski boots, her ski suit, skating skirts and wool stockings. Do you think they can be found?"
October 30 wire: "Check should be there by this time it has absolutely been mailed terribly sorry that its inconveniencing you. Wire collect if there is any further trouble. Zelda is with me and sends affection. Scott Fitzgerald."
Mrs. Owens had written Fitzgerald on October 26 that although Fitzgerald had apparently paid her a portion of his outstanding balance with her (the bank had not formally received the money yet), she sought the entire debt settled. The total was approximately $825, according to a personal note of Mrs. Owens from the time.
One observation: Fitzgerald had recovered sufficiently from his broken collarbone to do his own typing, but apparently had been seduced by the attraction of dictation that he continued when no longer necessary (at least in this instance). [Estimate $150/200].

"HOW VALUABLE YOU HAVE BEEN TO ME"

196. _____. Fine 4-page ALS, ca. November 10-15, 1936, to Isabel W. Owens. In pencil script on both sides of plain legal-size sheets, approximately 600 words, in fine condition, entirely clean and clear, few original folds, signed "Scott Fitz".
First 2½ pages concern Fitzgerald's questioning of the $825.01 Mrs. Owens, in a letter of November 4, 1936, claimed was owed to her. In part: "Thanks for your letter. I still cant see how with typing out and no carrying or dictation my work could have averaged four hours a day. And when did we even mention a rate of pay that would work out to $33.00 a full week.
"... Well, I hate to have our relations come to this point and the bill is now paid. It probably more nearly approximates how valuable you have been to me -- nevertheless knowing my utterly straitened circumstances I think you chose a poor time to spring on me an utterly new scale of salary that we had not even discussed. However no one but you can gauge what time I have cost you and let me repeat that if I were a richer man (Continued).

your help to me would have been worth anything you chose to ask for it, but you know how inept I am in financial matters ...
"Through a friend (Kalman in St. Paul) I raised $6,000 on the legacy and it's melted away like ice in a heatwave. (Present balance $22.00. Hotel bill up to $250 and sanitarium still $1300, and the arthritis fever never below 101° for two months. I have used for secretary the part time of a Miss Shank here who does court reporting and we cannot find anything to indicate that you had told me of impending charges ...
"I certainly let you down this summer in not making the payments you'd counted on and I value your friendship too much to let it slip away on the question of a hundred dollars more or less ...
"If my last story (not identified or determined), just finished, doesn't sell, all trips are off & I'd so like to see Scottie & get out of this cell. She led her class in 3 subjects out of 5 ...
"Always afftly yrs (but still good and sore at you) / Scott Fitz."
Postscript contains interrogatories of Baltimore friends, and salutations to Mrs. Owens' family.
Whatever story Fitzgerald finished, he did not get it published right away. The following month, when Scottie was in Baltimore for the holidays, Fitzgerald came north from North Carolina and gave the infamous tea dance for Scottie at the Belvedere Hotel, at which he got drunk, directed the guests to leave, and ordered the band to keep on playing while he sat alone in the middle of the hotel reception room. Fitzgerald spent the rest of the holidays at Johns Hopkins Hospital recovering from the flu and drying out (according to Matthew Bruccoli, in his 1981 biography).
A very fine letter. [Estimate $1000/1500].

197. FITZGERALD, F. SCOTT. Group of three (3) telegrams sent by Fitzgerald in southern California to Isabel W. Owens, September 9-14, 1939. All on Western Union standard 8vo forms, first 2 being the pasted printed strips, the 3d the carbon duplicate of telephoned wire. All with one or two folds, in very good condition save for few small edge tears and brief wear, Fitzgerald's printed name torn off and lacking from first telegram, last 2 signed "Scott Fitzgerald" in type.
Fitzgerald was living in a guest house at "Belly Acres", the estate of Edward Everett Horton in Encino. Scottie had visited him in August, several weeks before she started her sophomore year at Vassar. All telegrams primarily concern Scottie, and what family property she may take back to college with her, and what was off limits.
September 9 -- "Can you devote an afternoon to this. Scotty can have any classical records she wants ... she can have any pictures except Picasso etching or Braque drawing but no family pictures ... book boxes are inviolate ... Please don't let her override you as everything she takes to Vassar I must count as permanently lost."
September 12 -- "Will you wire me care of Samuel Goldwyn United Artists or am I talking into a complete fog. Are you there? Am sending money for Scottie and for other affairs. Please answer."
September 14 -- "Thank you. The young element is dominant and reeking with guile so don't let her chisel me out of any contraband as specified. Wire Encino address how much this will cost. Will be east in November and may move all goods west."
At the time, Fitzgerald had just picked up a week's free-lance work with Goldwyn to work on "Raffles"; he then became so engrossed in the writing of the first chapters of "The Last Tycoon" that he did not make the planned November trip. [Estimate $300/400].

198. _____. First page of typed letter of unknown length, May 13, 1940, from Fitzgerald to Isabel W. Owens. Single-spaced on single plain 4to sheet, several folds, approximately 350-400 words, brief tears and some chipping at edges, over-all slightly aged, all text very clear and dark.
Fitzgerald was in Hollywood, writing a draft of the screenplay for "Babylon Revisited" for independent producer Lester Cowan, who bought the rights to the story in March, 1940.
In part: "Writing in the hope we are friends again - I shouldn't have sent you that wire but Scottie and I were dueling and I was in a wretched humor. Anyhow you have forgiven so many of my sins that probably by now you've overlooked one more. (Continued).

"Specifically this letter is about the storage matter ... Myself I need the following: My files -- all of them -- there are only two or three more, letter files I think. And there's one more scrap book ... Though Zelda is better and is now at home in parole to her mother there is no prospect as far as I can see ahead of us setting up headquarters together ..." Near end of text, Fitzgerald states, "to recapitulate", perhaps indicating that the letter ended shortly on the missing second page.
Most of the text concerns specific family items (silver, books, pictures, refrigerator, beds, rug, etc.) and whether Mrs. Owens might sell some of the items to reduce Fitzgerald's eternal storage bills.
Although buried in the text, this letter contains one of the clearest and honest assessments of the state of his marriage seven months prior to his death.
Text of Fitzgerald's response to Mrs. Owens' reply to this letter in "Correspondence", pages 596-597. [Estimate $250/350].

WHERE FITZGERALD'S MONEY WENT IN EARLY 1934

199. (FITZGERALD). Original Fitzgerald family account book, primarily January-May, 1934, as separately maintained by Isabel W. Owens, as F. Scott Fitzgerald's secretary. Small 3-ring looseleaf green cloth notebook, containing 31 leaves of mostly separate accounts, all showing then-current accounts, and dates and amounts of partial or complete payments, on rectos with 4 of thinly-ruled paper, in pencil or black ink, entirely in the hand of Mrs. Owens. Further, includes one additional leaf with slightly later 1934 payments, and three pages of script and shorthand notes or dictated letters, probably done by Fitzgerald on the eve of his departure from Baltimore to stay at the Grove Park Inn, Asheville, in May, 1935. Unpretentious binding, in sound condition, contents very good throughout, completely legible, few leaves with small tears at punch holes.
Shows vividly the manner and cost of the way Fitzgerald lived just prior to the publication of "Tender Is the Night". No running total account is included, but the sum was in the thousands. The entries are mundane or exciting, depending on the reader's point of view: Bryn Mawr School, Helen Bevan (garage), Craig House ($489.34), Class of '17, Western Maryland Dairy, Gas & Electric Company, Dr. Herbert Gorgas ("dentist - Mrs. F"), Income tax ($186.45 average each quarter), Johns Hopkins Hospital, Liquor (45 different entries - total of $57.89), Park Meat Market, Dr. Charles O'Donovan (4 visits in January), Scottie's allowance ($2.25 per week, with occasional advances), Sheppard & Enoch Pratt Hospital (at least $1168.75 paid from January to April to eliminate balance due), Automobiles, etc.
The dictated correspondence includes apparent letter to Arnold Gingrich, as editor of "Esquire". In Mrs. Owens' own shorthand version, and so far undeciphered. No appropriate publication can be found either; the text includes 2 obvious references to H.L. Mencken, is addressed to "Arnold", and bears partial mailing address of "919 N. Mich" ("Esquire"'s offices were then at 919 N. Michigan Avenue, Chicago).
On the reverse of the one page bearing the Gingrich letter is a short note to be typed as a letter to Miss C.M. Egan, 575 W. 177th Street, New York. No mention of this name found in any source yet consulted.
Also laid into notebook are a typed account by Mrs. Owens of several small bills accrued by Fitzgerald (paid originally by Mrs. Owens) in 1935 or 1936, and 3 smaller looseleaf sheets with some other pencil accounting notes, also by Mrs. Owens, exact time span undetermined.
[Estimate $500/750].

FITZGERALD'S ADDRESS/TELEPHONE DIRECTORY

200. _____. Original small 4to notebook used by Isabel W. Owens to maintain address/telephone directory as secretary to F. Scott Fitzgerald, ca. 1933-1935. Black cloth and black and white patterned boards, thinly lined pages, worn at edges, partly shaken, all text very nice.
Much more than just an address book. As can best be determined, this item contains 6½ pages of mostly single line entries, in pen or pencil, primarily in Mrs. Owens' hand, containing names, addresses and/or telephone numbers for persons to be contacted for Fitzgerald. Most entries have been crossed out later with single pencil line, but all entries still legible and clear.
Further, at the front are 6 pages in which Mrs. Owens detailed the precise number of hours she worked for Fitzgerald day by day, from January 29, 1934 to February 2, 1935, plus another leaf further back containing similar entries from December 10, 1934 to May 14, 1935. Also, 16 pages containing
(Continued).

precise amounts and reasons for all expenditures by Mrs. Owens as secretary
and sometime houseparent for Scottie Fitzgerald, from September 20, 1935
to April 23, 1936.
Also, at the rear, 4 pages recording the number of hours Scottie spent
studying French during 1933-1934, broken down by type of study, and a
similar inserted pencil record for 1932-1933.
The expenses accrued by Mrs. Owens (with periodic running totals of what
she was owed by Fitzgerald) are prosaic and exciting at once, with numerous
entries for postage, paper and ribbon, gasoline, telephone and telegrams,
local merchants, paints for Zelda, and everything else which Mrs. Owens
handled and then sought reimbursement for.
The address list, in brief, covers all the persons Fitzgerald needed to
deal with, from local doctors and merchants, maids and nurses, Baltimore
friends, and many prominent names in national circles, e.g., Mencken,
Harold Ober, Charles Scribner, Edmund Wilson, Gilbert Seldes, Roland
Young, Alfred Stieglitz, Clark Gable, Dorothy Parker, and on and on, plus
many unrecognizable names. A primary source for study of Fitzgerald's
years in Baltimore, never before available to any biographer or student.
[Estimate,$1000/1500].

201. (FITZGERALD). Original 1935 Baltimore City property tax bill sent to F. Scott
Fitzgerald for taxes due on the house at 1307 Park Avenue. Oblong 8vo, single
sheet, printed text, pencil numbers and identity of taxpayer, few old folds,
reverse completely in carbon for copy, punch dated receipt at right side, in
quite good condition.
Fitzgerald's Bolton Hill house was assessed at $2000, with state and
city taxes amounting to $55.32, including interest and penalty. No date
is on the bill but it was paid on January 8, 1936, according to the cancel
punch.   [Estimate $45/75].

202. _____. Original typed 2-page itemized account of current debts of F. Scott
Fitzgerald as of August 17, 1936. Single 4to and long 4to sheets, single
spaced, with some later pencil adjustments, entirely typed and annotated by
Isabel W. Owens. Few horizontal folds, short (1/2") tear at top left blank
corner, old paper clip rust stains at same corner.
No over-all total is given, but the corrected figures amount to approximately $7845, not counting an additional $8000 to Harold Ober, and $9618.09
to Scribner's, as Fitzgerald had placed assignments on his life insurance
policy to cover them.
Within a month, Fitzgerald's mother died, and his inheritance helped him
to emerge from this financial pit, but Scottie's schooling and Zelda's illness soon put him in debt again.   [Estimate $50/90].

203. _____. Gathering of nine (9) letters or notes sent to Isabel W. Owens by authors
planning biographical studies of the F. Scott Fitzgeralds, 1948-1975. All one-
page, various formats, few folds, some with original envelopes, in very good
condition, one with old wrinkles and edge chips. Includes 3 TLSs by Arthur
Mizener, all 1948; one TLS by Dan Piper, December, 1949, who wondered whether
Fitzgerald's writing style underwent a noticeable change from writing in long-
hand ("The Great Gatsby") to dictating ("Tender Is the Night"); 2 TLSs from
Nancy Milford, 1963; and one TLS and 2 holograph postal cards from Howard
Boulden, 1974-1975. Lot also includes carbon copy of TLS from Mrs. Owens to
Mizener, expressing her willingness to discuss her life with the Fitzgeralds.
(Together, 10 items).   [Estimate $60/90].

3 AUTOGRAPH LETTERS BY ZELDA FITZGERALD

204. FITZGERALD, ZELDA S. 2 1/2-page ALS, (Craig House, Beacon, New York), no date,
ca. April 15, 1934, to Isabel W. Owens. Folded 8vo sheet, completely in pencil
script, signed in full on 2d page (before postscript), on recto of first page,
and both sides of second page. Light old water stains across both pages but
intact, all text legible and clear.
Written shortly after her transfer to Craig House from Sheppard and
Enoch Pratt Hospital, in mid-March, 1934. In full: "Mr. Fitzgerald writes
that you are very busy. When you get time, what I want is
"1) Baker's Book of Dramatic Technique; 2) Aristotle, in one volume; 3)
The Life of Pavlova by D'Andre; 4) The Nature of the Physical World by
Eddington - top hall.   (Continued).

"All except the Aristotle we have at home, so why not 'phone the book store to send the best they can find?
"Thanks for the paints. They have not arrived. Please send all these books. Also (and important) Emile Faure's History of Art, which we also have at home.
"Hoping the excitement is not wearing you out. Devotedly ...
"The Golden Treasury you sent is Scottie's and un-annotated. If its too complicated I can do with it, but if you can send my own, I'd rather have it. Will return the other.
"I mean, with this one, I can't indulge in the pleasure of thinking what a bad poet Masefield was because he's not there."
The reference to the "excitement" is probably to the April 12, 1934 publication of "Tender Is the Night". [Estimate $300/450].

205. FITZGERALD, ZELDA S. 3-page ALS, Craig House, Beacon, New York, no date, ca. late April, 1934, to Isabel W. Owens. Folded 8vo sheet, completely in pencil script, signed in full, on recto of first page, and both sides of second page. Old water and transfer stains but intact, all text legible and clear.
Probably written a few days after the letter in the above lot, as text begins: "One last task ..." Text concentrates on various books she wishes to have sent to her, plus short itemized list of painting supplies Zelda wanted Mrs. Owens to ship to her: "1 -- another large can of permalba; 2 -- an inch-wide flat camel hair brush; 3 -- another brush like the last one ($2) pointed".
In part: "If Mr. Fitzgerald has Menken's (sic) Treatise (on the Gods) I would like to read it very much. 2) Would you ask him to chose (sic) me a comprehensive volume of Aristotle as I would probably never finish the eleven volumes of the original ...
"I am very apologetic about bothering you so much. However, books are not such an unwieldly package to mail and Webers (local art supply store) will mail the rest. Also, turpentine and oil.
"Thanks a million times. You seem to have become my general source of supplies. Also, there is a green flowered golf-dress missing from the summer clothes.
"I hope all goes well on Park Avenue and I'm sorry to inconvenience you again. Sincerely ..."
Written while under hospitalization after her third nervous breakdown, in January, 1934. The rambling text is revealing, as are two pencil marginalia: at the top and middle of the first page, Mrs. Fitzgerald has boldly pencilled the names "Diaghilev" and "Doubrowska". The ballet was one of her passions; she thought she performed in front of a representative of Diaghilev's Ballet Russe in Paris in 1930, and her paintings of ballet figures are well represented in "The Romantic Egoists".
[Estimate $300/450].

206. _____. 2-page ALS, no date, probably July, 1936, to Isabel W. Owens. Small folded 8vo sheet, completely in pencil script, signed in full, on recto of first page and verso of second page. Old water and rust stains across both pages with brief effect on text plus one small hole through both leaves, text still legible and clear.
Probably written from Highland Hospital in Asheville, as the text begins: "Now that you are about to close the apartment ...", referring to F. Scott Fitzgerald's apartment in the Cambridge Arms, which he maintained until July, 1936.
Rest of text: "... would you be kind enough to send me my personal silver, the perfume Scottie gave me last birthday, and any belts & clothes of mine that happen to be still extant -- I can't find the top of my Austrian suit and it might have got left at Shephard (sic).
"With many thanks Mrs. Owens -- and regrets of the necessity of disturbing you. Devotedly ..." [Estimate $250/325].

NOTE: BIDS DO NOT INCLUDE 10 PER CENT BUYER'S PREMIUM

FINISH PASTEL DRAWING BY ZELDA FITZGERALD

207. **FITZGERALD, ZELDA S.** Original pastel drawing of group of brightly colored tropical flowers in Art Deco-style vase, ca. 1934, drawn while under psychiatric treatment at Sheppard and Enoch Pratt Hospital. Approximately 24 X 19" on light brown art board, unsigned, in fine condition.

    Rather unusual effort, lacking any background, unlike most of the reproduced work of Mrs. Fitzgerald of the period. Done in orange, blue, red, yellow, brown and purple chalks, art board surface slightly rough with faint ribbed pattern.

    Flowers drape over front of vase, which is an amalgam of curves and diagonals. The flowers as well emphasize curves and jutting lines; the petals have a spear-like configuration, similar to the Bird of Paradise flower.

    This drawing was exhibited in the Montgomery Museum of Art during an exhibition of Mrs. Fitzgerald's work in the 1970s.

    Provenance: direct descendant of Mr. & Mrs. Paul T. MacKie, Jr., close Baltimore friends of the Fitzgeralds; Mrs. MacKie dated F. Scott Fitzgerald before he married Zelda Sayre, and Mr. MacKie was a Princeton University friend of Fitzgerald. The MacKies are included in the address/telephone list offered in Lot #200. [Estimate $1500/2500].

UNIQUE ORIGINAL CARBON SECRETARIAL TYPESCRIPT OF "SCANDALABRA"

208. _____. "Scandalabra". Original secretarial carbon typescript, 1933. 4to, 62 double-spaced pages plus title sheet, all loose sheets. In very good condition, top and bottom sheets with some wear from storage and being handled, few pages with old rust spot at upper left from ancient paperclips.

    Unique copy, with minor yet apparently intentional dialogue changes in Act III, thereby differing with the 61-page version in the Zelda Fitzgerald Papers at Princeton University Library. The only other known version, and only other known original copy of the play, is the 91-page typescript serving as the copyright deposit copy (1932) at the Library of Congress. The earliest version is unpublished; the Princeton text (1933) has only been published in a 500-copy edition in 1980.

    The first 2 acts in the copy offered here are completely identical with the Princeton copy, and appear to be a second copy carbon, on "Hammermill Bond" paper. Act III, however, has been typed in carbon, on a variety of onion skin paper, and contains alterations (albethey minor) at three different locations in the dialogue. In the first case, one 2-sentence statement by "Andrew" is divided with the first sentence placed one line of dialogue ahead.

    The second change, 4 words are deleted from one line of "Baffles" comments. And the third alteration occurs in the last line of the play, with 3 words eliminated, and somewhat awkward as a result.

    The reasons for the changes are unknown, but the fact remains that this version of Act III differs not only in direct comparison with the actual Princeton version, but that the last 8 pages do not correspond even in the opening and closing lines on each sheet.

    The typescript is contained in the original return mailing envelope, sent to Zelda Fitzgerald from Roland Young, then head of The Theater Guild, and to whom the text was apparently submitted for consideration of publication or production. The return address is "La Paix, Rodgers Forge, Towson, Baltimore, Maryland", but with pencil forwarding address to 1309 Park Avenue, Baltimore. Envelope near complete, portion of address torn off but present.

    In her biography of Zelda Fitzgerald, Nancy Mitford the 1932 version "made the rounds of producers for a few months" that year; a copy was sent to agent Harold Ober in October, the same month Zelda's only novel, "Save Me the Waltz" was published, and the same month the copyright copy was deposited. There is no mention of another effort following the 6-day run of the play (its only contemporary production) in Baltimore, June 26-July 1, 1933, by the Junior Vagabond Players, at a converted carriage house on West Read Street just off Charles Street (house since leveled for parking lot).

    But the Fitzgeralds did not move to Park Avenue until December, 1933, so another effort was obviously attempted. Precisely when, however, cannot be determined since someone in years past tore off the stamps used for First Class postage, and thus the postmark as well. (Continued).

236 *Appendix 2*

```
WESTERN UNION

LD34 CF 46 NL DUPLICATE OF TELEPHONED TELEGRAM

    TDS VANNUYS CALIF SEP 14 1939

MRS ALLIEN OWENS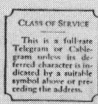

        GREENRIDGE ROAD TOWSON MD

THANK YOU STOP THE YOUNG ELEMENT IS DOMINANT AND REEKING
WITH GUILE SO DONT LET HER CHISEL ME OUT OF ANY CONTRABAND
AS SPECIFIED STOP WIRE ENCINO ADDRESS HOW MUCH THIS WILL
COST STOP WILL BE EAST IN NOVEMBER AND MAY MOVE ALL GOODS
WEST REGARDS

        SCOTT FITZGERALD

            115P 15TH
```

197

200

The 91-page version is believed by scholars to be solely Zelda's work, a very visible example of the competition she felt with her husband. But authorship of the 1933 version is still in debate: it is known that F. Scott Fitzgerald saw the dress rehearsal and led an all-night rewrite session prior to opening night. Whether the Princeton version and the one offered here represent Zelda's revised version(s) which survived until the dress rehearsal, or are they the rewritten husband-and-wife collaboration cannot be determined by this auction house.

The December, 1933 or later missing postmark is not really a help, either: Zelda could have easily sent a copy to Young prior to the dress rehearsal, or after the play's brief run. It would not be unusual for a producer to hold on to a new play for several months before returning it, especially if it was an effort by someone of repute.

[Estimate $1200/1800].

209. SAYRE, MINNIE MACHEN. 6-page ALS, Montgomery, December 4, 1935, from Zelda Fitzgerald's mother to Isabel W. Owens. In blue ink on both sides of folded 8vo sheets, with original hand-addressed envelope. Both the envelope and letter have received significant stains from past water damage, but both sheets of writing are still intact, small eroded holes on each sheet (few words affected), all writing very legible and mostly clear; envelope has become somewhat tired.

In part: "With both parents away and not well I like to be assured of Scottie's health and happiness. As you say it is hard not to be able to help Zelda. If her illness were anything else I might be with her constantly. But the doctor so far has not invited me to visit her and I must not do anything to hinder her progress ...

"(Scott) has no incurable malady as he improved so last summer. ...Perhaps I help Zelda more by staying quietly in my own home."

Other portions concern Christmas suggestions, the weather and mounting number of new cars on Montgomery streets. Written in large flowing script, with pages 1 and 2 on the outer halves of the folded sheet, and page 3 from top to bottom on the inner side; in likewise fashion, on the second sheet.

At the time, Zelda was an inpatient at Sheppard and Enoch Pratt Hospital, and Scott was living in Hendersonville, North Carolina. Scottie was going to school in Baltimore, and living with the Finneys or Mrs. Owens.

[Estimate $50/80].

"IN A MOST PITIABLE STATE"

210. SMITH, ROSALIND S. 3-page TLS, New York, October 2, 1936, from Zelda Fitzgerald's sister to Isabel W. Owens. 8vo, 2 single sheets, text on both sides of first leaf, signed in ink at base of recto of second sheet, both with single center fold, in fine condition.

Very extensive text regarding Zelda, F. Scott, and Scottie Fitzgerald: "... I take my first free moment to ... tell you the status of the Fitzgerald family as far as I know it ... I can't tell you the whole story I gathered this Summer in North Carolina, where I spent six weeks with my Mother in order to aid her in seeing Zelda ... the latter is in better condition than she has been in three years. She has gained 27 pounds ... is cheerful and busy with a number of interests - painting, gardening and sewing, in addition to a daily five-mile walk -- and loves the hospital where she is quartered in a pleasant residence with the privacy and equipments of home ... If the improvement continues, the doctor thinks she will be well enough to leave the hospital by February ... (but) since Scott himself is in critical condition, and we hardly dare anticipate more than a day ahead.

"As you doubtless know, he broke his shoulder about two months ago ... That has healed now, but he remains shut up in his room at the Grove Park, in a most pitiable state, and seems unable to force himself to leave there and follow his doctor's advice to go to a sanitarium. When I saw him last, at the end of August, he still had day and night nurses, and looked so ghastly and was so jittery that I lost all hope of his ever getting on his feet again ... I think he has reached the point where he does not realize the seriousness of his condition, or else is unable to act to relieve it. It made me ill to see him, but there is nothing that anybody can do about it.

"... This sounds like a hospital record, but the Fitzgeralds furnish no other kind of news. I appreciate all you have done for them over the years, and hope you will continue to write to Scottie because she seems to have more affection for you than for anybody else she knows ..."

[Estimate $125/175].

> A 13
>
> 211. WARREN, CHARLES M. ("BILL"). One-page TLS, Culver City, California, December 6, 1934, to Isabel W. Owens. Single 4to sheet with Metro-Goldwyn-Mayer Studios engraved letterhead, 2 horizontal folds, in excellent condition, with original hand-addressed stamped cover with Los Angeles postmark, envelope also very choice, with slight aging, hand-written ink personal return address with name on flap.
> Warren was literally F. Scott Fitzgerald's godson, and whom Fitzgerald took under his wing in 1934 as Fitzgerald's supervised re-write man when Warren was 18 years old.
> In part: "Dearest Mrs. Typewriter ... What in heaven's name is my brother doing in Scott's room? Is he learning how to write or to drink? Please, Isabel, if John stays over half an hour pat him on the head and send him home.
> "I don't suppose Scott is very well, although he never says in his letters. And I guess I was more frightened than sick when I wrote him I wanted to come home ... I've had enough of this dazzling film city for a while ..." Signed in blue ink script, "Bill Warren".
> In May, 1934, Fitzgerald had staked Warren to a Hollywood trip to help him try to land a writing job, and thus perhaps sell some studio on the film treatment of "Tender Is the Night" the two had prepared in Baltimore in April and early May. Matthew Bruccoli reports Warren never got a Hollywood job, and no studio was interested in their movie version. Thus, the M-G-M letterhead is a bogus use, and why Warren crossed out the studio's return address on the front of the envelope. Perhaps Warren acquired the letterhead during an interview with M-G-M story editor Samuel Marx, to whom Fitzgerald wrote a glowing letter of introduction, comparing Warren to Hemingway: "I haven't believed in anybody so strongly since Ernest".
> [Estimate $75/125].
>
> NS

Other Fitzgerald-Owens Letters in Catalogues

Nineteen additional letters from Fitzgerald to Owens were sold in the 1990s and 2000s by dealers and auction houses—principally by Ken Lopez (Catalogues 61, 67, 78). The dates assigned to certain letters by cataloguers may be unreliable. There is no way of determining if more Fitzgerald-Owens correspondence was sold apart from those items in catalogues.

The Fitzgerald-Owens letters have been scattered, and most of them are now unlocated. The catalogue descriptions and facsimiles provide a record of these documents. This report is based on the twenty-one catalogues we have located.

ALS, 2 pp. (ca. 9 November 1935)

Lame Duck Books Catalogue 20 (April 1995), $5,000.
Thomas A. Goldwasser [January 2005], $15,000.

> 205. **FITZGERALD, F. Scott.** *Autograph Letter, Signed,* 1935. Letter to his secretary in Baltimore, Isabel Owens, on two legal-size sheets, written in pencil, rectos only. An intriguing letter written during his stay at the Skyland Hotel in Hendersonville, NC. He arrived impoverished and rather unconfident, but immediately set out offering stories to various magazines. He mentions here the Post, which apparently rejected something he'd sent, and Esquire, which had sent him an advance he's enclosing to defray some of his debt through Owens. It was during his stay here that he would produce the articles that would form the basis of "The Crack-Up," for Esquire. Fitzgerald mentions a situation involving one of the string of flirtations and romantic entanglements in which he engaged while in North Carolina. "Everything was going well until the offspring of my Tryon friend arrived with the idea that I was playing fast and loose with mama. My God! when he probably couldn't be sure who his own father is -- and, beyond that, when I have an absolutely clear conscience in the matter. It was plenty upsetting, because there is literally nothing you can say or do across the generations (indecipherable). Anything said or done would have made it worse for the main 3 parties concerned so I had to let this snippy Etonian kid (and they're trained to be snooty) -- I had to let him sass me when I could have killed him, this time without beer openers!" It's not quite clear to whom Fitzgerald refers, though certainly possibly either Laura Guthrie or Beatrice Dance. The final remark above, though, refers to a well-known incident in which a drunken Fitzgerald -- he'd taken to drinking beer almost constantly, up to 20 bottles a day for a time while in NC -- attacked a hotel bellboy with a bottle opener. A good letter, offering revealing glimpses into Fitzgerald's personal life during one of the many difficult periods in his later years, and allusions to some of his least enviable moments. $5,000.00

Lame Duck Books Catalogue 20

ALS, 11 pp., n.d. [ca. 14 November 1935]

Lame Duck Books Catalogue 19 (December 1994), $25,000.
Ken Lopez Catalogue 78 [1995], $25,000.

> *Long Fitzgerald letter*
>
> 190. **FITZGERALD, F. Scott.** *Autograph Letter, Signed.* An exceptional eleven-page autograph letter (in pencil) to his secretary Isabel Owens, undated, but written during 1935, including an extraordinary two-page coda headed "About Scotty" containing instructions for the care of his daughter Frances Scott Fitzgerald at a somewhat difficult time in her adolescence. The letter, as so many of his letters, especially in the last decade of his life deals to some extent with financial difficulties and his often byzantine strategies for coping with them -- not to mention his usually hopeful assessment of his various prospects. Other parts are more personal: "But my health and morale have thrived -- I am alone & it's simply gorgeous. Certain times absolutely alone have become a necessity to me. Even at La Paix I really had it -- nobody not even Zelda bothered me in my suite, but that feeling has increased lately to the point of a mania." Much of the letter addresses his situation with his daughter: "I am at wits end about her...she is cross and unpleasant in tone...a general querroulousness," and; "Perhaps the fact that I have a little lost faith in myself lately has communicated itself to her. Certainly I am not good for her now...No one needs a mother more than she needs one now." He mentions his drinking several of times, "...not a soul in town even knows I'm a writer or a drinker, or susceptible, or poor or sick." And he characterizes a landlord whose premises he intends to vacate thus: "Whenever I think of that bland, unctuous, cowardly rogue it makes my blood boil. I dream about him at night." The two pages devoted to Scotty consist of a list (from the obsessive list-maker himself) of rules for her conduct now that she has not the regime of a boarding school to oversee it for her, along with Fitzgerald's justifications and glimpses of his creeping worries. He addresses one specific "symptom" of her recalcitrance: "There is something about this seeing one movie over and over again or playing one tune over and over again that is phoney. It's not only stultifying but it's an obsession. It absolutely must stop. I know all young girls live in a dream world but with Scotty it's a danger; she must be in touch with simple and practical realities in her spare time..." A propos of which last, he remarks, "what do they teach them in camps nowadays? To hunt Zebras? They used to teach us to clean and cook fish." An exceptional letter from one of the greatest American writers of the 20th Century, including two pages that can reasonably be characterized as a original manuscript. $25,000.00

Lame Duck Books Catalogue 19

ALS, 1 p. [ca. 15 November 1935]

Ken Lopez Catalogue 67 [1993], $5,500.

Nate's Autographs Catalogue 2 (5 February 1994), $2,750–$3,000.

University Archives Catalogue 116 (1994), $3,500. Envelope catalogued separately at $1,050!

Remember When Catalogue 34, Part I (7 January 1995), $1,500–$2,500.

Historical Documents International (28 April 1995), letter only, $2,500–$3,500.

> 142. **FITZGERALD, F. Scott. One-Page ALS on Legal-Size Stationery**, together with **hand-addressed envelope**, postmarked November 15, 1935, and **one-page holograph note**, giving Mrs. Owens permission to enter Fitzgerald's apartment at will. The letter is written in pencil from Hendersonville, North Carolina, and encloses a check for $50 (not present) and reports on Scotty, who is staying with friends in Tryon, N.C. Fitzgerald goes on to advise Mrs. Owens that "you will get a wire from Wilmington or word from a lawyer in Balt. relative to appartment [sic] squabble" and he says that he still needs "to bluff out of lease if humanly possible. In any case cant [sic] work there possibly with that music." A postscript closes with the information that he has sent a stock certificate to the bank with instructions to sell, and asks her to find out what they realized. Signed "Fitzgerald." The accompanying note is written in ink, also on legal-lize stationery, with a couple of small blotches. It instructs the reader that "This entitles my secretary Mrs I. W. Owens to enter my appartment in the Cambridge Arms at will," and is signed "Scott Fitzgerald" and dated "Nov 9th 1935." With hand-addressed envelope in ink in Fitzgerald's hand, much more neat and legible than the letter itself, or even the note. Three pieces signed; overall very good. $5500

Ken Lopez Catalogue 67

ALS, 2 pp. (postmarked 10 December 1935)

Ken Lopez Catalogue 67 [1993], $4,500.

Between the Covers Catalogue 56 (1997), $4,500.

> 143. **FITZGERALD, F. Scott. Two-Page ALS on Legal-Size Stationery** (one sheet, both sides), together with **hand-addressed envelope**, postmarked December 10, 1935. Again written in pencil from Hendersonville, Fitzgerald again writes about finances: "Have wired Ober [his agent] for money... Enclosing one [check] for Margaret & one for Stafford when you find there is enough there." He lists others whose bills he must pay, including two nurses, presumably for Zelda, and then he reports emphatically (underlined) "Also lost my list of bills and the bills themselves..." After that the letter becomes less frantic with worry and more chatty and personable: "...I've got the world's best grippe from the swimming, Zelda is only some better, but much better physically & Esquire clamoring for still unfinished article, so I am perfectly happy & at home." Signed "Scott Fitz" with a P.S. reporting "no news at all of Scotty." $4500

Ken Lopez Catalogue 67

ALS, 3 pp., n.d. [ca. 19 December 1935]

Ken Lopez Catalogue 61 [1992], $7,500.

Thomas A. Goldwasser Catalogue (January 2005), $15,000.

Thomas A. Goldwasser Catalogue (Winter 2005), $15,000.

> 116. **FITZGERALD, F. Scott. Autograph Letter Signed.** Three pages, on legal-size stationery, undated. In typical fashion, the letter starts on an extremely gloomy note:"Dear Mrs. Owens: The situation is as bad as can be. Here is my solution. To get any money for Xmas it seems necessary to sell this latest story — the one you read. Ober wants it revised, thinking it slight, & I agree with him. In process of doing so I got sick again & you can imagine my state of mind." He goes on to make detailed plans arranging to finish the revision and carry it from Asheville, North Carolina, where he has been staying, to Baltimore to deliver it to her so that she can deliver it to the publisher. In his state of mind he cannot deliver it himself ("I have no energy to face them...I can manage a letter, which if the story is good will make them wire a check..."). He then says "Once home I can rest a night & see Zelda & Scotty, Xmas & then make plans afresh. But I think that bad as I may be as an Xmas present at the time I will be better than to arrive a bankrupt & embarass of [sic] everyone." Boldly signed "Scott Fitzgerald." In this letter, it is clear that Fitzgerald has used Mrs. Owens as a reader for a story he's been working on, and he confides in her Harold Ober's reaction to the story (Ober was his agent). The extended passages formulating a plan for finishing the story, delivering the manuscript, and getting paid, as well as his lengthy explanation of his own "condition" show the writer as not just a creative artist but also a husband and father, concerned with the upcoming Christmas holiday. He ends the letter with a plea that Mrs. Owens be able to accomodate this plan: "Hope you can arrange your part of this. Look the letter over & note such points as train time and calling Miss Abercrombie [at the Post, who had apparently agreed to publish the story when it was ready]. There is literally no money unless this come off, & just about as I've scheduled it." A lengthy, revealing and touching letter, in which Fitzgerald emerges looking all-too-human, more than slightly desperate, and almost frail. $7500.00

Ken Lopez Catalogue 61; location: Bruccoli Collection

ALS, 1 p., n.d. [ca. 1936]

Ken Lopez Catalogue 61 [1992], $2,500.

> 118. **FITZGERALD, F. Scott. Autograph Letter Signed.** One page, 6" x 9 ½", undated. On gray pictorial stationery from the Grove Park Inn, in Asheville, North Carolina. A short handwritten note touching on a number of "business" matters, including literary: "Dear Mrs. Owens: Haven't finished the revision yet but Ober sold Make Yourself at Home to Pictorial for $2500 so there'll be some money very soon." A postscript written vertically up the side of the page says: "Ober hasn't yet received or deposited any money on this. Will wire about releasing checks." A second postscript, written in the upper right corner of the sheet, reads: "Remind Mrs. Smith about French matter, & Scottie about my muffler." The letter is folded twice for mailing, and a bit of paper is missing along one fold, just missing affecting any letters in the vertical postscript. There are also several discolored patches, where the paper apparently got damp at some point. Initialed by the author, "F.S.F."$2500.00

ALS, 2 pp., n.d. [ca. Spring–Summer 1936]

Ken Lopez Catalogue 61 [1992], $5,000.

> 117. **FITZGERALD, F. Scott. Autograph Letter Signed.** Two pages, legal-size stationery, undated. A remarkably personal letter from Fitzgerald to his secretary: he expresses concern for her health ("About your cold – I'm awfully sorry & I hope you're feeling quite well") and goes on to talk about his own feelings and the place he is staying, apparently a rest hotel, or retreat. "I am so damn well & restless I really think (this is no joke) I'll leave here in 10 days and spend the summer in New York City... It's beautiful here [North Carolina, apparently] but I hate it — haven't spoken to a soul, nor done any decent work, nor slept." He tells her that "a sign in the elevator says this is a great place for 'oversocietied women.' Tell Scotty to tip off Mrs. Eager." On the ever-present subject of money, this letter is optimistic to the point of poignancy: "I have check books that say $500. and notes that say $300. so my finances are a mystery but life & experience will straighten them." As other, later letters reveal, Fitzgerald's finances seem to have remained a mystery, and life and experience seem not to have sufficed to straighten them noticeably. He concludes this letter with some instructions for practical matters, ending with the particularly warm closing, "I miss you, personally & officially. Ever Your Friend," and <u>boldly signed "Scott Fitz."</u> $5000.00

TL, 1 p. (4 August 1936)

Harris Auction Galleries Sale Number 234 (10 May 1985), item 192, not sold. See pp. 228–29. Location: Bruccoli Collection.

TL, 1 p. (14 August 1936)

Harris Auction Galleries Sale Number 234 (10 May 1985), item 193, not sold. See p. 229. Location: Bruccoli Collection.

Wire (2 September 1936)

Harris Auction Galleries Sale Number 234 (10 May 1985), item 194, not sold. See pp. 229–30. Location: Bruccoli Collection.

ALS, 4 pp., n.d. [Fall 1936]

Sotheby's, New York, Sale Number 7001 (3 June 1997), $5,750 BP. Assigned date in catalogue is incorrect.

> *Property of Various Owners*
>
> 107
> **Fitzgerald, F. Scott**
> Autograph letter signed ("Scott Fitz"), in pencil, 4 pages (13 x 8½ in.; 330 x 216 mm), [no place, no date but early November 1934] to his typist, Mrs. Isabel W. Owens
>
> QUIBBLING OVER TYPING CHARGES. Irate with the bill his typist, Mrs. Isabel W. Owens, has presented for payment, Fitzgerald writes: "I still cant see how with typing out and no carrying or dictation my work could have averaged four hours a day. And when did we even even [sic] mention a rate of pay that would work out to $33.00 a full week." Not wanting to labor the point further, Fitzgerald notes the bill has been paid and even concedes the bill "probably more nearly approximated how valuable you have been to me . . . ." Yet Fitzgerald does not relent, noting, "nevertheless knowing my utterly straitened [sic] circumstances I think you chose a poor time to spring on me an utterly new scale of salary that we have not even discussed . . . ." Fitzgerald proceeds to harp on the unfairness of the abrupt wage hike imposed by his correspondent, lamenting, "you know how inept I am in financial matters . . . I raised $6,000 on the legacy and it's melted away like ice on a heatwave. (Present balance $22.00.) Hotel bill up to $250 and sanitarium still $1300, and the arthritis fever never below 101 for two months . . . ." Fitzgerald catches himself and concludes: "Well, let it go. I certainly let you down this summer in not making the payments you'd counted on and I value your friendship too much to let it slip away on the question of a hundred dollars more or less . . . ." He closes his letter outlining his plans to come north to Princeton, Baltimore or Philadelphia but notes, "If my last story, just finished, doesn't sell, all trips are off . . ."
>
> $6,000–8,000

244 Appendix 2

(4)

great batch of notes — shall I bring them or have them done here? I ought to have a regular secretary on salary but it seems impossible without a house.

If my last story isn't finished, doesn't sell, all hopes are off + I'd so like to see Scottie + get out of this cell. She led her class in 3 subjects out of 5, said she got a nice present from you, likes it as well as Bryn Mawr now (or rather can't decide). I enclose her letter — please mail it back.

Always aff'ly yrs
(but still good
and sore at you)

Scott Fitz —

P.S. The Mackies didn't mention paying for the furniture, did they? Nor Bill Warren give a reliable address — please get one if you can. Scarpulla was long dead, I hope so, + surely Swanie, O Connor! Nancy couldn't have called more than once, tho I admit Rita's calls average 3 times anyones elses. Best to Allien, your grandfather + your sisters.

Sotheby's Sale Number 7001

TLS, 1 p. (22 October 1936)

Thomas A. Goldwasser Catalogue [January 2005], $6,500.

> 88. FITZGERALD, F. SCOTT. TYPED LETTER SIGNED, to Isabel Owens. Asheville, N.C. October 22,1936. One page, paper clip mark, excellent condition. Signed in ink "Scott Fitzgerald". His plan: "I am going North without fail for Thanksgiving and spend at least one day in Baltimore.... If I have to have an all-day session with Ed Poe we will arrange some meeting that does not conflict with that, and I will stay two days." On clothes he wants from storage, and "there are other lost articles: (can't you hear me say 'full colon'?) one is part of a silver set", and money matters. About 300 words.
>
> $6500.00

TL, 1 p. (28 October 1936); wire (26 October 1936); wire (30 October 1936)

Harris Auction Galleries Sale Number 234 (10 May 1985), item 195, $90. See p. 230. Location of 28 October letter: Bruccoli Collection.

ALS, 4 pp. (postmarked 6 November 1936)

Lame Duck Books Catalogue 13 (July 1993), $6,500.
Gerald A. J. Stodolski Catalogue 4 (November 1995), $4,500.
R. M. Smythe Catalogue 157 (13 November 1996), $3,500.

> *Two Fitzgerald letters to his secretary*
>
> 166. FITZGERALD, F. Scott. *Autograph Letter, Signed.* Asheville, NC. Long letter to his secretary, Isabel Owens, written in pencil and covering four sides of two legal-size sheets of white paper. The entire letter concerns financial matters which have taken an unexpected turn for the worse. During much of his creative life, particularly during the drought preceding the publication of *Tender Is the Night* and for most of his final six years, finances weighed heavily on Fitzgerald. Apparently he had seen a glimmer of light at the end of the tunnel when an unexpectedly high bill from his secretary arrived sinking him into a deep funk. The painfully unsympathetic tone of this letter, which verges constantly on accusation, reveals much about the author's relationship with this woman who had been one of the few reliable friends in his later life. As in a number of other letters to her, his emotions are stripped bare; elsewhere he has revealed his innermost fears to her and spoken as to a confessor, here he speaks with little reserve -- he clearly wants to strike a different tone and cannot -- of the frustration her report has caused him, of the nature of their professional relationship in general, and recently when it has been somewhat unsatisfactory, in particular. He seems to feel someone must be to blame, and though there are hints that his husbandry has not been of the best, it cannot be himself -- perhaps there is no one else close enough or on whom he relies so much at this time and she must bear the brunt. He signs off after three pages, but remorseful, he resumes later, "I hate the tone of this letter, but this means so much to me at this time... You are accuracy indeed compared to me but I've known you to make mistakes in my check book of quite considerable sums and maybe you've made one in your accounts. Very gloomily yours, Fitz." An exceptional letter. A few small stains and a small bit of margin torn away, else very good. Hand addressed mailing envelope on Grove Park Inn (Asheville, NC) stationery included. The blurred postmark appears to read Nov. 6, 1936.
>
> $6,500.00

Lame Duck Books Catalogue 13

ALS, 4 pp. [ca. 10–15 November 1936]

Harris Auction Galleries Sale Number 234 (10 May 1985), item 196, $550. See pp. 230–31.

ALS, 2 pp., n.d. [Spring 1937]

Between the Covers Catalogue 27 [ca. September 1992], $4,500.

> 134. FITZGERALD, F. Scott. Unpublished two-page autograph letter **Signed** "Scott Fitz", undated to Allien Owens on the stationary of "Oak Hall Hotel" in Tryon, North Carolina. Octavo. Fitzgerald stayed in Tryon while visiting his wife Zelda who was convalescing in nearby Asheville. This letter deals with various expenses, his own, Zelda and Scotty's. He discusses the great debt he is under from Zelda's hospital bill. He mentions his relative good health, the fact that he has avoided liquor and beer, he relates how he has been driving a $90 1927 Packard to visit Zelda in Asheville once a week. He cautions Mrs. Owens about giving out his address, and in one particularly poignant sentence relays that "The second little Murphy boy died at last". An excellent letter in which Fitzgerald pours out the concerns of his day to day survival. Folded as mailed, a little foxing else very good.
> $4500.00

ALS, 1 p. [Summer–Fall 1937]

Between the Covers Catalogue 27 [ca. September 1992], $2,000.

> 133. FITZGERALD, F. Scott. Unpublished one-page autograph letter **Signed** "Scott Fitz", undated to Allien Owens on "The Garden of Allah" stationary. Small quarto. A brief letter in his characteristic large scrawl requesting Mrs. Owens to contact the storage company and sending condolences on the death of her grandfather. Folded as mailed.
> $2000.00

TLS, 1 p. (20 July 1937)

Between the Covers Catalogue 27 [ca. September 1992], $2,500.
Ken Lopez Catalogue 67 [1993], $2,000.

> 144. **FITZGERALD, F. Scott. One-Page TLS on MGM Stationery**, dated July 20, 1937, shortly after his arrival in Hollywood. A short letter that transmits his new address and remarks "Needless to say, things are going decidedly better. I am working on a Robert Taylor picture." He goes on to relay to her Scotty's address (c/o Harold Ober, his agent) and closes "Ever devotedly," signed "F Scott Fitzgerald" in ink. The signature has bled some but is still quite sharp and clear.
> $2000

Ken Lopez Catalogue 67

TLS, 1 p. (15 November 1938)

Ken Lopez Catalogue 61 [1992], $3,500.
Lame Duck Books Catalogue 12 (March 1993), $2,750.
Lame Duck Books Catalogue 21 (March 1995), $2,500.
Thomas A. Goldwasser Catalogue [January 2005], $5,500.

> 119. **FITZGERALD, F. Scott. Typed Letter Signed.** One quarto sheet, on Metro-Goldwyn-Mayer letterhead, dated November 15, 1938. Typed by a secretary, this letter appears to have been dictated and touches on several matters, in a somewhat perfunctory manner, and also responds quite specifically to a letter Owens must have just written him. He writes: "Dear Mrs. Owens: Thank you. My letter must have explained the New York telegram. Your note to the [here the typed word "letter" is crossed out, and Fitzgerald has written in, "Vanderbilt"] just arrived today." He wishes her well at her new location (she has moved to the country) and compliments her ("...I know you're extremely adaptable but I do believe you'll be happier there. I think, anyway, you'll have your usual calm intelligence and good humor..."). Other matters touched on include arrangements pertaining to furniture, a letter to be written to Scottie about some curtains, and a fur coat, for which she is to "send me a bill for what the whole thing cost you." He mentions having been "in Baltimore exactly two hours on my last trip," apparently to explain not seeing her, and concludes with a comment about his Hollywood work: "I am working on the script of 'Madam Curie' which I find very interesting." One newspaper reported about this that "F. Scott Fitzgerald...has drawn the scenario writing assignment for which most Hollywood writers would have given a right arm....He is adapting *The Life of Madame Curie* for Greta Garbo." One of calmest of the letters to Mrs. Owens; he attends to business, and one gets no sense of the tumult that surrounds this relatively placid moment. <u>Signed, "Ever yours, Scott Fitz."</u> A quite attractive letterhead, with M-G-M's trademark lion in a sunburst. Particularly suitable for framing. $3500.00

Ken Lopez Catalogue 61

TLS, 1 p. (21 November 1938)

Ken Lopez Catalogue 67 [1993], $2,000.

> 145. **FITZGERALD, F. Scott.** **One-Page TLS on MGM Stationery**, dated November 21, 1938. A short note in which Fitzgerald thanks Mrs. Owens "a million for everything" and comments somewhat cryptically on what must be a reference to her previous letter: "Do you mean you lend out dogs for nothing? Good Lord, is that a business? It seems amazing that you are shipping dogs to Denmark." The letter is <u>signed in pencil "Scott Fitz"</u> and there is a <u>holograph postscript in pencil</u>: "will you write to Scottie about coat & curtains?" The paper bears several spots of discoloration where it must have gotten wet, or possibly burned. The signature is bold and clear. $2000

3 wires (9–14 September 1939)

Harris Auction Galleries Sale Number 234 (10 May 1985), item 197, $150. See p. 231.

TLS, 1 p. (11 October 1939)

Kenneth W. Rendell Catalogue 272 [ca. 1998], $4,750.

F. SCOTT FITZGERALD. American author of *The Great Gatsby*. Typewritten Letter Signed, Scott Fitzgerald, one page, quarto, October 11, 1939. To Mrs. Owens, his secretary. "I think you owe me an explanation about this." Fine condition. Framed with a portrait in cream, gray and beaded gilt, measuring 20 inches wide by 15 1/2 inches high. $4750

TL—incomplete (13 May 1940)

Harris Auction Galleries Sale Number 234 (10 May 1985), item 198, not sold. See pp. 231–32. Location: Bruccoli Collection.

TLS, 1 p. (26 June 1940)

Ken Lopez Catalogue 67 [1993], $3,500.
Ken Lopez Catalogue 78 [1995], $3,500.
Thomas A. Goldwasser Catalogue [January 2005], $6,000.

146. **FITZGERALD, F. Scott. One-Page TLS** on plain stationery, dated June 26, 1940. Writing from Hollywood—but apparently typing his own letter, as opposed to the letters on MGM stationery, which were typed for him—Fitzgerald thanks Mrs. Owens "for your very full letter. You certainly went to a lot of trouble about the business and I'm awfully glad to know now where everything is. I'll keep your letter for all future reference to the matter." He then goes on to ask her if she would please get "Zelda's Scandalabra [from storage]...because she does want it. It is a pure concession to an invalid because it will never be produced again but if you are downtown and within range of the place I wish you would get it." After a paragraph of purely business details, Fitzgerald commiserates and reminisces: "I'm sorry you had more than your share of trouble in these troublous times. The days at LaPaix in 1933 seem comparatively tranquil now. You remember how we used to take time out in the middle of the summer mornings to go swimming in the quarry." Someone, presumably Mrs. Owens, has lightly underlined the last two sentences in red ink. Finally, Fitzgerald ends with the comment that "the people out here don't realize yet that there's a war on" and closes, "Ever your friend" signed "Scott Fitz" in pencil. A remarkably warm letter, written less than six months before Fitzgerald died. $3500

Ken Lopez Catalogue 67

TLS, 1 p., n.d. [Summer 1940]

Lame Duck Books Catalogue 13 (July 1993), $3,500.

> 167. **FITZGERALD, F. Scott.** *Typed Letter, Signed.* Hollywood, CA, 1940. A two-paragraph letter to his secretary, Isabel Owens, in Baltimore. He thanks her for seeing to the storage of some of his belongings and for "digging out Zelda's play." He reports that he has been "working on a Shirley Temple picture, which is sort of a gamble, that is I was paid a minimum and will get more if she does it. Strange as it may seem she's a lovely child, very well brought up and not at all the smirking brat she has been in her last pictures." <u>Signed</u> in ink "Scott Fitzgerald." One horizontal and two vertical folds, inch-long tear to top edge. Typed envelope included. $3,500.00

TLS, 1 p. (25 November 1940)

Ken Lopez Catalogue 61 [1992], $3,000.

Nate's Autographs Catalogue 2 (1994), $1,500–$2,000 estimate.

> 120. **FITZGERALD, F. Scott. Typed Letter Signed.** One quarto page, plain stationery, dated November 25, 1940. A short letter written from Hollywood, a month before Fitzgerald died. In it, Fitzgerald remembers a debt that Bill Warren, a young writer who stayed with him for a time in Malibu, still owes him. He tells Mrs. Owens: "It's occurred to me that Bill Warren still owes me $475. I've no idea whether or not he is in any position to pay it but if you ever felt like constituting yourself a private collection agency it would certainly be worth $100 to me to see some of it." He goes on to explain: "You can tell him the truth -- that I've been quite sick again, that I'm in debt and need it. Of course, he is quite possibly broke." He ends the letter will another mention of the storage company where his possessions are being kept, and their not having sent him an amended bill, and closes "With best wishes to you both. Ever your friend," <u>signed "Scott Fitzgerald."</u> Fitzgerald never recovered from this bout of illness. On December 14, he wrote a letter to Zelda in which he told her that the doctors had told him his heart was repairing itself, but that it would take some months. On December 21, as he was waiting for a doctor to arrive at his home, Fitzgerald died of a heart attack, at age 44. $3000.00

Ken Lopez Catalogue 61

Appendix 3
Copies of *This Side of Paradise* Inscribed at Princeton

Fitzgerald wanted to be at Princeton and was staying at the Cottage Club when his first novel was published on 26 March 1920. Eight copies of *This Side of Paradise* inscribed by him for Princetonians during March 1920 have been sold and resold.

1. Aiken Reichner copy*

Phoenix Book Shop Catalogue 83 (April 1967), $500.
Christie's, New York, Sale Number 1579 (2 December 2005), $15,600 BP.

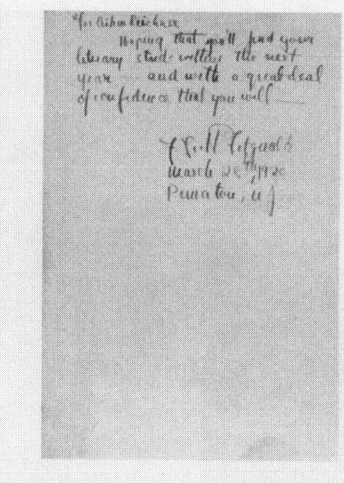

163
FITZGERALD, F. Scott. *This Side of Paradise.* New York: Charles Scribner's Sons, 1920.

8°. (A small dampstain on a few preliminary lower margins.) Original dark green cloth, spine lettered in gilt (spine a little dulled); quarter morocco slipcase. *Provenance:* Aiken Reichner, fellow student at Princeton (presentation inscription).

FIRST EDITION of the author's first book. PRESENTATION COPY, INSCRIBED BY FITZGERALD TO A JUNIOR SCHOOL-MATE AT PRINCETON, AIKEN REICHNER, on the front free endpaper: "For Aiken Reichner / Hoping that you'll find your literary stride within the next year—and with a great deal of confidence that you will— F. Scott Fitzgerald / March 28th, 1920 / Princeton, N.J."

Fitzgerald entered Princeton in the fall of 1913, where he was conditionally admitted to the Class of 1917. With his energy primarily devoted to extra-curricular social and literary pursuits, his grades suffered miserably there. After repeated failed attempts to make-up for missed classes or failing grades, he would eventually drop-out and join the army rather than complete his degree.

Fitzgerald was in residence at the Cottage Club at Princeton for the publication of *This Side of Paradise*, on March 26, 1920. It was presumably here that he met the younger Reichner and inscribed this copy two days after publication. The autobiographical Princeton set novel was an immediate success, and secured Fitzgerald's reputation as the voice of his generation. On the brink of his first great literary success, Fitzgerald confidently inscribed this copy to his junior schoolmate with words of encouragement. Reichner's family had a long connection with Princeton. Aiken followed his father there (Class of 1894), and his son, Aiken Jr., was later a member of the Class of 1947.

"The novel's defiant tone had the same powerful impact on rebellious postwar youth as Salinger's *Catcher in the Rye* did in 1951, and it became a bible and guidebook as the Twenties began to roar. Like Eliot's *Poems*, Owen's *Poems*, Huxley's *Limbo* and Lawrence's *Women in Love* (all of which appeared in 1920), Fitzgerald's novel captures the spirit of disillusionment that followed the Great War" (Meyers, p.56). Bruccoli A5.1.a.

$6,000-8,000

$15,600 BP

USC bid $11,000. Sold for $13,000—

Christie's (2 December 2005)

[*See "'Sleep of a University'—an Unrecorded Fitzgerald Poem" in the *Fitzgerald/Hemingway Annual 1970* for Fitzgerald's revision of Reichner's "Princeton Asleep" (*Nassau Literary Magazine*, November 1920).]

2. Bert Cohn copy

Parke-Bernet, New York, Sale Number 3130 (8 December 1970), $425.

> 39 FITZGERALD, F. SCOTT. This Side of Paradise.
> New York, 1920
> 8vo. FIRST EDITION OF THE AUTHOR'S FIRST BOOK. PRESENTATION COPY, inscribed by Fitzgerald to Bert Cohn, a schoolmate of his at Princeton, and dated March 25th 1920, Princeton, N.J. Original cloth, covers a little soiled. On the copyright page there is the publisher's statement: "Published April, 1920."

3. Unidentified inscribee, 26 March 1920

J & S Catalogue 23 [ca. 1974], $1,000.
J. Stephan Lawrence Catalogue 50 (1980), $1,200.
J. Stephan Lawrence Catalogue 56 (1981), $1,650.
   Possibly a repeated entry.

> 124. **FITZGERALD, F. Scott** — THIS SIDE OF PARADISE. New York, 1920, 8vo., cloth. First Edition. First printing, with "trait," p.13, line 1. (Bruccoli, A5.1.a.) PRESENTATION copy, SIGNED and dated March 26, 1920, by the author. Author's first novel. Enclosed in a folding box. $1,000.00

J & S Catalogue 23 [ca. 1974]

4. John Jay Johns copy

Phillips Sale Number 311 (1 October 1980), $1,600.
Phillips Sale Number 378 (21 May 1981), $825.

> • 189 FITZGERALD, F. SCOTT. This Side of Paradise. 8vo, original cloth (hinges slightly shaken as usual; sizeable tear along inner edge of 2 lower blank leaves; very short tear at bottom edge of upper fly-leaf and following 8 leaves; very slight fraying at head of spine). New York, 1920. FIRST EDITION, FIRST ISSUE. (Bruccoli A5.1.a.).
> *A SIGNED PRESENTATION COPY FROM FITZGERALD to his Princeton classmate, John Jay Johns,* reading, *"Ex laboris/F. Scott Fitzgerald./Cottage Club/Princeton, N.J./March 31st 1920". This copy was inscribed the month previous to the issue of the first issue, April 1920. Inscribed & signed by Johns; with his small handstamp.*
> $825.

Phillips (21 May 1981)

5. James H. Douglas copy

Quill & Brush Catalogue 39 (1980), $5,000.

Christie's, New York, Sale Number 5059A (22 May 1981), $1,000.

Peter L. Stern "Mostly New Arrivals with Selections from Stock" (May 2002), $55,000.

R. A. Gekoski Catalogue 30 (2005), £48,500.

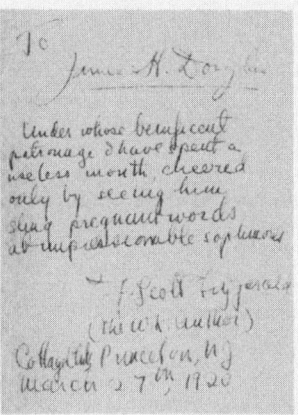

37. **FITZGERALD, F. SCOTT.** *This Side of Paradise*, Charles Scribner's Sons, New York, 1920. First edition, author's presentation copy: "To James H. Douglas Under whose beneficent patronage I have spent a useless month, cheered only by seeing him sling pregnant words at impressionable sophomores F. Scott Fitzgerald (the W.K. Author) Cottage Club, Princeton, N.J. March 27th, 1920." Wanting to be at Princeton on the day of publication of his first novel, the "well-known author" had moved in to the Cottage Club in late February. Douglas, who graduated from Princeton in 1920, was a fellow-member who went on to become Secretary of the U.S. Air Force. An excellent copy in chemise and slipcase. £48500

6. Samuel Graudia copy

Maurice F. Neville Catalogue Number 10 [1984], $1,750.

Swann Galleries Sale Number 1481 (10 November 1988), $1,900.

Swann Galleries Sale Number 1494 (23 March 1989), $2,000.

INSCRIBED ON THE DAY OF PUBLICATION

121A • ——. This Side of Paradise. 8vo, cloth, spine somewhat worn; front hinge starting; Art Deco bookplate on front pastedown; gilt-lettered ¼ morocco folding case by Sangorski & Sutcliffe. New York, 1920 **[600/900]**

 FIRST EDITION, FIRST PRINTING. INSCRIBED AND SIGNED BY FITZGERALD *on front free endpaper*, "For Samuel Graudia, 'The Wireless Red' from the w.k., F. Scott Fitzgerald. March 26th 1920. Princeton, N.J." According to Bruccoli A5.I.a., the book was published 26 March 1920.

Swann Galleries (10 November 1988)

7. Jerry English copy

Ken Lopez Catalogue 114 [March 2001], $25,000.

F. Scott Fitzgerald's First Book
This Side of Paradise
Inscribed in the Week of Publication

NY: Scribner, 1920. An autobiographical novel of youthful ideals and disillusion that helped define the jazz age and perfectly captured the tenor of postwar America, becoming both a critical success and a huge bestseller, going through fourteen printings in the first two years. Virtually overnight, Fitzgerald became both a celebrity and extremely wealthy – a success that he never duplicated with another of his books, even *The Great Gatsby*, and which he never quite lived up to thereafter, nor recovered from. The first printing was only 3000 copies. This copy is inscribed by the author in Princeton on April 1, six days after publication and two days before his wedding to Zelda: "For Jerry English / (Remember now/ its a solemn/ promise about/ June)/ F. Scott Fitzgerald/ April Fools day 1920/ Cottage Club, Princeton." Recased; blended ring to front cover, repaired nick at spine, still a near fine copy with the spine gilt still bright. A very nice copy of one of the most auspicious debuts in twentieth century American literature, and one of the scarcest to find inscribed, especially with a contemporary inscription. $25,000

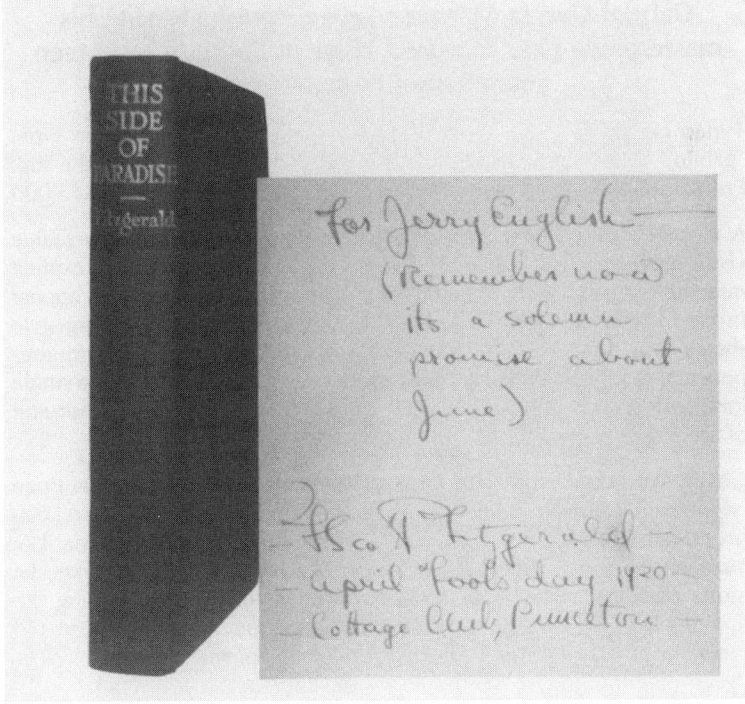

8. Christian Gauss copy

Masterpieces of Modern Literature: The Library of Roger Rechler. Christie's, New York, Sale Number 1098 (11 October 2002), $35,850.

Dean Gauss was the only Princeton faculty member Fitzgerald respected. There is an unsubstantiated report that Gauss had read *This Side of Paradise* ("The Romantic Egoist") in draft. See entry 128, item 88.

Appendix 4
Advance Copies of *Tender Is the Night*

The only advance copies in wrappers for a Fitzgerald book published during his lifetime were distributed for *Tender Is the Night* (Bruccoli A 15.1.a). They are complete texts—not dummies—and were probably intended for use as review copies and salesmen's copies. The Scribners records indicate that five hundred copies were ordered, but it is unlikely that that many copies were distributed because it is so rare: three institutional copies have been located (University of Virginia Library, the J. P. Morgan Library, and the Bruccoli Collection at the University of South Carolina). Seven catalogue appearances have been noted, and it is probable that one or more copies were recatalogued. No copy has been offered for sale since 1995.

These are the most collectible copies of *Tender Is the Night* in terms of priority and rarity; but collectors prefer the first printing in jacket: again the cult of the dust jacket.

Swann Galleries Sale Number 996 (11 September 1975), $800.
Johnson & O'Donnell Catalogue 4 (1981), $2,750.
William H. Allen Catalogue 260 [1983], $3,200.
Thomas A. Goldwasser Catalogue 2 (December 1991), $13,500.
Thomas A. Goldwasser Catalogue 4 (1993), $15,000.
Swann Galleries Sale Number 1697 (22 June 1995), not sold.
American and English Modern Literature from the Library of Mrs. Charles W. Engelhard. Christie's, New York, Sale Number I-8314 (27 October 1995), $4,830.

RARE ADVANCE ISSUE

118.   **Fitzgerald, F. Scott.** *Tender is the Night.* A Romance. Decorations by Edward Shenton. New York: Charles Scribner's Sons, 1934. Original pictorial wrappers. Fine condition. Bruccoli A14.1.a.+. Connolly, *100 Modern Books*, 79.

First edition of Fitzgerald's last completed novel, **an advance review copy bound in wrappers made from the dust jacket.**

Although the publisher's records show that 500 copies bound in wrappers were ordered, to distribute before publication, and 250 received, Fitzgerald's bibliographer was able to locate only a single extant copy, and only four can now be located. The most plausible explanation for the scarcity is that Scribner's decided to bind the extra copies in cloth. This is the only one of the eight of his books published in Fitzgerald's lifetime for which special advance copies were prepared. A beautiful example of this very rare state of one of the finest of American novels. $15,000

Thomas A. Goldwasser Catalogue 4 (1993)

Appendix 5
T. R. Smith

Fitzgerald's 1923 ALS to Boni & Liveright editor T. R. Smith responds to Smith's attempt to lure Fitzgerald away from Scribners, attacks popular author Waldo Frank, and praises Gertrude Stein's *Three Lives*. This letter, which was catalogued eight times between 1966 and 1996, is now unlocated.

 Phoenix Book Shop Catalogue 80 (September 1966), $500.
 Doris Harris Catalogue 15 [1973], $400.
 Beacon Bulletin, Catalogue 28, Issue 19 (Paul C. Richards Autographs [ca. 1973]), $575.
 J & S Graphics Catalogue 20 (1974), $850.
 J. Stephan Lawrence Catalogue 45 (1979), included in a $12,000 lot.
 Joseph the Provider Catalogue 18 (September 1980), $3,000.
 American and English Modern Literature from the Library of Mrs. Charles W. Engelhard. Christie's, New York, Sale Number I-8314 (27 October 1995), $2,415 BP.
 Heritage Book Shop (July 1996), $5,500.

•47
FITZGERALD, F. SCOTT. Autograph letter signed ("F Scott Fitzgerald") to "Dear Tom" (Thomas R. Smith, an editor at Boni & Liveright), Great Neck, L.I., n.d. [c. 1923]. *1 page, 4to, in brown ink, traces of tape on verso from previous mounting, show-through from verso of a long scratch; half morocco slipcase.*

FITZGERALD CHAMPIONS GERTRUDE STEIN, CASTIGATES WALDO FRANK

Smith, who hoped to woo Fitzgerald away from Scribner's, had sent him several new Boni & Liveright books. At the time Fitzgerald was living on the North Shore of Long Island, working on *The Great Gatsby*. "... The Waldo Frank novel is I'm afraid just his usual canned rubbish. He seems to be an ambitious but totally uninspired person under the delusion that by filching the most advanced methods from the writers who originated them *to express the moods of their definate* [sic] *personalities*, he can supply a substitute for his own lack of feeling and cover up the bogus 'arty-ness' of his work. He strains for a simile until his belly aches and brings up a mess of overworked words ... His horror of the cliche is entirely Freudian ... a man incapable of the disassociation of ideas can never think in any words except those that are immortally paired ... I'm afraid Horace [Liveright] has made a bad guess on him. I wish to God you'd republish Gertrude Stein's *Three Lives* and expose some of these jokers. Her book is utterly real. It's in her early manner before the attempt to transfer the technique of Mattisse [sic] & Picasso to prose made her coo-coo ..." (*Three Lives* was reissued in America in 1927 by Albert & Charles Boni.). Published in *Letters*, ed. M.J. Bruccoli and M.M. Duggan, p. 123.

$2,000-3,000

Christie's (27 October 1995)

Appendix 6
Horace Wade

Between 1922 and 1924 F. Scott Fitzgerald wrote encouraging letters to Horace Wade, a boy author who published his first novel, *In the Shadow of the Great Peril* (Chicago: Reilly & Lee, 1920) by the time he was eleven. Fifteen Fitzgerald letters to Wade or Wade's father were sold in Charles Hamilton Auction Number 142 (10 December 1981) for a total of $9,150. Individual letters were recatalogued twenty-nine times at increasing prices during the next twenty years. These sales have not been traced here because Fitzgerald's letters to Wade include little material of literary or biographical interest. Wade's letters to Fitzgerald have not been located.

Wade (1908–1993) became a minor celebrity with his first novel. William Randolph Hearst hired him for the *Chicago American,* and Wade interviewed such figures as Warren G. Harding and Babe Ruth. He also wrote for toy and boys' clothing catalogues. Wade did not become a literary figure, but he published at least ten books. His later reputation was based on his prominence as a race-track manager and horse-race caller at Monmouth and Gulfstream Park.

Hamilton Sale Catalogue 142 omitted part of the description for item 71 and repeated the illustration for item 67.

62 FITZGERALD, F. SCOTT. A.L.S., 2 full pages, penned on two 4to leaves, Great Neck, L.I., undated. To Horace Wade. "...my article was mostly kidding. So many people are taking cracks at youth these days that I thought I'd take a crack at them for a change. I've had the funniest letters from irate clergymen, schoolmasters and saloonkeepers about it...I hope you're not writing too much—fourteen ought to be an age of recieving [sic] impressions and of turning them over, as well as giving them out. Still, every case of our disease is different I suppose. My article didn't apply to brilliant people who may continue to function brilliantly up to seventy-five like Goethe. It was a low brow article written almost entirely in the Ring Lardnerish tortuous idiom for the low brow audience of a low brow magazine. I enjoy irritating the Babbits and the Boobs..." Fitzgerald concludes, "...Imagine being fourteen & having all the money you must have made. I thought your reply to G.B.S. [Shaw] was fine! And I hope you read him..." Some wear, marginal nicks, and small stains, otherwise about good. See listing in this catalogue under SHAW. ....(600/800)

63 FITZGERALD, F. SCOTT. A.L.S., about ½ page, 4to, 6 Pleasant Ave., Montgomery, Ala., undated. To Horace Wade: "Glad you liked *Tales of the Jazz Age*. Ring Lardner lives in Great Neck & is a good friend of ours. He's a great fella." Browned, with several marginal tears (affecting one word of the text), otherwise good. ....(300/400)

64 FITZGERALD, F. SCOTT. Brief A.L.S. on official postcard, Villa Marie, St. Raphael, France, undated and illegibly postmarked. Addressed by Fitzgerald on verso to Horace Wade of Chicago, bearing French postage. "The magazine reached me today. Your article is very well written & many thanks for the boost." Slightly worn, but very good. ....(300/400)

65 FITZGERALD, F. SCOTT. A.L.S., ½ page, 4to, Great Neck, L.I., undated. To Horace (Wade). "I am overcome by your shower of fishing similies. This is not a healthy sign—you cannot model an English prose style on the advertisements for Velvet Joe smoking tobacco. Leave Chicago and fly to Oxford immediately if you want to save your literary soul..." Minor wear, but very good. ....(400/500)

66 FITZGERALD, F. SCOTT. A.L.S., 1 full page, oblong 8vo, Great Neck, L.I., undated. To Horace (Wade). " 'A confidence in your own supreme ability in some one field, however limited, and an always untiring and always experimental interest in that field—this, it seems to me, lies at the root of all success.' If you use this, please don't add to it or change anything in it..." Minor wear and paper-clip stains, otherwise very good. This is actually a brief Fitzgerald A.Ms.S. ....(600/800)

67 FITZGERALD, F. SCOTT. A.L.S., penned on a U.S. one-cent postcard, Great Neck, L.I., undated. Addressed on verso to Horace Wade of Chicago, and postmarked, Oct. 27, 1922. "...If you'll send me your manuscript, *The Heavy Hand of Justice*, I'd esteem it a priveledge [sic] to take it into Scribners...You musn't be discouraged when bad authors praise your books—some of them may be better critics than they are authors. Even the approbation of Wm. Jennings Bryant [sic]—'Mud' Bryant [sic]—can be lived down as you are only fourteen and he will be dead, drawn & quartered by the time you are 21. Of course the Eleanor Glynn business is sadder and graver—but bear up—and if you haven't my deep prejudice against the conservative house of Scribner send on *The Heavy Hand of Justice*..." Slightly browned, otherwise very good. ....(500/600)

[See Illustration Top of Next Page]

[16]

[See Lot No. 67]

68 FITZGERALD, F. SCOTT. Pencilled A.L.S. "Scott Fitzgerald," 1 full page, 4to, Great Neck, L.I., undated. To Horace (Wade), acknowledging receipt of a manuscript, "...I am reading it immediately...Tell your father I received his letter and will bear in mind what he says. The ms. goes to Scribner during the week & they should give you an immediate decision on it..." In a postscript, Fitzgerald notes, "Excuse pencil but am sick in bed." Slightly worn and browned, with a light paper-clip stain, otherwise good. ....(275/350)

69 FITZGERALD, F. SCOTT. A.L.S. penned on a U.S. one-cent postcard, Great Neck, L.I., undated. Addressed on verso to Horace Wade of Chicago and postmarked Nov. 10, 1922. "Your book is now with Scribner. What they will do I cannot say but both Mr. Scribner and Mr. Perkins felt that it will have to stand on its own feet as a boys book and not be judged by the writers age...it is published by them. I read it and I think its remarkable that a boy of eleven should have written it... I'm glad you're having success with your short stories. I think it was a mistake to hold up 'The Heavy Hand of Justice' for three years. The story is well held together and has lots of action..." A few minor creases, otherwise almost fine. ....(300/400)

[See Illustration Top of Next Page]

70 FITZGERALD, F. SCOTT. A.L.S., penned on a U.S. one-cent postcard, Great Neck, L.I., undated. Addressed on verso to Horace Wade of Chicago and postmarked, Nov. 21, 1922. "Scribners would faint with horror if I showed them that list. The big publishers don't do things that way at all. The main thing is the book..." Heavily dampstained on the left ¼ of the card (affecting eight words of text), but the writing is dark and the signature fine. ....(200/250)

71 FITZGERALD, F. SCOTT. A.L.S., 2 full pages (on two 4to leaves), Great Neck, L.I., undated. To Edward O. Wade. "I'm calling up Scribners about the ms. It seems to me that Can the

264 *Appendix 6*

> Dear Horace:
> Great Neck, Long Island
> Enjoyed your most amusing letter. If you'll send me your manuscript The Heavy Hand of Justice I'd esteem it a priviledge to take it into Scribners. I'll bet its awfully good even if Sir Gilbert Parker did think so. You musn't be discouraged when bad authors praise your books—some of them may be better critics than they are authors. Even the approbation of Wm. Jennings Bryant—"Mud" Bryant can be lived down as you are only fourteen and he will be dead, drawn & quartered by the time you are 21. Of course the Eleanor Glynn business is sadder and graver—but bear up—and if you haven't any deep prejudice against the conservative house of Scribner send me The Heavy Hand of Justice to the above adress.
> Yrs ever Scott Fitzgerald

[See Lot No. 69]

72 FITZGERALD, F. SCOTT. A.L.S., 1 full page, oblong narrow 8vo, Gateway Drive, Great Neck, L.I., undated. To Horace (Wade). "Scribners have given me no report on your story but I am calling them up today...I hope your speech goes as big there as your 'Elephant' story went with me.

> your friend
> Scott Fitzgerald
> within the week.

Frankly, I think its got it all over the novel and that your style has matured enormously in it. Tho' of course that doesn't affect the fact that *The Heavy Hand of Justice* is a remarkable achievement for a boy of 11..." Paper-clip stain and a marginal tear, otherwise about fine. ....(300/400)

73 FITZGERALD, F. SCOTT. A.L.S., almost 1 full page, 4to, Great Neck, L.I., undated. To Mr. Wade (father of the recipient of most of this correspondence). "I'm afraid Scribner has decided against the book. It is remarkable for a boy of eleven but I feel he can do even better now that he's fourteen...It's too bad 'The Heavy Hand of Justice' couldn't have been published a few years ago and I am awfully sorry about Horace's disappointment. But then there are many in the writing game—even now I have things turned down constantly, especially a play that I've been working on six months..." Slightly worn and browned, with a few marginal tears, otherwise very good. ....(300/400)

[18]

74 FITZGERALD, F. SCOTT. A.L.S., 1½ pages, penned on two 4to leaves of slightly varying size, Great Neck, L.I., undated. To Horace (Wade). "...Revising is certainly hard and rather dull work. Congratulations on your 15th birthday. My 15th year was the most miserable of my life. And everything got gradually better until when I was 18 I began to feel reasonably sane and happy..." Fitzgerald recommends that Wade read Compton McKenzie's *Youths Encounter*, "...It will help counteract the influence of the blatant vulgarism of Chicago—the ugliest and most raucous city in the world, possibly excepting Liverpool and Manchester and Butte, Montana..." Minor wear, with a few marginal tears, otherwise good. ....(300/400)

75 FITZGERALD, F. SCOTT. A.L.S., 1 full page, 4to, Commodore Hotel, St. Paul, Minn., undated. To Edward Wade of Chicago, agreeing to meet, "both you and Horace" at the Plaza in N.Y.C. "...If youth hasn't learned enough to vote so old age has learned too much that is not true. I advocate disenfranchisement for all over military age & the lethal chamber at 60..." Slightly worn and foxed, with paper-clip stains, otherwise very good. ....(300/400)

76 FITZGERALD, F. SCOTT. Pencilled A.L.S. "Scott Fitz," 1 full page, folio, Hotel des Princes, Rome, Italy, undated. To Horace (Wade). "...You have matured in the last year & got rid of a lot of that forced slang...My new novel, *The Great Gatsby*, comes out in the Spring. Naturally I'm excited about it. Tell Russel Palmer I hope we'll meet sometime at Johns in those happy days when we get back..." Considerably worn and frayed, with some marginal tears and fold breaks, but very satisfactory. *Gatsby* appeared in 1925. ....(250/300)

Index

Abercrombie, Miss (unidentified), 24
"Absolution," 165
Across the River and into the Trees (Hemingway), xxiv
Adams, George Matthew, 14
Adventure Magazine, 59
Adventures of Huckleberry Finn (Twain), 165
Afternoon of an Author (ed. Mizener), 65, 125, 174
Ahearn, Patricia and Allen (book sellers), 10, 181–93
Air Raid (movie), 202–3
Aitkin, Zoë, 96
Albert and Charles Boni (publisher), 117, 260
A. L. Burt (publisher), 82, 171
Alexander Autographs (auction house), 109
Algonquin Hotel, 101
Allen, William H. (book seller), 257
All the Sad Young Men, xxix, xxx, 13, 19, 45, 49, 56, 117, 119, 137, 165, 169, 190, 215
All This and Heaven Too (movie), 111
Alphabet Bookshop, 85
A Lume Spento (Pound), 46
Americana Mail Auction (Rinsland), 38
American and English Literature from the Library of Mrs. Charles W. Engelhard (Christie's), 46–47, 53, 114–17, 161, 257, 259
American Art Association / Anderson Galleries (auction house), 3
American Book Company (publisher), 157
American Book Prices Current, xxiv, xxxii
American Booksellers Association, 56
American First Editions (Johnson), xxv
American Language, The (Mencken), 15
American Mercury, 6
American Tragedy, An (Dreiser), 144
Anderson, Sherwood, xxxiii, 103, 172

Anderson, W. R., xxxivn3
Anna Pavlova in Art and Life (Dandré), 233
Antiquarian Bookman, xxv
Any Amount of Books (book seller), 100
Apollo Theatre, 10
Apprentice Fiction of F. Scott Fitzgerald, The (Kuehl), 94
Argosy Books (book seller), 14
Argyll, Duchess of, 90
Aristotle, 233–34
Armed Services Editions, xxiii, xxxivn4
Arrowsmith (Lewis), 4, 44
As Ever, Scott Fitz— : Letters between F. Scott Fitzgerald and His Literary Agent Harold Ober, 1919–1940 (ed. Bruccoli and Atkinson), 211, 217
Atkinson, Jennifer McCabe, 211, 217
"At Your Age," 65, 154
Auction of Literary and Artistic Materials for the Benefit of Antiwar Congressional Candidates, An (Gotham Book Mart), 26–27, 163
"Author's Apology, The," xxxi, 13, 56, 81
"Author's Foreword," 75–76
"Author's Mother, The," 159
"Autographed by the Author" (Goodspeed's Book Shop), 4

Babbitt (Lewis), 111
"Babes in the Woods," 94
"Babylon Revisited," 84, 110–13, 116, 178, 193, 231
"Baby Party, The," 165
Baker, George Pierce, 233
Balch, David, 39
Balcon, Micky, 129
Ballantyne, Barbara Trego, 138
Ballantyne, Bobby, 137
Ballantyne, Howard, 136–38
Ballantyne sale, xxxiii, 135–38

268 *Index*

Ballet Russe, 234
Baltimore Symphony Auction, 15, 44
Bantam (publisher), xxiii
Barney Google (cartoon character), 85
Barrett, C. Waller, xxv
Barrie, J. M., 20, 142
Barrymore, John, 132
Barton, Bruce, 54
Barton, George, 212
"Basil and Cleopatra," 65–66, 156, 173–74
Basil and Josephine Stories, The (ed. Bryer and Kuehl), 58, 167, 174
Batchelder, Robert F. (book seller), 23, 72, 87
Baughman, Judith S., xxxivn10, 105, 163–65, 172, 215
Bauman Rare Books, 74, 79–80
Baxter, Warner, 208
Bayne, Rebecca "Ree," 92
Beach, Rex, 195
Beach, Sylvia, 120
Beacon Bulletin, 14, 25, 259
Beautiful and Damned, The, xxvii, xxvii, xxx, 3–5, 7, 9, 13–14, 16, 20–21, 26, 44–45, 48, 53–54, 59–60, 79, 81, 88, 100, 104, 109, 114, 116–17, 135, 143, 158–59, 171–72, 175, 183, 187, 213, 226
Beerbohm, Max, 120
Beginning of Wisdom, The (Benét), 127
Bell Haven Eight, The (Barton), 212
Benchley, Robert, 96, 177
"Benediction," 158
Benét, Stephen Vincent, 71, 127
Benét, William Rose, 71
Ben-Hur (silent movie), 40, 82, 87–88, 132
Bennett, Jeanne, 44
Bennett, Robert, 175–76
Bennett & Marshall (book seller), 26, 46, 176
Benson, Robert Hugh, 158
Bernard Quaritch (book seller), 32, 34
Bernheimer, Earle J., 7.
"Bernice Bobs Her Hair," 139, 159, 206, 212
Between the Covers (book seller), xxvi, 99, 151, 240, 246
Bibble, Minnie (character), 174
bibliographical terms, xvii
Biggs, John, Jr., 94, 112, 141
Bilphism, 109
Bishop, John Peale, xxi, 141, 145
Bissel, Imogene (character), 32, 34
Bissell, Dorothy, 79–80
Black Sun Books, 10, 26, 37, 87–88
Blaine, Amory (character), 8, 72, 130
Blum, Ralph, 40

Bodenheim, Maxwell, 9
Boesen, Charles S. (book seller), 5, 8–9
Bonhams & Butterfields (auction house), 200–206
Boni, Albert & Charles (publisher), 117, 260
Boni & Liveright (publisher), 43, 117, 172, 259–60
Bookman's Price Index, xxxii
Book of Princeton Verse II, A (ed. Van Dyke et al.), 47
Book-of-the-Month Club, 71
Boots rental library, xviii
Borgé, Isabelle (character), 32, 34–35
Boulden, Howard, 233
Bowers, Fredson, xiii
Bowers, Gwen (character), 153, 218
Bowie, M. Taylor, 55
Boyd, Ernest, 51
Boyd, Julian, xxi
Boyd, Madeleine, 51
Boyer, Charles, 111
Brady, William A., 208
Brigham Young (Werner), 29, 30
Brightbill, Kenneth, 48, 88, 114, 161
Bromfield, Louis, 51, 169
Bromfield, Mary, 51, 169
Brooke, Rupert, 142
Brooks, Nell, 21
Brooks, Van Wyck, xxvi, xxx, 115
Brooks, Virginia, 43
Broom, 68
Brown, Arthur William, 53–54, 116–17
Brown, Edith M., 53
Brown, Gilbert, 56
Brown, Henry Tatnall, Jr., 165
Brown, Mary, 18
Brown, Tatnall, 141, 164–65
Brownell, George, 182, 184, 186–90, 192
Brownell, Pauline Phillips, 182–88, 190–92
Browning, Robert, 120
Bruccoli, Matthew J. (as author/editor), xiii, xviii, xixn1, xxxivn2, xxxivn8, 58, 61, 94, 100, 105, 110–12, 114–16, 123, 127, 149, 153, 163–65, 172, 174–75, 182, 211, 213, 215–17, 226, 229, 231–32, 234, 238, 260
Bruccoli Clark (publisher), 40
Bruccoli Clark Layman (publisher), xxxivn8
Bruccoli Collection (Matthew J. and Arlyn Bruccoli Collection of F. Scott Fitzgerald, Thomas Cooper Library, University of South Carolina), xiii, xviii, xxvi, 10–11, 27, 38, 69, 80, 82, 85, 88, 99, 102, 109, 119–20, 122, 129, 131, 162, 168–69, 182, 212, 242, 245, 248, 257
Bruington, Walter, 45

Brush, Katharine, 54
Bryan, William Jennings, 262–64
Bryer, Jackson R., 58, 94, 162, 167, 174, 182
Bryn Mawr School, Baltimore, Md., 83, 244
Buchanan, Daisy Fay (character), xxviii, 34–35
Buchanan, Tom (character), 165
Buck, Gene, 46, 80–81
Buck, Helen, 80–81
Buck, Pearl S., xxv
Burden, Carter, 46
Burt, A. L. (publisher), 82, 171
Bush, Lovilla, 101
Butler, Hugo, 127
Butterfields (auction house), 69, 73
By a Stroke of Luck (Stewart), 145

Cabell, James Branch, xxv
Cagle, William, xiv
Caliban Bookshop, 99
Cambell, D. B. (character), 154
Cambell, Randy (character), 154
"Camel's Back, The," 39, 54, 214
Campbell, Alan, 96
Cape, Jonathan (publisher), 120
"Carmel and Ralph—(Four grand guys)—," 40
Carraway, Nick (character), 165
Carroll, Robert S., 63
Carter Burden Collection (J. P. Morgan Library), 46
Catalogue Number Six: Modern Authors (Wenning), 17
Catalogue Sixty Six A (Feldman), 16, 21
Catcher in the Rye, The (Salinger), 142, 252
Celt and the World, The (Leslie), 94
"Centaur in Brass" (Faulkner), 6
Chandler, Raymond, xixn3, 200
Charles Hamilton Auctions, xxix, 16, 21–23, 27, 29–31, 41, 43, 52–55, 67, 74, 76, 117, 261–65
Charles S. Boesen (book seller), 5, 8–9
Charles Scribner's Sons. *See* Scribners (Charles Scribner's Sons, publisher)
Chatto & Windus (publisher), 53, 96, 118
Chekhov, Anton, 103
Chicago American, 261
Chicago Daily News, 43, 114
Chinese Nightingale, The (Lindsay), 3
Chord, J. T., 11
Chorus Girl's Romance, The (silent movie), 8
Christie, Manson & Woods (auction house), 21
Christie's (London; auction house), 71, 89–90
Christie's (New York; auction house), xxix, xxxii, 10, 38, 46–47, 53, 66, 79–80, 90, 97, 100, 110–17, 135–38, 141–47, 149–50, 161–62, 178, 196–98, 207, 212–14, 216, 218, 220, 252, 254, 256, 259–60
Christie's East (New York; auction house), 127, 133
Christmas Carol, A (movie), 127
Christmas Garland, A (Beerbohm), 120
Clark, C. E. Frazer, xixn1
Clarkson, Elizabeth Craig, 179–80
Clemens, Samuel, 46
Cleonike (Cleon Damianakes), 169
Cohasco (auction house), 97
Cohn, Bert, 253
Cohn, Marguerite, xxxii
Collector, 20, 45
College Humor, 200
College of One (Graham), 149
Collier's, 123, 203–4
Collins (W. Collins Sons, publisher), 95
Collins, Seward (Sewie), 51, 169
"Colonial Ancestors of Francis Scott Key Fitzgerald, The" (Smith), 45
Colonial and Historic Homes of Maryland (Swann), 41–42
Colum, Mary, xxix
Columbia Studios, 110, 112
Connage, Rosalind (character), 72
Connelly, Marc, 29–30
Connolly, Cyril, 165
Conrad, Joseph, 127
Cooper Library. *See* Thomas Cooper Library, University of South Carolina
Copp Clark (publisher), xvii
Coppola, Francis Ford, 208
Correspondence of F. Scott Fitzgerald, The (ed. Bruccoli and Duggan), 45, 61, 111–12, 115–16, 127, 149, 175, 213, 229, 232, 260
Cosmatos, George. *See Library of George Cosmatos, The* (Sotheby's)
Cosmopolitan, 110., 112
Cottage Club, Princeton University, 251–55
"Count of Darkness, The," xxx, 17
"Course in Languages, A" 206
Cowan, Ann R., 110
Cowan, Lester, 110–13, 231
Cowley, Malcolm, xxi, xxii, 49–50, 167
"Crack-Up, The," xxiii, 7, 152, 178, 206, 221, 239
Craig. *See* Kelly, George
Craig House, Beacon, N.Y., 233–34
Craig's Wife (Kelly), 30

Craven, Frank, 21
Craven, Mary, 21
Crawford, Joan, 8
"Crazy Sunday," 6, 116, 178, 220
Crazy Sundays (Latham), 98, 134, 146
Croy, Homer, 208
Cugat, Francis, xxviii, 144, 165
Cugat, Xavier, 165
Cukor, George, 8, 86
Cummings, E. E., 43, 172
Cummins, James (book seller), 92–93, 101, 134–35
Cup of Gold (Steinbeck), xvi
"Curious Case of Benjamin Button, The," 214
Curtis, William, 38–39
"Cyclone in Silent Land," 220

Dana, Viola, 8
Dance, Beatrice, 239
"Dance, The," 206
Dancy, Bryan, 22–23
Dandré, Victor, 233
Darcy, Monsignor Thayer (character), 158
Darrow, Whitney, 106
David Copperfield (Dickens), 111
David Schulson Autographs (book seller), 103, 107, 199
Davis, Bette, 111
Davis, Curtis Carroll, 15
Davis, Harold, 21, 47
Davis, Owen, 208
Dear Scott / Dear Max (ed. Bryer and Kuehl), 162
Death in the Afternoon (Hemingway), 15
de Beck, Billy, 85
"Debutante, The," 94
"Demon Lover, The," 20
"Dentist Appointment," 123
Departmental Ditties and Ballads and Barrack Room Ballads (Kipling), 69
Desmarais, Rebecca, 55
"Devil, The," 130
Diaghilev, Sergei, 234
Dial (publisher), xxiii
"Diamond as Big as the Ritz, The," 114, 161, 214
"Diamond as Big as the Ritz, The" and Other Stories, xxiii, xxxivn4
Diary of Otto Braun, The (ed. Vogelstein), 38
Dickens, Charles, 111
Dictionary of Literary Biography Yearbook 2002 (ed. Bruccoli and Garrett), xxxivn8
Dietrich, Marlene, 21
D'Invilliers, Thomas Parke (character), 130

Disenchanted, The (Schulberg), xxiii, xxiv
Diver, Nicole (character), 98, 176, 194
Diver, Richard (Dick; character), 102, 176, 193–94
Dix, Dorothy, 126
Dolmetsch, Carl R., 94
Donald G. Drapkin Library, The (Christie's), 196–98
Donlevy, Brian, 112
"Don't expect me / I've gone fancy," 22
Doris Harris (book seller), 41, 259
Dorothy Parker: What Fresh Hell Is This? (Meade), 96
Dos Passos, John, xxi, xxv, xxxiii, xxxivn1, 144
Doubrovska, Felia, 234
Douglas, James H., 254
Dramatic Technique (Baker), 233
Drapkin, Donald G., 196–98
Dreiser, Theodore, 144
Duggan, Margaret M., 45, 61, 111–12, 115–16, 127, 149, 213, 229, 232, 260
Dukedom Large Enough (Randall), xxv, xxxivn2
Du Maurier, Daphne, 111
Durbin, Deanna, 112

Earle J. Bernheimer Collection of First Editions of American Authors Including . . . Robert Frost, The (Parke-Bernet), 7
Early, Jubal A., 42
Ecks, Beatrice, 226
Eddington, Arthur Stanley, 233
Edge, J. H., 16
Edmonds, Walter D., xxv
Egan, C. N., 232
Eldridge, Paul, 89
11th Co-operative Catalogue of Members of the Middle Atlantic Chapter of the Antiquarian Booksellers Association of America (Black), 21
Eliot, T. S., xixn3, xxix, 131, 142, 176, 196, 252
Ellis, Havelock, 38
Emerson, John, 74, 177
Emerson, Miss, 209
Emmerich, F. J., 16
Encyclopædia Britannica, 51, 169
"End of Hate, The," 123
Engelhard, Mrs. Charles W., 46–47, 53, 114–17, 161, 257, 259
English, Jerry, 255
Enoch Pratt Free Library, xxvi
"Esquimo Boy, The," 206
Esquire, 7, 125, 159, 205, 220–21, 232, 239

Ethel Walker School, Simsbury, Conn., 227
Etting, Ruth, 176
Evil Eye, The, xvi

Farewell Address of George Washington, The / The First Bunker Hill Oration of Daniel Webster, (ed. Pine), 157
Farewell to Arms, A (Hemingway), 169
Farrar, Greta, 97
Farrar, John, 23–24
Far Side of Paradise, The (Mizener), xxiii, xxiv, 32
Faulkner, William, xvi, xixn3, xxii, xxv, 6, 53, 56, 89, 200
Faure, Élie, 234
Fay, Monsignor Cyril Sigourney Webster, 16, 89, 100, 158–59
Fay, Ted (character), 167
Feinberg, Charles, xiv, xv
Feldman, Lew David (book seller), 16, 21–22, 46
Ferber, Edna, xxv, 95
"Festival of St. James," 120
Fie! Fie! Fi-Fi!, xvi, xxxi, 11–12, 47, 227
Fielding, Henry, xiii
Fields, W. C., 110
Finney, Margaret, 240
First and Last (Lardner), 108
"1st Draft Continuity" of *The Light of Heart,* xxvi
First Editions, Association Copies, Autograph Letters, and Manuscripts (House of Books), 11
First Editions, 1643–1943, Including 53 First Books of American and British Authors (Boesen), 5
First Editions & Manuscripts . . . Belonging to J. T. Chord (Parke-Bernet), 11
First Editions: Modern American Literature (Joseph the Provider), 28
First Editions of American and English Authors Mainly in Superb Condition: The Distinguished Collection of H. Bertram Smith, New York (Parke-Bernet), 4–5
Fish, Doris Frost (character), 162
Fish, Joseph (character), 162
Fitzgerald, Edward (father of FSF), 31, 42
Fitzgerald, Frances Scott (Scottie; daughter of FSF and ZF), xix, xxi, xxxiii, xxxivn10, 15, 18, 35, 45, 73, 78, 105–6, 139, 151, 153, 196, 205, 211, 215, 223, 225–26, 231, 233–34, 237, 239–42, 244, 246–47 correspondence, 227–28
Fitzgerald, F. Scott (FSF)
—address book/telephone directory, 232–33, 236
—books inscribed by both FSF and ZF, xxxii, 99, 133
—books inscribed by FSF, xxx–xxxi, xxxivn10, 3–5, 7–9, 11, 13–14, 21, 26, 27–28, 37–39, 44–50, 53, 56–57, 60, 63, 68, 73–74, 78–81, 88–89, 91–93, 95–96, 98–101, 121–22, 125–28, 131–39, 141–43, 145–48, 151, 156–62, 164–65, 171–72, 175–78, 180–82, 185–88, 194–98, 207, 212–16, 223–27, 251–56
—broadside, 49
—carbon copies, 58, 89
—contracts, 175, 200–204
—correspondence, xxi, xxx, xxxiii, 8–9, 15–20, 23, 26–29, 31–32, 34, 39, 41–43, 45, 49, 52, 54, 59, 61, 63, 71–73, 78–81, 83–89, 97, 103–9, 110–19, 127, 130, 141, 149–53, 156, 162–63, 169, 172, 181–84, 199–209, 217–21, 223–25, 228–33, 236, 238–49, 259–65
—drawings, 23–24, 33, 36, 54–56, 60, 139–40, 179
—flasks, 156, 16
—manuscripts, xxi, 22–25, 32–35, 37, 39–40, 67, 76–77, 123–24, 132, 156–57
—proofs, xvi–xvii, xxi, 7, 27–28, 75–76, 100, 102
—revised typescripts, xvi, xxi, xxx, 6, 17, 64–66, 124–25, 154–56, 166–67, 173–74
—screenplays, 87, 110–13
Fitzgerald, Mary "Mollie" McQuillan (mother of FSF), xxvi, 5, 15, 34, 73–74, 92, 156, 159–60, 213, 227, 229
Fitzgerald, Scottie. *See* Fitzgerald, Frances Scott (Scottie; daughter of FSF and ZF)
Fitzgerald, Zelda Sayre (ZF), xxx, 18, 20, 23, 27, 29, 49–50, 72, 78, 89, 92, 96, 105–6, 128, 132, 139, 145, 151–53, 155, 159, 182, 194, 196, 198–99, 206, 217, 219–20, 223, 227–29, 232–33, 235, 237, 239–41, 246, 248–49, 255; art, xxxii, 63, 170, 226; books inscribed by both ZF and FSF, xxxii, 99, 133; books inscribed by ZF, 178; correspondence, xxxii–xxxiii, 41, 47, 51, 169, 233–34; typescripts, 235, 237
"Fitzgerald and the Press" (Dos Passos), xxxivn1
Fitzgerald/Hemingway Annual, 226, 252
Fitzgerald Newsletter, 44
"Fitzgerald Revival, 1940–1974, The: A Study in Literary Reputation" (Anderson), xxxivn3
Flappers and Philosphers, xxxi, xxxii, xxxivn6, 8, 14, 39, 48, 73, 81, 88, 104, 119, 128, 133, 139, 156, 158–59, 184, 188, 212, 226

Fleming, Ian, 114
Fleming, John F., 9
Foch, Nina, 72
Ford, Ford Madox, 19
Ford's Theater, 123
Forrest, Nathan Bedford, 21
Forster, E. M., 19
Fortune, 194
Fowler, Elsie, 21–22
Fowler, Ludlow, 21–22
"Fractured Fairy Tales," 151
Francis, Gloria A., xixn1
Frank, Waldo, xxxii, 117, 259–60
Freeman, Samuel T. (auction house), 59
"Fresh Boy, The," 64
"Freshest Boy, The," 64, 156–57, 166–67, 174
"Freshman's Tragedy, The," 65, 174
Frohman, Charles, 78
From F. Scott Fitzgerald to a Nurse Unknown to His Biographers: Two Letters, Two Telegrams and Eight Inscribed Books (Quill & Brush), 181
Frost, Charlotte (character), 162
Frost, Horatio (Dada; character), 162
Frost, Jerry (character), 162
Frost and Fire: 50 Depressive and Manic Depressive Writers of Genius . . . A Celebration (Lakin & Morley), 105–6
F. Scott Fitzgerald (LeVot), 94
"F. Scott Fitzgerald: A Check List" (Piper), xxv
F. Scott Fitzgerald: A Descriptive Bibliography (Bruccoli), xiii, xvii, xviii, 44
"F. Scott Fitzgerald and the Origins of the Jazz Age" (Piper), xxii
F. Scott Fitzgerald A to Z (Tate), 157, 159, 162, 167, 174
F. Scott Fitzgerald Centenary Exhibition (ed. Bruccoli), 162, 165, 169, 212
F. Scott Fitzgerald in His Own Time (ed. Bruccoli and Bryer), 94
"F. Scott Fitzgerald's 'Babylon Revisited': A Long Expostulation and Explanation" (Larson) 193
F. Scott Fitzgerald's Ledger: A Facsimile (ed. Bruccoli), 58
Fülöp-Miller, René, xxxii, 99
Funk & Wagnalls (publisher), 109
Furies, The (Aikins), 96

Gable, Clark, 8, 233
Gaddis, William, 19
Gale (publisher), xxxivn8
Galsworthy, John, 20, 142
Garbo, Greta, 21, 56, 247

Garden of Allah, Hollywood, 200, 246
Garrett, George, xxxivn8
"Gateway Series of English Texts, The," 37
Gatsby, Jay (character), xxviii, 9, 27, 46, 117, 127, 129
Gatsby le Magnifique (trans. Llona), 226
Gauss, Christian, 141–42, 256
Gekoski, R. A. (book seller), 69, 88, 101, 223, 254
Gellert, Mr., 200
Gentlemen Prefer Blondes (Loos), 177
George Cukor Collection, The (Houle), 86
George Houle (book seller), 86
George M. Rinsland (auction house), 38
George Robert Minkoff (book seller), 82, 87, 151,
Gerald A. J. Stodolski (book seller), 245
Gibbons, Mike, 63
Gibbons, Tommy, 63
Gingrich, Arnold, 232
Girl, Girl, Girl (Tarkington), 54
Gish, Dorothy, 169
Glenn Horowitz (book seller), xiv, xxvi, 8, 14, 87, 92, 94–96, 120–21, 131
Glyn, Elinor, 262–64
Goethe, Johann Wolfgang von, 262
Goldberg, Ira and Larry, Auctioneers, 29–30
Golden Treasury, The (Palgrave), 234
Goldfinger (Fleming), 114
"Gold Hat, The," 219
Goldwasser, Thomas A. (book seller), 238, 241, 245, 247–48, 257–58
Goldwyn, Samuel, 67, 204, 217, 231
Gone with the Wind (movie), 86, 148, 203
Good Soldier, The (Ford), 19
Goodspeed's Book Shop, 4, 10–11, 61–62
Goodwin, Jonathan, xiii, xxx, 23, 46–51, 114–15, 161
Gorton, Bill (character), 145
Gosse, Edmund, 120
Gotham Book Mart, 5, 163
Graham, Sheilah, 98, 132, 149, 177
Grant, Ulysses S., 46
Grapes of Wrath, The (Steinbeck), 176
Graudia, Samuel, 254
Great American Short Novels, xxiii
Great Gatsby, The, xvii, xix, xxi, xxii, xxiii, xxiv, xxv, xxvi, xxvii, xxviii, xxix, xxx, xxxi, xxxiv, xxxivn4, xxxivn5, 3–5, 8–9, 13, 15, 20, 27–29, 34–35, 38, 41, 43–46, 49, 53, 59, 61–62, 73, 79–81, 85–87, 89, 96–97, 101, 105–6, 109, 112, 115, 118–20, 125, 127, 129, 132, 136, 141, 144, 154, 162, 164–65, 169, 172, 176, 189, 196, 200, 208–9, 219, 226, 233, 248, 255, 260, 265

Great Gatsby, The (advance copy), 55–56
Great Gatsby, The (Broadway production), 86
Great Gatsby, The (opera), 208
Great Gatsby, The (Scribner Library Edition), xxiii
Great Gatsby, The (Scribner "Student's Edition"), xxiii
Great Modern Short Stories (ed. Overton), 65
Green, Dexter (character), 117
Green, Margarate Orr, 7, 44
Grey Walls (publisher), xxiii
Griffiths, Florence, 104
Grosset & Dunlap (publisher), xxiii
Grove Park Inn, Asheville, N.C., 41, 63, 124, 126, 182, 228–29, 232, 237, 241, 245
Guardian, 118
Gunsmoke (television show), 98, 146
Guthrie, Laura, 239

"Hair" (Faulkner), 6
Hamilton, Charles, Auctions, xxix, 16, 21–23, 27, 29, 31, 41, 43, 52–55, 67, 74, 76, 117, 261–65
Hamlet, The (Faulkner), 6
Hammett, Dashiell, xixn3
"Handle with Care," 221
Hansen, Harry, 43, 53, 114, 116
Hanson, Silas M., 25
Harbison, John, 208
Harding, Warren G., 261
Harlow, Jean, 201
Harold Ober Associates, 211
Harper's Magazine, xxxiii
Harrington, Peter (book seller), 131–32, 194, 207
Harris, Mrs. Arthur J., 71
Harris, Doris (book seller), 41, 259
Harris, Jed, 108
Harris Auction Galleries, 83–84, 170, 223–38, 242, 245–48
Harry Ransom Humanities Research Center, University of Texas, Austin, 15–16
Haverford College, 164
Hawthorne at Auction (Clark), xix
Haydn, Joseph, 149, 150
"Head and Shoulders," 8, 39, 88, 206
Hearst, William Randolph, 261
Heavy Hand of Justice, The (Wade), 262–64
Hecht, Ben, xxv
Heinemann, William (publisher), 120
Held, John, Jr., 161–62
Hemingway, Ernest, xixn2, xixn3, xxii, xxiv, xxv, xxvi, 5, 8, 15, 43, 46, 98, 103,

105–6, 142, 144–46, 168–69, 172, 176, 194, 209, 238
Hemingway at Auction (Bruccoli and Clark), xixn1
Henderson, F. R., 95
Henry, O. (William Sydney Porter), 95, 103
Henry W. Wenning (book seller), xiii, xxix, xxx, xxxiii, 17–19, 46
Hergesheimer, Joseph, xxv
Heritage Book Shop, Long Grove, Ill., 16
Heritage Bookshop, Los Angeles, Calif., 3, 23, 44, 179, 259
"Her Last Case," xxx, 17
Hersey, Marie, 32–35, 40, 180
Heyward, Leland, 205
Highland Hospital, Asheville, N.C., 63, 152–53, 178, 218, 229, 234
Hill, W. E., 14, 54
Hime, Mark (book seller), 90
"His Russet Witch" ("O Russet Witch"), 214
Historical Documents International (auction house), 240
History of Art (Faure), 234
Hobby, Pat (character), 172
Hollywood, xxi, xxvi, 40, 79, 105–6, 132, 148–49, 169, 178, 200–202, 205–6, 218, 223, 227, 231, 246, 248–49
Holmes, Sherlock (character), 31
Hooper, Edna, 8, 13
Hoover, J. Edgar, 54
Horowitz, Glenn (book seller), xiv, xxvi, 8, 14, 87, 92, 94–96, 120–21, 131
Horton, Edward Everett, 151, 171–72, 231
"Hotel Child, The," 89
Houle, George (book seller), 86
House of Books (book seller), xxxii, 3, 11, 43, 46
Hovey, Carl, 54
Howell, Warren (book seller), 89
Hughes, Gareth, 8
Humanities Research Center, University of Texas, Austin, 15–16
Hume, Cyril, 127
Hunter, Anson (character), 22
Hunting Quartet (Mozart), 150
Hurley, James A., 122–24, 126
Hurley, James B., 122–26
Hurley, Margaret, 125
Hurst, Fanny, 14, 95
Huxley, Aldous, 142, 252

Ibsen, Henrik, 120
"Ice Palace, The," 133, 139, 159, 212
"I'd Die for You," 218
"I Didn't Get Over," 125
Idler, The (Johnson), xxxiii

274   Index

"I'm all wet . . . ," 57
Important Modern First Editions . . . The Collection of Jonathan Goodwin (Sotheby Parke Bernet), xiii, xxx, 23, 46–51, 114–15, 161
Impromptu (Paul), 127
Indelible (Paul), 127
Indispensable Fitzgerald, The (ed. Parker), xxxivn5
Ingalls, Bob, 165
in our time (Hemingway), xvi, 5
In Our Time (Hemingway), 144, 169, 172
"Inside the House," 217
"International Petting Cues," 31
In the Shadow of the Great Peril (Wade), 261
Intimate Lies (Westbrook), 172, 177
"Intimate Stranger, The," 205, 220
Inventory of the Robert L. Samsell Collection of F. Scott Fitzgerald, 44–45
Ira and Larry Goldberg Auctioneers, 29–30
Irving Thalberg Building (MGM), 127

Jack Potter (book seller), 8
Jacques, Leland (character), 154
James, Henry, 27, 142, 163
James Cummins (book seller) 92–93, 101, 134–34
James Joyce Books & Manuscripts (Horowitz), 120
J & S Graphics, xiii, xxx, 253, 259
J. B. Lippincott (publisher), 211
Jelly-Bean, The," 54, 89, 114, 161, 214
Jenkins, Oliver, 61–62
Jenkins Company (book seller), 61
Job, book of, 31
"John Jackson's Arcady," 56
Johns, John Jay, 253
Johnson, Merle, xxv
Johnson, Samuel, xxxiii
Johnson, Walter H., Jr., 227
Johnson & O'Donnell (book seller), 67–68, 257
Jonathan Cape (publisher), 120
Jones, Judy (character), 32, 34–35
Joseph M. Maddalena (book seller), 40, 42, 87, 89
Josephson, Matthew, 67–68
Joseph the Provider (book seller), 28, 97–98, 223, 259
Joyce, James, 120–21, 127
J. P. Morgan Library, 46, 257
J. Stephan Lawrence (book seller), xiii, xxx, xxxi, 253, 259
Judge Lynch (Rogers), 133

Junior Vagabond Players, 235

Kalman, Oscar, 231
Kelland, Clarence Budington, 54
Kelly, George, 30
Kelly, Scott, xxxivn9
Kemp, Harry, 3
Ken Lopez (book seller), 238–42, 246–49
Kennedy, Marguerite, 73
Kenneth (unidentified), 107
Kenneth W. Rendell (book seller), 32, 35, 39, 66, 133, 139–41, 152–55, 212, 215, 218, 248
Kern, Jerome, xiii
Kerouac, Jack, xix
Kerr, Joan P., 226, 234
Kerr, Robert, xxvi
Key, Francis Scott, 42, 45
Key, Philip, 45
Key, Philip Barton, 45
Kimball, Zella R., 16
King, Ginevra, 32, 34–35
"Kingdom in the Dark, A," xxx, 17
Kipling, Rudyard, 69–70, 103
Knopf, Albert A. (publisher), 99, 200
Knopf, Edwin, 200
Kohn, John S. Van E., xiv, xv, xix
Kroll, Nathan, 149–50
Kuehl, John, 58, 94, 162, 167, 174
Kunetka, Lawrence, xxix, xxx, xxxii

Lackritz, Richard M., 141, 149–50
Ladies' Home Journal, 123
Laemmle, Carl, 8
Lakin & Morley (book seller), 105–6
Lame Duck Books, 102, 238–39, 245, 247, 249
Lame Duck / Jaffe (book seller), xxxii
Lang, Miss (unidentified), 41
Lardner, Ring, 108, 144, 176, 194, 226, 262
Lark, The (Haydn), 149–50
Larson, Thomas A., 193
Lasch, Tillie, 67
Lassell Seminary for Young Women, Auburndale, Mass., 34–35
Lassie Come Home (movie), 127
Last Time I Saw Paris, The (movie), 110
Last Tycoon, The, xxii, xxiii, 6, 89, 110, 112, 149, 176, 204–6, 231
Latham, Aaron, 98, 134, 146
Lawrence, D. H., 142, 176, 252
Lawrence, J. Stephan, xiii, xxx, xxxi, 253, 259
Leaves of Grass (Whitman), 165
Lee, Basil Duke (character), 32, 58, 84, 153, 156–57, 167, 174, 178

Lee, Robert E., 46
Lengel, William C., 52, 208
Leonard, Elmore, 200
Leslie, Shane, 16, 94, 100, 104, 158–59
letters, about spelling errors in *Tender Is the Night*, 71–73
Letters of F. Scott Fitzgerald, The (ed. Turnbull), 20, 34, 41, 71, 118, 159, 163, 165
LeVot, André, 94
Lew David Feldman (book seller), 16, 21–22, 46
Lewis, Sinclair, xxv, xxvi, 4, 44, 95, 111, 115,
Lewis, Sylvia, 26, 45
Liberty (magazine) 123
Library of Congress, xiv
Library of George Cosmatos, The (Sotheby's), 195
Life in Letters, A (ed. Bruccoli and Baughman), xxxivn10, 105, 163–65, 172, 215
Light in August (Faulkner), 6
Light of Heart, The (Williams), xxvi, 87
Ligue Nationale Contre L'Alcoolism, 151
Lilly Library, Indiana University, xiv, xxxivn7, 211
Limbo (Huxley), 142, 252
Lincoln, Abraham, 123
Lindsay, Vachel, 3
Lion Heart Autographs (book seller), 119, 132
Lippincott, J. B. (publisher), 211
Literary Heritage (book seller), 23
Literary Manuscripts and Autograph Letters of Eminent Authors (Scribner Book Store), 6
Literature Including the Detective Fiction Library of Richard M. Lackritz, M.D. Part III (Christie's), 141, 149–50
Liveright, Horace (publisher), 117, 260
Llona, Victor, 169, 226
Long, Ray, 52
Loos, Anita, 67, 74, 177
Lopez, Ken (book seller), 238–42, 246–49
Lorimer, George Horace, 52, 119
Lorry, Annie (character), 154
Lorry, Arthur (character), 154
Los Angeles Book Fair (2006), xxvii
"Lost Road, The" (Kipling), 69, 70
Love of the Last Tycoon, The, 149
Lozynsky, Artem, xixn1
Lutz, Stuart, Historic Documents (book seller), 200

MacArthur, Charles, 18, 67
Macaulay (publisher), 68
Mackenzie, Compton, 265

MacKie, Paul T., 170, 244
MacKie, Paul T., Jr., 235
MacLeish, Ada, 194
MacLeish, Archibald, 194, 194
Madame Curie (movie), 247
Maddalena, Joseph M. (book seller), 40, 42, 87, 89
"Majesty," 206
"Make Yourself at Home," 153, 241
Manhattan Transfer (Dos Passos), 144
Mankiewicz, Joseph, 132
Mannes, Clara Damrosch, 26
Mannes, David, 26, 162
Mannes, Marya, 26–27, 156, 162–63
Mannheimer, Fritz, 114
Marble Faun, The (Faulkner), xvi
Mark Hime (book seller), 90
Marks, Jeffrey, 102
Mark Twain House, 46
Marx, Groucho, 218
Marx, Gummo, 218
Marx, Samuel, 8, 98, 146, 238
Marx, Zeppo, 218
Masefield, John, 234
Masterpieces of Modern Literature: The Library of Roger Rechler (Christie's), xxxiii, 97, 141–47, 172, 256
Matisse, Henri, 117, 260
Matthai, Claire Eager, 83
Maupassant, Guy de, 103
Maurice F. Neville Collection of Modern Literature, The (Sotheby's), xiii, xxxiii, 10, 26, 37, 47, 66, 74, 141, 155
May, E. C., 7
"May Day," 114, 161, 214
Mayou, David (book seller), 90
McArthur, Greta, 8
McCall's, 123, 205
McGraw, Thomas A., 162
McLenden, Paul C., xxxiii
McLenden, Paul C., Jr., 178
Meade, Marion, 96
Meekins, Russell, xxvii
Mellow, James, 120
Melville, Herman, xxii
Mencken, H. L., xxvi, xxix, 15, 59, 95, 115, 131, 176, 232–34
Meredith, George, 142
Metro-Goldwyn-Mayer (MGM), xxvi, 8, 98, 110, 127, 129, 146, 148, 164, 176, 201, 202, 238, 246–48
Metropolitan Book Auctions, 122
Metropolitan Magazine, 53, 54, 116, 143
Meyers, Jeffrey, 142, 144, 149, 196, 252
MGM. *See* Metro-Goldwyn-Mayer
Microcard Editions, 44

Milford, Nancy, 92, 178, 233, 235
Miller, James E, xxii
"Millionaire's Girl, The" (Zelda Fitzgerald), 89
Mind and Face of Bolshevism, The (Fülöp-Miller), xxxii, 99
Minkoff, George Robert (book seller), 82, 87, 151
Miron, Fernando, 195
Mitchell, Jake, 22–23
Mizener, Arthur, xxiii, 32, 34–35, 58, 65, 100, 125, 174, 233
Modern First Editions: 20'th Anniversary Catalogue (Young), 39
Modern Library (publisher), 85, 101, 125, 129
Modern Literature: First Editions & Presentation Copies of American & English Authors (Black Sun Books), 37
Morgan, J. P., Library, 46, 257
Morley, Christopher, xxiv, 164
Morrow, Bradford (book seller), 58
Movie Weekly, 39
Mozart, Wolfgang Amadeus, 149, 150
Muir, Marjorie Howey, 35
Murphy, Gerald, 105–6, 162
Murphy, Patrick, 246
Murphy, Sara, 162
Myers, Carmel, 40, 82, 88, 132
My Little Chicadee (movie), 110
"My Very Very Dear Marie," 32, 39–40

Nancy (unidentified), 128
Napoleon III, 123
Nassau Herald, 227
Nassau Literary Magazine (the *Lit*), 15, 94, 252
Nate's Autographs (auction house), 240, 249
Nathan, George Jean, 6
National Portrait Gallery, Washington, D.C., 56
Nature of the Physical World, The (Eddington), 233
Neall, Adelaide, 119
Neville, Maurice F., 37, 47, 53, 73, 80–81, 84, 155–78, 254
Neville sales (2004). See *Maurice F. Neville Collection of Modern Literature, The* (Sotheby's)
New Adam, The (Untermeyer), 3
New Directions (publisher), xxiii, 178
"New Leaf, A," 89
Newman School, Hackensack, N.J., 16, 34, 37, 127, 157–58, 167
New Republic, xxi, xxxivn1, 50

New Yorker, 18, 96, 220
New York Times Book Review, xxiv
Nigger of the "Narcissus," The (Conrad), 127
"Night at Chancellorsville, The," 75, 123
"Night before Chancellorsvile, The," 75, 123
19th Century Shop (book seller), 135
Normand, Mabel, 74
North, Abe (character), 176, 194
Northam, Edgar H., 83–84
"Note on the Disenchanted, A, Francis Scott Key Fitzgerald, 1896–1940" (Barrett), xxv

Oak Hall Hotel, Tryon, N.C., 79, 246
Ober, Anne, xxxiii, 205, 211–12, 215
Ober, Harold, xxvi, xxxiii, 65, 139, 152–54, 174, 200, 205–6, 211–15, 217–21, 228, 233, 235, 240–41, 246,
Ober, Harold, Associates, 211
"Offshore Pirate, The," 8, 139, 206, 212
"Of wonders is Silas M. Hanson the champ," 25
O'Hara, John, xxi, 177
O'Hara, John Myers, 3, 5
"Old Beau, The," 65, 154
Oliver, E. S., 31
Onassis, Jacqueline Kennedy, 122
"One Interne," 83, 86, 193
"On Your Own," 220
"Orange pajamas and heaven's guitars," 132
"O Russet Witch" ("His Russet Witch"), 214
"Outside the House," 217
Overton, Grant, 65
Owen, Wilfred, 143, 252
Owens, Isabel W., 18, 73, 223–49
Oxford University, 129, 262

Page, Clara (character), 229
Palgrave, Francis Turner, 234
Palmer, Russel, 265
Papantonio, Michael, xiv, xv
Paramount Pictures, 202–3, 219
Parke-Bernet (New York; auction house), xix, xxix, 3–5, 7, 11–14, 23–24, 27–28, 253
Parker, Dorothy, 96, 169, 177, 233
Parker, Gilbert, 263–64
Parrott, Stephan, 89–90
Paskman, Daley, 72
Passage to India, A (Forster), 19
Passing God, The (Kemp), 3
"Pasting It Together," 221
Patch, Gloria (character), 16
Patterson, Russell, 54

Patton Memorial Library, Henderson, N.C., 187
Paul, Elliot, 127
Paul C. Richards Autographs (book seller) 14, 25, 259
Paul Rassam (book seller), 89–90
Paul Reynolds Agency, 212
Pavlova, Anna, 39
"Pearl and the Fur, The," 152–53, 218
Penrod and Sam (Tarkington), 94
Pepper & Stern (book seller), 68, 91, 104, 217
Perkins, Maxwell, xxiii, 18, 20, 43, 75–76, 95, 118, 133, 139, 144, 162, 164, 172, 213, 263
Perry, Josephine (character), 84, 153, 167, 174, 178, 206
Peter Harrington (book seller), 131–32, 194, 207
Peter L. Stern (book seller), xxvi, 46–47, 127, 129, 151, 213, 216, 254
Peters, Marion (character), 111, 113
Petrie (character), 111, 113
Petronius, 27
Philadelphia Story, The (movie), 145
Philippe stories, 219–20
Phillips (auction house), 77, 253
Phipps Clinic, Baltimore, 99, 169, 198
Phoenix Book Shop, 252, 259
Picasso, Pablo, 117, 260
Pictorial Review, 153, 219, 241
Pilgrimage of Henry James, The (Brooks), xxx
Pine, Frank W., 157
Piper, Henry Dan, xxii, xxv, 233
Poe, Edgar Allan, Jr., 229–30, 245
Poems (Eliot), 142, 252
Poems (Owen), 142, 252
Poems, 1911–1940 (FSF),40
Pony Express (movie), 98, 146
"Porcelain and Pink," 128
Portable F. Scott Fitzgerald, The (ed. Parker), xxiii, xxxivn5
Porter, Katherine Anne, xxv
Porter, William Sydney, 95, 103
Portrait of the Artist as a Young Man, A (Joyce), 120, 127
Potter, Jack (book seller), 8
Pound, Ezra, 46
Pratt, Mr. (unidentified), 87
Price Was High, The (ed. Bruccoli), 123
"Princeton Asleep" (Reichner), 252
"Princeton–the Last Day," 94
Princeton Tiger, 31, 180
Princeton University, xxi, xxiii, 18, 31–32, 47, 69, 94, 137–39, 142, 145, 157, 162, 174, 179–80, 225, 235, 237, 243, 251–55
Princeton University Library, xxi, xxii, xix, 20, 49, 120
Princeton University Library Chronicle, xxv, xxxivn2, 58
Profiles in History (Maddalena; book seller), 40, 42, 87, 89
Prouse, Mrs. H. H., 45
Publishers' Weekly, 8
Pushing, Major General (character), 162

Quaritch, Bernard (book seller) , 32, 34
Quill & Brush (book seller), 10, 75–76, 104, 181, 181–93, 254

Raffles (movie), 204, 231
R. A. Gekoski (book seller), 69, 88, 101, 223, 254
Randall, David A., xxi, xxiv, xxv, xxxivn2
Random House (publisher), xxii, xxxivn2
R & R Enterprises (auction house), 208
Rare Books, First Editions (Boesen), 9
Rassam, Paul (book seller), 89–90
Rathje, Fred A., 60
Rawhide (television show), 98, 146
Rawlings, Marjorie Kinnan, xxix
Rebecca (Du Maurier), 111
Rechler, Roger, xxxiii, 97, 141–47, 172, 256
Recognitions, The (Gaddis), 19
"Recollection, A" (Beerbohm), 120
Redbook, 17
Red-Headed Woman (movie), 177, 201
Reese, William (book seller), xxvi, 67–68, 212, 215
Reichner, Aiken, 251
Reilly & Lee (publisher), 261
Reinsch, Pauline, 72
Remember When Auctions, 108, 240
Rendell, Kenneth W. (book seller), 32, 35, 39, 66, 133, 139–41, 152–55, 212, 215, 218, 248
Rennie, Dorothy, 29–30
Rennie, James, 29–30
Rennie, Thomas, 27, 99
Renoir, Jean, 127
Reporter, The, 206
Reuben, Walter (book seller), 60
Reynolds, Paul, Agency, 212
Richards, Paul C., Autographs (book seller), 14, 25, 259
Richardson, Alice, xxx, 17–19
Richardson, Dorothy, 85, 182
"Rich Boy, The," 22, 165, 215
Ridgely, Pleasance, 41
Ring, Frances Kroll, 149–50

Rinsland, George M. (auction house), 38
Ritz Bar, 111
R. M. Smythe (auction house), 209, 245
Robber Barons, The (Josephson), 68
Robert, Harvey C., 130
Robert F. Batchelder (book seller), 23, 72, 87
Roberts, Kenneth, xxv
"Robert says she's pretty," 76–77
Robertson, William George, 123
Robinson, Lennox, 61–62
Rocky and Bullwinkle Show, The (television show), 151
Rogers, John William, 133
"Romantic Egoist, The," 16, 142, 158, 256
Romantic Egoists, The (ed. Bruccoli, Smith, and Kerr), 226, 234
Roosevelt, James, 204
Roosevelt, Mrs. Theodore, Jr., 54
Rosenbach, A. S. W., xxiv
Rosenbach: A Biography (Wolf and Fleming), xxxivn6
Rosenfeld, Paul, xxix, 131
Royal Society of Literature, 118
Russe, Charlotte, 67
Ruth, Babe, 261
Ryan, Lajya, 44

Safety First, xvi, xxxi, 47
St. Denis, Ruth, 39
St. Paul, Minn., 28, 32–36, 78, 179–80
St. Paul Academy, St. Paul, Minn., 31
Salinger, J. D., xixn3, 142, 252
Samsell, Robert L., 3, 26, 44–45
Samuel Goldwyn Inc., 204
Samuel T. Freeman (auction house), 59
Sanctuary (Faulkner), 6
Saturday Evening Post, xxi, 8, 17, 39, 52, 58, 64–65, 89, 119, 123–24, 133, 139, 152, 154, 167, 174, 193, 211–12, 218, 220–21, 241
Satyricon (Petronius), 27
Save Me the Waltz (ZF), xxxii, xxxiii, 21–22, 50–51, 63, 169, 178, 217, 235
Sayre, Minnie Machen (ZF's mother), 38, 78, 92–93, 178, 237
Scandalabra (ZF), 235, 248–49
"Scandal Detectives, The," 32, 34
Schmurmeier, Gustave (Bob), 34
Schuberts, the (theatrical producers), 78
Schulberg, Budd, xxi, xxiii, 110–11
Schulberg, Victoria, 110, 111
Schulson, David, Autographs (book seller), 103, 107, 199
Scott, Charles T., 4
Scott Fitzgerald (Meyers), 142, 149, 196, 252

Scott Fitzgerald (Turnbull), 16, 32, 34, 81, 182
Scott Fitzgerald and His World (Mizener), 32
Scribner, Charles, II, 233, 263–64
Scribner Book Store, xxiv, 6
Scribner Firsts: 1846–1936 (Scribner Book Store), 3–4
Scribner Rare Book Department, xxi
Scribners (Charles Scribner's Sons, publisher), xxi, xvii, xviii, xxii, xxviii, xxxiii, xxxivn7, 3–4, 16, 20–21, 27–28, 37, 39, 43–45, 49, 58, 68, 73, 79–81, 83, 86, 89, 91, 95, 98, 100, 104–6, 114–16, 122, 125, 127–28, 131, 133–39, 142–46, 148–49, 151, 158–59, 161–62, 164–65, 168–69, 171–72, 176–77, 194, 196, 198, 207, 211–16, 226–27, 252, 254–55, 258–60, 262–63
Scribner's Magazine, 71, 100, 102
Seldes, Amanda, 105, 106
Seldes, Gilbert, xxix, 105–6, 233
Selznick, David O., 148
Selznick, Myron, 148
Selznick International, 148
"Sensible Thing, The," 165
Seven Gables Bookshop, xiv, xv, 88
Seven Lively Arts, The (Seldes), 105
Shakespeare, William, xviii
Shank, Martha Marie, 229, 230
Shaw, George Bernard, 20, 262
Shenton, Edward, 21, 125, 258
Sheppard-Pratt Hospital, Baltimore, 63, 170, 153, 229, 233–35
shimmee (dance), 39
Short Stories of F. Scott Fitzgerald, The (ed. Bruccoli), 174
Signature of America, The (Hamilton), 23
Silcox, Miss, 199
Silvette, David, 56
Silvette, Helen, 56–57
Simon, Horace F., 18
Simon & Schuster (publisher), xxxivn10
Skyland Hotel, Hendersonville, N.C., 239
"Sleeping and Waking," xxxii, 7
"'Sleep of a University'–an Unrecorded Fitzgerald Poem," 252
Smart Set, The (ed. Mencken and Nathan), 94, 128, 158
Smart Set, The: A History and Anthology (Dolmetsch), 94
Smith, H. Bertram, 4–5
Smith, Mrs. (unidentified), 241
Smith, Newman, 46, 48–49, 115
Smith, Rosalind Sayre, 21, 46, 48–49, 115n, 237

Smith, Scottie Fitzgerald. *See* Fitzgerald, Frances Scott (Scottie; daughter of FSF and ZF)
Smith, Thomas R., 43, 117, 172, 259–60
Smythe, R. M (auction house), 209, 245
Snooks, Mr. (character), 162
Soldier's Pay (Faulkner), 53
"Some Basic Notes on Three Modern Genres: Interview, Blurb, and Obituary" (Garrett), xxxivn8
Some Sort of Epic Grandeur: The Life of F. Scott Fitzgerald (Bruccoli), 45, 110, 114, 116, 153, 216, 231
Sotheby Parke Bernet (Los Angeles; auction house), 38
Sotheby Parke Bernet (New York; auction house), xxix, 21, 32, 38–39, 46, 53, 55–57, 63–66, 69–70, 114–16, 161, 167, 174, 219, 221
Sotheby's (London; auction house), 118
Sotheby's (New York; auction house), xxix, 10, 32, 37, 40, 66, 74, 78, 88, 122–26, 128, 130, 141 148, 155–80, 195, 217–18, 220–21, 243–44
Southerner, The (movie), 127
Spafford, Robert, 200
spelling errors in *Tender Is the Night*, 71–73
Sprague, Annabel Fitzgerald (sister of FSF), 229
Springfield Rifle (movie), 98, 146
Spurrier, Steve, 174
Squires, Tom (character), 154
Stafford, Mr., 240
Star Is Born, A (movie), 96
Stein, Gertrude, xxxii, 19, 117, 209, 259–60,
Steinbeck, John, xvi, xxv, 176
Stern, June, 168
Stern, Peter L.(book seller), xxvi, 46–47, 127, 129, 151, 213, 216, 254
Stevenson, Robert Louis, 133, 142
Stewart, Donald Ogden, xxvi, 105–6, 145
Stieglitz, Alfred, 233
Stockhausen, William E., 39
Stodolski, Gerald A. J. (book seller), 245
Stone, George E,, 132
Stonehill (book seller), xxx
Stories of F. Scott Fitzgerald, The (ed. Cowley), xxii, 167
Streets of Laredo (movie), 98, 146
Stuart, James Ewell Brown, 42
Stuart Lutz Historic Documents (book seller), 200
"Study in the Fictional Techniques of F. Scott Fitzgerald, A" (Miller), xxii

Sturges, Preston, 112
Stutz-Bearcat, 139
Sugarman, A. L., 9
Suman, Maud, 73
Sun Also Rises, The (Hemingway), 68, 134, 145, 169, 176, 194, 207
Superior Galleries (auction house), 83
Surratt, Mary, 123
Swann, Don, 41–42
Swann, Rita, 207
Swann Galleries (auction house), xxvi, xxvii, xxix, 14, 73, 87, 101, 254, 257
Swanson, H. N., 200–206
"Swimmers, The," 89
Tales of the Jazz Age, xviii, 5, 48, 61–62, 91, 114, 119, 128, 259, 161–62, 186, 214, 227, 262
Tamiroff, Akim, 112
Taps at Reveille, xvii, xxx, xxi, xxxii, 13, 15, 26, 45, 50, 64, 73–75, 83–84, 86–87, 92, 98, 110, 116, 119, 126, 146, 174, 177–78, 192–93, 212, 225, 227
Tarkington, Booth, 54, 94
"Tarquin of Cheapside," xviii
Tate, Mary Jo, 157, 159, 162, 167, 174
Taylor, Cecilia Delihant, 49, 229
Taylor, Robert, 246
Temple, Shirley, 19, 110, 112, 249
Tempo (ed. Jenkins), 61
Tender Is the Night, xix, xvii, xviii, xxiii, xxv, xxvi, xxix, xxx, xxxi, xxxiv, xxxivn5, 5, 8, 13, 19, 21, 27, 37–38, 50–51, 63, 67–68, 71–74, 83, 87–89, 100, 102, 104–5, 108–9, 119, 122, 125, 131–34, 138, 142, 145, 148, 151, 154, 163, 169, 175–76, 183, 191–94, 196, 198, 206–7, 209, 216, 220, 223, 225–27, 245
Tender Is the Night (advance review copies), xxvi, xxix, 115–16, 257–58
Tender Is the Night (screenplay), 98, 134, 146, 238
Tender Is the Night: With the Author's Final Revisions (ed. Cowley), xxii
Terry, George, 102, 122, 129
Thalberg, Irving, 127, 201
"Thank You for the Light," 220
"That Kind of Party," 58
theosophy, 109
These Thirteen (Faulkner), 6
Thigpen, Elizabeth, 62
"This book tells that Anita Loos," 67
This Side of Paradise, xvi, xxii, xxiii, xxxi, xxxii, 3, 5, 7, 11, 13–14, 16, 20–21, 28, 32, 34–35, 37, 44, 47, 54, 56, 59, 61, 79–82, 87–89, 92, 94–95, 98, 104, 106,

This Side of Paradise (continued)
  119, 127, 130, 132–33, 137, 139, 142,
  158–59, 183, 185, 212, 229, 251–56
This Side of Paradise (musical), 72
Thomas A. Goldwasser (book seller), 238,
  241, 245, 247–48, 257–58
Thomas Cooper Library, University of
  South Carolina, xiii, 10–11, 27, 38, 69,
  80, 82, 85, 88, 99, 102, 109, 119–20,
  122, 129, 131, 162, 168–69, 182, 212,
  242, 245, 248, 257
Thomson (publisher), xxxivn8
Three Comrades, 177
Three Lives (Stein), 117, 259–60
Three Novels by F. Scott Fitzgerald, 49
Three Stories & Ten Poems (Hemingway),
  xvi, xixn2, 5
"Thumbs Up," 123, 228–29
"Tiare Tahiti" (Brooke), 142
Tighe, Katherine, 145
Tipton, Terrence R., 58
Tom Jones (Fielding), xiii
"Too Cute for Words," 119
"Tooth and the Thumb, The," 123
Torrents of Spring, The (Hemingway), 172
Town, The (Faulkner), 56
Town & Country, 38
Train, Arthur, 54
transition, 68
"Travel Together," 220
"Treatise on the Gods" (Mencken), 234
Triangle Club (Princeton University), 12,
  31, 34, 47, 162, 180
Trimalchio, xvii, xixn4, 27
"Trouble," 206
True Story of Appomattox, The, 46, 49
Truex, Ernest, 10–11, 162
Tudury, Moran, 59
Turnbull, Andrew, 16, 20, 29, 32, 34–35,
  41, 71, 81, 118, 159, 163, 165, 182,
  196
Turnbull, Bayard, 196, 198
Turnbull, Eleanor, 196
Turnbull, Frances, 196
Turnbull, Margaret, 159, 196–98
Twain, Mark, 46, 165
Tyrone Guthrie Theater, 208

Ulysses (Joyce), 120
unidentified inscribee, 253
United Artists, 201–2, 231
University Archives (book seller), 240
University of Virginia Library, xiv, 10, 257
Untermeyer, Louis, 3
US Lithographic, xxxivn9
U.S. Steel Hour (radio show), 72

Van Doren, Carl, 115, 122
Van Duym, Alfred, 168
Vanity Fair, 145
Van Vechten, Carl, xxv, 132
Van Winkle, Courtland, 31
Vassar College, 228
Vaughn, Bernard, 44
Vegetable, The, xxxii, 3, 10, 13–14, 46, 48,
  56, 61–62, 74, 78, 81, 95, 162, 212, 262
Viking (publisher), xxiii, xxxivn5
Vizetelly, Frank H., 109
Vogelstein, Julie, 38

Wade, Edward O., 261, 263–65
Wade, Horace, xxix, 261, 262–65
Wales, Charles (character) , 111
Wales, Honoria (character), 110–12
Wales, Victoria (character), 110, 112
Wallace, David, 78, 88
Walter Reuben (book seller), 60
Ward-Belmont School, Nashville, Tenn., 53
Warner, Albert, 175
Warner, F. J. "Jack," 143, 172
Warner Bros., 175
Warren, Anne Crawford, 134
Warren, Charles Marquis, 8, 97–98,
  134–35, 146–47, 238, 249
Warren, Devereux (character), 98, 134
Warren Howell (book seller) 89
Washborn, Stuart A., 168
Washington, George, 37, 157
Washington's Farewell Address, 37
Waterman, Ivia, 104
Waverly Auctions, 67, 75–76
"Way through the Wood, The" (Kipling),
  69, 69, 70
*We Moderns: Gotham Book Mart,
  1920–1940*, 5
Webster, Daniel, 37, 157
Webster's First Bunker Hill Oration, 37
"Weekend at Ellerslie, A" (Wilson), 96
Weidler, Virginia, 111
Wells, H. G., 20
Wenning, Henry, xiii, xxix, xxx, xxxii, 17–19,
  46
Werner, M. R., 29
Wescott, Glenway, xxi
West, Mae, 110
West, Nathanael, 96
Westbrook, Robert, 172, 177
Westover School, Westover, Conn., 34, 35
Wharton, Edith, 142
"What to Do about It," 220
"What You Don't Know Won't Hurt You,"
  206
"When the Cruel War—," 123

"Where They Belong: The Acquisition of the F. Scott Fitzgerald Papers" (Bruccoli), xxxivn2
Whistler, James Abbott McNeill, 27, 163
White, Madame, 73
Whitman, Walt, xiv, 165
Whitman at Auction (Francis and Lozynsky), xixn1
Widmark, Richard, 72
Wife of the Centaur (Hume), 127
Willert, Lady Florence, 131, 132
William E. Stockhausen Collection of English & American Literature, Part II, The (Sotheby Parke Bernet), 39
William H. Allen (book seller), 257
William Heinemann (publisher), 120
William Reese (book seller), xxvi, 67–68, 212, 215
Williams, Emlyn, 87
William Young (bookseller), 32, 39–40
Wilson, Anne, 91
Wilson, Edmund, xxiii, 6, 94, 96, 120, 145, 178, 223
Winchell, Walter, 87
Winslow, Harry W., 23, 24
Winter Carnival (movie), 164, 202
"Winter Dreams," 32, 34–35, 54, 116–17, 215

Wolf, Edwin, 2nd, xxxivn6
Wolfe, Thomas, xviii, xxv, 99
Women, The (movie), 86, 177
Women in Love (Lawrence), 142, 252
Wooten, Alice Richardson. *See* Richardson, Alice
World (publisher), xxxivn6
Wrath of John Steinbeck or St. John Goes to Church, The (Bennett), 176
Wright, C. A., 31
Wyllie, John Cook, xiv, xv

Yale Literary Magazine, 15
Yale Record, 31
Yale University, 167, 174
Yank at Oxford, A (movie), 129
Young, Roland, 233, 235
Young, William (book seller), 32, 39–40
Young Tom Edison (movie), 127
Youth's Encounter (Mackenzie), 265

Zelda (Milford), 92, 178, 235
"Zelda Sayre Fitzgerald: A Check List" (Piper), xxv
Zeppo Marx Agency, 218
Ziegfeld, Florenz, 78, 81
Zola (Josephson), 68
"Zone of Accident," 206

About the Editors

Matthew J. Bruccoli (1931–2008) was the Emily Brown Jefferies Distinguished Professor Emeritus of English at the University of South Carolina and the leading authority on the House of Scribner and its authors. He was the editorial director of the *Dictionary of Literary Biography* and the author or editor of some one hundred books, including *Some Sort of Epic Grandeur: The Life of F. Scott Fitzgerald*; *The Romantic Egoists: A Pictorial Autobiography from the Scrapbooks and Albums of F. Scott and Zelda Fitzgerald*; and *The Sons of Maxwell Perkins: Letters of F. Scott Fitzgerald, Ernest Hemingway, Thomas Wolfe, and Their Editor*.

Judith S. Baughman is the author of *F. Scott Fitzgerald* in the Literary Masters series, editor of the 1920s volume in the American Decades series, and coeditor of books about Fitzgerald, Hemingway, and John Hall Wheelock.